The Harrowsmith

COOKBOOK

Volume Two

Classic & Creative Cuisine

By the Editors & Readers of Harrowsmith Magazine

Compiled from the private recipe collections of the Editors, Readers,
Contributors and Staff of *Harrowsmith*, Canada's National Award Winning Magazine
of Country Living and Alternatives

CAMDEN HOUSE

©1983 by Camden House Publishing (a division of Telemedia Publishing Inc.)

Revised and reprinted 1984
Third printing 1985
Fourth printing 1988
Fifth printing 1990
Sixth printing 1991

Canadian Cataloguing in Publication Data

Main entry under title:
   The Harrowsmith cookbook
''Editor, Pamela Cross; associate editors, Jennifer Bennett, James Lawrence.''—p. [3].
Contents: v. 1-2. Classic & creative cuisine—v. 3. More classic and creative cuisine.

ISBN 0-920656-28-5 (Hardcover)
ISBN 0-920656-23-4 (v. 2, pbk.)

1. Cookery. I. Cross, Pamela. II. Bennett, Jennifer.
III. Lawrence, James. IV. Harrowsmith.

TX714.H39 1981   641.5   C82-004954-9 rev

Trade distribution by
Firefly Books
250 Sparks Avenue
Willowdale, Ontario
Canada M2H 2S4

Printed and bound in Canada by
D.W. Friesen & Sons Ltd.
Altona, Manitoba, for
Camden House Publishing
(a division of Telemedia Publishing Inc.)
7 Queen Victoria Road
Camden East, Ontario
K0K 1J0

Cover illustration by Roger Hill

Printed on acid-free paper

The Harrowsmith

COOKBOOK

Volume Two

Editor
PAMELA CROSS

Photography
ERNIE SPARKS

Food Design
MARIELLA MORRIN

Drawings
JOANNE T.L. FITZGERALD

Copy Editors
JOHN ARCHIBALD, CAROLE PAQUIN

Design & Layout
PHILIP WOOD, JUDITH GOODWIN
LINDA MENYES, PAMELA McDONALD

Typesetting
CHARLOTTE DuCHENE

Test Kitchen Assistant
WENDY CLIFFORD

Photography Credits
PHOTOGRAPHIC PROPERTIES COURTESY OF:
KITCHEN CARGO, 86 BROCK ST., KINGSTON, ONTARIO; PRESENTS, 348 KING ST. E., KINGSTON, ONTARIO
DESIGN PLUS, 91 PRINCESS ST., KINGSTON, ONTARIO
McCALLUM'S CHINA AND GIFTS LTD., 79 BROCK ST., KINGSTON, ONTARIO; PATRICIA FRONTINI
PHOTOGRAPHIC LOCATIONS COURTESY OF:
ST. LAWRENCE PARKS COMMISSION, OLD FORT HENRY, KINGSTON, ONTARIO
PARKS CANADA, BELLEVUE HOUSE NATIONAL HISTORIC PARK, KINGSTON, ONTARIO
SPECIAL ASSISTANCE: GLENN E. ANGLIN, HELENE PRATT, CLARE STILL, JOE QUATTROCI
CATHERINE & ROSS McILQUHAM, DOUG CLARK, STEVE McCREADY, ED FREIL, JOHN COLEMAN

Contents

Introduction

Nothing to do but work,
Nothing to eat but food. . . .

– **Benjamin Franklin King**
The Pessimist

Trying a new recipe can be likened to going on a journey into strange territory; the accuracy of the map one carries is as important as the desirability of the destination. This is a book created by cooks who are pessimistic about neither food nor their ability to chart the way to delicious results for others.

The 719 recipes featured here represent the best of some 6,000 submissions from the readers, contributors, friends and staff of *Harrowsmith* Magazine. Those included were chosen because they produce interesting, flavourful, wholesome and attractive dishes. They are recipes that work – not just for their originators but in the Harrowsmith Test Kitchen and in the homes of the editors who have already added many of them to their own repertoires. Just as with *The Harrowsmith Cookbook, Volume 1*, a Canadian bestseller, this has been a cooperative effort in which thousands of good cooks generously shared the best their recipe boxes had to offer.

In forwarding her own favourites, Helene Conway-Brown of Elnora, Alberta, recalled a tale she had heard years earlier. "A woman was hired to look after some children whose mother was having a baby. The children were delighted to discover that this woman cooked exactly like

their mother. When the mother returned home, she was more than a little mystified, and queried the babysitter as to how she managed to cook all of her children's favourite meals. 'Easy,' the housekeeper replied. 'I took out all your cookbooks, opened them to the stained pages and used those recipes.'

"Well," wrote Ms Conway-Brown, "I have opened my own recipe binder to the 'stained' pages and hope they will find a place in *The Harrowsmith Cookbook*."

Others related stories of mothers and grandmothers bringing recipes from their ancestral homes in Europe: "As a young woman, my mother and her family were refugees in France," wrote Simone Van Bolhuis of Granton, Ontario. "They lived with a well-to-do French family, and my mother spent time at the elbow of the chef, watching and helping at times. She used many of his ideas later, when cooking for us. The recipes we are submitting are a happy blend of French and Flemish cooking."

Such pedigrees make for interesting dishes that have passed the critical test of time. Many other recipes are of more recent vintage – recipes that have been adapted to make use of natural ingredients and to incorporate the seasonality of home-grown vegetables.

In choosing which recipes to include, Pamela Cross was guided by her own instincts – developed as the owner of a small natural foods restaurant and as *Harrowsmith*'s food editor for the past four years. She admits to making the occasional arbitrary decision, but in most cases, recipes were set aside because they duplicated overly popular themes or repeated entries in *Volume 1*. Also avoided were submissions calling for convenience food ingredients such as powdered toppings or instant gravy. Each of the most promising selections was then tested in Harrowsmith's new in-house kitchen and the results presented to the editorial, business and circulation staff members as part of an "experimental lunch" programme. Judging was thus done by a mixed panel of critics – gourmands, gourmets, vegetarians and beef lovers alike – and although at times raucous, the final verdicts were remarkably consistent.

Many recipes that looked very good indeed on paper simply failed to excite the collective taste buds of our lunchtime arbiters. Writers, printers, job applicants and others passing through the Village of Camden East were pressed into service as instant food experts, and one, faced with an unexpected array of unusual dishes, effused his agreement with Liberace, who once said: "Too much of a good thing is simply wonderful."

One new feature in this book, one the readers expressed a desire for, is a chapter of menus – a dozen of them – for everything from an intimate Candlelight Dinner for Two to a Party Menu for Twenty and, for those cozy evenings by a crackling fire, the Post Cross-Country Skiing Dinner. The recipes for these tried-and-tested complete dinners, which are not only nutritionally well rounded but also aesthetically and gustatorially satisfying, were selected from both volumes of *The Harrowsmith Cookbook*. Volume number and page number are listed for each recipe.

To all who participated in making this book possible, our heartfelt thanks. Those whose recipes were not used should know that the overall quality of the contributions was so high that many excellent entries simply could not be made to fit into this volume. Readers may rest assured that the best are being reserved for use in *Harrowsmith* Magazine itself or, perhaps, in future cookbooks.

In the meantime, bon appétit and bon voyage. May you find your journey through these exceptionally fine recipes a culinary adventure, and may you enjoy reading, preparing and serving these recipes as much as we did.

Eggs
&
Cheese

Cheese. The adult form of milk.

— **Richard Condon**
A Talent for Loving

CHEESE PIE

1 egg
Salt & pepper
1 cup grated cheese

1 cup milk
¾ cup flour

Butter a 9-inch pie plate. Blend milk, flour, egg, salt and pepper. Stir in half of cheese. Pour into pie plate and bake at 350 degrees F until puffed and golden, about 25 minutes. Sprinkle remaining cheese over top. Continue baking until cheese melts — 3 to 4 minutes. Serve immediately.

Serves 2.

— Barb Alguire
Delta, Ontario

VAL'S ONION CHEESE PIE

Crust:
¾ cup flour
½ tsp. salt
½ tsp. dry mustard
1 cup grated sharp Cheddar cheese
½-1 cup melted butter

Filling:
2 cups thinly sliced onions

2 Tbsp. butter
1 cup cooked thin egg noodles
2 eggs
1 cup hot milk
1 cup grated Cheddar cheese
Salt & pepper

To make crust, mix together flour, salt, mustard and cheese. Slowly pour in melted butter until a workable dough results. Press into a deep 9-inch pie plate.

For filling, sauté onions in butter and add noodles. Place in pie shell. Beat eggs, then add hot milk and cheese while continuing to beat. Add salt and pepper to taste. Pour over onion and noodle mixture. Bake at 350 degrees F for 40 minutes.

Serves 6 to 8.

— Kirsten McDougall
Kamloops, British Columbia

TOMATO CHEESE PIE

Filling:
2 Tbsp. butter
¼ cup chopped green onions
1 cup bread crumbs
¼ cup chopped parsley
1 tsp. basil
⅛ tsp. salt
Pepper
10 firm red tomatoes, peeled

Topping:
1 cup flour
1½ tsp. baking powder
½ tsp. salt
2 Tbsp. butter
¼ cup milk
½ cup grated Cheddar cheese

Melt butter in skillet. Add onions and cook for 3 or 4 minutes. Stir in bread crumbs and cook until golden. Remove from heat; stir in parsley, basil, salt and pepper.

Cut tomatoes into slices ½-inch thick. Place half the slices in greased pie plate. Sprinkle with half the bread crumb mixture. Repeat.

To make the topping, sift together flour, baking powder and salt. Cut in butter to make fine crumbs. Add milk to make a soft dough, then work in cheese. Knead until smooth, wrap and refrigerate for 1 hour. On lightly floured surface, roll dough to a 9-by-12-inch rectangle, ½-inch thick. Cut into 12 strips ½-inch wide. Make lattice top for pie, crimping edges to pan. Bake at 350 degrees F for 30 to 35 minutes, or until crust is golden.

Serves 6 to 8.

— Jill Leary
Creston, British Columbia

CAULIFLOWER CHEESE PIE

2 cups packed, grated potatoes
1 tsp. salt
3 eggs
¼ cup grated onion
1 cup chopped onion
1 clove garlic, minced
3 Tbsp. butter

Thyme
Pepper
Paprika
½ tsp. basil
1 cauliflower, broken into florets
1 heaping cup grated Cheddar cheese
¼ cup milk

Salt the grated potatoes with ½ tsp. salt. Let stand for 10 minutes, then squeeze out excess water. Beat 1 egg and add along with grated onion. Pat into well-oiled pie plate and bake at 375 degrees F for 30 minutes or until golden brown.

Sauté chopped onion and garlic in butter. Add herbs (including ½ tsp. salt) and cauliflower and cook for 10 minutes. Spread half the cheese in pie plate, then cauliflower mixture, then remaining cheese. Beat together 2 remaining eggs and milk and pour over all.

Bake at 375 degrees for 30 to 40 minutes, or until set.

Serves 4.

— Nancy Beltgens
Coombs, British Columbia

SPINACH FETA CHEESE QUICHE

Pastry for 9-inch pie shell
2 Tbsp. olive oil
½ cup finely chopped mushrooms
1 shallot, chopped
¼ cup pine nuts
2 cups finely chopped spinach

2 eggs, beaten
¼ lb. feta cheese, crumbled
¼ cup milk
Parmesan cheese
Nutmeg

Heat oil and sauté mushrooms, shallot and pine nuts. Steam spinach until limp but still bright green. Beat together eggs, feta cheese and milk. Add vegetables and spoon into pastry-lined pie plate. Top with Parmesan cheese and nutmeg. Bake at 350 degrees F for 40 to 45 minutes.

Serves 4 to 6.

— P.S. Reynolds
Guelph, Ontario

SPINACH QUICHE

Pastry for 9-inch pie shell
2 Tbsp. finely chopped onion
1 cup grated cheese
2 eggs
1 cup yogurt

1 Tbsp. flour
½ tsp. salt
¼ tsp. pepper
Dash nutmeg
1 cup chopped cooked spinach

Bake crust at 450 degrees F for 10 minutes. Let cool and sprinkle onion and cheese over crust.

Beat eggs, then add yogurt, flour and seasonings. Stir well. Add and stir in spinach. Pour this mixture into the baked pie shell.

Bake at 450 degrees for 15 minutes. Reduce heat to 350 degrees and bake for 30 minutes longer.

Serves 4 to 6.

— Susan Lord
Quesnel, British Columbia

VEGETABLE CHEESE PIE

Pastry for 9-inch pie shell
1½ cups broccoli, cut into
  bite-sized pieces
1½ cups cauliflower, cut into
  bite-sized pieces
1 cup sliced carrots
1½ cups sliced mushrooms

1 Tbsp. butter
1 Tbsp. vegetable oil
3 Tbsp. whole wheat flour
1 cup milk
Salt & pepper
Thyme
1 cup shredded Swiss or Cheddar cheese

Steam broccoli, cauliflower and carrots until tender but crisp; drain and arrange in pie shell. Sauté mushrooms in butter and oil. Stir in flour and cook for about 1 minute. Add milk slowly and bring to a boil, stirring constantly. Cook for about 2 minutes.

Remove from heat; add seasonings and half the cheese, stirring until smooth. Pour sauce over vegetables. Sprinkle with remaining cheese.

Bake at 425 degrees F until sauce is bubbly and cheese is golden brown – about 20 minutes.

Serves 4.

— *Lise Gall*
Alexis Creek, British Columbia

DELICIOUS ONION QUICHE

Pastry for 9-inch pie shell
4-6 onions
4 Tbsp. butter
1 tsp. salt
1 tsp. pepper

1 cup grated Gruyère cheese
¾ cup milk
¾ cup whipping cream
6 eggs

Line pie plate with pastry and bake at 400 degrees F for 5 minutes. Set aside.

Thinly slice onions and cook in butter over medium heat until transparent. Add salt and pepper; mix and drain. Spread over bottom of pie shell. Add cheese.

Mix together milk, cream and eggs and pour over onions.

Bake at 350 degrees for 30 minutes, or until custard is set.

Serves 6 to 8.

— *Jane Cardona*
Toronto, Ontario

CARROT QUICHE

Pastry for 9-inch pie shell
4 cups sliced carrots, cooked
4 eggs
¼ cup whipping cream

1 tsp. salt
¼ tsp. pepper
¼ tsp. nutmeg
1 cup grated Swiss cheese

Line pie plate with pastry and arrange carrots in shell. Beat together eggs and cream. Mix in salt, pepper, nutmeg and cheese and pour over carrots.

Bake at 425 degrees F for 10 minutes. Reduce heat to 350 degrees and bake for another 30 to 35 minutes. Let stand for 10 minutes before serving.

Serves 6.

— *Elizabeth Clayton Paul*
Nepean, Ontario

POTATO PIE

Pastry for 10-inch pie shell
1 lb. cottage cheese
2 cups mashed potatoes
½ cup sour cream
2 eggs
2 tsp. salt
⅛ tsp. cayenne
½ cup scallions, sliced
3 Tbsp. grated Parmesan cheese

Line pie plate with pastry. Process cottage cheese in blender until smooth, then beat in mashed potatoes. Beat in sour cream, eggs, salt and cayenne. Stir in scallions. Spoon into pastry shell and sprinkle with cheese.

Bake at 450 degrees F for 50 minutes or until golden brown.

Serves 4 to 6.

— Marsha Plewes
Gormley, Ontario

EGGPLANT TOMATO QUICHE

Pastry for 9-inch pie shell
1 cup chopped tomatoes
1 Tbsp. chopped parsley
½ tsp. oregano
½ tsp. basil
1 Tbsp. butter
½ cup chopped mushrooms
1 clove garlic, minced
1 shallot, chopped
1 small eggplant, unpeeled
3 eggs
1 cup grated Cheddar cheese
Bread crumbs

Simmer tomatoes, parsley, oregano and basil for 20 minutes. Heat butter and sauté mushrooms, garlic and shallot. Add to tomato mixture and let cool.

Thinly slice unpeeled eggplant and bake at 350 degrees F for 10 minutes. Line pie plate with pastry and cover with eggplant slices.

Beat eggs and mix with tomatoes. Spoon half of this over eggplant, then add ½ cup cheese. Repeat layers and top with bread crumbs. Bake at 375 degrees F for 40 to 45 minutes.

Serves 6 to 8.

— P.S. Reynolds
Guelph, Ontario

CHICKEN QUICHE

Pastry for 9-inch pie shell
3 eggs
3 Tbsp. cornstarch
½ tsp. salt
⅛ tsp. pepper
½ tsp. thyme
¼ tsp. sage
1½ cups chicken stock
1 cup grated Cheddar cheese
½ cup chopped green pepper
1-2 cups minced cooked chicken

In large bowl, beat eggs until creamy. Mix cornstarch, salt, pepper, thyme and sage and slowly stir in chicken stock until smooth. Slowly beat into eggs. Add remaining ingredients and mix. Pour into pastry shell.

Bake at 425 degrees F for 15 minutes; lower temperature to 325 degrees and bake 30 to 45 minutes longer or until filling is set. Cool for 5 to 10 minutes before serving.

Serves 4 to 6.

— Janice Chammartin
Ste. Anne, Manitoba

MUSHROOM BEEF QUICHE

Pastry for 9-inch pie shell
½ lb. ground beef
1 cup thinly sliced onions
2 Tbsp. butter
¾ cup grated Cheddar cheese

2 eggs
1½ tsp. prepared mustard
2½ cups cream of mushroom sauce
  (*Volume I*, page 92)

Line pie plate with pastry. Brown ground beef and set aside. Sauté onions in butter until tender. Spread beef on pie shell, then spread onions over meat and sprinkle with cheese.

Blend together eggs, mustard and mushroom sauce. Pour over ingredients in pie plate.

Bake at 350 degrees F for 45 to 60 minutes or until firm. Let stand for 5 minutes before cutting.

Serves 4 to 6.

— *Kathy Labelle*
Montreal River Harbour, Ontario

FETTUCCINE SOUFFLE

SERVED WITH A GREEN SALAD AND GARLIC BREAD, THIS SOUFFLE MAKES A COMPLETE meal — especially for real pasta lovers.

½ lb. fettuccine noodles
1⅓ cups milk
1 clove garlic, minced
½ cup & 3 Tbsp. Parmesan cheese
¼ lb. Fontina cheese, grated
¼ lb. unsalted butter,
  cut into small pieces

Salt & pepper
1-2 tsp. chopped parsley
½ cup peas, steamed
6 large eggs, separated
1 Tbsp. milk

Cook fettuccine until just tender — about 5 minutes. Bring milk to a boil. Mix drained fettuccine with hot milk, garlic, ½ cup Parmesan cheese, Fontina cheese and butter. Season with salt and pepper to taste, then add parsley and cool. Add peas and egg yolks to cooled noodles and mix. Beat egg whites until stiff, then fold carefully into noodle mixture.

Butter soufflé dish and dust with remaining 3 Tbsp. of Parmesan cheese. Pour soufflé into dish. Bake at 350 degrees F for 45 minutes, then increase heat to 425 degrees and cook for 5 more minutes.

Serves 6.

— *Robyn Pashley*
Namu, British Columbia

WHITE FISH SOUFFLE

1 lb. white fish
3 Tbsp. butter
3 Tbsp. flour
½ cup milk

3 eggs, separated
½ cup peas
½ tsp. salt

Cook fish gently in lightly salted boiling water until it flakes. Melt butter, blend in flour and gradually add milk. Cook, stirring constantly, until smooth and thickened. Add yolks and beat well. Stir in fish, peas and salt. Beat egg whites until stiff, then fold into fish mixture. Pour into greased soufflé dish and place in pan of hot water. Bake at 350 degrees F for 45 minutes, or until soufflé is firm and well browned.

Serves 4.

— *Janice Graham*
London, Ontario

ZUCCHINI CUSTARD SOUFFLE

THIS SOUFFLE IS ALSO DELICIOUS SERVED COLD.

4 cups sliced zucchini
1 medium onion, finely chopped
3 large eggs, well beaten
2 Tbsp. flour

⅓ cup cream
1 cup cubed Cheddar cheese
Salt & pepper

Steam zucchini briefly and drain well. Gently combine with onion, eggs and flour. Stir in cream and cheese and pour into a buttered soufflé dish. Bake at 325 degrees F for 75 minutes, or until set and golden. Let stand for a few minutes before serving.

Serves 4.

— Kathleen Gray
Sointula, British Columbia

LEEK SOUFFLE

THIS SOUFFLE CAN BE MADE USING LEEKS THAT HAVE BEEN SLICED AND FROZEN FOR A pleasant midwinter taste of spring.

½ cup & 2 Tbsp. Parmesan cheese
2 leeks, sliced
6 Tbsp. butter
3 Tbsp. water
½ tsp. salt
¼ tsp. pepper

3 Tbsp. flour
1 cup milk
4 egg yolks, slightly beaten
Salt & pepper
6 egg whites

Coat inside of greased, 2-quart soufflé dish with 2 Tbsp. Parmesan cheese. Simmer leeks in 3 Tbsp. butter and water with salt and pepper, covered, until water evaporates — about 5 minutes.

Melt remaining 3 Tbsp. butter, then stir in flour. Cook over low heat, stirring constantly, for 2 minutes. Gradually stir in milk. Heat to boiling, stirring. Add leeks and ½ cup Parmesan cheese. Cook over medium heat, stirring constantly, until mixture boils. Remove from heat.

Stir ¼ cup of leek mixture into egg yolks, then gradually stir this back into leek mixture. Season with salt and pepper and cool to lukewarm.

Beat egg whites until stiff but not dry and fold into leek mixture. Pour into prepared soufflé dish. Bake at 400 degrees F for 35 minutes, or until golden and firm.

Serves 6.

— Pam Collacott
North Gower, Ontario

BULGUR MUSHROOM OMELETTE

1½ Tbsp. butter
3 green onions, sliced
Large handful mushrooms, sliced
¾ cup cooked bulgur
2 large eggs

2 Tbsp. milk
Salt
Basil
Curry
Grated Cheddar cheese

Melt butter and sauté onions and mushrooms. Add bulgur and heat through. Combine eggs, milk, salt, basil and curry and pour over bulgur-mushroom mixture. Cook, shaking pan, until custard is nearly set, then sprinkle with grated cheese. Cover pan and cook over low heat until cheese is melted.

Serves 1.

— Rosande Bellaar Spruyt
Rupert, Quebec

BASQUE OMELETTE

½ lb. bacon, cut into ¼-inch pieces
1 cup thinly sliced potatoes
1 medium onion, sliced
½ cup chopped celery
½ cup sliced green pepper
¼ cup sliced zucchini
1 clove garlic, minced
1 cup stewed tomatoes, drained

5-6 drops Tabasco sauce
Salt & pepper
8 eggs
¼ cup milk or cream
¼ tsp. salt
⅛ tsp. paprika
4 Tbsp. butter

Fry bacon to medium crispness and drain off all but 2 Tbsp. fat. Add potatoes, onion and celery and cook until tender. Add green pepper, zucchini, garlic, tomatoes, Tabasco sauce and salt and pepper and cook until vegetables are tender. Keep warm.

Combine eggs, milk, salt and paprika. Divide mixture into quarters. Melt 1 Tbsp. butter and cook first omelette by frying gently until firm and lightly browned on bottom. Slide onto plate and heap with one-quarter of hot vegetables. Repeat 3 times with remaining mixture.

Serves 4.

— Charlene Skidmore
Medicine Hat, Alberta

GERMAN OMELETTE

1 lb. sausage meat
1 medium onion, chopped
Salt & pepper
1 tsp. dry mustard
2 Tbsp. parsley

6 eggs
2 cups milk
3 slices bread, cubed
1 cup grated Cheddar cheese
1 cup grated mozzarella cheese

Brown sausage meat and drain off excess fat. Add onion, salt, pepper, mustard and parsley and cook until onion is tender.

Mix together eggs, milk, bread and cheeses. Add meat mixture and stir. Pour into a 9" x 13" baking dish and chill overnight. Bake at 350 degrees F for 45 minutes, or until knife inserted in centre comes out clean.

Serves 6 to 8.

— Lynda Watson
Kamloops, British Columbia

POTATO OMELETTE

1 medium potato
Butter
2 eggs
Milk
Salt & pepper
Sliced mushrooms

Slice the potato ⅛- to ¼-inch thick and lay on a lightly oiled cookie sheet. Dot with butter and bake at 350 degrees F until golden brown, turning once. Meanwhile, beat eggs with a little milk and season with salt and pepper. Sauté mushrooms.

Layer potato slices in an oiled frying pan. Add mushroom-egg mixture. Cover and cook slowly on both sides.

Serves 1.

— Veronica Clarke-Hanik
Toronto, Ontario

NEPTUNE OMELETTE

2 eggs
1 Tbsp. water
¾ tsp. parsley
Salt & pepper
2 Tbsp. mayonnaise

2 Tbsp. Parmesan cheese
2 Tbsp. crabmeat
6 asparagus tips, steamed until tender
Grated Cheddar cheese

Combine eggs, water, parsley and salt and pepper. Set aside. Mix together mayonnaise, Parmesan cheese and crabmeat and set aside.

Pour egg mixture into buttered skillet and cook over medium heat until nearly set. Lay asparagus spears on one side of omelette, spread with mayonnaise mixture and fold over. Cover pan and finish cooking. Sprinkle grated Cheddar cheese over top and allow to melt.

Serves 1.

— Bonnie Lawson
Medicine Hat, Alberta

CREAM CHEESE & WALNUT OMELETTE

3 eggs
3 drops Tabasco sauce
1 Tbsp. water
Salt

4 Tbsp. chopped walnuts
3½ Tbsp. butter
2 Tbsp. tamari sauce
2 oz. cream cheese, softened

Beat eggs, Tabasco sauce, water and salt and set aside. Brown walnuts in 2 Tbsp. butter, add tamari sauce and set aside.

Heat remaining 1½ Tbsp. butter in omelette pan until foamy. Pour in egg mixture and cook until almost set. Top with cream cheese and all but a few walnuts. Fold omelette over filling and cook for half a minute longer. Slide out of pan and top with walnuts.

Serves 1.

— Gillian Barber-Gifford
Rossland, British Columbia

BUCKWHEAT CREPES WITH MAPLE ORANGE SAUCE

Crêpes:
1½ cups buckwheat flour
½ tsp. salt
3 eggs & milk to make 4 cups
Oil

Maple Orange Sauce:
1 cup maple syrup
½ cup butter
¼ cup grated orange peel
Cottage cheese

Combine flour and salt in large bowl. Add 1 cup of egg-milk mixture at a time, whisking well. Continue adding liquid until mixture is consistency of heavy cream. Reserve extra liquid.

Pour ⅓ cup batter into hot pan and roll around to coat bottom evenly. Cook on medium-high until crêpe is golden brown on bottom and sturdy enough to flip — 30 to 45 seconds per side. If batter thickens as cooking continues, add some of reserved liquid.

To make sauce, place maple syrup, butter and orange peel in saucepan. Bring to a boil, lower heat and simmer for 5 minutes.

To serve, fill crêpes with cottage cheese and pour sauce over top.

Makes approximately 15 crêpes.

— Marilyn Rootham
Elora, Ontario

CHEESE CORN PANCAKES

2 cups flour
3 tsp. baking powder
1 tsp. salt
2 Tbsp. brown sugar
2 cups milk

2 eggs, slightly beaten
¼ cup oil or melted butter
2 cups corn
Small cubes Cheddar cheese

Combine flour, baking powder, salt and sugar. In another bowl, combine milk, eggs, oil and corn. Pour liquid ingredients over flour mixture and combine with a few strokes — batter should be lumpy.

Pour ¼ cup of batter onto greased griddle. While first side is cooking, top with 5 or 6 cheese cubes. Flip to cheese side and cook until golden brown.

Makes 8 to 10 pancakes.

— Rae Anne Huth
Fauquier, British Columbia

POPPY SEED PANCAKES

THE MOST FLAVOURFUL POPPY SEEDS ARE GROWN IN HOLLAND. THE SEED IS BEST WHEN steamed or roasted, then crushed to release its full flavour. For those who really enjoy poppy seeds, it is possible to buy a hand mill to grind the seeds at home.

1 cup whole wheat flour
1 Tbsp. sugar
½ tsp. salt
1 Tbsp. baking powder

1 egg, beaten
1 cup milk
2 Tbsp. oil
2 Tbsp. poppy seeds

Mix together flour, sugar, salt and baking powder. Beat egg and add milk, then oil. Add to dry ingredients. Add poppy seeds and stir until seeds are just moistened.

Pour batter by scant quarter cupfuls onto hot greased griddle. Cook until bubbly. Turn with pancake turner and cook until underside is golden. Place on platter and keep warm.

Makes about 15 three-inch pancakes.

— Suzanne Moore
Red Deer, Alberta

CORN MEAL PANCAKES

¼ cup flour
1 tsp. sugar
2 tsp. baking powder
¾ tsp. salt
½ tsp. baking soda

1 cup corn meal
3 eggs, beaten
1½ cups buttermilk
2 Tbsp. melted butter

Combine and mix flour, sugar, baking powder, salt and baking soda. Stir in corn meal. Add eggs, buttermilk and butter and stir until dry mixture is moistened. Pour ¼ cup batter onto hot griddle. Brown one side, turn and brown on other. Repeat with remaining batter.

Makes 12 pancakes.

— Judy Cushman
Wells, British Columbia

ALAND PANCAKE

THIS RECIPE WAS RECEIVED WHEN THE CONTRIBUTOR VISITED THE ALAND ISLANDS, Finland, one summer. After giving the Alanders a feast of Canadian pancakes and maple syrup, they reciprocated with their own pancake.

4 cups milk	1 cup butter
½ cup wheatlets	4 eggs
½ cup sugar	1 tsp. cardamom
1 tsp. salt	2 Tbsp. wheat meal

Boil 2 cups milk. Mix in wheatlets and bring to a boil for 2 minutes. Add sugar, salt and butter. Mix together eggs, cardamom and wheat meal in a bowl and add rest of milk. Mix everything with wheatlets.

Pour into a large, flat greased pan. Cook at 325 degrees F for 30 minutes. While it is baking, break the hills that will form. Cut into sections and serve with a topping of any berry jam and whipped cream.

Serves 4.

— *Lorne Davis*
Parkhill, Ontario

OATMEAL PANCAKES

1½ cups oatmeal	1 tsp. cinnamon
2½ cups milk	1 Tbsp. baking powder
1 cup flour	1 egg, beaten
1 Tbsp. brown sugar	¼ cup oil
½ tsp. salt	

Pour milk over oatmeal and let sit for 10 minutes. Sift flour, sugar, salt, cinnamon and baking powder together, then add to oatmeal mixture. Add egg and oil and mix well. Cook on hot griddle.

Makes 10 to 12 pancakes.

— *Judy Wuest*
Cross Creek, New Brunswick

BUCKWHEAT PANCAKES

2 eggs	¼ cup wheat germ
1¼ cups buttermilk	½ tsp. baking soda
2 Tbsp. oil	1 tsp. baking powder
½ cup buckwheat flour	½ tsp. salt
½ cup whole wheat flour	1 cup diced fruit (optional)

Beat together eggs, buttermilk and oil. Gradually mix in flours, wheat germ, baking soda, baking powder, salt and diced fruit. Fry on hot greased griddle.

Makes approximately 16 pancakes.

— *Marjorie Moore*
Calgary, Alberta

BANANA PANCAKES

2 eggs
2 cups buttermilk
1 Tbsp. baking soda
1 Tbsp. baking powder

2 cups flour
5 Tbsp. oil
1 cup mashed ripe bananas

Mix together eggs, buttermilk, baking soda and baking powder. Add flour and then oil, stirring only until blended. Fold in bananas. Spoon onto hot griddle or frying pan.

Makes approximately 12 pancakes.

— Marilynn Janzen
Celista, British Columbia

ZUCCHINI EGG CASSEROLE

THIS DISH HAS THE CONSISTENCY OF CREAMY SCRAMBLED EGGS. FREEZE ZUCCHINI in the summer for making this dish in winter. A 1-quart bag will hold the 2 pounds required for this recipe.

Oil
2 lbs. zucchini, thawed if frozen
1 medium onion, chopped
Salt
Basil
Oregano

Cornstarch
6 eggs, separated
½-¾ cup milk
6 Tbsp. flour
½ cup grated Parmesan cheese

Heat oil in skillet and sauté zucchini, onion, salt, basil and oregano until onion is translucent — about 15 minutes. Thicken with cornstarch if necessary.

Combine egg yolks, milk, flour and Parmesan cheese. Beat egg whites until stiff, then fold into egg mixture.

Pour zucchini mixture into greased baking dish, then spoon egg mixture over top. Stir together and bake at 350 degrees F for 30 to 45 minutes, or until firm.

Serves 6.

— Winn Horne
Dilke, Saskatchewan

HUEVOS RANCHEROS

2 medium onions, finely chopped
1 clove garlic, finely chopped
3 Tbsp. oil
1 large green or red pepper, sliced
1 cup stewed tomatoes, chopped
Salt & pepper

2 tsp. chili powder
¼ tsp. oregano
¼ tsp. cumin
6-8 eggs
Grated Cheddar cheese

Sauté onion and garlic in oil. Stir in pepper, tomatoes, salt, pepper, chili powder, oregano and cumin, and simmer until sauce is thick but not pasty. Poach or fry the eggs in butter without breaking the yolks. Spoon the simmered sauce into a shallow baking dish and nest the eggs in the sauce. Sprinkle with cheese. Bake at 250 degrees F until the cheese melts — about 15 minutes.

Serves 6 to 8.

— Carroll MacDonald
St. Léonard, Quebec

POACHED EGGS ITALIA

4 Tbsp. oil
1 clove garlic, minced
⅓ cup chopped green onions
3 cups chopped tomatoes

1 Tbsp. chopped parsley
Cayenne
¼ tsp. salt
6 eggs

Heat oil in heavy pan. Add garlic and onions and sauté for 2 minutes. Add tomatoes, parsley, cayenne and salt. Simmer over low heat for about 25 minutes. Replace lid if too much liquid is evaporating. Carefully drop the eggs into sauce, one at a time. Cover and return to boil. Simmer for 3 minutes, or until eggs are desired firmness. Serve on noodles or on toast with a salad.

Serves 6.

— Lisa Calzonetti
Elora, Ontario

FRENCH CREAMED SCRAMBLED EGGS WITH LEEK

5 Tbsp. butter
4 medium leeks, white part only,
  thinly sliced
20 eggs, beaten just to blend

8 oz. cream cheese,
  softened or chopped
1 Tbsp. minced fresh mint
Salt & pepper
Fresh mint sprigs to garnish

Melt 3 Tbsp. butter in heavy pan over low heat. Add leeks, cover and cook, stirring occasionally, until soft — about 20 minutes. Uncover and continue to cook, allowing liquid to evaporate. Remove leeks from pan.

Melt remaining 2 Tbsp. butter in same pan over low heat. Add eggs, cream cheese, mint and salt and pepper and cook, stirring, until eggs begin to set. Stir in leeks and cook until mixture forms soft curds. Adjust seasoning. Turn out onto heated platter and garnish with mint sprigs.

Serves 10.

— Lisa Calzonetti
Elora, Ontario

SHRIMP STUFFED EGGS

8 hard-boiled eggs, shelled
½ cup mayonnaise
1 Tbsp. chopped dill
¼ tsp. salt
1½ cups small shrimp, cooked

Halve eggs lengthwise, scoop out yolks and mash them thoroughly with a fork. Beat in mayonnaise, dill and salt.

Reserve 16 whole shrimp. Chop remaining shrimp finely and fold into yolk mixture.

Refill egg whites, garnish with reserved shrimp and fresh dill sprigs and refrigerate until thoroughly chilled.

Makes 16 appetizers.

— Claudette Spies
Nakusp, British Columbia

DEVILLED EGGS

6 eggs, hard cooked
½ cup mayonnaise
Salt & pepper
Curry
12 capers

Shell eggs and cut in half lengthwise. Scoop out yolks and place them in a small bowl. Mash lightly. Add mayonnaise, salt and pepper and curry, and mix well. Spoon carefully into yolks and garnish with capers.

Refrigerate until well chilled, then remove from refrigerator for 30 minutes before serving.

Makes 12.

HERBED CHEESE

THE CONTRIBUTOR OF THIS RECIPE USES FRESH GOAT'S MILK CREAM CHEESE, WHICH ADDS flavour. This, of course, is not imperative, but fresh herbs *must* be used.

1½ lbs. creamed cottage cheese,
  drained
1 lb. cream cheese
3 tsp. sour cream
3 cloves garlic, finely minced
½ tsp. salt
½ tsp. white pepper

1 tsp. minced basil
1 tsp. minced tarragon
½ tsp. minced thyme
½ tsp. minced sage
2 Tbsp. minced chives
2 Tbsp. minced parsley

Beat cheeses and sour cream until smooth, then beat in herbs. Cover and refrigerate for 24 hours to cure.

Place in a 3-cup mould lined with plastic wrap, refrigerate until set and remove from mould. Garnish with fresh herbs.

Makes 3 cups.

— Janet Ueberschlag
Breslau, Ontario

KNEDLYKY

THIS RECIPE FOR COTTAGE CHEESE DUMPLINGS IS A SIMPLIFIED VERSION OF A traditional Czechoslovakian dish prepared the way they used to be made during the harvest, when there was not much time to fuss in the kitchen. It is usually served as a side dish in place of noodles or potatoes.

1 cup cottage or ricotta cheese
1 egg
2 cups fine semolina

Mix cheese well with egg. If cheese curds are very large, break first with a pastry cutter or fork. Add semolina to make a workable dough — the exact amount will depend upon how moist the cheese is.

Form dough into walnut-sized balls, moistening hands with water to prevent sticking. Drop into a large pot of boiling salted water and cook for 7 minutes. Drain and serve.

Serves 6.

— Moira Abboud
Guelph, Ontario

TIOPETES

THIS GREEK RECIPE FOR CHEESE PUFFS MAKES DELICIOUS HORS D'OEUVRES — IT CAN even be reheated successfully.

3 eggs
½ tsp. salt
¼ tsp. pepper
1 lb. feta cheese

½ cup finely chopped parsley
½ lb. butter
½ lb. filo pastry

Beat eggs briefly in bowl. Sprinkle in salt and pepper. Crumble feta into small pieces and add to beaten eggs. Mix in parsley.

Melt butter in small pan over low heat. Cut filo into 3 equal strips about 3 to 4 inches wide. Cover two sections of the filo with a slightly dampened towel to prevent drying out and set aside until ready to use.

Working with the remaining one-third of the pastry, take one sheet, place on working area and butter with pastry brush. Place 1 Tbsp. of cheese mixture in bottom right hand corner of the buttered strip of filo, about an inch from the bottom of the strip. Fold left bottom corner over the cheese mixture to begin triangle. Then continue folding up, maintaining triangle shape. Lightly butter the finished triangle to seal the edge and place on an ungreased cookie sheet. Repeat process until all strips of filo are used. Cook in hot oil until golden brown — about 10 to 15 minutes.

Makes 3 to 4 dozen triangles.

— Zoe Mavridis Farber
Waterloo, Ontario

DEBBY'S QUICK VRENIKI

4 cups cottage cheese
4 eggs, beaten
½ cup melted butter

½ pkg. bow-tie macaroni, cooked
1 tsp. baking powder
1-1½ cups grated Cheddar cheese

Mix cottage cheese, eggs, butter, macaroni, baking powder and half of cheese. Place in baking dish and spread remaining cheese on top. Bake, uncovered, at 350 degrees F for 40 to 60 minutes, or until firm.

Serves 6.

— Mary Giesz
Winfield, British Columbia

POTTED CHEESE

1 lb. medium Cheddar cheese,
  grated
3 Tbsp. chopped scallions
3 Tbsp. chopped parsley
1 clove garlic, minced

1 tsp. Dijon mustard
2 Tbsp. softened butter
2 Tbsp. dry sherry
Tabasco sauce
Worcestershire sauce

Mix cheese, scallions, parsley, garlic and mustard in a bowl. Beat in butter, sherry and Tabasco and Worcestershire sauces. Stir the mixture until it becomes creamy, then pack it into a wide-mouthed jar or crock and refrigerate until ready to use.

Serve at room temperature with crusty bread.

— Valery Martinelli
Ganges, British Columbia

SPINACH SQUARES

2-3 eggs
6 Tbsp. whole wheat flour
1 lb. fresh spinach
1 lb. cottage cheese

½ lb. grated Cheddar cheese
½ tsp. salt
3 Tbsp. wheat germ

Beat eggs and flour in large bowl. Tear up spinach and add. Mix in cottage cheese, Cheddar cheese and salt. Combine well. Pour into a well-greased 9" x 13" baking pan and sprinkle with wheat germ. Bake, uncovered, at 350 degrees F for approximately 45 minutes. Cut into squares for serving.

Serves 6 to 8.

— Barbara Zikman
Winnipeg, Manitoba

OLIVE BALL SNACKS

BOTH THIS RECIPE AND THE ONE THAT FOLLOWS CAN BE MADE UP IN QUANTITY AND frozen. A quick reheating provides an almost instant party snack or hors d'oeuvres.

2 cups grated old Cheddar cheese
½ cup soft butter
1 cup flour

½ tsp. salt
½ tsp. paprika
48 green, pimento-stuffed olives

Combine cheese, butter, flour, salt and paprika and mix well. Wrap 1 tsp. of mixture around each olive. Place on cookie sheets and freeze. (Once frozen, the balls may be transferred to a covered container if they are to be stored for any length of time.)

Bake at 400 degrees F for 20 minutes.

Makes 48 balls.

— Jane Cardona
Toronto, Ontario

HOT CHEESE BALLS

½ lb. grated Cheddar cheese
¼ lb. butter
1 cup flour
Cayenne pepper

Mix cheese and butter, then flour and cayenne. Mix well and form into small balls. Bake on cookie sheet at 400 degrees F for 15 to 20 minutes. Serve hot.

Makes 24 balls.

— Mary Kelley
Ottawa, Ontario

Soups
&
Chowders

I live on good soup, not on fine words.

— **Molière**
Les Femmes Savantes

HUNGARIAN SOUP

3-4 medium potatoes
3 Tbsp. butter
2 Tbsp. flour
1 large tsp. Hungarian paprika
1-2 carrots, chopped
½ onion, chopped

1 small tomato, minced
1½ cups cubed turnip
Salt
8 cups water
1 cup spaghetti, broken into
 1-inch lengths

Peel potatoes, cut into small cubes and reserve in cold water. Melt butter in large pot and add flour, stirring until golden brown. Add paprika, potatoes, carrots, onion, tomato, turnip and salt. Add water.

Simmer, covered, until vegetables are partially done. Add spaghetti and cook until tender.

Serves 6.

— *Darlene Abraham*
Arkena, Ontario

MUSHROOM POTATO SOUP

½ lb. mushrooms, chopped
1 medium onion, minced
1 Tbsp. butter
5 cups water
2 potatoes, peeled & cubed
2 tsp. soya sauce
Worcestershire sauce

1 Tbsp. lemon juice
1 tsp. salt
Pepper
1½ Tbsp. cornstarch
⅛ tsp. nutmeg
Chopped chives

In a Dutch oven, cook mushrooms and onion in butter for about 5 minutes. Stir in water and bring to boil. Add potatoes, soya sauce, Worcestershire sauce, lemon juice, salt and pepper. Cover and simmer for about 45 minutes. Add cornstarch (in a paste made by adding a small amount of cold water) and stir until mixture thickens slightly. Top with nutmeg and chopped chives.

Serves 8.

— *Anne Ulmer*
Cannon Falls, Minnesota

SCOTCH SOUP

6 cups cold water
½ cup rolled oats
1 cup diced potatoes
2 cups diced turnips
¼ cup sliced carrot
¼ cup sliced celery

Bay leaf
2 Tbsp. butter
¼ cup chopped onion
2 cups tomatoes
½ tsp. salt

Combine water and oats in soup pot, bring to a boil and simmer for 30 minutes. Add vegetables and bay leaf and cook until vegetables are tender.

Meanwhile, in frying pan, melt butter and sauté onion. Add tomatoes and salt and cook for 15 minutes. Add to soup pot.

Serves 6.

— *Rose Strocen*
Canora, Saskatchewan

DILL CABBAGE SOUP

THIS HEARTY SOUP TAKES ONLY 30 MINUTES TO PREPARE. FOR AN EVEN MORE substantial soup, sauté a half-pound of sausage pieces and add them to the soup after the first 5 minutes of simmering.

½ small head cabbage
2 small onions, chopped
1 tsp. dill seeds
½ tsp. caraway seeds
2 Tbsp. butter
3 garlic cloves, minced
1 Tbsp. mild vinegar
1 Tbsp. red or white grape juice

1½ cups tomato juice
2 tsp. tamari sauce
3 cups stock
1 large potato, diced
Pepper
6 Tbsp. plain yogurt
2 Tbsp. minced parsley or dill

Cut the cabbage into small pieces. In a 3-quart saucepan, sauté the cabbage, onion, dill seeds and caraway seeds in butter, stirring occasionally, until cabbage is translucent and wilted — about 10 minutes. Add garlic, vinegar and grape juice. Cook for 1 minute. Add tomato juice, tamari sauce, stock and potato.

Cover and simmer until potato is tender, about 15 to 20 minutes. Add pepper to taste.

Serve topped with a spoonful of yogurt and some minced parsley or dill.

Serves 6.

— *Irene Louden*
Port Coquitlam, British Columbia

CABBAGE SOUP

1 lb. ground beef
1 onion, chopped
½ cup chopped celery
2 Tbsp. oil
1½ tsp. salt
¼ tsp. pepper
½ tsp. paprika

28-oz. can tomatoes
10-oz. can tomato paste
4 cups beef stock
3 Tbsp. chopped parsley
2 cups diced carrots
1 small cabbage, shredded

Sauté ground beef, onion and celery in oil. Drain off excess fat. Add remaining ingredients except cabbage, and simmer, uncovered, for 1 hour. Add cabbage and simmer for 1 hour longer.

Serves 8 to 10.

— *Patricia E. Wilson*
Belleville, Ontario

NOEL'S SOUP

1 cup finely chopped zucchini
1 cup finely chopped celery
¼ cup finely chopped green pepper
48-oz. can tomato juice

2 cups chicken or beef stock
1 small onion, chopped
Oregano
Salt & pepper

In a large pot, lightly sauté the zucchini, celery and green pepper. Add juice, stock and onion. Season with oregano, salt and pepper and simmer for 20 minutes.

Serves 4 to 6.

— *Patricia Daine*
Dartmouth, Nova Scotia

MULLIGATAWNY SOUP

THIS SOUP, ALSO KNOWN AS MULLIGATAWNY HOTPOT, IS TRADITIONALLY SERVED accompanied by *rice à la créole*. This is prepared by covering the raw rice with water, cooking it and then setting the covered pan at the side of the stove for an hour to allow it to dry out.

1 onion, sliced
¼ cup butter
1 carrot, diced
1 stalk celery, sliced
1 green pepper, chopped
1 apple, sliced
1 cup diced cooked chicken
⅓ cup flour

1 tsp. curry
⅛ tsp. mace
2 whole cloves
Minced parsley
Pepper
2 cups chicken stock
1 cup stewed tomatoes

Sauté onion in butter in large, thick pot. Add vegetables, apple and chicken. Stir in flour and spices and gradually add chicken stock. Add tomatoes and simmer, covered, for half an hour or more.

— *Cheryl Peters*
Courtenay, British Columbia

MUSHROOM LEEK SOUP

2 bunches leeks
½ cup butter
½ lb. mushrooms, chopped or sliced
¼ cup flour
1 tsp. salt

Cayenne
1 cup chicken stock
3 cups milk
1 Tbsp. dry sherry
Salt & pepper

Wash leeks well; slice and use white part only. In ¼ cup butter, sauté leeks until tender but not browned. Remove and set aside. In remaining butter, sauté mushrooms until soft — about 10 minutes. Blend in flour, salt and cayenne. Gradually stir in stock and milk. Cook, stirring, until mixture thickens and comes to a boil. Add leeks, sherry and salt and pepper to taste. Simmer for 10 minutes.

Serves 4.

— *Vanessa Lewington*
Timmins, Ontario

MUSHROOM RICE SOUP

1 clove garlic
1 large onion
1 Tbsp. oil
1 lb. mushrooms
1½ cups chicken stock

1 cup milk
1 cup cooked rice
Salt & pepper
Juice of ½ lemon
Parsley to garnish

Crush garlic, chop onion and sauté both in oil. Set aside.

Slice mushrooms into stock, bring to a boil and cook for 10 minutes. Pour half of the mushrooms and liquid together with the garlic and onion into the blender. Add milk and blend until creamy. Pour back into soup pot, mixing with the unblended mushrooms and liquid and the rice. Season and heat through. Remove from heat and add lemon juice.

Serves 4.

— *Lorraine Murphy*
Mississauga, Ontario

VEGETABLE BASIL SOUP

3 Tbsp. butter
1 onion, chopped
½ cup chopped celery
1 carrot, sliced
1 potato, peeled & cubed
2 ripe tomatoes, diced
4 cups chicken stock
½ tsp. salt
⅛ tsp. pepper

1 tsp. dry basil
1 tsp. oregano
¾ tsp. thyme
½ small head cauliflower, chopped
¼ lb. fresh green beans, sliced
2 small zucchini, sliced
½ lb. fresh green peas
Parmesan cheese

Melt butter in large soup pot over medium heat. Add onion, celery and carrot, and cook until limp. Add potato, tomatoes, stock, salt, pepper, basil, oregano and thyme to the pot. Partly cover and simmer for 20 minutes. Add cauliflower, green beans and zucchini and simmer for 10 minutes. Add peas and simmer for 5 minutes. Sprinkle Parmesan cheese over each serving.

Serves 4 to 6.

— Linda Stanier
Lacombe, Alberta

ZUCCHINI SOUP

THERE CAN NEVER BE TOO MANY ZUCCHINI RECIPES FOR THOSE WHO GARDEN. THIS soup can be made from either freshly harvested or frozen zucchini. The addition of cream cheese makes the flavour irresistible.

1 large onion, sliced
1 clove garlic, crushed
4 Tbsp. butter
4 medium zucchini, chopped
1 tsp. basil

½ tsp. oregano
4 cups chicken stock
4 oz. cream cheese
Salt & pepper

Sauté onion and garlic in butter for 5 minutes. Add zucchini and herbs and cook over low heat for 5 minutes. Stir in chicken stock and heat through. Blend with cream cheese until smooth. Return to pot, add salt and pepper and heat.

Serves 4.

— Sharon Sims
Hazelton, British Columbia

ONION SOUP

4-6 large onions
3-4 Tbsp. butter
4-5 cups chicken stock
¼ tsp. thyme
2 egg yolks, beaten with a little water

Halve onions and slice thinly. Sauté in butter until golden. Add stock and thyme, bring to a boil and cook for 15 minutes.

Blend about three-quarters of the soup in blender and return it to soup pot. Bring back to a boil and stir in egg yolks. Serve.

Serves 4.

— Gabriele Klein
Montreal, Quebec

PARSLEY SOUP

4 cups chicken stock
2 cups firmly packed,
  chopped parsley
½ cup chopped onion
½ tsp. salt
Pepper

1 cup milk
2 cups peeled & diced potatoes
2 Tbsp. butter
¼ cup flour
1 Tbsp. dry sherry
Parsley

Place chicken stock, parsley, onion, salt and pepper in heavy saucepan. Bring to a boil, reduce heat and simmer, covered, for 30 minutes. Strain and reserve stock.

Place milk and potatoes in small saucepan, cover and cook over medium heat until potatoes are tender – about 15 minutes. Set aside.

Melt butter, stir in flour and cook over low heat, stirring constantly, until smooth and bubbly. Slowly stir in stock, heat to boiling and cook, continuing to stir, until slightly thickened – about 2 minutes. Reduce heat. Add potato mixture and sherry and heat through. Garnish with parsley.

Serves 4.

— *Pam Collacott*
North Gower, Ontario

FRUIT & VEGETABLE SOUP

THIS RECIPE WAS CREATED FOR THE ADVENTUROUS SOUP QUAFFERS OF THE Sunflower Restaurant.

Oil
6 large onions, finely chopped
3 large leeks, finely chopped
1 bunch celery, finely chopped
6 cups chopped assorted root crops
  (yams, potatoes, turnips, carrots)
4 cups chopped sweet & hot peppers
4 quarts vegetable stock
2 cups apple cider

2 cinnamon sticks
6 cloves
1 cup chopped parsley
Several sprigs thyme
4-6 cups coarsely chopped assorted
  dried & fresh fruits (apricots, apples,
  plums, dates, figs, grapes)
Salt & pepper
Orange slices

In hot oil, sauté onions, leeks and celery. Add chopped vegetables and stock. Bring to a boil, cover, lower heat and simmer until vegetables are tender.

Add apple cider, cinnamon sticks, cloves, parsley and thyme. Stir in fruit and salt and pepper to taste. Cook until flavours are well blended. Garnish with orange slices.

Serves 10 to 12.

— *Deborah Washington*
Bath, Ontario

STRAWBERRY SOUP

2 pints strawberries
2 cups yogurt
½ cup orange juice
½ cup sugar
½ cup water
⅛ tsp. cardamom

Combine all ingredients and mix well in blender. Chill and serve.

Serves 4 to 6.

— *M. Cummings*
Stouffville, Ontario

RHUBARB SOUP

IN FINLAND, AS IN OTHER SCANDINAVIAN COUNTRIES, FRUIT SOUP IS POPULAR AND MAY be served either as a dessert or at the beginning of a meal.

2 lbs. red rhubarb
8 cups water
1 stick cinnamon
2 slices lemon
1½ cups sugar

2 Tbsp. cornstarch
⅓ cup cold water
1 egg yolk, beaten
½ cup heavy cream, whipped

Cut rhubarb in 1-inch pieces and cook in 8 cups water until tender. Drain liquid through sieve, discarding pulp. Return juice to saucepan and cook with cinnamon and lemon for 5 minutes. Add sugar.

Mix cornstarch with ⅓ cup water and stir into hot juice. Cook, stirring constantly, for 5 minutes. Remove cinnamon and lemon.

Just before serving, combine beaten egg yolk with whipped cream and stir into hot soup.

Serves 8 to 10.

— Ingrid Birker
Montreal, Quebec

PORTUGUESE CHICKEN WITH LEMON & MINT

12 cups water
½ cup chicken stock
¼ cup butter
3 large onions, chopped
3 large carrots, sliced

1 chicken
3-4 Tbsp. raw rice
6 Tbsp. lemon juice
Mint

Bring water to boil, add chicken stock and reduce heat to low. In another pan, sauté onions in butter until soft. Add to stock along with carrots, chicken and rice.

Cook until meat is tender — 2 to 3 hours. Remove chicken, discard bones and skin, chop meat and return to soup. Add lemon juice.

Sprinkle with chopped mint when serving.

Serves 8 to 10.

— Cindy McMillan
Procter, British Columbia

CHICKEN CURRY SOUP

3 lbs. chicken
10 cups water
½ cup butter
1 onion, chopped
1 Tbsp. flour
1 Tbsp. curry powder
26-oz. can tomatoes

1 green pepper, diced
1 lb. carrots, diced
2 apples, diced
2 stalks celery, diced
1 tsp. mace
½ tsp. pepper
¼ cup rice

Cook chicken in water until tender — about 2 hours. Remove chicken from stock and set stock aside. Debone chicken, fry in butter and return to stock. Brown onion in remaining butter.

Combine flour and curry powder, adding a little water to form a paste. Add to onion and mix well.

Stir remaining ingredients into onion mixture, then add stock and chicken. Bring to a boil, reduce heat and simmer until vegetables are tender and rice is cooked.

Serves 8.

— Kathryn MacDonald
Yarker, Ontario

CHICKEN CORN SOUP

1 quart chicken stock
2 cups corn
1 medium onion, chopped
1 green pepper, diced
1 cup cooked chicken

⅓ cup chopped parsley
Salt & pepper
2 Tbsp. cornstarch, dissolved in water
1 Tbsp. soya sauce

Bring stock to a boil and add corn, onion, green pepper, chicken and seasonings. Simmer for 5 minutes.

Thicken with cornstarch-water mixture and add soya sauce. Heat through.

Serves 4.

— Andrew Camm
Teeswater, Ontario

HEARTY MEATBALL SOUP

2 Tbsp. oil
1 medium onion, chopped
1 stalk celery with top, chopped
28-oz. can tomatoes
2 cups beef stock
1 lb. ground beef

1 egg
Grated Parmesan cheese
Salt & pepper
½ cup elbow macaroni
Chopped fresh parsley

Heat oil in large saucepan and sauté onion and celery for 5 minutes, or until tender. Add tomatoes and stock and cook over medium heat until mixture comes to a boil. Reduce heat and simmer.

Meanwhile, combine beef, egg, 1 Tbsp. Parmesan cheese, 1 tsp. salt, and pepper to taste. Shape into small (about 1-inch) meatballs and fry until browned. Drain off fat and drop into soup. Cover and simmer for about half an hour. Add macaroni, cover and simmer for 20 minutes longer, or until macaroni is tender.

To serve, sprinkle with Parmesan cheese and chopped parsley.

Serves 6.

— Judith Asbil
Ste. Agathe des Monts, Quebec

CHINESE HOT & SOUR SOUP

THE VARIATIONS OF THIS RECIPE ARE ALMOST ENDLESS. CHICKEN AND CHICKEN STOCK may be used in place of the beef and beef stock. Any crunchy vegetables may be added to, or replace, those mentioned below. If an egg-drop effect is desired, simply pour in a well-beaten egg after the soup has been removed from the heat and stir it in lightly. The two constants in the recipe are the hot pepper sauce and the vinegar to provide the hot and sour taste.

2 cloves garlic, halved
3 oz. beef flank, diced
2 Tbsp. oil
4 cups beef stock
2 tsp. dark soya sauce
½ tsp. Worcestershire sauce
¼ cup red wine
1 tsp. hot pepper sauce

Vinegar
2 oz. tofu
4 oz. fresh Chinese noodles
12 Chinese mushrooms
1 carrot, sliced
2 slices large onion
3 leaves Chinese cabbage
12 snow peas

Sauté garlic and beef in oil until garlic is golden. Add stock, soya sauce and Worcestershire sauce. Bring to a boil and cook for 10 minutes. Add wine, pepper sauce, vinegar to taste and tofu. Bring back to a boil. Add remaining ingredients except snow peas and cook briefly. Add snow peas and serve immediately.

— Lawrence Gellar
Toronto, Ontario

OXTAIL SOUP

3 oxtails, cut up
1½ Tbsp. salt
⅛ tsp. pepper
½ cup barley
2 cups diced onions
2 cups sliced carrots

1½ cups diced turnip
1 cup diced celery with tops
2 cups shredded cabbage
2 cups canned tomatoes
1 tsp. parsley

Wash oxtails well in cold water. Cover with fresh, cold water, bring to a boil and simmer for 1½ hours. Add salt and pepper and simmer for another 2½ to 3 hours, or until oxtails are barely tender. Remove from heat, add barley and let stand, covered, in a cool place overnight.

In the morning, remove layer of fat from stock. Remove oxtails, discard bones, chop meat and return to stock. Put stock on medium heat.

As stock heats up, add onions, carrots, turnip, celery, cabbage and tomatoes. Bring to a boil and add parsley. Lower heat and simmer for 1 hour.

Serves 8 to 10.

— *Brian Lawrence*
Mississauga, Ontario

MEAL IN A SOUP

1 lb. ground beef
2 medium onions, sliced
3 stalks celery, sliced
2 large carrots, sliced
1 medium potato, diced
1 parsnip, diced
1½ cups cauliflower florets
19-oz. can tomatoes

1½ tsp. salt
⅛ tsp. pepper
½ tsp. basil
¼ tsp. rosemary
½ tsp. thyme
½ tsp. sage
6 cups water
1 cup macaroni

Brown ground beef and drain well. Add remaining ingredients except macaroni. Cover and bring to a boil. Reduce heat and simmer for 30 minutes.

Add macaroni about 7 to 10 minutes before end of cooking time.

Serves 4 to 6.

— *Susan Ching*
Darlingford, Manitoba

BEEF LENTIL SOUP

1 lb. ground beef
1 medium onion, chopped
1 clove garlic, finely chopped
1 cup chopped mushrooms
28-oz. can tomatoes
1 medium stalk celery, sliced
1 large carrot, sliced

1 cup dried green lentils
3 cups beef stock
¼ cup red wine
1 bay leaf
2 Tbsp. snipped parsley
2 tsp. sea salt
¼ tsp. pepper

Cook and stir ground beef, onion and garlic in large pot until beef is light brown; drain. Stir in remaining ingredients. Heat to boiling, then reduce heat. Cover and simmer, stirring occasionally until lentils are tender — about 40 minutes.

Serves 4 to 6.

— *Lois Verfaillie*
Kelligrews, Newfoundland

INDIAN LENTIL SOUP

THIS SOUP MAKES AN EXCELLENT ACCOMPANIMENT TO A CURRY, AND IS DELICIOUS topped with a spoonful of yogurt. For a hearty lunch, serve this soup with warmed pita bread.

2 cups lentils
8 cups chicken or vegetable stock
1 onion, chopped
1 stalk celery, chopped
1 carrot, shredded
1 tsp. salt

¼ tsp. pepper
1 tsp. curry
½ tsp. cumin
½ tsp. coriander
¼ tsp. turmeric
¼ tsp. garlic powder

Put lentils in soup pot, cover with stock and bring to a boil. Add vegetables. Lower heat to simmer and add all spices. Simmer until lentils are soft, and soup is thickened with dissolved lentils – about 1 hour.

Serves 8.

— *Marcy Goldman-Posluns*
Dollard Des Ormeaux, Quebec

LEGUME GRAIN SOUP

2 cups split peas
¼ cup brown rice
¼ cup pot barley
4 Tbsp. oil
1 medium onion, chopped
3-5 cloves garlic, crushed
2 stalks celery, chopped

½ green pepper, chopped
2 pork hocks
1 Tbsp. dried parsley
1 Tbsp. tamari sauce
1½ tsp. salt
⅛ tsp. pepper
Few drops Worcestershire sauce

Bring 4 cups water to a boil. Add split peas, rice and barley; cover and simmer.

Meanwhile, in a large soup pot, heat oil. Sauté onion, garlic, celery, green pepper and pork hocks for 10 minutes. Add 10 cups hot water, split pea mixture and remaining ingredients. Simmer, covered, for 1½ to 2 hours, stirring occasionally.

Remove meat and bones from soup, discard bones, chop meat and return to pot.

Serves 12.

— *John Osborne*
Markdale, Ontario

LEEK & LENTIL SOUP

2 Tbsp. butter
2 Tbsp. oil
2 large leeks, chopped
1 medium onion, chopped
1 clove garlic, minced
1 cup lentils, washed
¼ cup pot barley
6 cups chicken stock

1 large carrot, sliced
1 large potato, chopped
1 stalk celery, chopped
2 cups canned tomatoes, chopped
Thyme
1 bay leaf, crumbled
Salt & pepper
Chopped parsley

In a big, heavy soup pot, melt the butter and oil. Add leeks, onion and garlic. Cook for a few minutes to soften.

Add lentils, barley and stock. Bring to a boil, then cover and simmer for about half an hour.

Add vegetables and seasonings. Cover and simmer about an hour longer, or until the vegetables are tender. Add parsley during last few minutes. Season to taste.

Serves 12.

— *Sylvia Petz*
Willowdale, Ontario

LAMB & LENTIL SOUP

1 cup dried lentils
1½ lbs. lamb shoulder, trimmed of fat
  & diced
2 Tbsp. vegetable oil
1 large onion, chopped

1 small turnip, peeled & diced
2 carrots, peeled & diced
6 cups beef broth
Salt & pepper

Rinse lentils in cold water, place in bowl and cover with fresh, cold water. Soak for 2 hours, then drain.

In a pot, cook the lamb in oil over medium heat until evenly browned. Add the onion and cook until soft. Stir in the drained lentils, turnip, carrots, broth and salt and pepper.

Simmer, stirring frequently, for 3 hours, or until the lamb is fork-tender. Adjust seasonings.

Serves 6.

— Janet Ueberschlag
Breslau, Ontario

BEAN SOUP

3 cups dry white pea beans
10 slices bacon
3 cups chopped onion
1½ cups diced celery
10 cups liquid (use bean stock,
  adding water if necessary)

1 Tbsp. salt
1 tsp. pepper
2½ quarts milk
¼ cup chopped parsley
1½ cups grated carrot
  or other vegetable

Soak beans. For each cup of beans, add 2½ to 3 cups of water. Let stand for 12 hours, or overnight. Or, for a quick soak, slowly bring to a boil and cook gently for 2 minutes. Remove from heat and let stand 1 hour. Drain beans, reserving liquid.

Fry bacon until crisp, then drain. Sauté onion and celery in bacon fat until onion is transparent. Add bean liquid, beans and seasonings. Cover and cook until beans are tender and water is almost absorbed, about 2 hours. Add milk, parsley and carrot and bring to a boil. Sprinkle with crumbled bacon and serve.

Serves 16.

— Nancy Willard
Haileybury, Ontario

SOUPPA FAKKI

THIS THICK GREEK BEAN SOUP SERVED WITH FRESH BAKED ROLLS AND A SALAD CAN take the chill out of a cold winter's day.

1 lb. brown lentils
1 medium onion, coarsely chopped
2 stalks celery with tops, chopped
2 cloves garlic, minced

½ cup olive oil
3 Tbsp. tomato paste
1 Tbsp. wine vinegar
Salt & pepper

Put lentils in a 2-quart saucepan and cover with water 2 inches above lentils. Add onion, celery, garlic, olive oil, tomato paste and pepper. Cover, bring to boil, reduce heat and cook slowly over medium heat for 30 minutes.

Check occasionally and add more water if needed. Soup should be thick. Just before serving, add vinegar and salt to taste.

Serves 4.

— Jan Post
West River Station, Nova Scotia

AUSTRIAN CREAM CHEESE SOUP

6 Tbsp. butter
6 medium leeks, finely chopped
4 celery stalks, finely chopped
6 Tbsp. flour
8 cups chicken stock
1 tsp. salt

1 lb. cream cheese, at room temperature
2 cups yogurt, at room temperature
4 egg yolks, beaten
White pepper
Parsley, chopped

Melt butter in heavy soup pot and sauté leeks and celery until limp. Stir in flour and cook, stirring, for 2 to 3 minutes. Add stock and salt, bring to a boil and simmer for 15 minutes.

Whisk cream cheese, yogurt and egg yolks until smooth. Add 2 cups of soup to cheese mixture, blend thoroughly and return to the pot. Stir until smooth and heat through, but do not boil. Sprinkle with pepper and parsley.

Serves 10.

— *Charlene Skidmore*
Medicine Hat, Alberta

CHEDDAR ONION SOUP

3 cups hot water
2 tsp. salt
8 potatoes, peeled & sliced
¼ cup butter
8 onions, sliced

5 cups milk
Parsley & celery leaves
¼ tsp. pepper
1½-2 cups grated Cheddar cheese

Combine water, salt and potatoes and cook until potatoes are tender. Meanwhile, melt butter and cook onions until tender.

Combine onions, potatoes, 2 cups milk, parsley, celery leaves and pepper and blend until smooth. Return to pot and add remaining 3 cups milk. Heat to scalding but do not boil. Reduce heat, stir in cheese and cook until cheese is melted.

Serves 6.

— *Marion Destorenis*
Curran, Ontario

CHEESE & VEGETABLE CHOWDER

4 Tbsp. butter
¼ cup finely chopped onion
1 cup chopped green pepper
1 cup pared, sliced carrots
1 cup pared, diced potatoes
1 cup peas

5 Tbsp. flour
3 cups chicken stock
3 cups grated, sharp cheese
2 cups milk
Salt & pepper
Chopped parsley

In a large saucepan, melt the butter and cook the vegetables, covered, stirring occasionally, for 20 to 25 minutes or until tender. Remove from heat and stir in flour, mixing well. Cook 1 minute, stirring occasionally.

Add chicken stock to vegetable mixture and bring to a boil, again stirring to prevent any sticking. Gradually add grated cheese and cook over medium heat until cheese has melted. Add milk and seasonings. Bring just to boiling point but do not boil. Sprinkle with parsley.

Serves 6 to 8.

— *Rebecca Gibson Spink*
Burlington, Ontario

BROCCOLI GARBANZO SOUP

¼ cup butter
¼ cup flour
1 tsp. salt
⅛ tsp. pepper
2 tsp. turmeric

4 cups milk
1 cup cream
2 cups broccoli, steamed & cut into
   ½-inch pieces
1½ cups cooked garbanzo beans, drained

Melt butter in 3-quart saucepan. Stir in flour, salt, pepper and turmeric. Cook slowly until mixture is smooth and bubbly. Using a wire whisk, gradually stir in the milk. Bring to a boil, stirring constantly, and cook for 1 minute. Add the cream, broccoli and garbanzo beans and heat through gently.

Serves 4.

— *Kristine Reid*
Floyd, Virginia

CREAMY CAULIFLOWER SOUP

THE ADDITION OF WORCESTERSHIRE SAUCE TO THIS RECIPE GIVES THE SOUP A PLEASANT bite. For those wishing a milder flavour, it could be omitted.

1 head cauliflower, cut into
  bite-sized pieces
¼ cup butter
1 medium onion, chopped
2 Tbsp. flour

2 cups chicken stock
2 cups milk or cream
½ tsp. Worcestershire sauce
¾ tsp. salt
1 cup grated Cheddar cheese

Cook cauliflower in about 1 cup water. Drain and reserve liquid. Set cauliflower aside. Melt butter, add onion and cook until soft.

Blend in flour, add stock and bring to a boil, stirring well. Stir in 1 cup cauliflower liquid, milk, Worcestershire sauce and salt. Add cauliflower and cheese and heat through.

Serves 6.

— *Ann Kostendt*
St. Thomas, Ontario

CREAM OF LEEK SOUP

THE LEEK IS CONSIDERED BY MANY TO BE KING OF THE SOUP ONIONS. BECAUSE of their growing method, it is essential to wash leeks extremely carefully to rid them of all the trapped dirt.

5 large leeks
¼ cup butter
Salt & pepper
3 cups milk
1 Tbsp. flour
2-3 egg yolks, beaten

Wash and cut up leeks and cook in butter in heavy pan until soft but not browned. Add water to cover and salt and pepper. Simmer for 15 minutes. Blend well. Add milk and flour and bring to a boil. Just before serving, add egg yolks, beating the soup well as you add the yolks.

Serves 4.

— *Annick Hardie*
Farrelton, Quebec

GREEN MEADOW SOUP

¼ cup minced green onions with tops
1½ Tbsp. unsalted butter
1½ Tbsp. flour
2 cups fresh peas
½ head Boston lettuce, shredded
½ cup spinach leaves

3 cups chicken stock
¼ tsp. salt
½ cup whipping cream
2 egg yolks
White pepper

Sauté onions in butter until soft, about 5 minutes. Stir in flour and cook, stirring constantly, for 2 minutes. Add 1½ cups peas, lettuce, spinach and salt. Stir in stock and heat to boiling. Reduce heat and simmer, covered, for 45 minutes. Cool slightly. Purée vegetable mixture in blender or food processor until smooth.

Beat cream, egg yolks and pepper in small bowl until smooth. Combine with puréed mixture in pot. Cook over low heat, stirring constantly, until soup is hot. Do not boil. Stir in remaining ½ cup peas.

Serves 4.

— Pam Collacott
North Gower, Ontario

MUSHROOM BISQUE

4 cups chicken stock
½ lb. mushrooms, chopped
1 onion, minced
¼ cup butter

¼ cup flour
1 cup milk
1 tsp. thyme
Salt & pepper

Combine stock, mushrooms and onion and simmer for 20 minutes.

In another pot, melt butter and stir in flour. When smooth, gradually add milk, stirring constantly, and cook until thick. Gradually stir into soup. Add seasonings.

Serves 4.

— Billie Sheffield
North Gower, Ontario

CREAM OF ALMOND SOUP

ESPECIALLY DELICIOUS SERVED COLD IN THE SUMMER, THIS UNUSUAL SOUP IS ALSO tasty served hot and can be quickly and easily prepared.

2 cups blanched almonds
3 Tbsp. butter
1 small onion or 1 stalk celery, sliced
3 Tbsp. flour
12 cups hot chicken stock

1 tsp. salt
½ tsp. pepper
2 cups thin cream, heated
1 tsp. almond extract

Sliver 30 almonds and toast at 225 degrees F until brown. Grind remaining almonds. Melt butter in large saucepan, add onion or celery and cook until soft. Stir in flour. Add chicken stock, ground almonds and seasonings and cook, stirring, until mixture boils. Simmer for 1 hour, stirring occasionally, strain and add hot cream, toasted almonds and extract. Serve hot, or chill and serve cold.

Serves 8.

— Hazel Baker
Coombs, British Columbia

OL' MAGIC TOMATO SOUP

28-oz. can tomatoes
1 onion
1 bay leaf
2 cloves
¼ tsp. baking soda
½ tsp. sugar

2 Tbsp. butter
2 Tbsp. flour
1 quart milk, heated
½ tsp. salt
¼ tsp. paprika

Put tomatoes, onion, bay leaf and cloves in saucepan and cook for 10 minutes. Purée and strain. Add soda and sugar.

Melt butter and add flour. Cook for 2 minutes. Add hot milk. Season with salt and paprika. Mix this cream sauce into the tomato mixture and serve immediately.

Serves 6.

— Vera Fader
Surrey, British Columbia

DILLED TOMATO SOUP

THIS SOUP CAN BE MADE EQUALLY SUCCESSFULLY WITH CANNED OR FROZEN TOMATOES as with fresh. The dill, however, must be fresh — this is what gives the soup its delicious, definitive flavour.

10 large ripe tomatoes
1 large onion
2 cloves garlic, minced
3 Tbsp. butter
5 Tbsp. flour

2 tsp. tomato paste
5 cups chicken stock
1 cup whipping cream
4 Tbsp. dill weed
Salt & pepper

Coarsely chop 8 tomatoes without removing skins. Chop onion and sauté with garlic and 4 of the tomatoes in butter for 3 minutes. Remove from heat. Blend in flour, tomato paste and stock and bring to a boil. Lower heat, add 4 tomatoes and simmer for 15 minutes. Add cream.

Peel and chop remaining 2 tomatoes and add to soup with dill, salt and pepper. Heat through, stirring well so cream does not curdle.

Serves 8.

— Ingrid Birker
Montreal, Quebec

CORN TOMATO CHOWDER

¼ lb. bacon
1 small onion
2 cups corn
2 cups tomatoes
2 cups diced potatoes
2 tsp. salt

½ tsp. paprika
⅛ tsp. pepper
1 tsp. basil
3 cups boiling water
1 cup cream

Fry bacon until crisp, then crumble. Sauté onion in drippings and add the rest of the ingredients except cream. Simmer until potatoes are tender. Add cream and warm over low heat.

Serves 6 to 8.

— Sally Ireland
Owen Sound, Ontario

VEGETABLE CHOWDER

3 slices bacon, diced
½ cup chopped onion
1 cup creamed corn
1 cup chopped green beans

1 cup tomatoes
½ tsp. salt
¼ tsp. pepper
4 cups hot milk

Fry bacon in a large saucepan, add onion and sauté until tender. Add remaining ingredients and heat to almost boiling, stirring constantly.

Serves 4.

— Vicki deBoer
Gibsons, British Columbia

HAM & POTATO CHOWDER

1 large onion, chopped
3 Tbsp. butter
½ cup water
6 medium potatoes, cut in
  ½-inch cubes
4 Tbsp. flour blended
  with ½ cup milk

3½ cups milk
2 cups cubed, cooked ham
1 tsp. salt
½ tsp. thyme
¼ tsp. pepper

Sauté onion in butter until tender. Stir in water and potatoes, cover and cook for 10 to 15 minutes. Stir in flour-milk mixture. Add milk, ham, salt, thyme and pepper and stir well.

Cover and cook for 5 to 10 minutes, or until potatoes are tender and soup is hot.

Serves 6.

— Janice Chammartin
Ste. Anne, Manitoba

SEAFOOD CHOWDER

½ lb. fresh halibut or cod
½ lb. fresh salmon
½ lb. fresh crabmeat
Lobster meat
Clams
2-3 Tbsp. butter
1 onion, finely chopped
2-3 stalks celery, chopped
Celery leaves, finely chopped

1 small clove garlic, minced
3-4 potatoes, peeled & diced
2 large carrots, sliced
1 bay leaf
2 cups milk or cream
2 Tbsp. cornstarch
1 tsp. salt
¼ cup butter

Chop and combine halibut, salmon and crabmeat, adding lobster and clams to taste. Set aside.

Melt butter in large, heavy pot and sauté onion, celery, celery leaves and garlic until tender. Add potatoes, carrots and bay leaf and cover with water. Cover and simmer until vegetables are tender but crisp — 15 to 20 minutes.

Add fish mixture and continue to simmer until fish is flaky. Combine milk and cornstarch and stir into soup. Add salt and butter. Simmer until thoroughly heated.

Serves 4.

— Donna Parker
Pictou, Nova Scotia

FISH CHOWDER

2 Tbsp. butter
2 medium onions, coarsely chopped
28-oz. can tomatoes, with juice
2 cups chicken stock
1 tsp. fresh basil
Pepper

2 cloves garlic
Worcestershire sauce
1 lb. frozen fish fillets, cut into
  1-inch pieces
½ cup long grain rice

Melt butter in large saucepan, add onions and cook until soft — about 5 minutes. Add tomatoes with their juice, stock, seasonings and fish. Add rice and bring to a boil. Reduce heat, cover and simmer over low heat for 20 to 25 minutes, or until fish flakes easily with a fork.

Serves 6.

— Janet Ueberschlag
Breslau, Ontario

PICKEREL CHEEK CHOWDER

PICKEREL CHEEKS ARE SO SMALL THAT THEY ARE USUALLY DISCARDED. THE TRUE FISH connoisseur, however, knows that they constitute the tastiest part of the fish.

2 cups diced potatoes
½ tsp. vinegar
1½ tsp. salt
¼ cup butter
1½ cups pickerel cheeks
1 cup chopped celery

1 cup chopped onions
¼ cup diced back bacon
¼ cup flour
2 cups milk
2 cups light cream
¼ cup chopped chives

Place potatoes in pot and cover with water. Add vinegar and salt and cook until tender.

Melt butter and sauté pickerel cheeks for 2 to 3 minutes. Remove and set aside. Sauté celery, onions and back bacon. Add flour and stir. Add milk and cream gradually, stirring constantly. Add potatoes, undrained, and mix thoroughly, then add pickerel cheeks. Garnish with chives.

Serves 4.

— Robert Currier
Nakina, Ontario

TUNA CHOWDER

2 stalks celery, sliced
2 large potatoes, cubed
3 large carrots, sliced
1 large onion, diced

2 cups corn
1 cup cooked, flaked tuna
3 cups cream of mushroom sauce (see
  Volume 1, page 92)

Boil celery, potatoes, carrots, onion and corn in a small amount of water until tender. Add tuna and mushroom sauce. Cook over medium-low heat until hot.

Serves 6.

— Carrie Osburn
Belwood, Ontario

CREOLE BOUILLABAISSE

¼ cup oil
2 onions, chopped
3-4 cloves garlic, crushed
1 stalk celery, diced
2 green peppers, cut in chunks
2 Tbsp. parsley
2 tsp. oregano

2 tsp. marjoram
1 bay leaf
4 Tbsp. flour
28-oz. can tomatoes
3 cups chicken stock
1 lb. cod, cut in bite-sized pieces
Salt & pepper

Heat oil. Add onions, garlic, celery, green peppers, parsley and spices. Sauté for a few minutes, then add flour. Cook slightly, stirring well. Add tomatoes and chicken stock. Stir and heat until bubbly. Add fish, cover and cook gently for 15 minutes. Season with salt and pepper to taste.

Serves 6.

— Beth Hopkins
Courtenay, British Columbia

HADDINGTON REEF BOUILLABAISSE

2 Tbsp. salad oil
2 cloves garlic, minced
1 onion, sliced
1 green pepper, diced
28-oz. can tomatoes
½ cup white wine
2 carrots, sliced

2 Tbsp. minced fresh parsley
1 tsp. salt
½ tsp. basil
⅛ tsp. fresh ground pepper
1 lb. cod fillets
½ cup water
4 tsp. cornstarch

In a 5-quart pan, heat oil and garlic, add onion and green pepper and cook until tender. Stir in tomatoes, wine, carrots, parsley, salt, basil and pepper, heat to boiling point and simmer for 15 minutes.

Cut cod into bite-sized chunks and add to mixture, bringing it to a boil. Reduce heat, cover and simmer for 10 minutes. Blend water with cornstarch, and slowly stir into stew to thicken.

Serves 6.

— Paula Compton
Sointula, British Columbia

ITALIAN FISH SOUP

1 lb. fish fillets
3 Tbsp. lemon juice
2-3 stalks celery, sliced
1 medium onion, thinly sliced
3-4 medium carrots, sliced
1½ Tbsp. butter
19-oz. can tomatoes

4 cups water
1 tsp. pepper
1½-2 tsp. oregano
½ tsp. basil
Bay, thyme, rosemary
1 tsp. garlic powder
¼-½ cup uncooked egg noodles

Cut fish into serving-sized pieces and sprinkle with lemon juice.

In a large pot, sauté celery, onion and carrots in butter, stirring until coated. Add tomatoes, water and spices and simmer for 20 minutes. Add noodles and simmer for another 10 to 15 minutes. Add fish and simmer for 20 minutes longer.

Serves 4.

— Marjorie Maund
Yellowknife, Northwest Territories

SPICY HALIBUT SOUP

THE USE OF A WHOLE, DRIED CAYENNE PEPPER GIVES THIS DISH ITS DISTINCTIVE HOT flavour. The amount of pepper used can be varied to suit individual tastes.

1 cup diced onion
Butter
6 cups chicken stock
1 dried red cayenne pepper,
  broken into pieces

½ lb. halibut, cut in small chunks
2 Tbsp. flour
½ tsp. basil
½ tsp. chervil
Thyme

Sauté onion in butter until transparent. Add chicken stock and cayenne and bring to a boil. Add halibut, lower heat and simmer for 10 minutes.

Mix the flour with a small amount of the soup stock and then gradually stir the flour mixture into the soup. Add spices.

Serves 4.

— Nancy Newsom
Courtenay, British Columbia

BERGEN FISH SOUP

Fish Stock
½ cup coarsely chopped turnip
½ cup coarsely chopped carrots
1 large yellow onion,
  coarsely chopped
1 potato, peeled & chopped
1 tsp. salt
6 whole black peppercorns
1 Tbsp. chopped parsley stems
1 bay leaf
3 stalks celery with leaves
2 lbs. fish trimmings (heads,
  bones, etc.), washed
4 quarts cold water

Soup
4 Tbsp. butter
4 Tbsp. flour
Fish stock
½ cup finely chopped carrots
¼ cup finely chopped parsnips
1 lb. boneless halibut, cod or haddock,
  in one piece
½ cup finely sliced leeks, white parts only
2 egg yolks
Salt & pepper
3 Tbsp. finely chopped parsley
6 Tbsp. sour cream

To prepare the fish stock, combine turnip, carrots, onion, potato, salt, peppercorns, parsley, bay leaf, celery and fish trimmings in a large, heavy saucepan. Add water and bring to a boil. Cover the pan, lower heat and simmer for 30 to 40 minutes.

Strain the stock, discarding the vegetables and fish trimmings. Wash the saucepan and return the stock to it. Boil rapidly for 20 minutes to reduce stock to 6 cups. Strain again and set aside.

To make the soup, melt butter in large, heavy saucepan. Add flour and stir until mixed. Gradually add stock, stirring constantly as stock thickens. Add carrots, parsnips and fish. As soon as soup reaches a boil, lower heat and simmer, uncovered, for 10 minutes. Add leeks and simmer for 3 to 4 minutes longer. Remove from heat, lift out fish and set aside on a platter.

In a small bowl, beat egg yolks with wire whisk. Beat in ½ cup of hot soup, one tablespoon at a time. Pour this back into the soup in a thin stream, beating continuously with a whisk.

With a fork, separate fish into flakes and add to soup. Season with salt and pepper and reheat, but do not boil. To serve, garnish with parsley and sour cream.

Serves 6.

— Louise Oglaend
Hjelmeland, Norway

SALMON SOUP

Quickly and easily assembled from ingredients usually in the pantry, this soup is handy to serve to unexpected guests. Add a salad and hot biscuits for a complete meal.

1 small onion, minced
2 Tbsp. butter
2 Tbsp. flour
4 cups milk

2 cups cooked, flaked salmon
Salt & pepper
½ cup cream

Cook onion in butter until soft. Add flour and stir well. Gradually add milk, stirring constantly, and cook for 1 minute. Add salmon, salt and pepper and cook until heated through and thickened. Stir in cream and heat.

Serves 4.

— *Judy Bachelder*
Georgeville, Quebec

GEORGE'S APHRODISIAC OYSTER SOUP

The contributor is so confident of the results of this soup that he strongly recommends that it be eaten only after the children are asleep in bed.

1 cup sliced mushrooms
3 Tbsp. butter
1 Tbsp. oil
1 pint fresh oysters
4 cups milk

½ tsp. salt
Pepper
⅛ tsp. oregano
Cayenne

Brown mushrooms in butter and oil. Drain oysters, reserving liquid, and add to mushrooms. Sauté briefly and set aside.

Heat milk to scalding, then add the oyster-mushroom mixture and the oyster liquid. Slowly heat to boiling point, adding salt, pepper, oregano and cayenne.

Serves 4.

— *George Belcher*
Lac La Biche, Alberta

CAPE HOUSE INN ICED BUTTERMILK WITH SHRIMP SOUP

The contributor of this recipe discovered this soup while on holiday in Nova Scotia last summer. The owner of the Cape House Inn in Mahone Bay generously shared his recipe.

3 cups shrimp
3 quarts buttermilk
1½ English cucumbers,
  coarsely chopped
3 Tbsp. fresh dill weed

2 Tbsp. dry mustard
3 Tbsp. chopped dill pickle
1 Tbsp. salt
1 tsp. pepper
Cayenne

Cook shrimp in boiling water until tender. Peel and chop into 1-inch pieces. Combine all ingredients, adding cayenne to taste. Mix well and chill. Serve garnished with thin cucumber slices.

Serves 12.

— *Billie Sheffield*
North Gower, Ontario

COLD BUTTERMILK SOUP

2½ cups buttermilk
¼ green pepper, sliced
½ cucumber or zucchini, sliced
Salt & white pepper
Parsley

Place ½ cup buttermilk and remaining ingredients in blender and purée at high speed. Add remaining buttermilk and blend briefly. Chill thoroughly.

Serves 2.

— *Mrs. M.H. Moloney*
London, Ontario

LEBANESE SOUP

THIS IS A TASTY COLD SOUP TO SERVE ON HOT SUMMER DAYS, WHEN MINT IS plentiful in most Canadian gardens.

½ English cucumber, seeds removed,
  cut into small pieces
3 cups plain yogurt
6 cups chicken stock

4 cloves garlic, minced
4 Tbsp. finely chopped mint leaves
Salt & pepper
1 ripe avocado

Salt the cucumber pieces lightly and let stand, refrigerated, for a few hours. Rinse and drain.

Combine yogurt with the stock; add cucumber, garlic and mint. Add salt and pepper to taste. Refrigerate until thoroughly chilled.

Immediately before serving, peel an avocado, cut it into small pieces and add to the soup. Serve cold.

Serves 6.

— *Ulla Sterm Troughton*
London, Ontario

Vegetables & Salads

My salad days,
When I was green in judgement. . . .

– William Shakespeare
Anthony and Cleopatra

ARTICHOKE SALAD

THE ARTICHOKE HAS BEEN CULTIVATED IN FRANCE SINCE THE BEGINNING OF THE sixteenth century. There are several types of artichokes, each best suited to a different method of preparation. Both of these recipes make use of canned artichoke hearts — readily available in most food stores. Of course, the same results can be had from fresh, whole artichokes that are cooked and stripped down to the heart.

2 14-oz. cans artichoke hearts
4 medium tomatoes, quartered
1 onion, sliced to form rings
5 Tbsp. corn oil
2 Tbsp. lemon juice

1 Tbsp. red wine vinegar
½ tsp. salt
¼ tsp. pepper
1 tsp. basil
1 Tbsp. chopped parsley

Drain artichoke hearts and chop into quarters. Toss in a salad bowl with tomatoes and onions.

Combine remaining ingredients and pour over artichoke mixture. Mix well. Chill to let flavours blend.

Serves 4.

— Linda Droine
Owen Sound, Ontario

MARINATED ARTICHOKES

2 Tbsp. lemon juice
2 Tbsp. oil
Garlic salt
1 Tbsp. sugar

¼ tsp. oregano, crushed
¼ tsp. tarragon, crushed
2 Tbsp. water
1 can artichoke hearts, drained

Combine all ingredients and mix well. Cover. Chill several hours or overnight.

To serve, lift artichoke hearts out of marinade and place on beds of lettuce. Sprinkle lightly with paprika.

Serves 2.

— Joan Morrison
North Gower, Ontario

MARINATED BROCCOLI

1 bunch broccoli
½ cup oil
6 Tbsp. vinegar
1 tsp. minced garlic
¾ tsp. salt
¼ tsp. pepper
½ tsp. tarragon

½ tsp. thyme
½ tsp. dry mustard
⅓ cup sliced green onions
½ cup slivered almonds
Pimento strips
Tomato wedges

Cut florets from stems of broccoli. Slice stems on the diagonal about ¼-inch thick. Steam 3 to 5 minutes or until tender but crispy.

To make marinade, combine other ingredients, except almonds, pimento, and tomatoes, in large bowl. Add hot broccoli and toss to mix. Cover and chill for at least 4 hours.

Lift broccoli from marinade and arrange on serving dish. Garnish with almonds, pimento and tomato.

Serves 4 to 6.

— Cheryl Peters
Courtenay, British Columbia

MARINATED BRUSSELS SPROUTS

1 lb. Brussels sprouts
3 Tbsp. salad oil
1½ Tbsp. lemon juice
Salt & pepper

1 clove garlic, crushed
1 tsp. dried tarragon
¼ cup Parmesan cheese

Clean and steam Brussels sprouts. Meanwhile, mix other ingredients together for dressing. Combine dressing and hot, drained Brussels sprouts in a bowl. Cool, then cover and refrigerate.

Serves 6.

— Pamela Morninglight
Queen Charlotte, British Columbia

TANGY VEGETABLE SALAD

1 carrot, grated
2 stalks celery, chopped
1 cup small cauliflower florets

1 tomato, chopped
¼ cup vinegar
3 Tbsp. oil

Mix vegetables. Combine remaining ingredients to make dressing.

Marinate vegetables overnight, stirring occasionally.

Serves 8 to 10.

— Linda Townsend
Nanoose Bay, British Columbia

MARINATED LEEKS

10 large leeks
3 Tbsp. apple cider vinegar
½ cup oil
1½ Tbsp. chopped parsley or chives

1 tsp. salt
Pepper
1 tsp. liquid honey
½ tsp. dry mustard

Clean leeks well and steam until tender — 10 to 15 minutes. Combine vinegar, oil, parsley or chives, salt, pepper, honey and mustard. Pour over leeks, chill and serve.

Serves 4.

— Leslie Dunsmore
Denman Island, British Columbia

SALPICON

THIS MEXICAN MARINATED VEGETABLE DISH IS ESPECIALLY ATTRACTIVE IN THE HEIGHT of summer, when most garden vegetables can be added to the marinade.

½ cup olive oil
½ cup vegetable oil
½ cup cider vinegar
¼ cup fresh lemon juice
Salt & pepper
1 cup cooked, thinly sliced potatoes
1 cup cooked, thinly sliced green beans

1 cup cooked, thinly sliced carrots
1 cucumber, peeled & thinly sliced
1 Bermuda onion, cut into thin rings
1 green pepper, cut into thin rings
1 red pepper, cut into thin rings
1 cup cooked, thinly sliced beets

Combine oils, vinegar, lemon juice and salt and pepper. Combine cooked and raw vegetables except beets and chill for several hours in marinade. Garnish with beets at serving time.

Serves 8 to 10.

— Holly Andrews
Puslinch, Ontario

RUTH'S FALL VEGETABLE VINAIGRETTE

1 cup small broccoli florets
1 cup small cauliflower florets
1 cup thinly sliced carrots
1 cup turnip, cut into 2-inch sticks
1 onion, sliced in rings
¼ cup vinegar
½ cup oil

1 clove garlic, minced
1 tsp. salt
⅛ tsp. pepper
¼ tsp. dried tarragon
¼ tsp. dried basil
1 Tbsp. chopped parsley
Dry mustard

Cook vegetables, except onion, in boiling water. Drain and cover with cold water until chilled. Drain again and combine with onion in large bowl.

Combine remaining ingredients for marinade. Pour over vegetables and mix gently. Cover and chill for several hours.

Serves 8.

— Marlene Spruyt
Ottawa, Ontario

SPECIAL WINTER SALAD

1 tsp. Dijon mustard
1 tsp. brown sugar
¾ cup vinegar
¾ cup orange juice, or juice
  from canned mandarin oranges
1½ cups oil

1 tsp. poppy seeds
1 tsp. curry
1 head romaine lettuce
2 ripe avocados
4 fresh (or 1 tin) mandarin oranges

Shake together mustard, sugar, vinegar, juice, oil, poppy seeds and curry. Tear romaine lettuce into bite-sized pieces. Slice avocados and oranges and arrange on lettuce. Pour dressing over top.

Serves 4.

— Kathe Lieber
Montreal, Quebec

VEGETABLES A LA GRECQUE

THIS COLOURFUL DISH, WHICH CAN MAKE USE OF MANY DIFFERENT COMBINATIONS OF vegetables, can be served as an appetizer or as a salad.

1½ cups water
¼ cup olive oil
Juice of 4-6 lemons
4 cloves garlic
1 bay leaf
Celery top
1 tsp. thyme
Sprig of fennel
1 tsp. salt

½ tsp. white pepper
Sprig of parsley
Tabasco sauce
1 lb. asparagus, sliced
6 leeks, sliced
6 zucchini, sliced
8 carrots, sliced
12-16 small onions
3 fennel heads, quartered

Combine all ingredients except vegetables and bring to a boil. Boil for 5 minutes, add vegetables and lower heat. Cook until vegetables are tender but crisp.

Cool. Remove garlic and chill salad.

Serves 8.

— Elizabeth Imboden
Uxbridge, Ontario

COPPER PENNIES SALAD

2 lbs. carrots, sliced
1 cup sugar
¾ cup vinegar
1 tsp. mustard

½ cup vegetable oil
1 tsp. Worcestershire sauce
1 green pepper, thinly sliced
1 onion, finely chopped

Boil carrots in salted water until just tender. Cool and then mix with other ingredients.

Serves 6.

— Isabell Lingrell
North Battleford, Saskatchewan

CARROT CONFETTI SALAD

A SIMPLE BUT DELICIOUSLY CRUNCHY SALAD, THIS IS PARTICULARLY GOOD DURING THE winter, when fresh vegetables are few and far between.

Grated carrot, allow 1 large
  carrot per person
1 small onion, finely chopped
1 stalk celery, finely chopped

½ green pepper, finely chopped
½ cup cubed Cheddar cheese
Mayonnaise, thinned with milk
Black pepper

Toss all ingredients together, chill well and serve.

Serves 1.

— Nicolle Fournier
Dunedin, New Zealand

TURKISH YOGURT & CUCUMBER SALAD

3 medium cucumbers
¼ tsp. salt
1 clove garlic, chopped
1 Tbsp. vinegar
½ tsp. dill

1 pint unflavoured yogurt
2 Tbsp. olive oil
1 Tbsp. chopped fresh mint leaves,
  or ½ tsp. dried mint

Peel, quarter and slice cucumbers. Sprinkle with salt. Rub serving bowl with garlic and then swish vinegar around bowl. Add yogurt, oil, dill and mint. Stir until thick. Add cucumbers and toss gently until well coated.

Serves 6.

— Fern Acton
Creston, British Columbia

CELERY & YOGURT SALAD

½ cup yogurt
2 tsp. olive oil
2 generous Tbsp. crumbled blue cheese
2 Tbsp. grated sharp Cheddar cheese

¼ tsp. salt
4 cups chopped celery
1 cup sliced mushrooms
½ sweet red pepper, chopped

Combine yogurt, olive oil, cheeses and salt. Mix with vegetables and serve.

Serves 4.

— Shan Simpson
Leslieville, Alberta

CAULIFLOWER PECAN SALAD

THE CAULIFLOWER IS A VEGETABLE OF ORIENTAL ORIGIN, WHICH HAS BEEN CULTIVATED in Europe since the sixteenth century. Although it is the white head that is commonly eaten either hot, or, as in these recipes, cold, the leaves and stalks are also edible. They should be prepared as broccoli would be.

1½ cups cauliflower florets
¾ cup chopped green pepper
1 cup toasted pecan halves
1 cup grated carrots
1 cup chopped celery

Horseradish Mustard Dressing:
¾ cup mayonnaise
4 Tbsp. horseradish
½ cup sour cream or yogurt
½ tsp. prepared mustard
Salt & pepper

Blanch cauliflower in boiling water for 2 minutes. Drain and chill. When ready to serve, combine all ingredients and toss with dressing.

To make dressing, combine all ingredients and mix well.

Serves 4 to 6.

— Lorraine Murphy
Mississauga, Ontario

CAULIFLOWER SPINACH TOSS

4 cups spinach, torn into
  bite-sized pieces
½ head lettuce, torn into
  bite-sized pieces
1 small head cauliflower,
  cut into small florets
3 carrots, peeled & sliced diagonally

⅔ cup vegetable oil
⅓ cup white vinegar
¼ tsp. salt
¼ tsp. paprika
½ tsp. dry mustard
2 cloves garlic, minced

Combine salad ingredients in a bowl. Place dressing ingredients in a jar with a tight-fitting lid. Shake well to combine. Toss salad with sufficient dressing to coat pieces evenly.

Serves 6 to 8.

— Nan & Phil Millette
Corunna, Ontario

HOT SPINACH SALAD

1 clove garlic, peeled & slivered
¼ cup oil
1 lb. spinach, washed, drained
  & torn into bite-sized pieces
1 cup sliced raw mushrooms

6 slices bacon
2 green onions, finely chopped
¼ cup vinegar
¼ tsp. salt
Pepper

Let garlic stand in oil for 1 hour. Discard garlic. Toss spinach and mushrooms in a bowl and refrigerate.

Fry bacon until crisp, remove from pan and crumble. Reserve 1 Tbsp. of fat. Stir in onions and sauté for 2 to 3 minutes. Add oil, vinegar, salt and pepper and bring to a boil.

Toss with spinach and mushrooms. Sprinkle with bacon.

Serves 4 to 6.

— Carol Frost
Chilliwack, British Columbia

SPINACH AND FRUIT SALAD WITH PIQUANT DRESSING

4 slices bacon
4 cups torn spinach
1 cup mandarin orange segments,
  drained & chopped
½ cup sliced onion
1 cup oil

3 Tbsp. lemon juice
1 tsp. salt
2 tsp. paprika
1 small onion, chopped
1 tsp. dry mustard
1 clove garlic, crushed

Fry bacon until crisp, drain and crumble. Combine with spinach, mandarin orange segments and sliced onion.

To make dressing, combine remaining ingredients, refrigerate and shake vigorously before using.

Serves 6 to 8.

— Janice Graham
London, Ontario

SPINACH, ORANGE & MANGO SALAD

IF ONE CAN FIND THE MANGOES, THIS IS A DELICIOUSLY EXOTIC SALAD, ESPECIALLY in the dead of winter, when it conjures up thoughts of tropical holidays.

1 lb. fresh spinach
2 navel oranges
2 mangoes
6 strips bacon
Dressing:
3 tsp. onion

½ tsp. salt
Pepper
1 Tbsp. Dijon mustard
2 Tbsp. white wine vinegar
1 tsp. lemon juice
⅔ cup olive oil

Wash, dry and tear up spinach. Peel and section oranges. Peel mangoes, remove pits, and cut into bite-sized strips. Cook bacon until crispy, drain, then crumble.

For the dressing, combine onion, salt, pepper, mustard, vinegar and lemon juice in a small bowl. Mix well, then beat in the olive oil very slowly. Continue beating until dressing thickens. Pour over spinach, oranges, mangoes and bacon, and toss. Let stand for 10 minutes and serve.

Serves 6.

— Ingrid Birker
Montreal, Quebec

AVOCADO SALAD

1 avocado
1 green pepper
2 stalks celery
10 raw mushrooms
1 cup oil
¼ cup apple cider vinegar
½ tsp. dry mustard

1 tsp. honey
½ tsp. paprika
½ tsp. salt
1 Tbsp. finely chopped onion
2 cloves garlic, finely chopped
Tarragon, thyme, basil, marjoram

Peel and dice avocado. Dice pepper, celery and mushrooms and combine with avocado.

Combine remaining ingredients and mix well. Pour over vegetables and toss lightly.

Serves 2.

— Denise Hensher
Charlton, Ontario

SALADE MEDITERRANEE

½ cup sliced mushrooms
¼ cup sliced almonds
1 cup sliced stuffed olives
1 tsp. tarragon

Juice of ½ lemon
½ tsp. basil
2 Tbsp. tarragon vinegar
6 Tbsp. olive oil

Boil mushrooms for 2 to 3 minutes, add sliced almonds and boil for another minute. Drain. Mix mushrooms and almonds with sliced olives.

Combine remaining ingredients in screw-top jar; shake to mix. Add dressing to olive, almond and mushroom mixture and toss together.

Refrigerate 24 hours before serving.

Serves 8.

— Gérard Millette
St. Anne-de-Bellevue, Quebec

ANTIPASTO

SERVED WITH CRACKERS OR ITALIAN BREAD, SWISS CHEESE AND A VARIETY OF SALAMIS, antipasto provides a flavourful start to an Italian meal.

8 oz. olive oil
1 large cauliflower, cut into
  bite-sized pieces
2 cups chopped black olives
2 cups chopped green olives
2 cups diced onion
2¼ cups sliced mushrooms
2 large green peppers, chopped
2 large red peppers, chopped

1 cup pimentos
4 cups tomato paste
4 cups stewed tomatoes, drained
  & chopped
1 cup chili sauce
3 cups chopped sweet pickles
Pepper
Cayenne
4 7-oz tins water-packed tuna

Mix together oil, cauliflower, olives and onion and stir-fry for 10 minutes, then add mushrooms, peppers, pimentos, tomato paste, tomatoes, chili sauce and pickles. Bring to a boil and simmer for 10 minutes, then add spices and tuna, bring back to a boil and simmer for 10 more minutes. Pack in jars and process in water bath or freeze. Serve, at room temperature, with cheese and whole wheat crackers.

— Charlene Skidmore
Medicine Hat, Alberta

APPLE BACON SALAD

⅔ cup garlic oil (oil which has had
  2-3 peeled, sliced garlic cloves
  standing in it overnight)
2 tsp. lemon juice
3 red apples, quartered, cored
  & thinly sliced
½ lb. bacon, cooked until crisp

1 head lettuce, torn into
  bite-sized pieces
½ cup grated Parmesan cheese
1 bunch scallions, chopped
½ tsp. pepper
¼ tsp. salt
1 egg

Mix garlic oil and lemon juice, and drop freshly cut apples into mixture. Combine all ingredients in salad bowl and toss until all traces of egg disappear. Serve immediately.

Serves 4.

— Denise Feeley
Kearney, Ontario

DELICIOUS APPLE SALAD

THIS LIGHT SALAD IS DELICIOUS WITH ROAST DUCK OR TURKEY.

1 cup whipping cream
3 tsp. sugar
½ cup mayonnaise
8 medium-sized Delicious apples, diced

Whip the cream and add sugar. Add mayonnaise and mix well. Stir in the cut-up apples and mix until well coated.

Serves 5 to 7.

— Pam Stanley
Vernon Bridge, Prince Edward Island

WATERMELON BOAT SALAD

½ watermelon
1 cantaloupe
1 honeydew melon
1 cup orange or pineapple juice
2 peaches or nectarines

2 apples
2 pears
1 bunch green grapes
6-10 large strawberries
½ cup Kirsch or Cointreau

Clean watermelon out using melon baller. Save juice. Ball cantaloupe and honeydew melons and place fruit in orange juice. Peel and slice peaches, apples and pears and add to above. Wash grapes and strawberries and add. Place fruit in watermelon boat and pour liqueur over top. Cover with plastic wrap and let marinate for 1 to 2 hours.

— Kirsten McDougall
Kamloops, British Columbia

BEYOND COLESLAW

3 cups finely grated cabbage
1 cup finely chopped cauliflower
1 red or green pepper, chopped
⅔ cup oil

⅓ cup apple cider vinegar
Salt & pepper
Garlic powder

Toss together cabbage, cauliflower and pepper. Combine oil, vinegar and seasonings to taste. Pour over vegetables and toss.

Serves 4 to 6.

— Dyan Walters
Kitchener, Ontario

SIMPLE TOMATO & MOZZARELLA SALAD

2 Tbsp. olive oil
1 Tbsp. red wine vinegar
1 clove garlic, finely chopped
4-5 basil leaves, chopped

½ tsp. salt
¼ tsp. black pepper
4 tomatoes, sliced
8 thin slices mozzarella cheese

Whisk together oil, vinegar, garlic, basil, salt and pepper. Arrange tomato and cheese slices in a bowl. Drizzle with dressing and let marinate, refrigerated, for 1 hour.

Serves 4.

— Francie Goodwin-Rogne
Calgary, Alberta

JELLIED GAZPACHO

1 envelope gelatin
1 cup cold beef stock
¼ tsp. salt
2 Tbsp. vinegar
⅛ tsp. dried basil leaves
1 clove garlic, crushed

14-oz. can tomatoes
2 Tbsp. finely sliced green onions
¼ cup diced, unpeeled cucumber
¼ cup diced green pepper
¼ cup diced celery

Sprinkle gelatin over stock in saucepan. Place over low heat and stir constantly until gelatin has dissolved — about 5 minutes. Remove from heat and stir in salt, vinegar, basil and garlic.

Chop large tomato pieces and add with juice to seasoned gelatin mixture. Chill to consistency of unbeaten egg whites. Stir in green onions, cucumber, green pepper and celery. Cover and chill until set.

Serves 6.

— Nan & Phil Millette
Corunna, Ontario

JELLIED BEET SALAD

1 envelope gelatin
¼ cup cold water
½ tsp. salt
⅓ cup sugar
¼ cup vinegar
¾ cup water or beet liquid

2 cups cooked, diced beets
¾ cup finely diced celery
1 Tbsp. minced onion
1 Tbsp. horseradish
Parsley
Pickled beets

Sprinkle gelatin over cold water in saucepan. Place over low heat and stir until gelatin dissolves.

Remove from heat and stir in salt, sugar, vinegar and water or beet liquid.

Chill to consistency of unbeaten egg white. Stir in beets, celery, onion and horseradish. Turn into 3-cup mould and chill until set.

Remove from mould and garnish with fresh parsley and pickled beets.

Serves 6 to 8.

— Lynn Tobin
Thornhill, Ontario

BLUSHING SALAD

2 cups pickled beets, well drained
2 medium-sized apples, sliced
¼ cup mayonnaise
¼ cup sour cream

Combine beets and apple slices. Combine mayonnaise and sour cream and gently stir into beets and apples. Chill well.

Serves 4.

— Maggie Christopher
Kemble, Ontario

LITHUANIAN BEET SALAD

THIS SALAD MAKES A COLOURFUL AND FLAVOURFUL MAIN DISH FOR A WINTER luncheon.

2 lbs. beets
¾ cup dry navy beans
3-4 medium potatoes
1 quart dill pickles

Salt
1 cup sour cream
Parsley

Cook beets, beans and potatoes separately and cool. Dice beets and potatoes into small pieces and place in large bowl. Add the cooked beans. Finely dice the pickles and add to the bowl. Add salt to taste.

Add the sour cream, as a dressing, no more than ½ hour before serving. Mix thoroughly. Decorate with parsley if you wish.

Serves 10.

— *Giedre Abromaitis*
Ottawa, Ontario

BEET & CABBAGE SALAD

6 beets, cooked & peeled
1 onion, finely chopped
2 cups shredded cabbage
2 tsp. sugar
1 tsp. salt

1 tsp. dry mustard
1 Tbsp. flour
1 egg, beaten
¼ cup vinegar
1 cup sour cream

Chill beets and cut into cubes. Combine with onion and cabbage. For dressing, mix together sugar, salt, mustard and flour and combine with egg and vinegar. Add sour cream and cook over medium heat, stirring constantly until thickened.

Pour hot dressing over combined cold vegetables and toss until well blended.

Serves 8 to 10.

— *Ingrid Birker*
Montreal, Quebec

SPICY CUCUMBER SALAD

CUCUMBERS HAVE BEEN CULTIVATED IN NORTHWEST INDIA FOR MORE THAN 3,000 years. Either regular or English cucumbers can be used with equal success in this recipe.

2 medium cucumbers
1 tsp. soya sauce
1 Tbsp. vinegar
1 Tbsp. sugar

2 tsp. sesame oil
¼ tsp. Tabasco sauce
½ tsp. salt

Peel cucumbers, halve lengthwise and scoop out and discard pulp. Cut crosswise into ¼-inch slices. Mix soya sauce, vinegar, sugar, oil, Tabasco sauce and salt in a small bowl. Add the cucumbers and toss well. Chill before serving.

Serves 4.

— *Beth Lavender*
Smiths Falls, Ontario

HERB AND GARLIC SALAD DRESSING

⅓ cup vinegar
⅔ cup salad oil
½ tsp. salt
½ tsp. sugar
1 clove garlic, chopped
¼ tsp. pepper

¼ tsp. dry mustard
¼ tsp. basil
¼ tsp. oregano
½ tsp. lemon juice
1 Tbsp. water

Combine all ingredients in a jar with tight-fitting lid. Shake well to combine. Refrigerate. Shake well before each use.

Makes 1 cup.

— *Joan Morrison*
North Gower, Ontario

MAPLE SYRUP DRESSING

THIS SIMPLE DRESSING MAKES A PLEASANT TOPPING FOR A COLE SLAW OF GRATED cabbage and carrot, raisins and sunflower seeds.

⅓ cup oil
⅓ cup cider vinegar
⅓ cup maple syrup

Mix and store in a covered container in the refrigerator.

— *I.F. Robinson*
Nepean, Ontario

GARDEN SALAD DRESSING

THIS DRESSING IS PARTICULARLY TASTY TOSSED WITH A LETTUCE AND MUSHROOM SALAD.

½ cup oil
¼ cup vinegar
¼ cup chopped parsley
2 green onions with tops, chopped
1-1½ Tbsp. chopped green pepper

1 tsp. salt
1 tsp. dry mustard
½ tsp. sugar
Paprika
Cayenne

Combine all ingredients, shake well and refrigerate. Shake well before tossing into salad.

— *Charlotte DuChene*
Yarker, Ontario

LEMON MUSTARD DRESSING

¼ cup oil
¼ cup lemon juice
1 tsp. basil
1 tsp. oregano

½ tsp. pepper
1 clove garlic, crushed
4 tsp. Dijon mustard
2 cups mayonnaise

Combine all ingredients and blend well. Refrigerate.

Makes 2½ cups.

— *Irene Louden*
Port Coquitlam, British Columbia

CHILI FRENCH DRESSING

⅓ cup salad oil
2 Tbsp. vinegar
2 Tbsp. catsup
2 tsp. grated onion
1 tsp. prepared mustard
¾ tsp. chili powder

½ tsp. salt
⅛ tsp. dry mustard
Pepper
Paprika
4 drops Tabasco sauce

Combine all ingredients in jar. Cover, shake and chill. Keep refrigerated and shake before using.

Makes ⅔ cup.

— *Nan & Phil Millette*
Corunna, Ontario

SPINACH SALAD DRESSING

⅓ cup oil
¼ cup vinegar
¼ tsp. Tabasco sauce
¼ tsp. dry mustard
½ tsp. salt
1 clove garlic, crushed

Mix all ingredients well.

— *Valerie Cameron*
Hamilton, Ontario

MOTHER'S FRENCH DRESSING

1 cup oil
⅓ cup vinegar
1½ tsp. dry mustard
¼ tsp. pepper

1½ tsp. salt
1 tsp. paprika
2 cloves garlic, minced

Combine all ingredients together and beat until creamy. Place in glass jar and store in refrigerator for 1 to 2 days.

Strain dressing through sieve to remove garlic and chill.

Makes 1 cup.

— *Mary Matear*
London, Ontario

CURRY VINAIGRETTE

1 Tbsp. curry powder
1 Tbsp. Dijon mustard
1 Tbsp. chopped parsley
1 Tbsp. chopped green onion

9 Tbsp. wine vinegar
1 cup olive oil
Juice of 1 lemon
Salt & pepper

Combine all ingredients and shake to mix well. Store in the refrigerator.

Makes approximately 1½ cups.

— *Wendy Neilson*
Pender Island, British Columbia

CREAMY CULTURES DRESSING

¾ cup sour cream
¼ cup yogurt
2 cloves garlic
2 Tbsp. olive oil
1 Tbsp. paprika
Salt & pepper

Combine all ingredients and blend well. Keep refrigerated.

Makes 1 cup.

— *Georgia White*
Simcoe, Ontario

CREAMY GARLIC DRESSING

THIS IS A SALAD DRESSING FOR REAL GARLIC LOVERS.

1 egg
1 tsp. mustard
1 tsp. salt
1 tsp. celery seeds

1 Tbsp. honey
2 or 3 cloves garlic
3 Tbsp. vinegar
1 cup oil

Put egg, mustard, salt, celery seeds, honey, garlic, vinegar and ½ cup oil in blender. Blend until smooth, then gradually add remaining oil.

Makes 1 cup.

— *Crystal Burgess*
Kincardine, Ontario

CREAMY SALAD DRESSING

½ cup mayonnaise
½ cup sour cream
1½ Tbsp. vinegar
1½ Tbsp. lemon juice
¼ cup chopped chives

Combine all ingredients and mix well. Cover and let stand, refrigerated, for 1 day.

Makes approximately 1 cup.

— *Carol A. Smith*
Whitehorse, Yukon Territory

WHIPPED DRESSING

2 egg yolks
¼ cup Dijon mustard
½ cup vinegar
Salt & pepper
1½ cups sunflower oil

Beat egg yolks, then add mustard and beat until smooth. Add vinegar and salt and pepper. Very slowly, taking 10 to 12 minutes, add the oil while beating. Refrigerate.

Makes 2½ cups.

— *Susan Budge*
Terra Cotta, Ontario

Delicious Onion Quiche, page 14

Indonesian Rice Salad, page 112

Dilled Tomato Soup, page 43

Chicken Pinwheels, page 155

Vegetable Pasta, page 216

Old Fort Henry Brown Bread, page 271

Castilian Hot Chocolate, page 293

Pavlova & Yogurt Chantilly, page 245

GREEN GODDESS DRESSING

1 cup mayonnaise
½ cup sour cream or yogurt
2 Tbsp. chives, finely chopped
¼ cup finely chopped fresh parsley
1 tsp. tarragon

1 clove garlic, crushed
1 Tbsp. lemon juice
1 Tbsp. white or tarragon vinegar
Salt & pepper

Combine all ingredients and mix well. Keep refrigerated.

Makes 1½ cups.

— Marlene Spruyt
Ottawa, Ontario

FETA CHEESE DRESSING

¾ cup oil
Juice of 1 lemon
2 tsp. anchovy paste
½ cup feta cheese
2 cloves garlic, crushed

½ tsp. dry mustard
½ tsp. dill weed
½ tsp. salt
½ tsp. pepper

Combine all ingredients and blend until smooth.

Makes 1 cup.

— P.C. Suche
Winnipeg, Manitoba

PARMESAN DRESSING

2 cups mayonnaise
½ cup cider vinegar
½ tsp. basil
½ tsp. oregano
2 cloves garlic, crushed
½ cup Parmesan cheese

Combine all ingredients and mix well with wire whisk. Store, covered, in refrigerator.

Makes 2½ cups.

— Wendy Neilson
Pender Island, British Columbia

AVOCADO YOGURT SALAD DRESSING

1 very ripe avocado
1 cup unflavoured yogurt
⅓ cup diced onion
⅓ cup diced green pepper
¼ cup mayonnaise

2 tsp. fresh dill weed
½ tsp. lemon juice
2 cloves garlic, minced
Salt & pepper

Blend avocado, yogurt, onion and green pepper for 20 seconds. Add remaining ingredients and blend until smooth.

Makes 1½ to 2 cups.

— Jill Leary
Creston, British Columbia

WHITE WINE SAUCE

½ cup white wine
½ cup grated Gruyère cheese
¼ tsp. dry mustard

¼ tsp. parsley
1 tsp. finely minced green onion
Salt & pepper

Heat wine and add cheese slowly, whisking to a smooth consistency. Add mustard, parsley, green onion and salt and pepper. Cover, keep warm and serve over steamed vegetables.

— Charlene Skidmore
Medicine Hat, Alberta

PEANUT SAUCE

ANY NUT BUTTER MAY BE USED IN PLACE OF PEANUT BUTTER — CASHEW IS A favourite. Serve this sauce over rice, spaghetti, tofu, as a fondue dip or over steamed vegetables.

½ cup peanut butter
1 small onion, grated
1 clove garlic, crushed
¼ cup instant milk powder

½ tsp. honey
2 Tbsp. lemon juice
2 tsp. soya sauce

Blend all ingredients in saucepan over low heat, adding hot water until mixture has consistency of heavy cream. For a smoother sauce, use blender to mix.

Makes 1 cup.

— Lorna Wollner
Moberly Fire-Lookout, Alberta

BABA GHANNOUJ

1 large eggplant
⅓ cup lemon juice
2-3 cloves garlic

3-4 Tbsp. bean stock or water
6 Tbsp. tahini
Paprika

Cut ends off eggplant and bake at 350 degrees F for 20 to 30 minutes, or until soft and partly collapsed. Peel and mash.

Mix together lemon juice, garlic, bean stock or water and tahini until smooth. Add eggplant and continue mixing, adding liquid as needed. Chill for at least 3 hours. Top with paprika and serve with raw vegetables or crackers.

— Marlene Spruyt
Ottawa, Ontario

CHEDDAR VEGETABLE DIP

1 cup mayonnaise
1 cup sour cream
1 cup finely grated Cheddar cheese
2 Tbsp. chopped spring onion

1 tsp. lemon juice
Worcestershire sauce
¼ tsp. garlic powder
Salt & pepper

Mix all ingredients and let sit, refrigerated, overnight. Taste and adjust seasonings before serving. Place on a platter and surround with fresh vegetables.

Makes 3 cups.

— Bonnie Lawson
Medicine Hat, Alberta

TUNA VEGETABLE DIP

6-oz. can white tuna
2 cups sour cream
4 Tbsp. mayonnaise

1 tsp. garlic powder
1 Tbsp. dill weed
1 Tbsp. chopped parsley

Mash tuna, then blend well with sour cream, mayonnaise, garlic, dill and parsley. Refrigerate for a few hours, then serve with raw vegetables.

Makes 3 to 4 cups.

— Jocelyn Raymond
Portland, Ontario

NANCY'S DILL DIP

1½ cups sour cream
½ cup mayonnaise
2 Tbsp. Dijon mustard
½ cup chopped, fresh dill weed

¼ cup thinly sliced green onion
2 tsp. lemon juice
½ tsp. salt
¼ tsp. pepper

Combine all ingredients, mixing well. Refrigerate, then serve with raw vegetables.

Makes 2 cups.

— Michèle Raymond
St. Sulpice, Quebec

VEGETABLE DIP

1 cup sour cream
¼ cup finely chopped green pepper
¼ cup finely chopped radishes
¼ cup grated carrots
2 Tbsp. chopped green onion

2 Tbsp. finely chopped parsley
½ tsp. salt
¼ tsp. pepper
½ tsp. lemon juice

Combine all ingredients and chill well. Serve with raw vegetables or crackers.

Makes 1½ cups.

— Kathy Major
Cherhill, Alberta

CREAMY LIVERWURST DIP

8 oz. liverwurst, coarsely chopped
1 cup sour cream
2 Tbsp. minced green onion
1 Tbsp. drained, chopped capers

¼-½ cup chopped water chestnuts
½ tsp. salt
Parsley

Beat liverwurst, then add sour cream and mix until blended. Add onion, capers, water chestnuts and salt, and chill. Garnish with parsley and serve with raw vegetables.

— Mary Howes
Picton, Ontario

ALMOND & MUSHROOM PATE

1 Tbsp. finely chopped onion
2 cloves garlic, crushed
½ lb. mushrooms, very finely chopped
2 Tbsp. butter

1 Tbsp. heavy cream
½ cup ground almonds
Salt & pepper
1 Tbsp. dry sherry

Sauté onion, garlic and mushrooms in butter until liquid evaporates, but do not let it brown. Cool. Add cream, almonds, salt and pepper and sherry. Mix well. Form into a ball, cover and chill. Serve with crackers or raw vegetables.

— *Louise Olson*
Vancouver, British Columbia

VEGETARIAN PATE

EQUALLY DELICIOUS AS A CRACKER SPREAD OR A SANDWICH FILLING, THIS PATE IS quickly and easily prepared.

1 cup sunflower seeds
1 potato, peeled
½ cup whole wheat flour
1½ cups hot water

1 large onion, minced
½ cup butter, melted
1½ tsp. basil
1 tsp. thyme

Chop the sunflower seeds finely by hand or in food processor. Grate the potato. Combine all ingredients and place in greased loaf pan. Bake at 350 degrees F for 1½ hours. Pâté will be moist. Serve hot, or chill in refrigerator overnight before serving.

— *Suzanne Dignard*
Ottawa, Ontario

STUFFED ARTICHOKE HEARTS

8 artichoke hearts, drained
¼ cup mayonnaise
¼ cup grated Parmesan cheese

Place artichoke hearts upright in small baking dish. Combine mayonnaise with Parmesan cheese and spoon into hearts. Broil until stuffing is lightly browned.

Serves 4 as an appetizer.

— *Joanne T. Gordon*
Toronto, Ontario

STIR-FRIED ASPARAGUS

2 Tbsp. oil
2 lbs. asparagus, cut into
  1½-inch pieces
1 large clove garlic, crushed
1 Tbsp. minced ginger root

Salt
½ cup chicken stock
1 tsp. cornstarch
2 Tbsp. soya sauce
1 tsp. sugar

Place oil in hot wok and heat until hot but not smoking. Stir-fry asparagus, garlic, ginger root and salt for 3 to 4 minutes until slightly tender. Combine stock, cornstarch, soya sauce and sugar and add to wok. Cover and simmer, stirring occasionally, for 2 minutes, or until asparagus is tender but still crisp.

Serves 4.

— *Valerie Gillis*
Renfrew, Ontario

DEVILLED GREEN BEANS

1 lb. green beans
3 tsp. butter
2 tsp. prepared mustard
½ tsp. Worcestershire sauce
Salt & pepper

Cook beans in boiling water until tender but crisp. Drain. Add remaining ingredients and stir gently until blended.

Serves 4.

— *A. Dianne Wilson-Meyer*
Saskatoon, Saskatchewan

BAKED GREEN BEANS

1½ lbs. green beans
8-oz. can water chestnuts
5 green onions
½ lb. mushrooms, sliced
½ cup butter
½ cup flour

2 cups milk
¾ cup grated Cheddar cheese
2 tsp. soya sauce
½ tsp. salt
1 cup slivered almonds

Cut beans diagonally, wash and cook. Slice water chestnuts and add to drained beans. Place in greased casserole dish. Sauté onions and mushrooms in butter, then stir in flour, milk and cheese. Cook over low heat until thickened, stirring occasionally. Stir in soya sauce and salt. Pour sauce over bean mixture and mix gently. Sprinkle almonds on top. Bake at 375 degrees F for 20 minutes.

Serves 6.

— *Midge Denault*
Lee Valley, Ontario

GREEN BEAN CASSEROLE

½ cup sliced onion
1 tsp. finely chopped parsley
2 Tbsp. butter
2 Tbsp. flour
½ tsp. grated lemon peel
Squeeze of lemon juice

Salt & pepper
1 cup sour cream
5 cups green beans, partially cooked
2 Tbsp. melted butter
½ cup dry bread crumbs
½ cup grated sharp cheese

Cook together onion, parsley, butter, flour, lemon peel, lemon juice and salt and pepper, then add sour cream and green beans. Pour into greased casserole dish and spread evenly, smoothing the top. Combine melted butter and bread crumbs and sprinkle over the top, then distribute the cheese evenly. Bake at 325 degrees F for 30 minutes, or until cheese is melted and browned.

Serves 8 to 10.

— *Rebecca Gibson Spink*
Burlington, Ontario

GREEK BEANS

3 Tbsp. olive oil
1 small onion, minced
1 small clove garlic, minced
2 Tbsp. minced green pepper
1 lb. green or wax beans,
　cut into 2-inch lengths

¾ cup chopped tomato
1 cup boiling water
2 tsp. wine vinegar
1½ tsp. chopped, fresh mint leaves
Salt & pepper

Heat oil in medium saucepan, and sauté onion, garlic and green pepper until soft — about 5 minutes. Add remaining ingredients, cover and cook for 20 to 30 minutes, or until beans are tender. Add salt and pepper to taste.

Serves 4 to 6.

— Valerie Sherriff
Courtenay, British Columbia

SWEET & SOUR GREEN BEANS

1 lb. green beans
2 green onions
2 Tbsp. butter
2 Tbsp. chili sauce

Steam beans for about 5 minutes, or until tender but crisp. Sauté chopped green onions in butter over low heat until soft and clear. Add green beans and chili sauce and toss until well blended.

Serves 4 to 6.

— Jennifer Webber
Westhill, Ontario

GREEN BEAN TIMBALES

THE WORD TIMBALE COMES FROM THE ARAB *thabal*, MEANING DRUM, AND DESCRIBES the traditional round metal dish used in the preparation of this and similar recipes.

4 cups cut-up green beans
2 Tbsp. butter
1 onion, sliced
1 clove garlic, chopped
½ cup cream

½ tsp. nutmeg
1 tsp. Dijon mustard
1 Tbsp. toasted sesame seeds
Salt & pepper
2 eggs

Steam green beans for about 5 minutes, or until tender but crisp. In large frying pan, melt butter and sauté onion, garlic and green beans for 2 minutes. Place mixture in food processor or blender and add cream, nutmeg, mustard, sesame seeds and salt and pepper. Purée thoroughly, then add eggs and blend.

Spoon mixture into 6 well-greased 6-ounce custard cups, cover with foil and place in deep pan filled with water to reach halfway up cups. Bake at 350 degrees F for 30 minutes, or until knife inserted in middle comes out clean. Remove from water and wait 5 minutes before removing foil. Remove from moulds or serve as is.

Serves 6.

— Megan Sproule
Bath, Ontario

ZIPPY BEETS

THIS IS A QUICK AND EASY WAY TO ADD SOME SPARKLE TO FROZEN BEETS IN THE MIDDLE of the winter.

3 Tbsp. butter
2 Tbsp. mustard
2-3 Tbsp. honey

1 tsp. Worcestershire sauce
Salt
2 cups hot cooked beets

Combine butter, mustard, honey, Worcestershire sauce and salt in saucepan. Blend well and heat to boiling. Add beets, stir to cover and serve.

Serves 2.

— *Lynn Andersen*
Lumsden, Saskatchewan

CRUNCHY BROCCOLI

THIS DISH CAN BE PREPARED UP TO THE BAKING STAGE EARLY IN THE DAY OR EVEN THE day before and refrigerated, leaving little work for the cook at dinner time.

3 cups chopped broccoli
3 Tbsp. butter
3 Tbsp. grated onion
2 Tbsp. flour
½ tsp. salt

¼ tsp. pepper
1 cup sour cream
¾ cup bread crumbs
¼ cup Parmesan cheese

Cook broccoli for 4 minutes, drain and place in greased casserole dish. Melt 2 Tbsp. butter in pan and sauté onions for 1 minute. Blend in flour, salt and pepper. Stir in sour cream until thick, then pour over broccoli. Melt remaining 1 Tbsp. butter, remove from heat and stir in bread crumbs. Sprinkle on casserole and top with cheese. Bake, uncovered, at 350 degrees F for 20 to 25 minutes.

Serves 4.

— *Kathy Payette*
Kitchener, Ontario

BROCCOLI ONION DELUXE

2 cups sliced onion
1 bunch broccoli, chopped
3 Tbsp. butter
3 Tbsp. flour
1¼ cups milk

4 oz. cream cheese
2 Tbsp. melted butter
1 cup soft bread crumbs
Parmesan cheese

Boil onion in salted water until tender. Cook broccoli until tender. Melt butter, stir in flour and milk and cook, stirring, until slightly thickened. Add cream cheese a little at a time, stirring until well mixed.

Place broccoli in greased casserole dish, top with onion and pour sauce over all. Combine butter and bread crumbs and place on top of casserole. Sprinkle Parmesan cheese over top and bake at 350 degrees F until lightly browned – about 30 minutes.

Serves 6.

— *Jill Harvey-Sellwood*
Toronto, Ontario

BROCCOLI WITH LEMON BUTTER

16 Brazil nuts, shelled
½ cup butter
¼ cup lemon juice
2 tsp. grated lemon rind
1 lb. broccoli, chopped

Place Brazil nuts in small saucepan and cover with cold water. Bring to a boil, lower heat and simmer for 2 minutes. Drain, then slice nuts thinly. Spread in a single layer on a shallow pan and bake at 350 degrees F for 10 minutes, or until lightly browned, stirring frequently. Cool.

Melt butter, add lemon juice and rind and keep hot. Steam broccoli until tender. Serve broccoli with lemon butter poured over it and sprinkled with Brazil nuts.

Serves 4.

— Barbara Zikman
Winnipeg, Manitoba

BROCCOLI WITH WILD RICE

WILD RICE MAKES THIS AN ELEGANT DISH WHICH IS ESPECIALLY GOOD WITH SEAFOOD. It is also delicious with other vegetable dishes and fresh bread.

¼ cup raw wild rice, cooked
½ cup raw white rice, cooked
1 cup very finely chopped onion
1 Tbsp. parsley
⅛ tsp. thyme
¼ tsp. garlic powder
Pepper

1 tsp. paprika
2 cups thick white sauce
 (*Volume I*, page 92)
1 cup chopped mushrooms, sautéed
1 tsp. salt
2 cups grated Cheddar cheese
2 stalks broccoli, cooked & chopped

Mix together rices, onion, parsley, thyme, garlic powder, pepper and paprika. Combine white sauce, mushrooms, salt and pepper and 1½ cups cheese. Layer these 2 mixtures, with the broccoli, in casserole dish. Top with remaining ½ cup cheese. Bake at 350 degrees F for 40 minutes.

Serves 4.

— Mary Hague
Grand Lake, Nova Scotia

CHEDDAR ALMOND BROCCOLI CASSEROLE

2 lbs. broccoli florets, steamed
 until barely tender
¼ cup butter
¼ cup flour
1 cup milk
¾ cup vegetable stock

2 Tbsp. lemon juice
2 Tbsp. sherry
Pepper
1 cup shredded Cheddar cheese
¼ cup ground almonds
Parmesan cheese

While broccoli is steaming, melt butter in saucepan and blend in flour. Add milk and stock and cook, stirring, until smooth and thick. Add lemon juice, sherry and pepper. Blend in Cheddar cheese and all but 1 Tbsp. of the almonds. Place broccoli in casserole dish and pour sauce over it. Sprinkle with Parmesan cheese and remaining almonds. Bake, uncovered, at 375 degrees F for 20 minutes.

Serves 4.

— Holly Andrews
Puslinch, Ontario

ORANGE BROCCOLI PARMIGIANA

2 heads broccoli, cut
  into bite-sized pieces
2 egg whites
½ cup mayonnaise
6 Tbsp. Parmesan cheese

1 tsp. parsley
1-2 tsp. grated orange peel
1 orange, peeled and sliced
2 Tbsp. butter

Cook broccoli until barely tender. Meanwhile, in a small bowl, beat egg whites until soft peaks form. Fold in mayonnaise, cheese, parsley and orange peel.

Drain broccoli and arrange in an ovenproof serving dish. Arrange orange slices over broccoli and dot with butter. Top with egg white mixture. Bake at 450 degrees F for 5 minutes, or until lightly browned.

Serves 6.

— Marilynn Janzen
Celista, British Columbia

INDIAN CABBAGE

IN INDIAN COOKING, IT WAS TRADITIONAL TO ADD THE SALT, DISSOLVED IN WATER, when the dish was about to be served as the blessing was never asked on food that had the salt already in it.

1 Tbsp. clarified butter
1 tsp. black mustard seeds
1 medium onion, chopped
1 medium cabbage, cut
  into ½-inch squares

1 tsp. turmeric
¾ cup water
½ tsp. salt

Place butter and mustard seeds in heavy pot. Cover and cook until all the seeds have popped. Add onion and fry until just turning brown.

Meanwhile, cover cabbage with cold water. When onion is browned, add drained cabbage and cook, stirring frequently, until dry. Dissolve turmeric in ½ cup water and add to pot. Continue cooking, covered, over medium heat until cabbage is tender. Stir in ½ tsp. salt dissolved in ¼ cup water. Serve.

Serves 6 to 8.

— Ethel Hunter
Warkworth, Ontario

COUNTRY CABBAGE CASSEROLE

2 lbs. cabbage, coarsely shredded
1 large onion, coarsely chopped
¼ lb. mushrooms, sliced
6 Tbsp. butter
¼ cup flour

1½ cups milk
Salt & pepper
½ cup wheat germ, toasted
¼ cup Parmesan cheese

Sauté cabbage, onion and mushrooms in 1 Tbsp. butter until tender — about 15 to 20 minutes.

Meanwhile, prepare white sauce using 3 Tbsp. butter, flour and milk. Cook, stirring, until thickened and season with salt and pepper.

Add white sauce to sautéed vegetables and mix well. Pour the mixture into a greased 9" x 13" baking dish. Melt remaining 2 Tbsp. butter and mix with wheat germ and Parmesan cheese. Sprinkle over cabbage mixture and bake at 350 degrees F until bubbly and heated through — about 20 minutes.

Serves 6.

— Pamela Mason
Ninga, Manitoba

ZESTY CARROTS

6-8 carrots, cut lengthwise
¼ cup water
2 Tbsp. grated onion
2 Tbsp. horseradish
½ cup mayonnaise
½ tsp. salt
¼ tsp. pepper
¼ cup cracker crumbs
1 Tbsp. melted butter

Cook carrots until tender and place in shallow baking pan. Mix water, onion, horseradish, mayonnaise and salt and pepper and pour over carrots.

Mix crumbs with melted butter and sprinkle on top of casserole. Bake at 375 degrees F for 20 minutes.

Serves 4 to 6.

— *Anne Lawrence*
Binghampton, New York

CALIFORNIA CORN

1 large onion, sliced
1 clove garlic, minced
2 Tbsp. olive oil
½ cup thinly sliced green pepper
1 lb. mushrooms, sliced
1 cup minced parsley
½ cup dry bread crumbs
½ tsp. oregano
14-oz. can creamed corn
4 medium tomatoes, peeled & sliced
½ lb. sharp Cheddar cheese, grated
1 tsp. salt

Sauté onion and garlic in oil until tender. Add green pepper and mushrooms and cook over low heat for 5 minutes. Combine parsley, bread crumbs and oregano in a bowl.

To assemble, place half the creamed corn in a greased casserole dish, then add half the green pepper-mushroom mixture, half the tomatoes, half the cheese, ½ tsp. salt and half the bread crumb mixture. Repeat layers. Cover and bake at 300 degrees F for 45 minutes. Remove cover and bake for 15 minutes more.

Serves 4.

— *Enid Campbell*
Belmont, Nova Scotia

BAKED CORN

¼ cup chopped onion
2 Tbsp. flour
1 tsp. salt
2 Tbsp. butter
2 tsp. paprika
¼ tsp. dry mustard
Pepper
¾ cup milk
2 cups corn
1 egg

Combine all ingredients and bake at 350 degrees F for 20 to 25 minutes.

Serves 4.

— *Kathy Cowbrough*
Stirling, Scotland

MEXICAN CORN CUSTARD

2 eggs, beaten
3 cups creamed corn
1 cup cooked corn
½ tsp. salt
1 clove garlic, minced

½ tsp. baking powder
⅓ cup melted butter
4 oz. chopped green chilies
½ cup chopped green or red pepper
⅓ lb. sharp Cheddar cheese, grated

Combine all ingredients in order listed and pour into buttered, 2-quart casserole dish.

Bake at 375 degrees F for 45 minutes; reduce temperature to 325 degrees and continue to bake for another 30 to 45 minutes, or until set.

Serves 6.

— *Joyce Falkowski*
Gold River, British Columbia

CAULIFLOWER CASSEROLE

1 large cauliflower
2 cups sliced mushrooms
⅓ cup finely chopped celery
¼ cup butter
2 Tbsp. flour
½ tsp. salt

½ tsp. dry mustard
1¼ cups milk
1 cup grated Cheddar cheese
½ cup cracker crumbs
2 Tbsp. melted butter

Break cauliflower into florets and cook until tender. Drain. Sauté mushrooms and celery in butter until tender. Blend in flour, salt and mustard. Gradually stir in milk and cook until mixture comes to a boil, stirring constantly. Add cheese and stir until melted. Put cauliflower into buttered, 1½-quart casserole dish and pour sauce over. Combine cracker crumbs with melted butter and sprinkle over casserole. Bake at 350 degrees F for 30 minutes.

Serves 4.

— *Joan Airey*
Rivers, Manitoba

DANDELIONS IN BATTER

Dandelion heads
½ cup flour
¾ tsp. salt
¼ tsp. pepper

½ tsp. baking powder
1 egg, well beaten
½ cup milk
Oil

Gather a few cups of blooms early in the morning, rinse in cold water, then soak in salt water for about 2 hours.

Prepare egg batter by sifting together flour, salt, pepper and baking powder. Blend in egg and milk and mix well. Dip blossoms into batter, then drop, a few at a time, into deep oil heated to 375 degrees F. Fry until golden brown, turning once.

— *Glenda G. Green*
Perth Road, Ontario

GARBANZO BEAN EGGPLANT ROLL-UPS

EGGPLANTS, ALSO CALLED AUBERGINES, ARE EXTREMELY VERSATILE. THIS RECIPE FOR stuffed eggplant is one unusual method of preparation. It is such an attractive vegetable that it is also the perfect vehicle for almost any combination of fillings, with or without the eggplant pulp as one of the ingredients.

1 large eggplant	3 Tbsp. butter
¼ cup oil	1 clove garlic, minced
1 cup dry garbanzo beans, cooked	3 Tbsp. flour
6-oz. can tomato paste	1 tsp. garam masala
¼ cup sesame seeds	¼ cup white wine
2 tsp. garlic powder	1¾ cups milk
2 tsp. tamari sauce	¼ cup Parmesan cheese
1 tsp. pepper	Chopped mint
1 cup grated mozzarella cheese	

Peel eggplant and slice ¼-inch-thick lengthwise. Fry in oil until tender.

Mash garbanzo beans until smooth. Add tomato paste, sesame seeds, garlic powder, tamari sauce, pepper and mozzarella cheese and mix together. Place a heaping spoonful of filling on each slice of eggplant and roll up. Place close together in greased casserole dish.

To make sauce, melt butter, add garlic and lightly brown. Stir in flour until smooth, reduce heat to low and add garam masala and wine. As sauce begins to thicken, slowly add milk and heat until slightly thickened, stirring often. Add Parmesan cheese. Pour over rolled eggplant, sprinkle with mint and bake at 350 degrees F for 30 minutes.

Serves 4.

— *Kay Chornook*
Englehart, Ontario

EGGPLANT TOFU CASSEROLE

TOFU, OR BEAN CURD, IS A COMPLETE-PROTEIN PRODUCT AND IS THEREFORE A VALUABLE food for those wishing to reduce the amount of meat in their diets. This recipe is but one of many ways to serve tofu. Another recipe is to stir-fry tofu along with a selection of vegetables and rice for a quick and easy complete meal.

1 onion, chopped	1 medium eggplant
5 cloves garlic, chopped	¼ cup oil
Butter	2 cups cooked rice
19-oz. can tomatoes	14-oz. tofu
Salt & pepper	1-2 Tbsp. tamari sauce
Oregano	1 cup grated mozzarella cheese

Fry onion and 3 cloves garlic in butter until onion is limp. Add tomatoes and simmer for 30 minutes, seasoning with salt, pepper and oregano.

Peel eggplant and chop into large cubes. Heat oil and fry eggplant until soft, adding a small amount of water if necessary to keep pan from drying out.

Place rice in bottom of greased 9" x 13" casserole dish. Cover with thin slices of tofu and sprinkle with 2 chopped cloves garlic. Pour tamari sauce over, then top with eggplant. Pour tomato sauce over this and sprinkle cheese over the top. Bake at 350 degrees F for 45 minutes.

Serves 6.

— *Lylli Anthon*
Duncan, British Columbia

BAIGAN SUBJI

THIS IS A THICK, RICH EGGPLANT CURRY THAT IS POPULAR IN NORTHERN INDIA.

5 Tbsp. oil
2 large onions, chopped
1 tsp. minced fresh ginger
1 tsp. turmeric
1 tsp. ground coriander
¼ tsp. cayenne

4 tomatoes, peeled & coarsely chopped
3 large eggplants, cubed
Salt
1 cup water
1 Tbsp. lemon juice
3 Tbsp. chopped coriander leaves

Heat oil and sauté onion and ginger. Add turmeric, coriander, cayenne and tomatoes and cook until tomatoes are liquid and sauce is thick.

Add eggplants, salt and water and cook, covered, until eggplant is soft — about 40 minutes. Add lemon juice and sprinkle with coriander leaves just before serving.

Serves 6 to 8.

— Ingrid Birker
Montreal, Quebec

EGGPLANT WITH GINGER SAUCE

2 medium eggplants
Oil
1¾ cups chicken stock
2 Tbsp. soya sauce
1 Tbsp. honey

1 Tbsp. cornstarch
1 Tbsp. peeled, minced ginger root
¼ tsp. salt
1 green onion, finely chopped

Cut eggplants lengthwise into ½-inch-thick slices, then cut each slice in half lengthwise.

In skillet over medium-high heat, cook eggplant in ¼ cup oil a few slices at a time until browned on both sides, adding more oil if needed. As they brown, remove slices to paper towels to drain.

In same skillet, mix remaining ingredients and cook over medium heat, stirring constantly, until mixture thickens. Return eggplant to skillet and heat through.

Serves 4.

— Christine Taylor
Norbertville, Quebec

BRAISED LEEKS

1 bunch leeks
4 Tbsp. butter
½ cup chicken stock

Trim, wash and cut down the middle of white parts of leeks. Melt butter, add chicken stock and bring to a boil. Add leeks, return to boil, cover, reduce heat and simmer for 15 to 20 minutes.

Serves 4.

— Doris Hill
Ayr, Ontario

SPINACH STUFFED MUSHROOMS

1 lb. fresh spinach
24 medium to large mushrooms,
  cleaned & stemmed, reserving stems
Butter

½ cup grated Parmesan cheese
⅔ cup crumbled feta cheese
½ cup finely chopped green onion
½ cup chopped fresh parsley

Steam spinach, chop finely, then drain well in sieve, pressing out moisture with wooden spoon. Finely chop mushroom stems and sauté in small amount of butter. Combine all ingredients, except mushroom caps, in bowl and mix well.

Brush outsides of mushroom caps with butter, then fill with spinach mixture, mounding it up in centre. Place on baking sheet and bake at 375 degrees F for 20 minutes, or until mushrooms are soft. Serve warm.

Makes 24.

— Susan Gillespie
Comox, British Columbia

CRAB STUFFED MUSHROOMS

4 oz. cream cheese
2 Tbsp. chopped almonds
1 tsp. chopped chives
8 oz. chopped crabmeat
Salt & pepper

Lemon juice
16 large mushroom caps
10 oz. spinach
2 cloves garlic, minced
4 oz. butter

Mix cream cheese, almonds and chives until smooth. Add crabmeat, salt and pepper and lemon juice.

Drop mushrooms into boiling water for 2 minutes, remove and rinse in cold water. Dry and stuff with cream cheese mixture.

Drop spinach into boiling water for 1 minute, drain and rinse with cold water to stop cooking. Squeeze dry. Sauté briefly in butter, tossing until hot. Place in greased 8" x 8" casserole dish, top with stuffed mushrooms and bake at 500 degrees F for 3 to 5 minutes. Heat garlic with butter until butter is melted. Pour over mushroom caps and serve.

Serves 4 as an appetizer.

— Estelle Lemay
Masson, Quebec

SPANISH MUSHROOMS IN GARLIC SAUCE

3 Tbsp. olive oil
2 cloves garlic, minced
1½ Tbsp. flour
1 cup beef stock
½ dried hot red chili pepper,
  seeded & cut into 3 pieces

2 Tbsp. minced parsley
2 tsp. lemon juice
½ lb. mushrooms

Heat 2 Tbsp. oil in skillet over medium-high heat. Add garlic and sauté until golden. Remove from heat, stir in flour and mix until smooth. Return to heat and cook for 2 minutes. Gradually add stock, blend in chili pepper, 1 Tbsp. parsley and lemon juice and stir until smooth and thick. Set aside.

Heat remaining 1 Tbsp. oil in skillet, add mushrooms and stir-fry until lightly browned. Add mushrooms to sauce and simmer for 5 minutes. Sprinkle with remaining 1 Tbsp. parsley and serve.

Serves 4.

— Pam Collacott
North Gower, Ontario

CREAMED MUSHROOMS

1 onion, finely chopped
½ lb. mushrooms, finely chopped
3 Tbsp. butter
1 Tbsp. sherry
½ cup sour cream

1 tsp. Worcestershire sauce
Tabasco sauce
Salt & pepper
1 tsp. thyme

Fry onion and mushrooms in butter until onion is limp. Add sherry and cook for 1 more minute. Add remaining ingredients and simmer slowly until thick — about 30 minutes.

Serve with crackers.

— *Mary Cummings*
Stouffville, Ontario

CREAMED MUSHROOMS & CHESTNUTS

THIS IS AN UNUSUAL CULINARY USE FOR CHESTNUTS, WHICH ARE TRADITIONALLY roasted and eaten whole or used as an ingredient in stuffings for fowl. Possessing considerable food value (3¼ pounds of chestnuts supply the daily caloric needs of the average adult), chestnuts, unfortunately, are so high in starch content as to be indigestible for many people.

1 lb. chestnuts
Cold water
5 Tbsp. butter
1 lb. mushrooms, quartered
2 Tbsp. flour

½ tsp. salt
⅛ tsp. pepper
1½ cups light cream
1 Tbsp. chopped parsley

Prick chestnut shells with sharp knife, cover with cold water and bring to a boil over moderate heat. Boil for 15 minutes, drain and cool. Remove shells and skins and cut into quarters.

Melt butter in skillet, add mushrooms and cook until lightly browned. Add flour and salt and pepper and stir until blended. Gradually add cream and cook over moderate heat, stirring constantly, until thickened. Fold in chestnuts and heat. Garnish with parsley.

Serves 6 to 8.

— *Doris McIlroy*
Kanata, Ontario

ROASTED RED ONIONS

6-8 medium red onions, peeled
⅔ cup oil
⅓ cup vinegar
Salt & pepper
Rosemary

Boil onions for 5 minutes and drain. Place in lightly greased baking dish, or in roasting pan with meat, and roast at 350 degrees F for 30 minutes, or until onions are browned, adding a little butter if desired.

Meanwhile, combine oil, vinegar, salt and pepper and rosemary. Place cooked onions in serving dish and pour dressing over them.

Serves 6 to 8.

— *Linda Valade*
Mississauga, Ontario

BAKED STUFFED ONIONS

4 medium yellow onions
1 cup coarse dry bread crumbs
¼ tsp. sage
¼ tsp. savory

¼ tsp. thyme
¼ tsp. paprika
¼ tsp. salt
3 Tbsp. melted butter

Peel onions, cover with boiling water and boil rapidly, uncovered, for 15 minutes. Drain and cool slightly.

Cut onions in half and remove centres, leaving shells of 2 or 3 layers. Chop centres coarsely and combine with bread crumbs and remaining ingredients. Spoon into shells and place in greased, shallow baking dish. Cover and bake at 350 degrees F for 35 to 40 minutes.

Serves 4.

— Mary Rogers
Hastings, Ontario

MAPLE GLAZED PARSNIPS

THE SELECTION OF SMALL, UNIFORMLY SIZED PARSNIPS FOR THIS RECIPE RESULTS in a delicious, tender dish.

8 small parsnips, trimmed & pared
⅓ cup maple syrup
1½ Tbsp. unsalted butter
2 tsp. lemon juice
¼ tsp. grated lemon zest

Cook parsnips, covered, in ½ inch of boiling water over medium-high heat until tender but crisp — 3 to 4 minutes. Remove from heat and drain well.

Combine remaining ingredients in same skillet and heat over medium heat until simmering. Return parsnips to skillet and cook, uncovered, turning frequently, until parsnips have absorbed the glaze — about 4 minutes.

Serves 4.

— Lucia M. Cyre
Logan Lake, British Columbia

BREADED PARSNIPS

8 small parsnips
1 egg, beaten
2 cups seasoned bread crumbs
Oil

Wash and pare parsnips. Boil until slightly softened, drain and let sit on paper towels to dry. Dip in egg and then bread crumbs. Place in baking dish, which is covered with ¼ inch of oil. Bake at 350 degrees F until golden brown — about 30 minutes — turning once.

Serves 4.

— Evelyn Coleman
Minden, Ontario

HEAVENLY PARSNIPS

12 medium parsnips, peeled
1 cup crushed pineapple, undrained
½ cup orange juice
½ tsp. salt

½ tsp. grated orange peel
2 Tbsp. brown sugar
2 Tbsp. butter

Cook parsnips in boiling water until tender — 25 to 30 minutes. Drain, split lengthwise and place in greased 9" x 13" greased baking dish. Combine remaining ingredients except butter and pour over parsnips. Dot with butter. Bake at 350 degrees F for 30 to 35 minutes, spooning sauce over parsnips several times.

Serves 6.

— Midge Denault
Lee Valley, Ontario

YOUNG GARDEN PEAS WITH HONEY & MINT

1 Tbsp. sesame oil
½ small onion, chopped
1 lb. young peas, shelled

2 sprigs fresh mint
1 tsp. honey
Salt

Heat oil and lightly brown onion. Add peas, mint and honey. Season with salt and cook for 5 to 7 minutes, or until peas are soft, but not mushy, adding 2 Tbsp. water if necessary. Remove the cooked mint and garnish with sprigs of fresh mint.

Serves 2 to 4.

— Lorraine Murphy
Mississauga, Ontario

POTATO CASSEROLE

2 cups mashed potatoes
2 cups cottage cheese
½ cup sour cream
1 small onion, minced

1-2 eggs, well beaten
Salt & pepper
Romano or Parmesan cheese

Combine all ingredients and place in greased casserole dish, cover with grated Romano or Parmesan cheese if you wish and bake at 350 degrees F for 1 hour.

Serves 4.

— Margaret Graham
Greenwood, British Columbia

CARLOS' POTATOES

4 large potatoes
4 cloves garlic, peeled & cut in half
1½ tsp. salt
1 Tbsp. oil

Cut potatoes into quarters, place in saucepan with garlic, salt, oil and water to barely cover. Cover pan, bring to a boil and simmer until tender. Serve potatoes with liquid.

Serves 4.

— Winifred Czerny
Pointe Claire, Quebec

COLCANNON

6 medium potatoes, peeled & chopped
⅓ cup milk
1 Tbsp. butter
½ tsp. salt
2 cups shredded cabbage

3 slices bacon
½ cup chopped onion
1 cup soft bread crumbs
¼ tsp. paprika
2 Tbsp. melted butter

Cook potatoes in boiling water until tender. Mash with milk, butter and salt.

While potatoes are cooking, steam cabbage until tender but crisp. Fry bacon until crisp, then crumble. Drain off about half the bacon fat. In remaining bacon fat, fry onion until soft.

In greased casserole dish, mix hot mashed potatoes, cooked cabbage, bacon and onion. Mix bread crumbs, paprika and melted butter and sprinkle over casserole. Bake, uncovered, at 400 degrees F until topping is golden — about 10 minutes.

Serves 8.

— Sherran McLennan
Prince George, British Columbia

HOT GERMAN POTATO SALAD

6 medium potatoes
¼ lb. bacon, chopped
¼ cup sliced green onions
⅓ cup vinegar
⅓ cup beef stock
1 Tbsp. sugar

½ tsp. salt
½ tsp. celery salt
Pepper
Parsley
Paprika

Boil potatoes until tender. Peel, slice and keep warm in serving dish. Cook bacon until crisp, remove, drain and add to potatoes, reserving fat.

In fat, fry green onions. Add vinegar, stock, sugar, salt, celery salt and pepper. Bring to a boil and pour over potatoes. Toss lightly to combine and top with parsley and paprika.

Serves 6.

— Irma Leming
Meaford, Ontario

POTATO LACE

½ cup chopped green onion
3 eggs
3 Tbsp. flour
⅓ cup chopped parsley

1 tsp. salt
½ tsp. pepper
3-4 large potatoes
Butter

In stainless steel bowl, combine onion, eggs, flour, parsley, salt and pepper. Grate potatoes onto towel; twist with one hand and press with the other to remove excess starch. Add potatoes to egg mixture.

Heat butter in skillet, drop in 3 Tbsp. batter and spread with back of spoon to make patties very thin. Fry until golden brown — about 2 minutes on each side.

Makes 10 to 12 patties.

— Mrs. James Fuller
Highland Park, Illinois

DOROTHY'S FAVOURITE STUFFED SPUDS

6 medium-large potatoes
1 lb. mushrooms, sliced
1 onion, finely minced
1-2 cloves garlic, crushed
2 tsp. butter

1 Tbsp. soya sauce
½ cup yogurt
3-4 green onions, sliced
¾ lb. grated old Cheddar cheese
Salt

Scrub potatoes and steam for 35 minutes, or until almost tender. Place on a baking sheet and bake at 350 degrees F until tender.

Sauté mushrooms, onion and garlic in butter with 1 tsp. soya sauce. When potatoes are cool enough to handle, split apart lengthwise and scoop out the insides. Mash with yogurt. If potatoes are very dry, add more liquid, although they should not be as moist as regular mashed potatoes. Mix in mushroom mixture, green onions, the remaining 2 tsp. soya sauce and three-quarters of the cheese. Taste for seasoning and add salt if needed. Place mixture back into the potato shells, top with remaining cheese and bake at 350 degrees F until heated through and cheese is melted.

Serves 6.

— *Cindy Panton-Goyert*
Kitimat, British Columbia

POTATOES MOUSSAKA

4 potatoes, thinly sliced
Oil
1 medium onion, thinly sliced

1 clove garlic, crushed
Parmesan cheese
14-oz. can tomatoes

Fry potatoes in oil until tender, add onion and garlic and cook until onion is limp.

In greased casserole dish, alternate layers of potatoes, cheese and tomatoes, ending with cheese. Bake at 350 degrees F until bubbly — about 30 minutes.

Serves 4.

— *Linda Hodgins*
Calgary, Alberta

SCALLOPED POTATOES & TOFU

1 onion, sliced
2 Tbsp. butter
4 oz. tofu, cubed
¼ cup wheat germ
2 large potatoes, thinly sliced

Milk
½ tsp. salt
Pepper
½ cup grated cheese

Sauté onion in butter until transparent. Add tofu and sauté for 5 minutes. Stir in wheat germ until well blended. Add potatoes and cook for several minutes longer, stirring carefully so as not to break the slices.

Turn ingredients into a greased casserole dish, adding salt and enough milk to nearly cover — about 1½ cups. Bake, covered, at 325 degrees F for about 45 minutes, or until the potatoes are tender. Uncover during the last 15 minutes and sprinkle with grated cheese if desired.

Serves 3.

— *Linda Goddu*
Ganges, British Columbia

RAPURE

The name for this dish based on grated potatoes originates with the verb "râper," which means "to grate." This version calls for pork, but chicken or clams can also be used.

½ lb. diced salt pork
1 onion, chopped
12 potatoes, peeled

1 egg
Flour
Salt & pepper

Boil the pork for a few minutes, then discard the water. Sauté the pork for another few minutes, then mix with onion in a greased 9" x 13" baking pan.

Grate potatoes and beat in egg. Add flour, salt and pepper and mix. Pour over pork and mix well. Cook at 250 degrees F for 4 to 5 hours.

Serves 6.

— Rachelle Poirier
Scoudouc, New Brunswick

SAVOURY STUFFED PUMPKIN

1 small pumpkin (approximately
  8-10 inches in diameter)
1-1½ lbs. lean ground beef (enough to
  stuff both pumpkin halves)
1 cup fine, dry bread crumbs
½ cup diced onion
½ cup diced green pepper
1 cup sliced mushrooms
2 cups canned tomatoes
½ cup catsup
1 Tbsp. Worcestershire sauce

1 Tbsp. brown sugar
1 Tbsp. parsley flakes
½ tsp. basil
½ tsp. oregano
1 tsp. chili powder
½ tsp. cayenne
1 Tbsp. sesame seeds
Garlic powder
Salt & pepper
Parmesan cheese

Slice pumpkin in half vertically, clean out seeds and stringy insides and set aside. Cook ground beef and drain off excess grease. Set aside. Sauté onion, green pepper and mushrooms. Return ground beef to pan and add remaining ingredients except Parmesan cheese. Simmer until most of the liquid has evaporated. Fill pumpkin halves, sprinkle with Parmesan cheese and cover with aluminum foil. Bake at 400 degrees F for about 2 hours, or until pumpkin is cooked.

Serves 6.

— Bonnie Lawson
Medicine Hat, Alberta

SPINACH & EGG CASSEROLE

¼ cup butter
¼ cup flour
½ tsp. salt
¼ tsp. paprika
2 cups milk

1 cup bread crumbs
2 cups chopped, cooked spinach
4 eggs, hard boiled, peeled & sliced
4 slices Cheddar cheese

Melt butter, stir in flour, salt, paprika and milk and cook, stirring constantly, until thickened.

In greased baking dish, assemble casserole as follows: half the bread crumbs, half the spinach, half the eggs, one-third of the sauce, half the cheese, rest of spinach, rest of eggs, one-third of the sauce, rest of cheese, rest of sauce and rest of bread crumbs. Bake at 325 degrees F for 35 to 40 minutes.

Serves 4.

— J. Kristine MacDonald
Baddeck Bay, Nova Scotia

DILL & CREAMED SPINACH

THIS RECIPE COMBINES DILL AND SPINACH, WHICH OFTEN ARRIVE IN THE GARDEN AT THE same time, with delicious results.

3 Tbsp. oil
2 Tbsp. flour
1 large clove garlic, minced
2-3 Tbsp. finely chopped dill

2 cups coarsely chopped, steamed spinach
1 Tbsp. brown sugar
1 cup cream
Salt

Heat oil, add flour and stir over high heat until flour browns. Add garlic and cook for 30 seconds. Add dill, remove from heat and let cool slightly. Stir in spinach, brown sugar and cream. Salt to taste, bring to boil and simmer for 2 to 3 minutes.

Serves 4.

— Ann Kostendt
St. Thomas, Ontario

GLAZED SQUASH WITH CRANBERRIES

THIS DISH IS EXCELLENT SERVED AS PART OF A TRADITIONAL THANKSGIVING OR Christmas dinner.

4 8-oz. pieces Hubbard squash
½ cup light maple syrup
2 Tbsp. butter
¼ tsp. salt

½ cup sugar
1 Tbsp. cornstarch
⅓ cup water
1½ cups cranberries

Peel squash, discarding seeds and stringy portion. Rinse and pat dry, then arrange in greased baking dish.

In saucepan over medium heat, combine syrup, butter and salt; heat to boiling, then pour over squash. Cover dish with foil and bake at 350 degrees F for 45 to 55 minutes, or until squash is almost tender.

Meanwhile, prepare cranberries. In saucepan over medium heat, combine sugar, cornstarch and water and heat to boiling, stirring constantly. Add cranberries and cook until they are just tender — about 5 minutes.

Spoon cranberries over squash. Continue to bake squash, covered, for 10 minutes, or until the pieces are tender.

Serves 4.

— Frances Walker
Halifax, Nova Scotia

SPINACH BALLS

1 lb. spinach, steamed & chopped
1 small onion, chopped
3 eggs
1 cup seasoned bread crumbs

¼ cup Parmesan cheese
Garlic salt
Thyme
⅓ cup melted butter

Combine all ingredients and mix well. Form into small balls and freeze separately on a cookie sheet. Place in an airtight container and use as required by baking at 350 degrees F for 15 minutes.

Serves 8 to 10 as an appetizer.

— Mrs. J. Wynes
Dauphin, Manitoba

SPINACH WITH PEANUT SAUCE

2 lbs. fresh spinach
2 Tbsp. butter
1 large onion, chopped
Cayenne

1 Tbsp. whisky
1 tsp. soya sauce
½ cup fresh coconut milk
½ cup unsalted peanuts, crushed

Cook spinach, without water, until limp. Cool, then drain to remove all moisture. Melt butter in a pan, and when foam subsides, add onion and cayenne. Cook until onion is soft. Stir in whisky, soya sauce, coconut milk and peanuts. Cook, stirring constantly, for 2 to 3 minutes. Add spinach to frying pan and cook until heated through, about 4 to 5 minutes.

Serves 6 to 8.

— *Ingrid Birker*
Montreal, Quebec

SUMMER SQUASH PUREE

THIS PUREE CAN BE MADE IN THE LATE SUMMER AND EARLY FALL, WHEN THE ZUCCHINI are threatening to overrun the garden. Kept in the freezer, it can be thawed out when needed and added to soups or casseroles thoughout the winter for a garden-fresh taste.

2 large onions, thinly sliced
6 Tbsp. butter
¼ cup water
3 cloves garlic, minced
2½ tsp. salt

½ tsp. pepper
6 lbs. summer squash
2 green peppers, thinly sliced
1 cup chopped parsley

Cook onions in butter until soft. Add water, garlic, salt, pepper, squash and green peppers. Cover and cook for 3 minutes. Lower heat to medium and cook for 12 to 15 minutes, or until squash is tender.

Remove from heat, add parsley and cool. Purée in blender half a cup at a time. Cool. Freeze in 2-cup amounts.

Makes 12 cups.

— *Dianne Griffin*
Pefferlaw, Ontario

BUTTERNUT SQUASH MEDLEY

3 large onions, sliced
1 large clove garlic, crushed
2-3 Tbsp. butter
2 cups cubed butternut squash,
  steamed until tender
1 brick tofu, cubed
½ cup cooked brown lentils

1 cup stewed tomatoes, with juice
2 Tbsp. tamari sauce
1 tsp. curry
1 tsp. oregano
Grated mozzarella or Cheddar cheese
Parsley

Sauté onions and garlic in butter. Add squash, tofu, lentils, tomatoes, tamari sauce, curry and oregano. Simmer until slightly thickened. Cover with cheese and sprinkle with parsley.

Serves 4 to 5.

— *Rosande Bellaar Spruyt*
Rupert, Quebec

BUTTERNUT SQUASH WITH CHEESE & WALNUTS

1 small butternut squash
1 small onion, chopped
1 cup shredded hard cheese
½ cup chopped walnuts

Peel and slice squash and steam until just tender. Oil a casserole dish. Layer squash, onion, cheese and walnuts, ending with a layer of cheese and walnuts on top. Bake, uncovered, at 300 degrees F for 15 minutes.

Serves 4.

— *Brenda Thaler*
Waterloo, Ontario

LOVE IT SQUASH

THIS IS AN UNUSUAL STUFFED SQUASH RECIPE THAT TAKES ADVANTAGE OF THE celery-like lovage plant. The addition of grapes and sherry gives the dish a slightly sweet taste.

1 large Hubbard squash,
  halved & seeded
5 onions, chopped
6-8 cloves garlic, minced
2 hot peppers, chopped

Fistful lovage, chopped
1 lb. sweet red grapes, halved & pitted
½ cup sherry
Olive oil

Bake squash at 375 degrees F for 1½ hours, or until flesh is tender. Scrape out insides without piercing shell. Chop up pulp and combine with onions, garlic, peppers and lovage. Add grapes and sherry and dribble with olive oil. Return to shells and bake at 350 degrees F for 1 hour, or until piping hot, with a pan of water on the rack below the squash to prevent it from drying out.

Serves 4 to 6.

— *Deborah Washington*
Bath, Ontario

RUM SQUASH

4 cups mashed, cooked squash
2 Tbsp. rum
2 Tbsp. maple syrup
½ tsp. salt
1 Tbsp. cream

½ cup well-drained, crushed pineapple
5 Tbsp. butter
½ cup brown sugar
½ cup chopped walnuts

Mix squash, rum, syrup, salt, cream, pineapple and 2 Tbsp. butter and pour into a greased, 2-quart casserole dish. Melt remaining 3 Tbsp. butter over low heat and stir in brown sugar and walnuts. Cook, stirring, until creamy and pour over squash. Bake at 350 degrees F for 20 to 30 minutes, or until bubbly.

Serves 4.

— *Joan Patricia Cox*
Healey Lake, Ontario

TOFU & SWEET POTATO BALLS

A NATIVE OF INDIA, THE SWEET POTATO HAS ADAPTED TO GROW IN ALL WARM
countries. Very similar to yams, the two vegetables can be used interchangeably. The
leaves of the sweet potato can also be cooked and eaten like spinach.

24 oz. tofu, mashed
2 cups mashed, cooked sweet potatoes
¼ cup chopped onion
½ tsp. salt
Pepper
1 cup dried bread crumbs
Oil

Combine tofu, sweet potatoes, onion, salt and pepper. Form into 1-inch balls and roll in
bread crumbs. Remove excess crumbs, then let stand on paper towel for 10 minutes. In
wok, heat cooking oil to 350 degrees F — hot but not smoking — then deep-fry balls until
golden brown.

Serves 8 to 10 as an appetizer.

— Colin Webster
Kelowna, British Columbia

SWEET POTATO SOUFFLE

5 sweet potatoes, quartered
2 apples, peeled, quartered & cored
4 eggs, separated
1 tsp. vanilla
1 Tbsp. butter

Place sweet potatoes in large saucepan with water to cover and simmer until tender —
about 30 minutes. Let cool and peel. Place apples in a saucepan, cover with water and
simmer for about 8 minutes, until just tender. Put potatoes and apples through a food
mill together or purée together in food processor. Transfer to large mixing bowl and stir
in egg yolks. In another bowl, beat egg whites until stiff peaks form. Fold into sweet
potato-apple mixture. Beat in vanilla.

Place mixture in buttered, 2-quart soufflé dish. Dot with butter and bake at 350 degrees F
for 45 to 60 minutes, or until hot and bubbly and lightly browned on top.

Serves 6 to 8.

— Sue Summers
Enderby, British Columbia

SCALLOPED YAMS & APPLES

2 lbs. yams, peeled & sliced
6 medium apples, peeled & cut
  into thin wedges
Juice of 1 lemon
⅓ cup brown sugar
⅓ cup butter
¼ tsp. nutmeg
Salt & pepper

Arrange half the yams, cut side down in greased, shallow, 2-quart casserole dish. Add
half the apples. Mix remaining ingredients and sprinkle half on mixture. Repeat layers,
cover and bake at 350 degrees F for 1 hour.

Serves 6 to 8.

— Judy Morrison-Cayen
Courtenay, British Columbia

BAKED SWISS CHARD

THIS IS AN EXCELLENT WAY TO USE AN OVERABUNDANCE OF CHARD DURING THE summer. The recipe may be varied by adding mushrooms, tomatoes, olives and chopped bacon.

1 lb. Swiss chard	2 eggs
¼ cup butter	Salt & pepper
1 large onion, sliced	¾ cup grated Cheddar cheese

Cut stems from chard, then cut stems into ¼-inch pieces and leaves into 1-inch strips. Melt butter, add onion and stems and cook until onion is transparent. Add leaves and cook for 3 minutes. Place in greased, 2-quart baking dish. Beat eggs, add salt and pepper and then pour over chard. Sprinkle with grated cheese and bake at 400 degrees F for 10 minutes.

Serves 2 to 4.

— Sandra Lintz
Nelson, British Columbia

SCALLOPED TOMATOES WITH HERBS

2 medium onions, sliced	2 cups coarse, soft bread crumbs
½ green pepper, diced	2 Tbsp. chopped parsley
2 stalks celery, diced	1 tsp. chopped chives
¼ cup butter, melted	3 cups peeled & chopped tomatoes
¼ tsp. pepper	2 Tbsp. butter
½ tsp. thyme	

Sauté onions, green pepper and celery in butter with pepper and thyme. Cook, stirring occasionally, until onions are transparent and remove from heat.

Combine bread crumbs, parsley and chives. Stir half this mixture into onions.

Arrange alternate layers of chopped tomatoes and onion-bread crumb mixture in a greased casserole dish, ending with tomatoes. Sprinkle with remaining bread crumbs and dot with 2 Tbsp. butter.

Bake at 350 degrees F for 45 minutes.

Serves 4.

— Cathy Gordon
Kingston, Ontario

GREEN TOMATO CURRY

THIS RECIPE PROVIDES A DELICIOUS USE FOR END-OF-THE-SEASON UNRIPE TOMATOES. It can be frozen very successfully and does not take a great deal of time to prepare.

¼ cup butter	8 cups green tomatoes
2 medium onions, chopped	½ cup brown sugar
4 Tbsp. curry powder	2 Tbsp. lemon juice
1 tsp. cumin	½ tsp. paprika
1 cup water	Salt

Sauté onions in butter for 10 minutes. Add curry powder and cumin and cook for 5 minutes longer. Stir in water and remaining ingredients. Simmer for 30 minutes, stirring occasionally and adding more water if necessary. Serve over rice.

Serves 4.

— Leslie Gent
Courtenay, British Columbia

ZUCCHINI FRENCH FRIES

4 medium zucchini
1½ cups flour
Salt
2 eggs

1½ Tbsp. water
1 cup Parmesan cheese
Garlic salt
Oil

Wash zucchini and remove ends, but do not peel. Cut into shoestring strips approximately 3 inches long. Sprinkle well with salt and roll lightly in ½ cup flour. Shake off excess flour and drop strips, several at a time, into eggs beaten lightly with 1½ Tbsp. water.

In wide, shallow pan, combine remaining 1 cup flour with Parmesan cheese and garlic salt. Roll zucchini in flour mixture to coat evenly and spread on paper towels to dry. Heat oil to 375 degrees F. Fry strips, a handful at a time, until crisp and golden. Drain on paper towels and keep warm until all are fried.

Serves 4 to 5.

— *Barb Krimmer*
Big Lake, British Columbia

ZUCCHINI SOUR CREAM CASSEROLE

3 medium zucchini, sliced
3 Tbsp. butter
¼ cup sour cream
1 Tbsp. grated Cheddar cheese
½ tsp. salt

⅛ tsp. paprika
1 egg yolk, beaten
1 Tbsp. chopped chives
½ cup cracker crumbs

Cook zucchini in steamer or small amount of boiling, salted water until tender but crisp. Drain and place in a greased, 1½-quart casserole dish.

Melt 1 Tbsp. butter in small saucepan. Stir in sour cream, cheese, salt and paprika. Cook over low heat, stirring constantly and without boiling, until cheese is melted. Remove from heat and stir in egg yolk and chives. Stir into zucchini. Toss cracker crumbs with remaining 2 Tbsp. melted butter. Cover zucchini with crumb mixture. Bake, uncovered, at 350 degrees F for 20 to 25 minutes.

Serves 3 to 4.

— *Diane Cancilla*
Kingston, Ontario

ZUCCHINI LASAGNE

2 cups cottage cheese
1 cup cooked, chopped spinach
1 lb. mozzarella cheese, grated
1½ lbs. ground beef
1 small onion, chopped
8-oz. can tomato sauce

½ tsp. salt
½ tsp. pepper
½ tsp. oregano
½ tsp. thyme
2½ lbs. zucchini, thinly sliced lengthwise

Combine cottage cheese, spinach and half the mozzarella cheese in a bowl. Brown ground beef and onion, drain off excess fat, then add tomato sauce, salt, pepper, oregano and thyme. Simmer for 5 minutes.

In a greased 9" x 13" casserole dish, layer half the meat mixture, half the zucchini, all of the spinach-cheese mixture, the rest of the zucchini, the rest of the meat and top with remaining ½ lb. of mozzarella cheese. Cover and bake at 350 degrees F for 30 minutes. Uncover and bake for another 45 minutes.

Serves 6.

— *Christine Peterman*
Victoria, British Columbia

ZUCCHINI PARMIGIANA

6 small zucchini
1 egg
1 Tbsp. water
¼ cup oil
1 medium onion, chopped
2 cloves garlic, finely chopped

13-oz. can tomato paste
1½ cups water
1 Tbsp. basil
Salt & pepper
1 cup Parmesan cheese
1 lb. mozzarella cheese, grated

Slice zucchini lengthwise ¼-inch thick. Combine egg and water and coat slices in mixture. Cook in hot oil until golden brown, then remove. Cook onion and garlic in remaining oil until tender. Combine with tomato paste, water and seasonings.

In a lightly greased 9″ x 13″ casserole dish, arrange half the zucchini. Spoon over half the tomato mixture and cover with half the cheese. Repeat layers.

Bake at 350 degrees F for 30 to 45 minutes, until heated through and golden.

Serves 4 to 6.

— Jane Durward
Lindsay, Ontario

STUFFED ZUCCHINI BLOSSOMS

THE BLOSSOMS THAT FALL OFF SQUASH VINES WITHOUT MATURING ARE THE MALE flowers not retained for seed development. They make decorative as well as edible cases for almost any type of stuffing — bread, meat or vegetable. Open each blossom and lightly stuff, then close the petals. Place on greased baking dish and cook at 350 degrees F until thoroughly heated.

VEGETABLE MEDLEY WITH BEER SAUCE

1 medium eggplant, peeled & cut
 into ½-inch slices
2 medium zucchini, cut
 into ½-inch slices
2 eggs
2-3 Tbsp. butter
13-oz. can tomato paste
½ lb. mushrooms, sliced
14½-oz. can stewed tomatoes

½ cup beer
½ green pepper, diced
1 medium onion, diced
2 tsp. oregano
½ tsp. basil
1 tsp. salt
4 oz. cream cheese, softened or sliced
4 oz. Monterey jack cheese, sliced
4 oz. Cheddar cheese, sliced

Dip eggplant and zucchini slices in beaten eggs and sauté for approximately 5 minutes on each side.

Make the beer sauce by combining the tomato paste, mushrooms, stewed tomatoes, beer, green pepper, onion, oregano, basil and salt in a saucepan. Bring to a boil and simmer for 10 minutes.

Assemble the casserole in a greased 9″ x 13″ pan as follows: half the eggplant, all of the cream cheese, half the zucchini, one-third of the beer sauce, the rest of the eggplant, half of the Monterey jack and Cheddar cheese, one-third of the beer sauce, the rest of the zucchini, the rest of the beer sauce and the rest of the cheeses.

Bake at 350 degrees F for 45 to 50 minutes.

Serves 6.

— Francie Goodwin-Rogne
Calgary, Alberta

ITALIAN VEGETABLE MEDLEY

THIS RECIPE IS REALLY JUST A GUIDELINE. ALMOST ANY GARDEN-FRESH VEGETABLE CAN be added or substituted — it is the banana pepper and garlic which give the dish its distinctive flavour.

3 Tbsp. oil
4 medium onions, cut in half
  & sliced lengthwise
1 banana pepper, sliced
6 cloves garlic, crushed
1 tsp. finely chopped ginger

2 Tbsp. curry
2 sweet peppers, thinly sliced lengthwise
Juice of 1 lemon
8 tomatoes, peeled & chopped
1 cup bean sprouts

Sauté onions, banana pepper, garlic and ginger lightly in hot oil. Add curry and sweet peppers. When vegetables are cooked, but still crunchy, add tomatoes and lemon juice. Cook over low heat until tomatoes are soft. Add bean sprouts and toss. Serve with pasta or rice.

Serves 4.

— *Sandra Hunter*
Toronto, Ontario

TOMATO SQUASH CASSEROLE

1 large onion, chopped
1 green pepper, chopped
1 large butternut squash, cubed
3 Tbsp. brown sugar

3 Tbsp. flour
28-oz. can tomato sauce
Salt & pepper

Sauté onion and green pepper. Add squash, sugar, flour, tomato sauce and salt and pepper and mix well. Place in buttered casserole dish and bake at 350 degrees F for 40 minutes.

Serves 4.

— *Valerie Repetto*
Oshawa, Ontario

CABBAGE TOMATO CASSEROLE

THIS IS AN EXCELLENT RECIPE FOR THE FALL, WHEN FRESH CABBAGE AND TOMATOES are plentiful.

3 cups finely shredded cabbage
1½ cups peeled &
  coarsely chopped tomatoes
¾ tsp. salt

¼ tsp. paprika
1 cup grated Cheddar cheese
1 cup bread crumbs
2 strips bacon, finely chopped

Boil cabbage in salted water for 5 minutes, then drain well. Heat tomatoes and add salt and paprika.

Place alternating layers of tomatoes and cabbage, beginning with tomatoes, in a greased baking dish. Sprinkle each layer with grated cheese and bread crumbs.Top casserole with chopped bacon. Bake at 350 degrees F until crumbs are brown — about 30 minutes.

Serves 6.

— *Janeen Clynick*
Clinton, Ontario

SIMPLE SUMMER CASSEROLE

2 ears corn
4 very ripe tomatoes
2 onions
4 stalks celery
½ cup cooked rice

2 cloves garlic, crushed
1½ tsp. chili powder
¾ tsp. salt
Pepper
2-2½ cups grated Cheddar cheese

Cut corn from cob, peel and chop tomatoes coarsely, slice onions in rings and cut celery into bite-sized pieces.

Place vegetables in 9-inch round casserole dish. Add rice, garlic, seasonings and 1 cup grated cheese. Stir until well mixed and press to form even top. Sprinkle remaining cheese over top. Bake at 350 degrees F for 45 to 50 minutes.

Serves 4.

— Linda Page
Courtenay, British Columbia

MOROCCAN TAGINE

THE CONTRIBUTOR LEARNED HOW TO MAKE THIS DISH WHILE LIVING IN MOROCCO. The word "tagine" refers to the covered clay pot in which the vegetables and tomato sauce were simmered over an open fire.

1 parsnip
1 potato
1 carrot
1 eggplant
1 zucchini
3 tomatoes
1 onion, chopped

1 clove garlic, chopped
2 tsp. cumin
½ tsp. turmeric
½ tsp. cayenne
5-6 prunes
5-6 olives

Chop or slice parsnip, potato, carrot, eggplant and zucchini. Steam tomatoes to remove skins and then mash with fork. In saucepan, sauté onion and garlic; add tomatoes and spices. Layer vegetables over tomato sauce as follows — parsnip, potato, carrot, eggplant, zucchini, tomatoes. Add a little water and the prunes and top with olives.

Cover and simmer on medium heat for about 30 minutes or until vegetables are tender.

Serves 2 to 3.

— Sylvia Dawson
Manitoulin Island, Ontario

CHEESE TOMATO & CORN SCALLOP

2 cups bread crumbs
2 cups canned tomatoes
2 cups whole kernel corn

¼ cup butter
1 tsp. salt
1 cup grated Cheddar cheese

Combine bread crumbs, tomatoes, corn, butter, salt and ⅔ cup cheese. Pour into greased, shallow baking dish. Sprinkle remaining cheese on top. Bake at 350 degrees F for 20 to 30 minutes, or until brown on top.

Serves 4.

— Helene Conway-Brown
Elnora, Alberta

TOMATO ALFALFA & CHEESE PIE

Pastry for double 9-inch pie shell
¼ cup finely chopped celery
½ tsp. parsley
½ tsp. basil
¼ tsp. salt
2 Tbsp. butter

2 cups peeled & sliced tomatoes
4 oz. alfalfa sprouts
1 cup grated Cheddar cheese
½ cup mushrooms, sliced
¼ cup bread crumbs

Sauté celery, parsley, basil and salt in butter until celery is limp. Line pie plate with half of pastry, then layer tomatoes, sprouts, cheese, mushrooms, bread crumbs and celery-herb mixture. Add top crust and bake at 375 degrees F for 45 minutes.

— *Tracy Brown*
Perth, Ontario

VEGETABLE POT PIE

THIS IS A DELICIOUS ALTERNATIVE TO THE TRADITIONAL BEEF OR CHICKEN POT PIE.

Pastry for 9-inch pie shell
6 small white onions
  or 1 medium onion, cut into eighths
2 cups chopped cauliflower
1 cup sliced carrots
1 cup quartered mushrooms
1 cup peas

½ cup slivered almonds
3 Tbsp. butter
4 Tbsp. flour
1 cup milk
1 Tbsp. parsley
Salt & pepper

Cook onion, cauliflower and carrots until just tender. Drain and save 1 cup liquid. Arrange cooked vegetables in greased 8" x 8" baking dish along with mushrooms, peas and almonds.

To make sauce, melt butter, stir in flour, then gradually add cooking liquid and milk. Continue to stir and cook, adding parsley and salt and pepper, until sauce is thickened. Pour over vegetables. Top with pie crust and bake at 425 degrees F for 20 to 25 minutes, or until crust is lightly browned. Cool for 10 minutes before serving.

Serves 4.

— *Julie Pope*
Fort McMurray, Alberta

COLACHE

THIS MIXED VEGETABLE DISH IS A MEXICAN RECIPE DATING FROM THE DAYS of the Aztecs.

1 cup chopped onion
2 medium tomatoes, peeled
  & coarsely chopped
1 green or red pepper, diced
2 cups diced zucchini
½ cup green beans
½ cup wax beans

2 cups corn
½ cup vegetable stock
1 tsp. oregano
⅛ tsp. chili powder
⅛ tsp. pepper
Salt

Cook onion and tomatoes in heavy pot until softened. Add green or red pepper, zucchini and beans and cook over medium-high heat, stirring, for 5 minutes. Add corn, stock, oregano, chili powder, pepper and salt and simmer for 10 minutes.

Serves 4 to 6.

— *Heather Quiney*
Victoria, British Columbia

GUI DING

THIS CHINESE VEGETABLE DISH CAN BE ACCOMPANIED BY RICE AND SWEET AND SOUR spareribs for a complete meal.

2 carrots
2 stalks celery
1 can bamboo shoots
1 can water chestnuts
4 green onions
2 Tbsp. plus 1 tsp. peanut oil
½ lb. cashews

2 Tbsp. cornstarch
¾ cup water
½ tsp. garlic powder
1¼ tsp. soya sauce
1 tsp. sugar
2 drops sesame seed oil

Cut carrots, celery, bamboo shoots, water chestnuts and green onions into ½-inch pieces. Cook carrots and celery in 2 Tbsp. peanut oil for 1 minute. Add bamboo shoots, water chestnuts, green onions and cashews and continue to cook over high heat, stirring frequently.

Meanwhile, combine cornstarch, water, garlic powder, soya sauce, sugar, remaining 1 tsp. peanut oil and sesame seed oil. Pour over vegetables and fry for another minute until well mixed and slightly thickened.

Serves 6.

— Mary Giesz
Winfield, British Columbia

KOHLRABI CARROT BAKE

3 medium kohlrabi, peeled & sliced
  into ½-inch fingers
4 medium carrots, sliced diagonally
¼ cup chopped onion
2 Tbsp. butter
2 Tbsp. flour
½ tsp. salt

Pepper
1½ cups milk
¼ cup parsley
1 Tbsp. lemon juice
¾ cup bread crumbs
1 Tbsp. melted butter

Cook kohlrabi in small amount of water for 15 minutes. Add carrots and cook for another 10 to 12 minutes until vegetables are tender. Drain.

Cook onion in butter until tender. Blend in flour, salt and pepper. Add milk and cook, stirring, until bubbly. Stir in vegetables, parsley and lemon juice. Turn into greased, 1-quart casserole dish. Combine bread crumbs and butter and sprinkle over casserole. Bake at 350 degrees F for 20 to 25 minutes.

Serves 6.

— Valerie Gillis
Renfrew, Ontario

LENTIL KALE & MUSHROOM STEW

THIS DISH CAN BE SERVED AS A VEGETABLE ACCOMPANIMENT OR AS A MAIN COURSE.

3 potatoes, cubed
6-8 dried Chinese mushrooms
2 carrots, sliced
½ cup lentils

1 clove garlic, crushed
4 Tbsp. butter
¼ cup soya sauce
1 bunch kale, chopped

Combine all ingredients except soya sauce and kale in large, heavy pot. Cover with water and simmer for several hours. Add soya sauce and kale and cook for another hour.

Serves 4.

— Arlene Pervin
Moyie, British Columbia

LAYERED VEGETABLE CHEESE BAKE

1 Tbsp. oil
1 large onion, coarsely chopped
1 large green pepper,
  cut into squares
1 small eggplant, peeled
  & cut into small cubes
½ lb. mushrooms, halved

1 large tomato, peeled & chopped
1 cup bread crumbs
1 tsp. salt
¾ tsp. thyme
⅛ tsp. pepper
2 cups grated Swiss cheese

Heat oil over medium heat, add onion and green pepper and sauté for 3 minutes. Add eggplant and mushrooms and sauté for another 3 minutes, stirring constantly. Add tomato and cook for 1 minute.

Mix bread crumbs with salt, thyme and pepper. Spread on bottom of greased casserole dish. Top with half the vegetable mixture, then half the cheese. Repeat. Bake at 350 degrees F for 30 to 40 minutes.

Serves 2.

— *Christine Davidson*
Campbell River, British Columbia

PLOUGHMAN'S PLATTER

THIS DISH USES UP LEFTOVER VEGETABLES IN A DELICIOUS AND EASY-TO-PREPARE MEAL. You may use more or less vegetables, depending on your preference and what you have available.

1½ cups vegetables
2 slices onion, chopped
½ clove garlic, chopped
3 Tbsp. soya sauce

2 potatoes, cooked & sliced
½ cup grated Cheddar cheese
Yogurt

Steam or fry vegetables, onion and garlic until tender, then toss with soya sauce.

Place potatoes in a single layer to cover bottom of greased, shallow baking dish. Place vegetable mixture on top of potatoes in another layer. Cover with grated cheese.

Broil until cheese is bubbly and dish is steaming hot. Serve with yogurt garnish.

Serves 2.

— *Jane Lott*
Toronto, Ontario

Beans
&
Grains

Work and pray,
Live on hay,
You'll get pie in the sky when you die.

— **Joe Hill**
The Preacher and the Slave

VEGETARIAN CHILI

1 cup pinto beans
1 cup navy beans
1 cup kidney beans
9 cups water
1 large onion, chopped
2 cloves garlic, minced

2 Tbsp. oil
2 stalks celery, chopped
1 large green pepper, chopped
2 26-oz. cans tomatoes
1 cup chopped mushrooms
Chili powder

Soak beans in water overnight. Sauté onion and garlic in oil. Add celery and green pepper and cook for 5 minutes. Add tomatoes, mushrooms and beans, bring to a boil and simmer for at least 2 hours. Season with chili powder to taste.

Serves 6.

— *Lynn Bakken*
Winlaw, British Columbia

MIXED BAKED BEANS

3 cups cooked white beans,
  with cooking liquid reserved
1½ cups cooked red kidney beans,
  with cooking liquid reserved
1½ cups cooked soy beans
  with cooking liquid reserved
½ cup chopped onion

½ cup catsup
¼ cup brown sugar
¼ cup molasses
1½ tsp. salt
1 tsp. dry mustard
¼ tsp. pepper
¼ lb. salt pork or bacon, cut into pieces

Combine beans, onion, ketchup, brown sugar, molasses, salt, mustard and pepper. Spread half of pork in casserole dish, add bean mixture and top with remaining pork. Add enough reserved cooking liquid to cover.

Cover and bake at 350 degrees F for 2 hours, adding liquid as needed. Remove cover and bake for an additional 30 minutes.

Serves 4.

— *Elizabeth Clayton-Paul*
Nepean, Ontario

SWEET & SOUR BEANS

½ cup maple syrup
¼ cup lemon juice
3 Tbsp. soya sauce
1 cup unsweetened pineapple chunks,
  drained with juice reserved
2-3 Tbsp. cornstarch
1 cup thinly sliced carrots

1 cup thinly sliced celery
1 onion, thinly sliced
2 cups cooked kidney beans
2 cups cooked garbanzo beans
Salt
4 cups steamed rice

Combine maple syrup, lemon juice and soya sauce with reserved pineapple juice in a saucepan. Add cornstarch dissolved in 2-3 Tbsp. water. Heat, stirring, until mixture boils. Add carrots and celery and simmer, covered, for 10 minutes, or until vegetables are tender but still crisp. Stir in pineapple, onion and beans and heat through. Season with salt to taste. Serve on rice.

Serves 4 to 6.

— *Patricia McKay*
Victoria, British Columbia

BEAN LENTIL STEW

THIS VEGETARIAN STEW IS FLAVOURFUL AND HEARTY. IT IS VERY EASY ON THE budget, especially in summer, when fresh vegetables are in abundance.

1 cup navy beans, rinsed
1 cup brown lentils, rinsed
28 oz. canned tomatoes
2 onions, chopped
2 stalks celery, chopped
½ cup diced green pepper
1-2 cloves garlic, minced
1 Tbsp. butter or oil

3 large carrots, cut into chunks
1 large potato, cut into chunks
1 cup diced turnip
2 tsp. salt
¼ tsp. pepper
1 tsp. crushed savory
½ tsp. crushed basil
¼ cup finely chopped parsley

Place navy beans in a large pot, cover with 4 cups water and bring to a boil. Boil for 2 minutes, turn off heat and let sit for 1 hour. Then simmer beans gently for about 2 hours, or until almost tender. Add lentils and tomatoes.

In heavy pan, sauté onions, celery, green pepper and garlic in oil. Add this to the bean mixture. Add remaining ingredients and simmer until lentils and vegetables are cooked, adding liquid as necessary.

— *Jan Gilbert*
Ashton, Ontario

NAVY BEAN PATE

8 cups cooked navy beans
3 cups roasted hazelnuts or walnuts
6 onions, chopped
2 cups chopped mushrooms
Butter
2 tsp. thyme
1 tsp. white pepper
1 tsp. nutmeg

1 tsp. cloves
1 tsp. ginger
1 bunch parsley, finely chopped
Salt
Tamari sauce
8 eggs
2 cups cream

Grind together navy beans and nuts. Sauté onions and mushrooms in butter, then add to bean mixture. Add thyme, pepper, nutmeg, cloves, ginger, parsley, salt and a dash of tamari sauce.

Beat eggs with cream and blend into above ingredients. Turn into 2 well-greased baking pans. Cover with buttered wax paper and bake at 350 degrees F for 45 to 60 minutes. Serve either hot or cold.

Makes 2 loaves.

— *Deborah Washington*
Bath, Ontario

REFRITOS NEGROS

1 Tbsp. lard or bacon fat
¼ cup chopped onion
2 cloves garlic, minced
2 Tbsp. diced, seeded jalapeño peppers
½ tsp. cumin

¼ tsp. cinnamon
⅛ tsp. cloves
½ tsp. salt
2 cups cooked black beans,
    drained with cooking liquid reserved

Melt lard or bacon fat and cook onion and garlic until onion is soft but not browned. Add peppers and spices and cook for a few minutes longer.

In food processor or blender, process spice mixture with beans, adding cooking liquid as needed to make a soft, moist mixture. Return mixture to saucepan and cook, stirring constantly, until heated through.

Serves 2.

— *Karen Kadlee*
Calgary, Alberta

BLACK TURTLE BEANS

MANY COUNTRIES OF THE WORLD INCLUDE BLACK BEANS AND RICE AS A DAILY DIETARY staple. The legume and rice combination forms a complete protein, one that is much more economical than meat. Serve this dish with stir-fried mustard greens or collards.

1 lb. black turtle beans
Stock
2 cloves garlic
1 tsp. salt
1 Tbsp. oil

Rinse beans thoroughly and cover by at least 1 inch with stock. Cook gently for 1½ to 2½ hours, or until tender.

Crush garlic with salt in mortar and pestle until paste is formed. Heat oil in small skillet and sauté garlic until lightly browned.

Remove large spoonful of beans from pot and mash into garlic-oil mixture until beans are well puréed. Return to bean pot. Simmer gently for another half-hour, adding water if beans become too thick. Serve with rice.

Serves 6 to 8.

— *Mrs. J.E. Tilsley*
Aurora, Ontario

BLACK BEAN DINNER

1 cup black beans
4 cups water
6-oz. can tomato paste
2 cloves garlic
1 Tbsp. soya sauce
Oregano

1 tsp. chili powder
2 onions, chopped
2 ribs celery, chopped
2 green peppers, chopped
1 Tbsp. grated ginger root

Boil beans in water for 2 hours. Add remaining ingredients and simmer until flavour is well blended. Serve with baked potatoes, pasta or brown rice.

Serves 4.

— *Kathe Lieber*
Montreal, Quebec

HOT CURRIED GARBANZO BEANS

1½ cups garbanzo beans
2 cups water
2 tsp. curry
1 tsp. turmeric

⅛ tsp. chili peppers
Salt & pepper
2 Tbsp. cornstarch
3 green onions, chopped

Soak garbanzo beans in water for 24 hours. Simmer in 2 cups water for approximately 1½ hours. Add curry, turmeric and chili peppers. Season with salt and pepper to taste. If sauce is too thin, thicken with 2 Tbsp. cornstarch dissolved in ¼ cup of water. Stir in green onions. Serve over millet or rice.

Serves 2.

— *Joanne Lavallée*
St. Côme, Quebec

INDONESIAN FRIED RICE

FOR A VEGETARIAN MEAL, THE MEAT CAN BE EASILY OMITTED FROM THIS RECIPE.

1 onion, chopped
3 cloves garlic
½ tsp. ginger
½ tsp. cardamom
½ tsp. turmeric
½ tsp. crushed red pepper
1 tsp. salt
¼ tsp. pepper

2 Tbsp. oil
2 Tbsp. lemon juice
1 Tbsp. soya sauce
1 cup cubed, cooked meat
3 Tbsp. chopped green pepper
3 Tbsp. chopped celery
¼ cup coconut milk
4 cups cooked rice

Crush together onion, garlic, ginger, cardamom, turmeric, red pepper, salt and pepper. Sauté in oil for 2 to 3 minutes. Add lemon juice, soya sauce and meat and cook for a few minutes longer. Add green pepper, celery, coconut milk and rice. Stir-fry until hot.

— Susan Bates Eddy
St. Andrews, New Brunswick

RAVISHING RICE

THIS RICE IS A MEAL-IN-A-DISH — WITH THE COTTAGE CHEESE AND TAMARI SAUCE providing protein.

1 cup raw rice, cooked
1 clove garlic
2 green onions, chopped
½-1 cup sliced mushrooms

3 Tbsp. butter
2 Tbsp. sesame seeds
1 cup cottage cheese
2 Tbsp. tamari sauce

As rice is cooking, sauté garlic, green onions and mushrooms in butter. Add sesame seeds, stirring until they coat mushrooms.

Add cottage cheese, tamari sauce and mushroom mixture to cooked rice and heat through.

Serves 3 to 4.

— Helene Dobrowolsky
Whitehorse, Yukon Territory

SESAME RICE

THIS IS A SLIGHTLY DRESSED-UP VERSION OF FRIED RICE. CASHEWS OR OTHER NUTS OR seeds may be used in place of sesame seeds.

1½ cups sesame seeds
½ tsp. cayenne
1 bay leaf
4 Tbsp. butter

1 tsp. salt
4 cups cooked rice
Juice of ½ lime

Sauté sesame seeds, cayenne and bay leaf in butter until seeds are golden. Stir in salt and rice and cook over high heat, stirring constantly, until rice is heated through. Sprinkle with lime juice and serve.

Serves 4.

— Susan Bates Eddy
St. Andrews, New Brunswick

ROSEMARY'S RUMBLETUM RICE

THIS RECIPE AND THE THREE THAT FOLLOW IT ARE BUT A FEW EXAMPLES OF RICE salads. The possible additions and combinations are limited only by the cook's imagination. This dish makes use of rice, olives, raisins, nuts and corn — an unusual but tasty mix.

2 cups cooked rice
¼ lb. olives, coarsely chopped
½ cup raisins
½ cup mixed nuts

1½ cups corn
1 small onion, finely chopped
Salt & pepper
Olive oil

Combine all ingredients, using just enough oil to bind them together. Chill thoroughly before serving.

— Mary Flegel
Montreal, Quebec

CURRIED RICE SALAD

1 carrot
2 stalks celery
3 green onions
1 cucumber
10 mushrooms
3 cups cooked brown rice, cooled

½ cup mayonnaise
½ cup yogurt
2 tsp. curry powder
2 Tbsp. parsley
Salt & pepper

Slice vegetables thinly and combine with rice. Mix together mayonnaise, yogurt, curry powder, parsley and salt and pepper. Toss with rice-vegetable mixture until all ingredients are coated. Chill well and serve.

Serves 8 to 10.

— Avril Houstoun
Edson, Alberta

INDONESIAN RICE SALAD

2 cups cooked brown rice
½ cup raisins
2 green onions, chopped
½ cup chopped onion
½ cup toasted sesame seeds
½ cup toasted almonds or cashews
½ cup sliced water chestnuts
1-2 cups bean sprouts
1 green pepper, chopped
1 red pepper, chopped
1-2 stalks celery, chopped

Dressing:
Parsley
¾ cup orange juice
½ cup oil
Juice and chopped peel of 1 lemon
2 cloves garlic, crushed
1 Tbsp. sesame oil
4 Tbsp. soya sauce
2 Tbsp. sherry

Combine rice, raisins, onions, seeds, nuts and vegetables. Blend remaining ingredients well to make dressing. Pour over rice-vegetable mixture and stir to coat. Chill several hours or overnight.

Serves 6 to 8.

— Megan Sproule
Bath, Ontario

CURRIED RICE & ARTICHOKE SALAD

6-oz. jar marinated artichoke hearts
2-3 stalks celery
½ green pepper
1 green onion
1 cup pitted black olives

4 Tbsp. slivered almonds
1 cup mayonnaise
½ tsp. curry powder
Salt & pepper
2 cups cooked rice

Chop artichoke hearts, reserving liquid from jar. Chop celery, green pepper, onion and olives. Combine all ingredients and mix well. Chill before serving.

— Elizabeth Lettic
Ladysmith, British Columbia

SPINACH & BROWN RICE CASSEROLE

1 cup brown rice
2½ cups water
2 Tbsp. oil
1 cup sliced mushrooms
½ cup chopped green onions
¼ cup roasted sunflower seeds

1 lb. spinach, chopped
¾ cup grated jack cheese
2 cups cubed, cooked chicken
6-oz. jar marinated artichoke hearts, drained
¾ cup grated Cheddar cheese

Cook rice in boiling water until tender. Remove from heat, uncover and cool slightly. Heat oil in small saucepan over medium heat. Add mushrooms and green onions and sauté until mushrooms are golden. Set aside.

Mix sunflower seeds into rice, then spread in a greased, shallow 2-quart casserole dish. Layer spinach, then jack cheese, then chicken over the rice. Spread mushroom mixture over this, then arrange artichokes. Sprinkle with Cheddar cheese and bake, covered, at 350 degrees F until bubbly and cheese has melted – about 45 minutes.

Serves 6.

— Julianne Ourom
Kitimat, British Columbia

BROWN RICE BURGERS

THIS BASIC RICE BURGER RECIPE CAN BE ADDED TO IN A NUMBER OF WAYS. Mushrooms, peas, green pepper, celery or almost any other vegetable, finely chopped, can be added, as can thyme or sage. Cornmeal or wheat germ can replace the oatmeal.

3 cups cooked rice
½ bunch parsley, finely chopped
3 carrots, grated
1 onion, chopped
1 clove garlic, minced

2 eggs
¼ cup oatmeal
¾ cup flour
Salt
1 tsp. dill weed

Combine all ingredients. Shape into patties and fry in oil.

Serves 4.

— Dixie Yeomans
Kamloops, British Columbia

BULGUR BURGERS

1 cup bulgur
2 cups brown rice
1 cup wheat germ
1 cup soy flour

½ cup oil
3 tsp. turmeric
2 tsp. salt
Cheese

Bring bulgur and rice to a boil in 7 cups water. Lower heat and simmer, covered, until water is absorbed — about 45 minutes. Add wheat germ, soy flour, oil, turmeric and salt and mix well. Shape into burgers and place on baking sheet. Bake at 350 degrees F for 15 minutes, top each burger with a slice of cheese and bake for 5 minutes more.

Makes approximately 18 burgers.

— Kristine Reid
Floyd, Virginia

NUT RISSOLES

1½ cups ground brazil nuts
1½ cups ground cashews
⅔ cup whole wheat flour
½ tsp. salt

1 small onion, grated
1 cup grated old Cheddar cheese
Bread crumbs
Cooking oil

Combine all ingredients in a bowl and stir in enough water to make a stiff dough. Shape into patties and roll in bread crumbs. Fry in oil until golden.

Makes 12 patties.

— Leslie Gent
Courtenay, British Columbia

KUSHERIE

THIS IS A TRADITIONAL EGYPTIAN RECIPE FOR RICE AND LENTILS. IT IS SERVED WITH A tomato sauce, fried onions and yogurt.

2 Tbsp. oil
1¼ cups lentils
4 cups boiling water
Salt & pepper
1½ cups rice

Sauce:
¾ cup tomato paste
3 cups tomatoes

1 green pepper, chopped
1 stalk celery, chopped
1 Tbsp. honey
1 tsp. cumin
¼ tsp. cayenne

Fried onions
Yogurt

Heat oil in heavy saucepan. Add lentils and cook over medium heat for 5 minutes, stirring often. Add 3 cups of boiling water and salt and pepper to taste. Cook for 10 minutes, uncovered, over medium heat. Stir in rice and remaining 1 cup water, cover and simmer for 25 minutes without stirring.

For sauce, combine tomato paste, tomatoes, green pepper, celery, honey, cumin and cayenne. Bring to a boil, reduce heat and simmer for 20 to 30 minutes.

Serve grains topped with tomato sauce and fried onions, with yogurt as an accompaniment.

Serves 4 to 6.

— Chris Nofziger
Elmworth, Alberta

LENTIL BARLEY STEW

¾ cup brown lentils
¾ cup chopped onion
¼ cup butter
6 cups water
28 oz. tomatoes
¾ cup barley
2 tsp. salt

¼ tsp. pepper
½ tsp. rosemary
½ tsp. garlic salt
Cayenne pepper
¾ cup chopped cabbage
½ cup grated carrots

Rinse lentils in warm water. Sauté onion in butter in large saucepan. Add water and lentils and cook for 20 minutes. Add tomatoes, barley, salt, pepper, rosemary, garlic salt, cayenne and cabbage. Simmer for 45 to 60 minutes. Add grated carrots and cook for 5 minutes longer.

Serves 6.

— Teri McDonald
Regina, Saskatchewan

HERBED RICE & LENTIL CASSEROLE

2⅔ cups water
¾ cup lentils
¾ cup chopped onion
½ cup rice
¼ tsp. salt

⅛ tsp. garlic powder
⅛ tsp. pepper
¼ tsp. oregano
2 Tbsp. chopped dill weed
1 cup grated Cheddar cheese

Combine all ingredients in a greased casserole dish and bake at 325 degrees F for 1½ to 2 hours, stirring twice.

Serves 2.

— Rose Strocen
Canora, Saskatchewan

SPANISH BULGUR CASSEROLE

THIS DELICIOUS CASSEROLE CAN BE FROZEN SUCCESSFULLY, EITHER COOKED OR uncooked, so it makes a handy dish to keep on hand for unexpected guests.

4 Tbsp. oil
1 cup chopped celery
1 cup chopped green pepper
½ cup chopped onion
3 cloves garlic, finely chopped
¼ lb. mushrooms, sliced
1½ cups raw bulgur
1 cup sliced black olives

2 cups tomatoes
½ cup sherry
½ cup water
2 tsp. oregano
Salt & pepper
2 cups grated Cheddar cheese
Parsley
Paprika

Heat oil in a large skillet. Sauté celery, green pepper, onion, garlic and mushrooms until limp. Add bulgur, olives, tomatoes, sherry, water, oregano, salt and pepper. Mix well and bring to a boil.

Pour into a large, greased casserole dish. Bake, covered, at 375 degrees F for 20 minutes. Uncover and sprinkle with cheese, parsley and paprika. Bake 15 minutes longer.

Serves 6 to 8.

— June Countryman
Waterloo, Ontario

BARLEY CASSEROLE

½ lb. bacon, finely chopped
½ cup finely chopped onion
1 cup finely chopped celery
½ lb. fresh mushrooms, sliced

1 cup pearl barley
3 cups beef stock
¼ cup finely chopped fresh parsley
  or 1 Tbsp. dried parsley

Sauté bacon and onion and place in casserole dish with other ingredients. Cover and bake at 350 degrees F for 2 hours, or until liquid is absorbed and barley is tender.

— *Devon Anderson*
Maple Creek, Saskatchewan

KIBBI

THIS ANCIENT LEBANESE DISH IS A GOOD MEAT EXTENDER AS A LITTLE GOES A LONG way. Ground lamb may also be used. Cold kibbi stuffed in pita bread and topped with yogurt, chopped lettuce and tomato is a delicious variation.

1½ cups raw bulgur
1 lb. ground beef
1 small onion, grated or finely chopped

1 Tbsp. salt
Cumin, pepper, allspice, cinnamon
Butter

Soak bulgur in cold water for 15 minutes. Drain, then squeeze dry with hands. Mix all ingredients very well, either kneading by hand or running several times through meat grinder. Pat into square cake pan. Score to bottom of pan in diamond pattern.

Bake at 350 degrees F for 45 to 60 minutes. Drain any excess grease.

Serves 8.

— *Sandra Wikeem*
Kamloops, British Columbia

GLAZED DINNER LOAF

1½ cups oatmeal
1 cup wheat bran
¼ cup wheat germ
¼ cup peanuts, coarsely ground
¼ cup almonds, coarsely ground
¼ cup tamari sauce
¼ cup sesame oil
2 eggs
½ cup tomato juice
1 onion, chopped
Oregano
Basil
Salt

Glaze:
½ cup tomato juice
1 Tbsp. dry mustard
2 Tbsp. honey
1 tsp. lemon juice
1 Tbsp. cornstarch

Combine all loaf ingredients and mix well. Place in greased loaf pan. Bake at 350 degrees F for 30 minutes.

To make glaze, heat tomato juice, dry mustard, honey and lemon juice in small saucepan. Mix cornstarch with a little bit of water and stir in. Continue cooking until thick.

Cover loaf with glaze and bake for 15 minutes longer.

Serves 6.

— *Joanne Lavallée*
St. Côme, Quebec

ALL-IN-ONE CEREAL

2 cups cracked wheat
1 cup rolled oats
½ cup toasted wheat germ
½ cup raw wheat germ

½ cup soy grits
½ cup wheat germ
1 cup coarse cornmeal

Combine all ingredients and store in cool place in jar with tight-fitting lid.

To cook, use 1 cup cereal to 4 cups water, adding ¼ to ½ tsp. salt to taste for each cup of grain. Bring salted water to a boil and stir in cereal slowly. Cook and stir for 1 to 2 minutes, then cover and cook on very low heat for 20 to 25 minutes.

Makes 6 cups of dry cereal.

— Kathy Cowbrough
Stirling, Scotland

SLOW-COOKER CEREAL

WHAT COULD BE BETTER ON A BUSY MORNING THAN GETTING UP TO A FLAVOURFUL breakfast of nutritious whole grains? This cereal is the old-fashioned kind that sticks to the ribs. The apples, raisins and coconut provide natural sweetening so the addition of honey or sugar is unnecessary.

¼ cup rye berries
¼ cup rolled oats
¼ cup corn meal
¼ cup brown rice
¼ cup sunflower seeds
¼ cup soy grits

2 Tbsp. flax seeds
¼ cup shredded coconut
¼ cup raisins
¼ cup chopped, dried apples
¾ tsp. salt
5 cups water

Combine all ingredients in slow cooker and cook overnight on low.

Serves 6 to 8.

— Jan Gilbert
Ashton, Ontario

HEALTHY BREAKFAST COOKIES

THESE COOKIES ARE SOLD AT THE SATURDAY MORNING KAMLOOPS FARMERS' MARKET. Packed full of grains and nuts, they provide a nutritious, if unusual, breakfast.

½ cup butter or oil
½ cup peanut butter
1½ cups honey
2 eggs
½ tsp. vanilla
1½ cups flour
1 tsp. salt

1 tsp. baking soda
3 cups rolled oats
1 cup coconut
¾ cup bran
¼ cup wheat germ
1 cup raisins
½ cup chopped peanuts

Cream butter or oil, peanut butter and honey. Add eggs and vanilla, then beat well. Stir in flour, salt and baking soda until very smooth. Add remaining ingredients and blend well.

Drop by teaspoonful onto greased cookie sheets. If a large, meal-sized cookie is desired, use ¼ cup of dough for each cookie. Bake at 375 degrees F for 10 to 20 minutes, depending on size of cookies.

— Dianne Lomen
Kamloops, British Columbia

Fish
&
Seafood

He was a bold man that first eat an oyster.

– **Jonathan Swift**
Polite Conversation

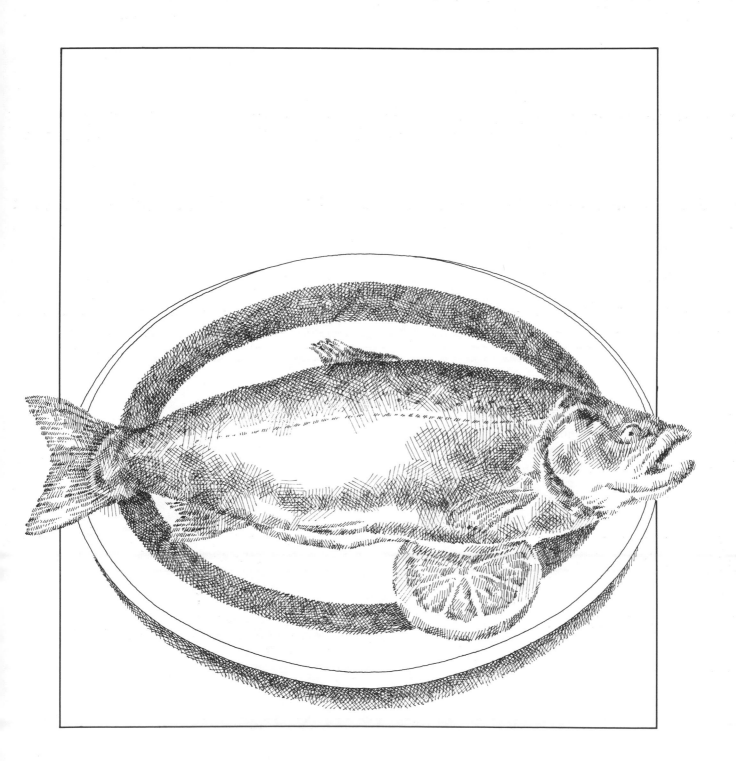

FILLETS OF SOLE WITH LEEKS & SHRIMP

2 cups sliced leeks, white part only
½ cup butter
8 oz. shrimp, cooked,
  shelled & chopped
2 Tbsp. chopped dill weed
1 cup whipping cream

⅔ cup dry white wine
Salt & white pepper
Lemon juice
4 sole fillets
Flour

Cook leeks in ¼ cup butter over medium heat for 5 minutes. Stir in shrimp and dill and cook for 1 minute. Add cream, wine, salt and pepper and lemon juice to taste and simmer for 10 minutes, or until thickened. Set aside and keep warm.

Dust sole with flour and sauté in remaining ¼ cup butter over medium-high heat until golden and flaky. Transfer to heated platter and pour sauce over.

Serves 4.

— *Pam Collacott*
North Gower, Ontario

SOLE SWIRLS IN TROPICAL SAUCE

2 lbs. sole fillets
Salt
1 cup coarsely grated carrot
¼ cup finely chopped onion
½ cup melted butter
½ tsp. salt
1 cup crushed pineapple, drained
  & juice reserved

Sauce:
1 cup pineapple juice
2 Tbsp. vinegar
1 Tbsp. brown sugar
1 Tbsp. cornstarch
2 tsp. soya sauce
½ medium green pepper, chopped

Sprinkle fillets with salt. Sauté carrot and onion in ¼ cup melted butter until tender, then add salt. Combine pineapple with vegetables and stuff fillets. Place in greased baking dish and drizzle with remaining butter. Bake for 20 to 30 minutes at 450 degrees F.

Combine and heat ingredients for sauce until thickened. Pour over fish and serve.

Serves 6.

— *Gillian Richardson*
Regina, Saskatchewan

BAKED SOLE WITH CURRANTS

½ cup currants
¾ cup white wine
1-1½ lbs. sole
Salt & pepper
Juice of 1 lemon
2 green onions, sliced

2 cloves garlic, crushed
3 Tbsp. oil
19-oz. can tomatoes
2 whole cloves
3 Tbsp. chopped parsley
2 Tbsp. flour

Soak currants in wine for at least 15 minutes. Place fish in greased baking pan and sprinkle with salt, pepper and lemon juice. Sauté onions and garlic in oil over low heat for about 3 minutes. Add remaining ingredients except flour and simmer for 10 minutes. Make a smooth paste of flour mixed with sauce juices and stir into sauce. Pour over fish and bake at 400 degrees F for 30 minutes.

Serves 4.

— *Marjorie Moore*
Calgary, Alberta

SOLE GRATINEE AUX CHAMPIGNONS

1½-2 lbs. sole fillets
½ cup dry white wine
Salt
4 Tbsp. butter
½ lb. mushrooms, sliced

2 Tbsp. lemon juice
3 Tbsp. flour
⅓ cup light cream
⅛ tsp. nutmeg
¾ cup grated Swiss cheese

Arrange fish in greased, shallow baking dish so that fish is no more than 1-inch and no less than ½-inch thick. Pour white wine over fish and sprinkle with salt. Cover and bake at 400 degrees F for 6 to 10 minutes, depending on thickness. Drain off juices and measure, adding water to make 1 cup. Place fish in baking dish and set aside.

In skillet, melt 2 Tbsp. butter and add mushrooms and lemon juice. Cook over high heat, stirring, until mushrooms are cooked and juice is evaporated. Let cool, then remove mushrooms from pan.

Melt remaining 2 Tbsp. butter in pan and stir in flour. Remove from heat and gradually add 1 cup fish stock, cream and nutmeg. Return to heat and cook, stirring, until thickened.

Cover fish evenly with mushrooms and sauce and top with cheese. Bake, uncovered, at 400 degrees F for 10 to 15 minutes, or until hot.

Serves 4 to 6.

— Heather Petrie
Pitt Meadows, British Columbia

CREAMY FILLET OF SOLE

4 sole fillets
1 green onion, chopped
1 Tbsp. chopped parsley
6 large mushrooms, sliced
1 tsp. salt

⅛ tsp. pepper
3 Tbsp. apple juice
2 Tbsp. butter, cut into pieces
3 Tbsp. cream
1 tsp. lemon juice

Place sole in buttered dish. Sprinkle with onion and parsley. Top with mushrooms and salt and pepper. Add apple juice and dot with 1 Tbsp. butter. Top with a piece of brown paper and bake at 500 degrees F for 15 minutes. Drain liquid and reduce to half by cooking over high heat. Add cream, lemon juice and remaining 1 Tbsp. butter. Mix and pour over fillets and place in hot oven or under broiler for 5 minutes to brown.

Serves 4.

— Andrea Stuart
Winnipeg, Manitoba

SCRUMPTIOUS SOLE

1 head broccoli, chopped & parboiled
1 lb. sole fillets
4 oz. shrimp
1 cup sliced mushrooms
2 cups cream of mushroom sauce
  (*Volume 1*, page 92)
¼ cup Parmesan cheese

½ tsp. chopped dill weed
½ tsp. salt
½ tsp. pepper
¼ tsp. nutmeg
1 Tbsp. lemon juice
1 Tbsp. Worcestershire sauce

Line a 9" x 13" baking pan with foil. Place broccoli in bottom and cover with fillets. Top with shrimp and mushrooms. Combine mushroom sauce, cheese, dill, salt, pepper, nutmeg, lemon juice and Worcestershire sauce and pour over fish. Close and seal foil and bake at 350 degrees F for 1 hour.

Serves 4.

— Karen Havelock
Balmoral, Manitoba

STUFFED SOLE

1 clove garlic, finely chopped
3 mushrooms, finely chopped
¾ cup finely chopped spinach
1 Tbsp. butter

6 medium shrimp, chopped
3 medium-sized sole fillets
Salt & pepper

Cook garlic, mushrooms and spinach in butter until soft. Add shrimp and stir to mix. Season fillets with salt and pepper. Place one-third of mixture on each fillet, roll up and secure with toothpick. Place in buttered baking dish, cover and bake at 350 degrees F for 15 to 20 minutes.

Serves 3.

— Gail Walter
Edmonton, Alberta

BABINE RIVER SALMON ROYAL

3-4 lbs. filleted salmon, char
  or rainbow trout
Salt
¼ cup butter
2 cups soft bread crumbs
¾ tsp. salt
½ tsp. pepper
1 Tbsp. finely chopped parsley
1½ Tbsp. lemon juice
1 cup drained baby clams
1 tsp. tarragon or dill

Drawn Butter Sauce:
3 Tbsp. butter
3 Tbsp. flour
1½ cups boiling water
¼ cup butter, cut into ½-inch cubes
½ tsp. salt
1 Tbsp. lemon juice
1 Tbsp. parsley
Lemon wedges

Sprinkle fillets with salt. Melt butter and combine with remaining ingredients. Lay one fillet, skin side down, on large piece of foil and shape foil up sides of fish. Pile stuffing evenly over fish and top with the other fillet. Bring foil up to overlap edges so that no open flesh is showing, only skin. Place on baking sheet and bake for 10 minutes per stuffed inch at 450 degrees F.

To make sauce, melt butter over low heat and stir in flour to make thick roux. Add boiling water gradually and stir constantly until smooth. Add the chopped butter gradually, stirring well after each addition. Season with salt and add lemon juice and parsley. Place on platter garnished with parsley and lemon wedges and serve with sauce.

Serves 6 to 8.

— Lori Messer
Topley Landing, British Columbia

COTTAGE SALMON CASSEROLE

1 cup cooked salmon
2 cups cottage cheese
1 Tbsp. minced onion
1 egg

½ cup bread crumbs
1 tsp. salt
Paprika

Combine all ingredients, reserving ¼ cup bread crumbs for topping. Place in greased casserole dish and top with reserved crumbs and a sprinkling of paprika. Bake at 350 degrees F for 30 minutes.

Serves 2.

— Isabell Lingrell
North Battleford, Saskatchewan

ORANGE CURRIED FISH STEAKS

ALTHOUGH HALIBUT IS A WHITE-FLESHED FISH AND SALMON A PINK, EITHER ONE CAN BE used equally successfully in this recipe.

4 halibut or salmon steaks, 1-inch thick
Oil
Salt & pepper
¾ cup mayonnaise
¼ cup catsup

2 tsp. grated orange peel
2 Tbsp. orange juice
¼ tsp. curry
1 orange, cut into wedges
Parsley

Brush fish steaks lightly with oil and sprinkle with salt and pepper. Place on well-oiled broiler and barbecue over moderately hot coals for 5 to 7 minutes on each side, brushing occasionally with additional oil.

Meanwhile, make the sauce by combining mayonnaise, catsup, orange peel, orange juice and curry.

Remove fish to serving plate, garnish with orange wedges and parsley and serve with the sauce.

Serves 4.

— Irene Louden
Port Coquitlam, British Columbia

SMOKED SALMON

SMOKED SALMON CAN SERVE AS THE BASE FOR A NUMBER OF DELICIOUS HORS D'OEUVRES. Of course, it is best known served as lox, with bagels and fresh cream cheese. Smoked salmon should be pale pink and should not be salty in taste. If it is red in colour and tastes salty, a smoke salt extract has been used in the processing.

It is easiest to slice smoked salmon if it is partially frozen — it should be sliced across the grain as thinly as possible. A few suggestions for serving smoked salmon as a canape follow.

1. Place on crackers or squares of toast, dust with freshly ground pepper and sprinkle with lemon juice.
2. Top salmon with a slice of stuffed olive.
3. Top with guacamole and serve on toast.

SMOKED SALMON CARIBBEAN

1½ lbs. smoked salmon
4 Tbsp. olive oil
1 Tbsp. lime or lemon juice
¼ tsp. pepper
½ Tbsp. Tabasco sauce
½ cup chopped green onions
½ cup chopped onions

2 tomatoes, chopped
1 ripe avocado, chopped
½ cup cooked garbanzo beans
½ cup chopped sweet red peppers
½ cup chopped artichoke hearts
Romaine lettuce

Chop salmon into bite-sized pieces. In a bowl, combine oil, lime or lemon juice, pepper and Tabasco sauce. Add salmon, onions, tomatoes, avocado, garbanzo beans, peppers and artichoke hearts. Toss and serve on lettuce leaves.

Serves 4.

— Noel Roberts
Burnaby, British Columbia

STUFFED SNAPPER WITH ORANGE & LIME

4 Tbsp. butter
5 oz. shrimp, sliced
1 cup sliced mushrooms
2 green onions, finely chopped
2 stalks celery, chopped
½ tsp. tarragon
½ tsp. basil
½ tsp. thyme

1 pineapple, half sliced & half diced
5-6 lbs. red snapper fillets
Juice of 1 lime
Juice & zest of 3 oranges
2 Tbsp. flour
1 cup whipping cream
2 Tbsp. sherry
Pepper

Melt 2 Tbsp. butter and sauté shrimp, mushrooms, green onions, celery and herbs. Add diced half of pineapple and sauté for 2 to 3 minutes.

Lay fillets flat and make a slit lengthwise down the centre of each, starting and ending 2 inches from either end and being careful not to cut all the way through. Run knife sideways down the slit out towards the edges of the fillet, creating a pocket. Stuff sautéed mixture into snapper, reserving ¼ cup. Cover with lime and orange juices. Bake, covered, at 350 degrees F for 30 minutes.

Gently mince the reserved stuffing and set aside. Place remaining 2 Tbsp. butter in skillet, add flour and cook until blended. Add cream, stirring until thickened and add reserved stuffing. Stir in sherry, pepper and grated orange zest.

When snapper is cooked, remove from pan to serving dish. Add pan liquid to sauce and reduce by simmering. Surround fish with sliced pineapple and pour sauce over top.

Serves 6 to 8.

— Jan van der Est
Vancouver, British Columbia

RED SNAPPER VERA CRUZ

4 tomatoes, peeled & chopped
1 onion, chopped
1 green pepper, sliced
5 Tbsp. butter
½ tsp. thyme

¼ cup white wine
1 bay leaf
1 lemon, quartered
1 tsp. parsley
4 lbs. red snapper, filleted

Make sauce by sautéing tomatoes, onion and green pepper in butter until onion is transparent. Add remaining ingredients except fish and cook for 5 minutes. Place fish in greased casserole dish, top with sauce and bake at 350 degrees F for 35 minutes.

Serves 4.

— Melody Scott
Bramalea, Ontario

CHINESE RED SNAPPER

¼ cup chopped green onions
1 clove garlic, chopped
1-inch piece ginger root, chopped

4 lbs. red snapper
¼ cup sesame seed oil
½ cup soya sauce

Combine green onions, garlic and ginger root and rub over fish, placing some inside fish. Bake at 400 degrees F for 1 hour. Remove onions, ginger and garlic from fish.

Heat sesame seed oil and soya sauce. Pour over fish and serve.

Serves 6 to 8.

— Claudette Spies
Nakusp, British Columbia

BAKED STUFFED ARCTIC CHAR

THE CONTRIBUTOR OF THIS AND THE FOLLOWING RECIPE LIVED ON BAFFIN ISLAND for 5 years, where char is fresh and readily available. This recipe is an adaptation of one for stuffed fish that came originally from McGowen House, a fishermen's boardinghouse on Lake Memphramagog in Quebec.

2 cups cracker crumbs
1 small onion, chopped
½ cup chopped parsley
4-5 sweet pickles, chopped

½ cup melted butter
¼ cup pickle juice
1 large Arctic char, cleaned
Soft butter

Combine crumbs, onion, parsley, pickles, melted butter and pickle juice. Stuff fish with this and sew opening together. Rub fish all over with soft butter. Place in foil-lined roasting pan and bake at 400 degrees F for 45 to 60 minutes, or until fish flakes.

Serves 6 to 8.

— Judith Asbil
Ste. Agathe des Monts, Quebec

BARBECUED ARCTIC CHAR

Arctic char, cut into fillets
Soya sauce
Lemon wedges

Marinate char in soya sauce for 1 hour or more, turning occasionally to make sure all parts of fish are covered. Cover barbecue grill with foil and grease lightly. Place drained fillets on grill for 5 minutes. Turn and grill for another 5 minutes, or until fish flakes with a fork. Serve with lemon wedges.

Serves 6 to 8.

— Judith Asbil
Ste. Agathe des Monts, Quebec

BAKED TROUT WITH ALMOND CREAM

⅓ cup slivered almonds
3 Tbsp. butter
1 Tbsp. minced green onion
3 rainbow trout, boned
Parsley
6 Tbsp. white wine

½ cup whipping cream
1 Tbsp. sour cream
1½ tsp. cornstarch
Salt & pepper
Lemon juice

Brown almonds in butter and set aside. Butter a piece of aluminum foil large enough to wrap around fish. Sprinkle with green onion and place fish on top. Stuff each fish with parsley, then pour over wine and butter from cooking almonds. Tightly close foil over fish and bake at 425 degrees F for 10 minutes per inch of thickness of fish.

Meanwhile, remove almonds to paper towel. Combine whipping cream, sour cream and cornstarch in saucepan. When fish is cooked, pour fish liquid into cream mixture and bring to a boil, stirring constantly. Cook until thickened and smooth. Add salt and pepper and lemon juice to taste.

To serve, remove parsley from fish. Top each fish with small ribbon of sauce and almonds. Serve remaining sauce separately.

Serves 6.

— The Art of Cooking School
Kingston, Ontario

FILLETS BAKED IN SOUR CREAM

4 tsp. butter
2 lbs. fish fillets (sole,
  haddock or flounder)
1 tsp. salt
½ tsp. Tabasco sauce

1 Tbsp. paprika
¼ cup Parmesan cheese
1 cup sour cream
¼ cup fine bread crumbs
Lemon & parsley

Grease 2-quart casserole dish with 1 tsp. butter. Arrange fish in dish. Blend salt, Tabasco sauce, paprika and Parmesan cheese into sour cream. Spread over fish. Top with bread crumbs and dot with remaining butter. Bake, uncovered, at 350 degrees F for 30 minutes, or until fish is easily flaked with a fork. Garnish with lemon slices and parsley sprigs.

Serves 4 to 6.

— *Judy Morrison Cayen*
Courtenay, British Columbia

FISH SPINACH CASSEROLE

6 oz. fine egg noodles
3 cups vegetable stock
4 Tbsp. butter
4 Tbsp. flour
½ cup yogurt or sour cream

1½ cups cooked spinach
1 cup cooked, flaked fish
3 eggs, hard-boiled & sliced
5 Tbsp. Parmesan cheese

Cook egg noodles in stock until just tender. Drain and reserve liquid.

Melt butter until it foams, add flour and stir until combined. Add warm stock and stir until thickened. Remove from heat and add yogurt or sour cream.

Assemble in a casserole dish by layering as follows: noodles, spinach, half the sauce, fish and eggs. Add 4 Tbsp. Parmesan cheese to remaining sauce and pour over top. Bake at 350 degrees F for 20 minutes. Sprinkle remaining tablespoon of cheese over top and broil until browned.

Serves 4.

— *Ann R. Jeffries*
La Ronge, Saskatchewan

CURRIED ALMOND COD

1 lb. cod
1 lemon, cut into quarters
1 tsp. salt
½ cup flour
Salt & pepper
1 tsp. paprika
Oil

2 medium onions, chopped
1 Tbsp. curry powder
1 Tbsp. flour
1½ cups stock
½ cup shredded almonds
1 Tbsp. chutney
2 tomatoes

Rub cod with lemon and sprinkle with salt. Let sit for 30 minutes to lose excess liquid. Wipe the fish and cut into 2-inch chunks. Combine flour, salt, pepper and paprika. Roll fish in seasoned flour. Fry in oil, drain and place in serving dish. Keep warm.

Fry onions in 2 Tbsp. oil until golden, add curry and cook for a few more minutes. Add flour and cook, stirring constantly, for 2 minutes. Stir in stock and simmer, uncovered, for 15 minutes. Add almonds and simmer for 15 minutes longer. Add chutney, salt and pepper. Add tomatoes and heat through. Spoon over the cod and serve.

Serves 4.

— *Kay Barclay*
Burlington, Ontario

GREEK PASTRY STUFFED WITH FISH & SPINACH

THIS RECIPE TAKES A BIT OF TIME TO PREPARE, BUT THE RESULTING DISH IS WELL WORTH the effort. Filo pastry can be found in most Italian and Greek specialty stores. It can be stored in the freezer for several months if necessary.

Filling:
1½ lbs. spinach, washed
 & coarsely chopped
Butter
1 bunch green onions, sliced
¾ lb. Boston bluefish, minced
½ green pepper, minced
4 eggs, lightly beaten
¼ cup lemon juice

Salt & pepper
1½ tsp. dill weed
1 tsp. garlic powder

Pastry:
2 cups butter
⅓ cup lemon juice
1 Tbsp. garlic powder
1 lb. filo pastry

To make filling, sauté spinach in butter until limp. Combine with remaining ingredients in bowl and set aside.

For dough, combine butter, lemon juice and garlic powder in saucepan. Cook over low heat until melted. Unwrap filo dough on large working area. Fold one sheet lengthwise in thirds and brush with butter mixture. Fold and butter a second sheet similarly. Place strips end to end, overlapping by ½ inch. Place 2 Tbsp. filling near one end and fold pastry into triangle shape, folding over and over until all dough is used. Place on greased cookie sheet. Repeat with remaining dough and filling. Drizzle with remaining butter mixture and bake at 350 degrees F for 30 minutes, or until golden brown and puffed.

Makes 12 triangles.

— Titia Posthuma
Maberly, Ontario

JAMAICAN SALTFISH & DUMPLINGS

2 green peppers
1 sweet red pepper
3 or 4 hot banana peppers
2-3 hot cherry peppers
2-3 cups oil
2 large onions, sliced
1 lb. cooked saltfish

Dumplings:
3 cups flour
1 cup corn meal
½ tsp. salt
1½ tsp. baking powder
1 cup warm water

Cut all peppers into large chunks. Place 2 cups oil in pot over medium-high heat. When oil is hot, add onions. Cook for 3 minutes, then add fish and peppers. Oil should just cover all ingredients. Cook for 5 minutes, then reduce heat to medium and cook a further 25 to 30 minutes.

While saltfish and peppers are cooking, prepare dumplings. In a large bowl, mix together flour, corn meal, salt and baking powder. Add just enough water to make a rather stiff dough. Knead for 1 minute, then shape dough into patties. Place 3 Tbsp. of the oil from the fish and peppers in a frying pan. Fry dumplings at medium heat, turning once, until golden brown on both sides. Drain fish and peppers with slotted spoon and serve with dumplings.

Serves 4 to 6.

— Ken Williamson
Ste. Clotilde, Quebec

HERRING IN SOUR CREAM

16-oz. jar herring, whole or fillets
6 large onions
6 apples
1 quart sour cream

3 Tbsp. vinegar
Salt & pepper
¼ cup crushed walnuts

Drain liquid from jar of herring, discarding spices, onion rings, etc. Dice herring and place in 4-quart porcelain or glass bowl. Peel onions and apples. Cut onions into thinly sliced rings; core and cube apples into ¼-inch cubes. Add to herring. Pour sour cream over top and mix well. Add vinegar, salt and pepper and walnuts. Cover and let stand for 8 hours at room temperature, then refrigerate.

Serves 12 as an appetizer.

— *Wido J. Heck*
Glen Robertson, Ontario

SEASIDE MANICOTTI

6 manicotti shells
10 oz. spinach
½ cup chopped onion
1 clove garlic
2 Tbsp. butter
3 Tbsp. flour
2 cups milk

1 cup Swiss cheese
¼ cup grated Parmesan cheese
2 Tbsp. butter, melted
½ tsp. salt
1 lb. perch fillets, cooked & flaked
Ground nutmeg

Cook manicotti shells and drain. Cook spinach and drain.

Meanwhile, prepare cheese sauce. Cook onion and garlic in 2 Tbsp. butter until tender but not brown. Blend in flour. Add milk all at once. Cook and stir until thick and bubbly. Stir in Swiss cheese until melted.

Combine ½ cup of sauce with the spinach, Parmesan cheese, 2 Tbsp. melted butter and salt. Fold in flaked fish. Stuff manicotti shells with this mixture.

Pour half of remaining sauce into baking dish. Put manicotti on top and pour remaining sauce over.

Cover and bake at 350 degrees F for 30 to 35 minutes. Sprinkle nutmeg over top before serving.

Serves 6.

— *Mary Ann Vanner*
Kingston, Ontario

BARBECUED SQUID

4 large squid
1 thumb-sized piece fresh ginger
1 clove garlic

2 Tbsp. saké or white wine
2 Tbsp. soya sauce

Clean and peel squid and slice into 1½" x 2½" strips. Peel and grate ginger and garlic. Place squid, ginger and garlic in bowl and sprinkle with saké and soya sauce. Mix, then marinate for 30 minutes in cool place. Place squid in a broiler pan and broil for 3 to 5 minutes, basting with sauce once during cooking.

Serves 4.

— *Isao Morrill*
St. Louis de Kent, New Brunswick

MARINATED SQUID

2 lbs. squid, cleaned & sliced
  into 1-inch strips
⅓ cup oil
¼ cup vinegar
1 Tbsp. lemon juice

¼ tsp. salt
Pepper
1 tsp. chopped chives
1 tsp. chopped sweet pepper
1 tsp. chopped parsley

Simmer strips of squid in boiling, salted water for 1 hour. Drain. Combine other ingredients in a bowl and add squid. Marinate for at least 1 hour in refrigerator.

Serves 6 to 8.

— Marjorie Bobowski
Port Colborne, Ontario

SPINACH TUNA PATE

Butter
2 lbs. spinach, stemmed & washed
¾ cup whipping cream
3 large eggs
4 oz. tuna, drained & flaked
½ cup minced scallions
4 anchovy fillets, drained

1 Tbsp. lemon juice
⅓ cup soft white bread crumbs
1 tsp. salt
⅛ tsp. pepper
Lemon wedges
Parsley sprigs

Butter bottom of loaf pan, line with wax paper and butter paper lightly.

Cook spinach in large saucepan of boiling, salted water until tender — about 3 minutes. Drain in colander and rinse under cold, running water to cool. Squeeze spinach with hands to remove as much moisture as possible, then chop coarsely. Set aside.

Purée cream, eggs, tuna, scallions, anchovies and lemon juice in blender or food processor until smooth. Turn tuna mixture into medium bowl. Add bread crumbs, salt, pepper and spinach and stir to mix well.

Pour spinach mixture into prepared pan and cover with aluminum foil. Place loaf pan in larger baking dish or small roasting pan and fill with boiling water halfway up sides of loaf pan. Bake in centre of oven at 375 degrees F until knife inserted in centre of pâté comes out clean but wet — about 1 hour. Remove from water bath and cool in pan on rack to room temperature. Refrigerate, covered, until chilled — about 3 hours.

At serving time, remove pâté from mould and place on serving platter. Cut into ½-inch slices and garnish with lemon wedges and parsley.

— Erika Maurer
Smithers, British Columbia

PIRAEUS SHRIMP

SERVED IN BOWLS WITH A LOAF OF ITALIAN BREAD FOR DIPPING, THIS DISH MAKES A delicious meal in itself. It takes its name from the Greek port where the contributors first tasted it.

2 medium onions, chopped
3 large cloves garlic, chopped
2½ Tbsp. olive oil
28-oz. can tomatoes, lightly chopped
Oregano & basil

Salt & pepper
¼ cup white wine
1 lb. shelled, deveined shrimp
8 oz. feta cheese, crumbled

Sauté onions and garlic in oil for 30 seconds over medium-high heat. Add tomatoes, oregano, basil, salt and pepper. Cook until boiling, then add wine. Stir in shrimp when liquid is boiling. Simmer for 5 minutes, or until shrimp turn pinkish white. Add cheese and cook for another 2 or 3 minutes.

Serves 4.

— John & Elaine Bird
Toronto, Ontario

STIR-FRIED PRAWNS

THE PRAWNS ARE COOKED IN THEIR SHELLS IN THIS RECIPE. TO ENJOY ALL THE DELICIOUS flavour, suck the shells before removing them to eat the prawns.

3 Tbsp. peanut oil
2 Tbsp. finely chopped ginger root
2 cloves garlic, chopped
1 lb. fresh prawns, deheaded & washed
1 Tbsp. soya sauce

1 Tbsp. dry sherry
½ tsp. salt
Pepper
Coriander

Heat oil in wok and stir-fry ginger root and garlic for 30 seconds. Add prawns and cook for 2 more minutes to brown shells lightly. Add soya sauce, sherry, salt and pepper and cook for another 2 minutes. Transfer to warm serving dish and garnish with coriander.

Serves 3 to 4.

— Helen Campbell
Loughborough Inlet, British Columbia

SHRIMP IN SHELLS AU GRATIN

½ lb. uncooked shelled shrimp
½ cup dry white wine
5 Tbsp. butter
2 Tbsp. flour
1½ cups light cream

Salt
1 Tbsp. finely chopped parsley
½ cup sliced mushrooms, sautéed
2 Tbsp. Parmesan cheese
½ cup coarse bread crumbs

Cook shrimp in wine for 5 minutes and set aside, reserving liquid. In heavy saucepan, melt 3 Tbsp. butter and stir in flour, cooking for 2 minutes. Gradually stir in ½ cup shrimp liquid then cream. Bring to a boil, then cook for 2 to 3 minutes, stirring constantly. Add salt to taste. Stir in parsley, mushrooms and shrimp.

Spoon mixture into 2 greased au gratin dishes or scallop shells. Melt remaining 2 Tbsp. butter and stir in Parmesan cheese and bread crumbs. Sprinkle this over each shell and place under broiler until crumbs brown.

Serves 2.

— Valerie Cameron
Hamilton, Ontario

SHRIMP COOKED IN BEER

THIS DISH MAKES AN EXCELLENT COLD APPETIZER OR PARTY SNACK.

2 bottles beer
2 bay leaves, crumbled
½ tsp. crushed red pepper
½ tsp. cayenne
2 Tbsp. mustard seeds

1½ lbs. jumbo shrimp,
  shelled & deveined
¼ cup wine vinegar
1 large clove garlic, peeled

Combine beer, bay leaves, red pepper, cayenne and mustard seeds in saucepan. Bring to a boil and simmer for 5 minutes. Add shrimp and simmer for 8 to 10 minutes, or until shrimp turns pink.

Remove from heat and add vinegar and garlic. Let stand for 30 minutes. Strain and chill well before serving.

Serves 8 to 10 as an appetizer.

— Mary Carney
Dryden, Ontario

SWEET & SOUR SHRIMP

1½ cups orange juice
1 Tbsp. soya sauce
2 Tbsp. vinegar
2 Tbsp. currant jelly
1 tsp. dry mustard
¼ tsp. ginger

1 Tbsp. cornstarch
1 Tbsp. water
1½ cups pineapple chunks
1 green pepper, cut into chunks
6 water chestnuts, sliced
1½ lbs. shrimp, cleaned & cooked

In heavy saucepan, combine orange juice, soya sauce, vinegar, jelly, mustard and ginger and heat just to boiling. Dissolve cornstarch in water and stir into hot mixture until thickened. Add pineapple, green pepper and water chestnuts and cook, stirring, for 1 minute. Add shrimp and remove from heat. Let stand for a few minutes and serve.

Serves 4 to 6.

— Christine Fordham
Black Creek, British Columbia

SHRIMP MARSEILLAISE

3 cups shrimp
½ cup butter
Salt & pepper
6 green onions, minced
1 clove garlic, minced
1 large tomato, peeled & chopped
¼ cup brandy
¼ cup white wine
1 Tbsp. Worcestershire sauce

1 Tbsp. lemon juice
1 Tbsp. parsley
½ tsp. basil
Coriander
Mace
Dill weed
4 dashes Tabasco sauce
1 bay leaf

Sauté shrimp in butter until pink. Salt and pepper lightly, add onions and sauté for 1 minute. Add garlic and cook for 30 seconds, then add tomato and cook for 1 minute. Add brandy and wine and ignite. Allow to burn for 30 seconds to 1 minute, then extinguish flame. Add remaining ingredients and heat through.

Serves 4 to 6.

— Marney Allen
Edmonton, Alberta

PRAWNS WITH CHEESE SAUCE

24 prawns in shell
1 Tbsp. butter
1 Tbsp. flour
1 cup milk
1 cup grated Cheddar cheese

Salt & pepper
Garlic powder
2 Tbsp. chopped green onion
½ cup bread crumbs

Remove heads from prawns and place prawns in pot of boiling, salted water for 30 seconds. Plunge immediately into cold water and shell.

Melt butter and blend in flour. Slowly add milk, stirring constantly. Cook until thickened, then add cheese, seasonings and green onions.

Place prawns in greased baking dish and pour cheese sauce over. Top with bread crumbs. Bake at 375 degrees F for 20 minutes — until hot and bubbly.

Serves 4.

— Carol Swann
Bella Coola, British Columbia

MAMA'S SCAMPI

1½ lbs. shrimp
½ cup melted butter
½ tsp. salt
Pepper

1 clove garlic, chopped
1 cup sliced mushrooms
¼ cup chopped parsley
¼ cup chopped chives

Shell and devein shrimp. In large heavy pot, melt butter and sauté shrimp for 5 minutes, or until shrimp are pink. Sprinkle with salt and pepper, place on heated platter and keep warm. Sauté garlic and mushrooms for 1 to 2 minutes, then add parsley and chives and cook for 1 minute longer. Pour over shrimp. Serve with rice.

Serves 4.

— *Kirsten McDougall*
Kamloops, British Columbia

GUYANESE COOK-UP

MAKE THE COCONUT MILK FOR THIS RECIPE BY COMBINING 3 CUPS BOILING WATER WITH 1 cup grated coconut — preferably fresh. When mixture is cool enough to handle, squeeze out all the liquid and discard the coconut.

1½ cups raw brown rice
3 cups coconut milk
½ tsp. salt

¾ cup sliced green beans
½ cup shrimp

Cook rice in coconut milk with salt for 25 minutes. Place green beans and shrimp on top of rice to steam for remaining cooking time — about 20 minutes. Stir when cooked and serve.

Serves 4.

— *Shiela Alexandrovich*
Whitehorse, Yukon

MANICOTTI WITH SHRIMP FILLING

18 manicotti noodles
2 cups ricotta cheese
1½ cups cottage cheese
½ cup Parmesan cheese
2 eggs
1 green pepper, chopped

3-4 green onions, chopped
¼ cup finely chopped fresh parsley
½ tsp. salt
½ tsp. pepper
1½ cups shrimp
2 cups white sauce (*Volume 1*, page 92)

Cook noodles in boiling water for 6 minutes, stirring so they do not stick to one another.

Combine cheeses, eggs, green pepper, onions, parsley, salt, pepper and shrimp. Carefully stuff the manicotti shells with this mixture. Arrange filled noodles in single layers in two greased 9" x 13" baking pans. Pour one cup of white sauce over each.

Bake, covered, at 350 degrees F for 45 minutes.

Serves 4 to 6.

— *Lorraine McFarland*
Telkwa, British Columbia

SHRIMP FONDUE

2 lbs. shrimp, cleaned & deveined
2 cups white wine
1 clove garlic
1 lb. Swiss cheese, cubed
3 Tbsp. cornstarch

½ tsp. Worcestershire sauce
1 tsp. salt
Pepper
1¼ tsp. nutmeg

Boil shrimp for 3 minutes, drain and keep warm. Heat 1½ cups wine and garlic in top of double boiler. Remove garlic and stir in cheese until melted. Combine remaining ½ cup wine, cornstarch, Worcestershire sauce, salt, pepper and nutmeg. Stir into cheese and cook until smooth. Pour into fondue pot and dip shrimp.

Serves 6.

— *Audrey Moroso*
Puslinch, Ontario

SHRIMP & ARTICHOKE TARTS

Pastry for 24 tart shells
2 cups cooked shrimp, drained
1 can artichoke hearts, drained
1 can smoked oysters, drained
2 cups grated jack cheese
4 green onions, chopped
1½ cups milk

4 eggs
2 Tbsp. chopped dill weed
Salt & pepper
Paprika
Olives, sliced
4 Tbsp. Parmesan cheese

Combine shrimp, artichokes, oysters, jack cheese and onions and place in pastry-lined muffin tins.

Combine milk, eggs, dill and salt and pepper and beat well. Pour over mixture in shells. Top with paprika, olives and Parmesan cheese and bake at 375 degrees F for 20 minutes. Let sit for 10 minutes before serving.

Serves 6 to 8.

— *Gillian Barber-Gifford*
Rossland, British Columbia

SHRIMP PATE

1 lb. shelled small shrimp, cooked
½ lb. butter, softened
Juice of 1 lemon
1 small clove garlic, minced

1 Tbsp. Madeira wine
Nutmeg
Salt & pepper
Crackers

In food processor or blender, combine shrimp, butter (broken into pieces), lemon juice, garlic and wine and process with on/off motion until blended but not puréed. Season with nutmeg and salt and pepper.

Pile pâté into individual servings or a serving crock, cover tightly and chill. Serve with crackers.

Serves 8.

— *Francie Goodwin-Rogne*
Calgary, Alberta

SCALLOPS IN WINE

2 lbs. scallops
2 cups white wine
¼ cup butter
4 shallots, finely chopped
24 mushroom caps, finely sliced

2 Tbsp. parsley
2 Tbsp. flour
2-4 Tbsp. whipping cream
½-1 cup bread crumbs
Butter

Wash scallops and simmer in wine for 5 minutes. Drain and reserve liquid.

Melt butter and sauté shallots, mushroom caps and parsley. Stir in flour. Add reserved liquid and whipping cream and cook until slightly thickened. Stir in scallops and place in greased, shallow casserole dish. Top with bread crumbs and dot with butter. Broil until golden brown.

Serves 4.

— Kathy Payette
Kitchener, Ontario

SCALLOPS COMPASS ROSE

THIS RECIPE COMES FROM A GUEST HOUSE ON GRAND MANAN ISLAND IN THE BAY OF Fundy. As the owners say, "It helps when you can scoop the fresh scallops from the fishermen's boats at $3.50 a pound!"

1½ Tbsp. oil
1½ lbs. scallops, each cut
  into 4 thin slices
2 tsp. salt

1 green onion, sliced diagonally
2 slices ginger root
1 Tbsp. cornstarch, dissolved
  in 4 Tbsp. water

Heat oil in skillet. Add scallops and cook for 1 minute. Add salt, onion and ginger root and cook for 2 minutes. Add cornstarch-water mixture and cook, stirring, until juices thicken — about 1 minute.

Serves 4.

— Linda L'Aventure & Cecilia Bowden
The Compass Rose
North Head, Grand Manan, New Brunswick

CURRIED CRAB

2 coconuts
1 cup water
1 small onion, chopped
2 cloves garlic, minced
1 inch ginger, peeled & grated

2 Tbsp. olive oil
Salt
1 Tbsp. curry
2 or more crabs, cleaned

Crack coconuts and save milk. Chop or shred coconut meat and place in blender. Add ¾ cup water and blend thoroughly. Remove from blender and squeeze all liquid from pulp, save and add to coconut milk. Replace pulp in blender and add remaining ¼ cup water. Blend, save liquid and discard pulp. Fry onion, garlic and ginger in oil until light brown. Add coconut liquid, pinch of salt and curry. Add crabmeat, bring liquid to boil, then reduce heat and cook until liquid thickens — about 10 minutes.

Serves 2.

— Pieter Timmermans
Ucluelet, British Columbia

CRAB POTATO CAKES

1 medium onion, finely chopped
2 Tbsp. butter
2 cups mashed potatoes
1 cup crabmeat, flaked
1 egg
¼ cup milk
½ tsp. parsley
½ tsp. pepper
¼ cup corn meal

Sauté onion in 1 Tbsp. butter. Combine potatoes, crabmeat, egg, milk, parsley and pepper to form a stiff, slightly sticky dough. Add onions, form into cakes and dredge in corn meal. Melt remaining 1 Tbsp. butter in heavy pan and cook cakes over medium heat until golden.

Serves 4 to 6.

— Nancy Chesworth Weir
Kensington, Maryland

CRAB VERMICELLI

2 cups chopped onion
½ lb. mushrooms, sliced
2 cloves garlic, minced
½ cup butter
½ lb. vermicelli, cooked
2-3 cups flaked crabmeat
½ cup sliced stuffed green olives
½ lb. Cheddar cheese, grated
½ cup sour cream
12-oz. can stewed tomatoes, drained
1½ tsp. salt
1½ tsp. basil

Sauté onion, mushrooms and garlic until onion is translucent. Add remaining ingredients, place in greased casserole dish and bake at 350 degrees F for 45 minutes.

Serves 4 to 6.

— Anita DeLong
Fort Fraser, British Columbia

SPICY CLAMS

4 Tbsp. olive oil
2 cloves garlic, chopped
½ tsp. chili peppers
2 Tbsp. wine
2 Tbsp. soya sauce
⅓ cup fish stock
Green onion, chopped
24 clams, cleaned, steamed & chopped

Heat oil in wok. Add garlic, chili peppers, wine, soya sauce, stock and onion and stir-fry briefly. Add clams and heat thoroughly.

Serves 4.

— Wendy Neilson
Pender Island, British Columbia

ANGELS ON HORSEBACK

12 oysters, shucked & rinsed
Flour
Salt & pepper
12 strips bacon, fried until almost crisp

Dust oysters with flour and salt and pepper. Wrap bacon strip around each oyster and hold together with a toothpick. Broil for 4 to 6 minutes, or until bacon is crisp.

Serves 3.

— Nina Christmas
Courtenay, British Columbia

LASQUETI OYSTER SAUTE WITH TARRAGON

24 oysters
Seasoned flour
¾ cup butter

Buttered toast
Tarragon mayonnaise
Lemon slices

Shuck oysters, discard liquor and pat dry. Dredge in flour, shaking off excess. Heat butter until foamy, add oysters and sauté on both sides over high heat until lightly browned.

Arrange on buttered toast and top with a spoonful of tarragon mayonnaise and a lemon slice.

Serves 4 to 6.

— *Katherine Dunster*
Golden, British Columbia

MARINATED OYSTERS

10 oysters
3 Tbsp. olive oil
2 Tbsp. tarragon vinegar
2 Tbsp. lemon juice
3-4 Tbsp. diced onions
2 Tbsp. chopped parsley

2-3 Tbsp. chopped chives
1 Tbsp. grated lemon peel
1 tsp. salt
½ tsp. white pepper
1-2 cloves garlic, crushed
Pumpernickel bread

Steam oysters in salt water until plump — 5 to 10 minutes — then cut into quarters. Combine remaining ingredients, except bread, for marinade and pour over oysters. Refrigerate for at least 4 hours. Serve on pumpernickel bread.

Serves 4.

— *Berit Christensen*
Cumberland, British Columbia

OYSTACADO

2 avocados
¼ cup mayonnaise
1 tsp. Dijon mustard
Salt & pepper

1 can smoked oysters, drained & chopped
1 Tbsp. lemon juice
1 cup sour cream
4 almonds

Cut avocados in half, scoop out pulp and mash. Add mayonnaise, mustard, salt and pepper, oysters and lemon juice. Fill each avocado shell with mixture and top with dollop of sour cream and an almond.

Serves 4.

— *Gillian Barber-Gifford*
Rossland, British Columbia

SMOKED OYSTER DIP

1 can smoked oysters,
  finely chopped & juice reserved
¾ cup chopped celery
½ cup chopped onion
4 slices crisp bacon, crumbled

8 soda crackers, crumbled
2-3 Tbsp. bacon drippings
2 eggs, hard-boiled & finely chopped
6 Tbsp. mayonnaise
Juice of 1 lemon

Combine all ingredients, mix well and refrigerate for 24 hours. Serve with vegetable sticks and crackers.

Makes approximately 3 cups.

— *Cynthia Gilmore*
Toronto, Ontario

OYSTER CREPES

Crêpe batter (*Volume 1*, page 17)
Filling:
¼ lb. bacon, chopped
1 onion, chopped
1 clove garlic, crushed
Salt & pepper
2 Tbsp. butter
2 cups oysters

¼ cup white wine
Parsley
Sauce Fondue:
2 tsp. butter
2 Tbsp. flour
1 cup cream
1 cup white wine
2 cups grated Swiss cheese

Prepare and cook crêpes as recipe directs. Set aside and keep warm.

Cook bacon until crisp; drain and set aside. Sauté onion, garlic and salt and pepper in butter. Add oysters and cook for 3 to 5 minutes. Add bacon, wine and parsley and simmer for 10 minutes.

To make sauce, melt butter, then add flour, stirring constantly. Gradually add cream, stirring, until well blended. Stir in wine. Add cheese and cook until melted and thickened.

To assemble, place filling in crêpes, roll up and top with sauce. Bake at 350 degrees F for 15 minutes.

Serves 4.

— Audrey Alley
Victoria, British Columbia

MOULES GRILLEE

2 dozen mussels
Lemon juice
Garlic powder

Butter
Thyme
Parsley

Scrub mussel shells and remove byssus threads. Open by inserting a small, sharp knife between shells on flat side one-third of the way from the pointed end. Cut through to the wide end and spread the shell open. Remove meat from one shell to the other so that all the mussel is on one side. Break shells apart and place shells containing meat on ovenproof serving dishes. Squirt with lemon juice and sprinkle with garlic powder. Dot with butter and top with thyme and parsley. Broil for 5 minutes and serve.

Serves 4 to 6.

— Nancy Witherspoon
Halifax, Nova Scotia

CLAM OR MUSSEL PIE

Pastry for double 9-inch pie shell
1½ cups clams or mussels
¾ cup diced potatoes
1 onion, chopped
2 cloves garlic, chopped

¼ cup chopped celery
3 Tbsp. butter
2 Tbsp. flour
Thyme
Salt & pepper

Scrub clams or mussels and cook in boiling water for 10 minutes, then shuck. Reserve liquid. Cook potatoes in fish liquid. Remove and set aside. Sauté onion, garlic and celery in butter. Stir in flour, thyme, salt and pepper and cook for 2 minutes. Slowly add cooking liquid and cook until thickened. Add potatoes and clams or mussels.

Place in pastry-lined pie plate and top with pastry. Bake at 400 degrees F until crust is browned.

Serves 4.

— Rachelle Poirier
Scoudouc, New Brunswick

PAELLA

AN ELEGANT PARTY DISH, THIS VERSION OF PAELLA USES ONLY SEAFOOD, WHEREAS there are some that also include chicken. After the baking, any clams and mussels that did not open should be discarded.

4-5 cups stock, half clam & half chicken
1 tsp. saffron
⅓ cup oil
2 cloves garlic
1 large onion, finely chopped
1 green pepper, cut into thin strips
2 lbs. white fish, cut into 2-inch pieces
Salt & pepper

2 cups raw rice
2 large tomatoes, peeled, seeded & diced
12 shrimp, shelled & deveined
12 scallops
1-2 cups partially cooked vegetables
 (peas, green beans, zucchini,
 artichoke hearts)
12 mussels or clams, scrubbed in shells

Bring stock to a boil, add saffron and set aside. In a large casserole dish, heat ¼ cup oil, fry garlic until browned, then remove and discard. Add onion, green pepper and white fish and cook until slightly browned. Season with salt and pepper. Add remaining oil and the rice and cook, stirring, for 2 to 3 minutes until rice is slightly browned. Add tomatoes and simmer for 2 to 3 minutes. Add stock and stir once.

Bury shrimp and scallops in rice, then add vegetables. Arrange mussels or clams around edge of dish, cover and simmer for 15 minutes, or until rice is cooked, adding stock as necessary. Uncover and bake at 450 degrees F for 10 minutes.

Serves 8.

— *Alice J. Pitt*
Kingston, Ontario

COMPANY SEAFOOD BAKE

¼ cup butter
1½ cups rice
3 cups chicken stock
2½ tsp. salt
⅜ tsp. pepper
12 Tbsp. butter
1½ cups sliced mushrooms
2 tsp. curry

½ tsp. ginger
2 6-oz. cans crabmeat, drained
5-oz. can lobster, drained
¼ cup dry sherry
¼ cup flour
¼ tsp. dry mustard
3 cups light cream
1 cup grated Swiss cheese

Heat ¼ cup butter in large saucepan, add rice and cook gently, stirring, until rice is golden brown. Add chicken stock, bring to a boil, turn down heat and simmer, covered, for 40 minutes, or until rice is tender and liquid absorbed. Add 1½ tsp. salt and ¼ tsp. pepper and stir together lightly with a fork. Spread rice mixture in bottom of greased, 9" x 13" baking dish.

Melt 6 Tbsp. butter in large skillet. Add mushrooms, curry and ginger and cook gently for 3 minutes, stirring. Remove from heat. Add crabmeat, lobster, ½ tsp. salt and sherry and blend lightly. Spoon over rice.

Melt remaining 6 Tbsp. butter in saucepan. Sprinkle in flour, ½ tsp. salt, ⅛ tsp. pepper and mustard and let bubble. Remove from heat and add cream all at once, stirring to blend. Return to moderate heat and cook, stirring, until thickened. Pour over seafood evenly and sprinkle with cheese. Bake at 400 degrees F for about 25 minutes, or until very hot.

— *Karen Havelock*
Balmoral, Manitoba

SHRIMP & CRABMEAT CREPES

Crêpe batter (*Volume 1*, page 17)
6 Tbsp. butter
3 Tbsp. flour
1 cup milk
¼ tsp. garlic powder

¼ tsp. basil
¼ lb. mushrooms, finely chopped
1 small onion, finely chopped
6 oz. can crabmeat, drained
1 cup small shrimp, cooked

Prepare and cook crêpes as recipe indicates. Cover, set aside and keep warm.

Make a white sauce by melting 3 Tbsp. butter. Blend in flour and cook over low heat for 5 minutes. Slowly add milk, garlic powder and basil. Set aside.

Sauté mushrooms and onion in remaining 3 Tbsp. butter. Add crabmeat and shrimp and heat through. Add to white sauce, fill crêpes, place in a greased, shallow baking dish, cover and bake at 300 degrees F for 30 minutes.

Serves 2 to 3.

— Diane Schoemperlen
Banff, Alberta

SEAFOOD CASSEROLE

¾ cup crabmeat, cooked
¾ cup small shrimp,
  cooked & shelled
2 Tbsp. grated sharp Cheddar cheese

2 sole fillets, split in half down the centre
1½ cups white sauce (*Volume 1*, page 92)
1 Tbsp. Parmesan cheese
1 Tbsp. parsley

Toss crabmeat and shrimp with cheese and place half in each of two greased individual casserole dishes. Mound mixture into loaf shapes and place one half split fillet on each side of each mound. Cover with warm white sauce and sprinkle with Parmesan cheese and parsley. Bake at 325 degrees F for 20 minutes.

Serves 2.

— June McKinnell
Toronto, Ontario

SEAFOOD SPAGHETTI SAUCE

1 cup water
1 cup dry white wine
1 bay leaf
Cloves
1 medium onion, finely chopped
1-2 cloves garlic, finely chopped
Salt & pepper
½ lb. shrimp
½ lb. squid, cut into small pieces

1 lb. sole fillets, cut into 1-inch pieces
3 Tbsp. butter
4 Tbsp. flour
2½ cups fish liquid
½ cup whipping cream
½ tsp. lemon juice
2 Tbsp. chopped parsley
1 tsp. tarragon
1 tsp. thyme

Bring water, wine, bay leaf, pinch of cloves, onion, garlic and salt and pepper to a boil. Add fish one type at a time and cook for 3 to 4 minutes each. Remove from liquid and set aside. Strain and reserve liquid.

Melt butter in double boiler, add flour and cook, stirring, for 5 minutes. Add 2½ cups reserved fish liquid while stirring, bring to a boil and simmer for a few minutes. Add cream, lemon juice, parsley, tarragon and thyme. Add fish, heat to boiling point and serve.

Serves 6.

— Harvey Griggs
Willowdale, Ontario

Poultry
&
Game

It is not only fine feathers that make fine birds.

— **Aesop**
The Jay and the Peacock

SUPREMES DE VOLAILLES AUX QUATRES FROMAGES

CONTRIBUTED BY A LONDON, ONTARIO, RESTAURANT, THIS RECIPE FOR DEBONED Chicken Breasts With Four Cheeses is incredibly rich, but delicious. It is relatively simple to prepare and can be assembled hours in advance — the final cooking stage takes only 5 minutes. Because it is so rich, it is best served with a salad or cooked vegetable and a light dessert of fruit.

¼ lb. plus 3 Tbsp. butter
6 chicken breasts, deboned,
  trimmed & pounded
Flour
Salt & pepper
1 cup flour
3 cups milk

2½ cups grated Jarlsberg cheese
1 cup plus 1 Tbsp. Parmesan cheese
¼ tsp. nutmeg
1 egg
1 cup grated white Cheddar cheese
1 cup grated old Gouda cheese

Melt 3 Tbsp. butter on high heat. Dredge chicken in flour and sauté. Season with salt and pepper and set aside.

In medium saucepan, melt ¼ lb. butter. Add 1 cup flour and stir over medium heat for 2 minutes. Pour in milk, stirring constantly, and bring to a boil. When sauce boils, lower heat, add 1½ cups Jarlsberg, 1 Tbsp. Parmesan, nutmeg, egg and salt and pepper. Continue cooking and stirring until cheese is melted. Mix together remaining cheeses.

To assemble, place chicken in shallow baking dish or in individual gratin dishes. Pour sauce over each breast, then sprinkle each with one-sixth of cheese mixture. Bake at 400 degrees F for 5 minutes, then broil to brown the top.

Serves 6.

— Auberge du Petit Prince
London, Ontario

CHICKEN MADAGASCAR

THIS RECIPE WAS DEVELOPED BY THE CONTRIBUTOR WHEN HE WAS THE TEACHING CHEF in a Victoria, British Columbia, high school. In his words, "When the budget got tight, I decided I could not afford beef tenderloin for pepper steak. I used chicken, and this recipe evolved." Deglazing the pan is simply adding liquor and/or stock to the concentrated juices in which the meat has been cooked to dilute them.

2 chicken breasts
2 Tbsp. unsalted butter
2 cloves garlic, minced
2 Tbsp. minced shallots
½ Tbsp. green peppercorns

Worcestershire sauce
1 oz. brandy
1 oz. strong chicken stock
½ cup whipping cream
Salt

Debone and skin chicken breasts. Pound between wax paper until meat is of even thickness. Melt butter and sauté garlic and shallots. Add chicken and brown lightly, but do not overcook. Remove meat and keep warm. Add peppercorns and Worcestershire sauce and mash peppercorns. Add brandy and chicken stock and cook over high heat to reduce liquid and deglaze pan. Reduce heat, add cream and salt and simmer, stirring constantly, until cream begins to thicken. Return chicken and continue to simmer until chicken is heated through.

Serves 2.

— Wayne Smith
Victoria, British Columbia

SHRIMP STUFFED CHICKEN

1¼ cups chopped, cooked shrimp
¼ cup chopped celery
1 tsp. salt
¼ cup chopped onion
½ cup softened butter

3 chicken breasts, deboned,
  skinned & halved
1 cup cream of mushroom sauce
  (*Volume I*, page 92)
½ cup chicken stock
½ cup sherry

Combine shrimp, celery, salt, onion and butter and divide evenly among chicken breasts. Roll up and secure with toothpicks.

Combine mushroom sauce, stock and sherry and blend well. Arrange chicken rolls in shallow baking dish and pour sauce over top. Bake at 350 degrees F for 1 hour.

Serves 6.

— Jane Falls
Bradford, Ontario

CHICKEN LEMONESE

4 chicken breasts
1 egg, beaten with 2 Tbsp. water
½ cup flour
½ cup grated Monterey jack cheese
½ cup Parmesan cheese
Garlic powder

¼ cup chopped parsley
1 tsp. paprika
Salt
3 Tbsp. butter
1 clove garlic, minced
3 lemons

Skin, debone and cut chicken breasts into bite-sized pieces. Place egg and water in shallow bowl. Mix together flour, cheeses, garlic powder, parsley, paprika and salt in another shallow bowl. Drop chicken pieces first into flour-cheese mixture, then into egg mixture, then back into flour-cheese mixture, coating well.

Melt butter and add garlic. Sauté chicken pieces until golden brown on both sides. Remove from pan and set aside. To liquid in pan add the juice of 2 lemons and simmer briefly. Add 1 sliced lemon, pour over chicken and serve.

Serves 4.

— Francie Goodwin-Rogne
Calgary, Alberta

CHICKEN BOLERO

2 chicken breasts
1 large green pepper
1 large onion
3 Tbsp. oil

1½ Tbsp. dill weed
2½ cups sour cream
Salt & pepper
4 cups cooked rice

Debone chicken and slice into narrow strips. Slice pepper and onion into narrow strips. Sauté in hot oil until chicken is golden and vegetables are tender. Add dill weed, sour cream and salt and pepper. Cook over low heat for 10 minutes without boiling. Serve with rice.

Serves 3 to 4.

— Katie Larstone
Langley, British Columbia

DIJON CHICKEN

3 Tbsp. milk
2 Tbsp. Dijon mustard
2 chicken breasts
¼ cup bread crumbs
1 tsp. tarragon leaves, crushed or crumbled

Whisk milk and mustard together. Dip chicken in mixture, then coat with mixture of bread crumbs and tarragon. Place in shallow baking dish and bake at 375 degrees F for 30 minutes, covered, then 15 minutes, uncovered.

Serves 2.

— Beth Rose
Tavistock, Ontario

BRANDIED CHICKEN BREASTS

4 chicken breasts, skinned, deboned & halved
¼ cup brandy
Salt & pepper
Marjoram
Thyme

6 Tbsp. unsalted butter
½ cup dry sherry
4 egg yolks
2 cups light cream
Nutmeg
Grated Gruyère cheese

Soak chicken in brandy, seasoned with salt and pepper, marjoram and thyme, for about 20 minutes.

Heat butter in large skillet and sauté chicken over medium heat for 6 to 8 minutes on each side. Remove to heated ovenproof platter and keep warm. To remaining butter in pan add sherry and the brandy that the chicken soaked in. Simmer over low heat until reduced by half.

Beat egg yolks into cream and add to pan juices, stirring constantly. Season with salt, pepper and nutmeg and cook, stirring, until slightly thickened. Pour sauce over chicken breasts, sprinkle with cheese and brown under broiler.

Serves 4.

— Jim Boagey
Aurora, Ontario

HERBED CHICKEN BREASTS

2 chicken breasts, deboned & halved
1 Tbsp. flour
¼ cup plain yogurt
¼ tsp. lemon juice
1 tsp. grated onion
Sage, thyme & basil

¼ tsp. salt
Pepper
3 Tbsp. grated Cheddar cheese
¼ tsp. paprika
⅓ cup fine cracker crumbs

Sprinkle chicken with flour to lightly coat both sides. Mix yogurt, lemon juice, onion, spices and salt and pepper in a bowl. Mix cheese, paprika and crumbs in a flat dish.

Dip chicken in yogurt mixture, then in crumb mixture to coat all sides. Put in greased baking dish, cover with foil and bake at 350 degrees F for 30 minutes. Uncover and bake until tender — about 15 minutes.

Serves 2.

— Maureen Thornton
Palgrave, Ontario

MANDARIN CHICKEN BREASTS

¼ cup flour
½ tsp. paprika
½ tsp. salt
6 chicken breasts, deboned
2 Tbsp. butter
1¾ cups chicken stock

1 Tbsp. minced onion
2 Tbsp. lemon juice
1 bay leaf
1 Tbsp. cornstarch
1 cup seedless grapes
1 can mandarin oranges

Mix flour, paprika and salt in pie plate. Dip chicken into mixture to coat, then brown slowly in butter. Stir in chicken stock, onion, lemon juice and bay leaf. Heat to boiling, cover and reduce heat. Simmer for 25 minutes, then remove bay leaf. Mix cornstarch with a little water to make a paste and stir into gravy. Cook, stirring constantly, for 3 minutes. Stir in grapes and oranges and heat until bubbly. Serve over rice.

Serves 6 to 8.

— Marsha Plewes
Gormley, Ontario

CHICKEN BREASTS A LA WALPER

THIS RECIPE ORIGINATED WITH THE CONTRIBUTOR'S GRANDMOTHER WHO OPERATED THE Walper Hotel, now called the Dominion Hotel, in Zurich, Ontario.

6 chicken breasts, skinned,
  deboned & cut in pieces
Seasoned flour
12 slices Swiss cheese

6 cups sauerkraut, well drained
1 cup sour cream or yogurt
2 Tbsp. butter

Arrange chicken breasts in well-greased, shallow baking dish. Sprinkle with seasoned flour. Top with 6 slices of Swiss cheese, then sauerkraut. Spoon sour cream over this and place remaining Swiss cheese over sour cream. Dot with butter and bake at 325 degrees F for 45 to 50 minutes, or until chicken is tender.

Serves 6 to 8.

— E.K. Walper
Lions Head, Ontario

CHICKEN WITH PEACHES & CREAM

3 whole chicken breasts
Garlic powder
1 cup raw rice
1 head broccoli

1 cup sour cream
½ cup mayonnaise
3 peaches, sliced
1 cup grated Cheddar cheese

Bake or broil chicken, seasoned with garlic powder, until tender. While chicken is baking, cook rice and place in greased casserole dish.

Steam broccoli pieces until barely tender and layer over rice. Blend sour cream and mayonnaise together and carefully fold in peach slices and drained, cooked chicken. Layer on top of broccoli, top with Cheddar cheese and bake at 350 degrees F until cheese is hot and bubbly — 20 minutes.

Serves 3.

— Annette Laing
Mission, British Columbia

CHICKEN BREASTS & VEGETABLES

THIS IS AN EXCELLENT AND ECONOMICAL FAMILY DINNER THAT IS EASY TO PREPARE.
If the honey and barbecue sauce are not to your liking, the chicken can be floured and sautéed in butter (rather than being put in the oven) for a different but just as satisfying result.

2 chicken breasts, deboned & halved
4 carrots, sliced
2 stalks celery, sliced
1 small onion, chopped
½ tsp. rosemary
½ tsp. thyme
½ tsp. parsley
½ tsp. marjoram
½ tsp. salt
½ cup white wine
¼ cup honey
¼ cup barbecue sauce

Place chicken, carrots, celery, onion, seasonings and wine in large saucepan. Cover with water and cook over medium heat for 30 minutes. Remove from heat and keep warm. Combine honey and barbecue sauce. Place chicken in shallow ovenproof dish and brush with honey-barbecue sauce mixture. Bake at 325 degrees F for 15 to 20 minutes. Serve with drained vegetables and mashed potatoes.

Serves 4.

— *Edwina Johnson*
Peterborough, Ontario

CHICKEN LAROUSSE

3 large chicken breasts, cut in half
Salt
Paprika
1 cup Parmesan cheese
1 lb. green beans, trimmed & Frenched
½ cup slivered almonds
1½ cups raw wild rice
¾ cup butter
1 small onion, chopped
1 small green pepper, chopped
1 cup chopped celery
Mushrooms, halved
Pepper
1 cup dry white wine

Sprinkle chicken with salt and paprika, roll in Parmesan cheese and set aside. Place green beans and almonds in shallow casserole dish. Cook wild rice according to package directions. Melt ½ cup butter, add onion, green pepper and celery and sauté until soft. Stir in mushrooms, wild rice and salt and pepper to taste. Place chicken over beans and almonds and spoon wild rice mixture around sides of casserole. Pour white wine over all, dot chicken with remaining butter and bake at 350 degrees F for 45 to 50 minutes.

Serves 6.

— *Sandra Binnington*
Parry Sound, Ontario

FORTY GARLIC CLOVES CHICKEN

⅔ cup olive oil
4 stalks celery, chopped
Parsley
1 Tbsp. tarragon
Salt & pepper
Nutmeg
½ cup Cognac
40 cloves garlic, peeled but not cut
2 chickens, cut up

Place oil, celery, parsley, tarragon, salt and pepper, nutmeg, cognac and garlic in heavy enamel cooker. Add chicken. Cover tightly with foil or with lid glued on with a paste of flour and water. Bake at 350 degrees F for 2 hours.

Serves 4 to 6.

— *Marie-Paula Chartier*
Grand Mère, Quebec

GOLDEN POPOVER CHICKEN

1 chicken, cut up
2 Tbsp. oil
Salt & pepper
3 eggs
1½ cups milk
1 Tbsp. oil
1½ cups flour
¾ tsp. crushed dried parsley

Mushroom Sauce:
1 cup cream of mushroom sauce
  (*Volume I*, page 92)
½ cup white wine
1 Tbsp. parsley
½ cup sliced mushrooms

Brown chicken pieces in oil, then season with salt and pepper and place in 9" x 13" casserole dish.

Blend remaining ingredients together in order given and pour over chicken. Bake at 350 degrees F for 55 to 60 minutes, or until chicken is cooked and batter has puffed up and turned golden brown.

Meanwhile make sauce. Combine all ingredients in saucepan and cook over low heat. Serve with chicken.

Serves 4.

— Marcy Goldman-Posluns
Dollard Des Ormeaux, Quebec

CRISPY WHEAT GERM CHICKEN

¼ cup soya sauce
2 Tbsp. oil
1 clove garlic, minced
3 lbs. chicken pieces
½ cup wheat germ

¼ cup dry bread crumbs
2 Tbsp. sesame seeds
½ tsp. pepper
½ tsp. paprika

Combine soya sauce, oil and garlic. Arrange pieces of chicken in single layer in broad, shallow baking dish. Pour soya mixture over top and let stand for 10 minutes, turning chicken pieces several times to coat all sides.

Meanwhile, mix together wheat germ, bread crumbs, sesame seeds, pepper and paprika. Lift chicken pieces from marinade, drain briefly, then turn over in wheat germ mixture to coat all sides evenly. Arrange chicken, skin side down, on well-greased, rimmed baking sheet. Bake, uncovered, at 350 degrees F for about 1 hour, or until done, turning after 30 minutes.

Serves 4.

— Lisa Reith
Cranbrook, British Columbia

SESAME YOGURT CHICKEN

½ cup yogurt
2 Tbsp. Worcestershire sauce
2 Tbsp. lemon juice
½ cup sesame seeds

½ cup bread crumbs
½ tsp. paprika
Salt & pepper
6 chicken legs or breasts

Combine yogurt, Worcestershire sauce and lemon juice in shallow bowl. In another bowl, mix sesame seeds, bread crumbs, paprika and salt and pepper.

Dip chicken in yogurt mixture, then coat with crumb mixture. Place in greased shallow pan in a single layer. Bake at 350 degrees F for 50 to 60 minutes, or until chicken is tender and surface crisp.

Serves 6.

— Jane Lott
Toronto, Ontario

CHICKEN PARMESAN

2 chickens, cut up
Oil
1 small onion, grated
4 Tbsp. butter

3 Tbsp. flour
1 cup Parmesan cheese
2 cups milk
2 egg yolks

Lightly brown chicken in hot oil, but do not cook right through. Remove from oil, drain on paper towels, then place in large baking dish.

Cook onion in butter, add flour and stir in well. Add ¾ cup cheese, then gradually stir in milk and cook over low heat, stirring constantly, until sauce is thick. Beat egg yolks slightly and add a little of the sauce to the yolks. Stir back into sauce gradually. Cook over low heat for 10 minutes, pour over chicken and sprinkle with remaining ¼ cup cheese. Bake, covered, at 325 degrees F for 1 hour.

Serves 6.

— L_ othy Hurst
Nanaimo, British Columbia

CHICKEN PUFF

1½ cups flour
2 tsp. baking powder
½ tsp. salt
2 eggs, separated & beaten
1 cup milk

1 cup chopped, cooked chicken
2 tsp. chopped onion
¼ cup grated, raw carrot
2 Tbsp. melted butter
Chicken gravy

Mix together flour, baking powder and salt. Add beaten egg yolks and milk and mix well. Add chicken, onion, grated carrot and melted butter and mix well. Fold in stiffly beaten egg whites. Bake in greased baking dish at 400 degrees F for about 25 minutes. Serve with hot chicken gravy.

Serves 2.

— Cathy Royer
Welland, Ontario

SPANISH CHICKEN

¼ cup chopped onion
1 Tbsp. brown sugar
½ tsp. salt
1 tsp. prepared mustard
1 Tbsp. chili sauce
1 tsp. Worcestershire sauce
¼ cup vinegar

1 cup tomato juice
¼ cup water
½ cup sliced, stuffed green olives
Flour
Salt & pepper
3½ lbs. chicken pieces
½ cup butter

Combine onion, sugar, salt, mustard, chili sauce, Worcestershire sauce, vinegar, tomato juice and water. Cook over low heat for 10 minutes, then add olives.

Meanwhile, combine flour and salt and pepper. Dredge chicken pieces in this. Melt butter, add chicken and brown well.

Arrange chicken in 9" x 13" baking dish and cover with sauce. Cover and bake at 350 degrees F for 45 minutes.

Serves 4.

— Barbara Taylor
Calgary, Alberta

SKIER'S ORANGE CHICKEN

A DELIGHTFUL MEAL TO RETURN HOME TO AFTER A WINTER DAY'S OUTSIDE ACTIVITY, this dish can be assembled in the morning and popped into the oven at the last minute. Serve with rice pilaf and a tossed salad.

1 cup orange marmalade
1 Tbsp. curry
1 tsp. salt
½ cup water
3 lbs. chicken pieces

Combine marmalade, curry, salt and water. Place chicken cut side down in greased 9″ x 13″ baking pan. Spoon marmalade mixture over chicken.

Bake, uncovered, at 350 degrees F for 45 minutes, spooning sauce over chicken several times. If sauce begins to stick to bottom of pan, add ¼ cup water.

Serves 4.

— *Mrs. E. Louden*
Port Coquitlam, British Columbia

ITALIAN STYLE CHICKEN CASSEROLE

1 onion, sliced
6-8 medium potatoes, peeled & sliced
1 chicken, cut up
1 head broccoli, cut
  into bite-sized pieces
1 green pepper, sliced
19-oz. can tomatoes

¼ tsp. oregano
¼ tsp. basil
¼ tsp. parsley
¼ tsp. pepper
½ tsp. salt

In greased casserole dish, arrange layers of onion, potatoes, chicken and broccoli. Cover with slices of green pepper and tomatoes. Sprinkle with spices. Cover and cook at 350 degrees F for about 2 hours. Remove cover for last 10 minutes to brown meat and potatoes.

Serves 4 to 6.

— *Julie Herr*
Acton Vale, Quebec

CASSEROLE ROAST CHICKEN

5 lbs. chicken pieces
2 tsp. salt
1 tsp. pepper
2 tsp. paprika
2 large cloves garlic, minced
4 Tbsp. butter

12 small white mushrooms
12 small onions
3-5 potatoes, quartered
5 carrots, quartered lengthwise
1 cup chicken stock
Parsley

Wash and dry chicken pieces. Combine salt, pepper, paprika and garlic and rub the chicken with this mixture. Melt the butter in a casserole dish and brown the chicken. Add the mushrooms, onions and potatoes and brown lightly. Add the carrots. Mix in the stock, cover and bake at 375 degrees F for 1 hour or until tender, basting frequently. Serve garnished with fresh parsley.

Serves 4 to 6.

— *Maureen Marcotte*
Farrellton, Quebec

POULET GRATINE AU FROMAGE

3-4 lbs. chicken pieces
Salt
Melted butter

1 cup grated Gruyère or Swiss cheese
1 Tbsp. dry mustard
¾ cup whipping cream

Place chicken pieces on rack in roasting pan and salt lightly. Bake, uncovered, at 350 degrees F for about 1 hour, or until well browned. Brush the chicken once with melted butter while it is cooking. When done, place the chicken in a shallow, heat-resistant serving dish. Sprinkle with ½ cup of the grated cheese. Return to the oven and turn off the heat.

Skim and discard fat from chicken juices in roasting pan. Stir dry mustard and whipping cream into juices. Bring to a boil on high heat and stir until shiny bubbles form — about 3 to 4 minutes. Remove from heat, stir in remaining ½ cup grated cheese and keep warm.

Broil chicken 4 to 5 inches from heat for about 1 minute, or until cheese bubbles. Pour sauce around chicken.

Serves 4.

— *Anne Calverley*
Calgary, Alberta

CHICKEN SUPREME

1 chicken, cut up
Juice of 1 lemon
¼ cup flour
¼ cup butter
1 clove garlic, minced
3 carrots, sliced
2 onions, sliced
1 stalk celery, sliced

¼ cup white wine or chicken stock
1 cup cream sauce
½ tsp. paprika
¼ tsp. basil
¼ tsp. rosemary
2 Tbsp. parsley
Salt & pepper

Brush chicken with lemon juice and coat with flour. Melt butter and brown chicken in skillet. Place in casserole dish and top with vegetables.

Pour wine into skillet with chicken drippings, add sauce and seasonings, mix well and pour over chicken. Bake at 350 degrees F for 1½ hours.

Serves 4.

— *Pat Dicer*
Mission, British Columbia

SOUTHERN BAKED CHICKEN

½ cup butter
1 small onion, finely chopped
1 clove garlic, finely chopped
¼ cup Parmesan cheese
¾ cup bread crumbs

¾ cup corn meal
3 Tbsp. minced fresh parsley
1 tsp. salt
1 tsp. pepper
2 chickens, cut up

Melt butter and sauté onion and garlic until tender. Combine cheese, bread crumbs, corn meal, parsley, salt and pepper. Dip chicken in butter and then roll in coating.

Bake at 350 degrees F for 1 hour.

Serves 8.

— *Valerie Marien*
Orangeville, Ontario

BAKED ALMOND CHICKEN

3½ lbs. chicken pieces
Flour
1 tsp. celery salt
1 tsp. paprika
1 tsp. salt
½ tsp. curry
½ tsp. oregano

½ tsp. freshly ground pepper
7 Tbsp. melted butter
¾ cup sliced almonds
1½ cups light cream
½ cup sour cream
3 Tbsp. fine, dry bread crumbs

Coat chicken pieces with flour. Blend celery salt, paprika, salt, curry, oregano and pepper with 6 Tbsp. melted butter. Roll chicken pieces in this, coating all sides. Arrange chicken in single layer in 9" x 13" baking dish and sprinkle evenly with almonds. Pour light cream between pieces.

Bake, covered, at 350 degrees F for 45 minutes. Uncover, add about ½ cup sauce from pan to sour cream, mix together and pour evenly over chicken. Combine bread crumbs with remaining 1 Tbsp. melted butter and sprinkle over chicken. Bake, uncovered, for 15 minutes longer, or until chicken is tender.

Serves 6.

— *Marilyn Nichols*
Tahsis, British Columbia

CHICKEN & SHRIMP CASSEROLE

10 oz. raw shelled shrimp
2 cups chicken stock
½ cup plus 1 Tbsp. butter
½ cup flour
1 cup whipping cream
2 egg yolks

½ cup plus 2 Tbsp. Parmesan cheese
Salt & pepper
2 tsp. parsley
3 cups chopped cooked chicken
2 Tbsp. ground almonds
¼ cup bread crumbs

Combine shrimp and ½ cup stock and boil for 1 minute. Drain, reserving stock. Melt ½ cup butter, add flour and stir to mix. Stir in all stock and cook until thickened. Add cream and bring to a boil. Lower heat and simmer, stirring, for 5 minutes. Beat egg yolks, stir in a little of the sauce, then return to pan. Add ½ cup cheese, salt and pepper and 1 tsp. parsley. Mix in shrimp and chicken and place in greased casserole dish. Combine remaining 1 tsp. parsley, 2 Tbsp. Parmesan cheese, 1 Tbsp. butter, almonds and bread crumbs until crumbly and sprinkle over casserole. Bake at 400 degrees F for 30 to 35 minutes.

Serves 4.

— *Linda Townsend*
Nanoose Bay, British Columbia

BALKAN CHICKEN STEW

4-5 lbs. chicken pieces
Salt & pepper
3 medium onions, thinly sliced
1 clove garlic, crushed

4 Tbsp. butter
1 cup white wine
2 cups sour cream
1 cup pitted ripe olives

Pat chicken dry and season with salt and pepper. Sauté onions and garlic in butter until transparent. Remove onions, add chicken and sauté until brown. Return onions to skillet, add wine and simmer for 1 hour. Cool to room temperature, then stir in sour cream and olives. Simmer gently for 20 minutes.

Serves 5 to 6.

— *Midge Denault*
Lee Valley, Ontario

SHERRIED CHICKEN

1 chicken, cut up
½ tsp. salt
⅛ tsp. pepper
½ tsp. paprika
Butter
1 cup chicken stock
½ cup sherry
Savory

Thyme
Rosemary
Parsley
Marjoram
1 bay leaf
¼ cup butter
1 cup sliced mushrooms

Sprinkle chicken on both sides with salt, pepper and paprika and brown in butter. Add stock and sherry and sprinkle with herbs. Cover and simmer for 45 minutes, turning chicken over during cooking. Add a little water if too dry. Stir in mushrooms 5 minutes before serving.

Serves 4.

— Lori Davies
Vanderhoof, British Columbia

EGGPLANT & CHICKEN

1 chicken, cut up
2 Tbsp. oil
2 cloves garlic, minced
1 unpeeled eggplant, cut
  into 1-inch cubes
1 onion, diced

6 tomatoes, peeled & sliced
½ cup dry red wine
1 tsp. oregano
1 tsp. basil
¼ tsp. pepper
Salt

In large pan, brown chicken on all sides in oil with garlic. Add eggplant and onion and sauté for 5 minutes. Add tomatoes, wine and spices, cover and let simmer for about 1 hour, stirring occasionally.

Serves 4 to 6.

— Julie Herr
Acton Vale, Quebec

JEFFERSON CHICKEN

4 chicken breasts, deboned
  & cut in half
Butter
2 Tbsp. sherry
½ cup white wine
¼ cup lemon juice

Grated rind of 1 lemon
Grated rind of 1 orange
1 cup light cream
Parmesan cheese
Orange & lemon slices

Brown chicken in butter, cover, lower heat and stew until cooked through. Remove chicken from pan and place on serving dish.

Combine sherry, wine, lemon juice and rinds. Add to juices in pan and bring to a boil. Lower heat and slowly stir in cream.

Sprinkle cheese over chicken and brown briefly under broiler. Pour sauce over chicken, garnish with orange and lemon slices and serve.

Serves 4.

— Elizabeth Ballantyne
Winnipeg, Manitoba

GALLINO EN CHICHA

This recipe for chicken in wine sauce is of El Salvadoran origin. Planning ahead is required as some of the ingredients will involve a trip to a specialty food shop.

5 lbs. chicken pieces
2 large onions
2 Tbsp. sesame seeds
2 dried sweet red peppers
2 peppercorns
4 small bay leaves
1 small Italian loaf of bread, soaked
  in sweet red table wine
1 cup apple cider vinegar

1 tsp. pepper
1 cup sweet red table wine
1 Tbsp. Worcestershire sauce
24 dried prunes
1 cup olives, pitted
½ cup capers
6-oz. can tomato paste
12-oz. jar pimentos

Simmer chicken slowly with onions in salted water, using just enough water to cover bottom of skillet. Add water as needed while cooking.

Grind the sesame seeds, red peppers, peppercorns, laurel leaves and bread into a paste.

When chicken is soft, add vinegar, pepper, wine, Worcestershire sauce, prunes, olives, capers, tomato paste, pimentos and sesame seed paste. Cover and cook slowly on top of stove for 1 hour.

Serves 6.

— *Kathy Cowbrough*
Stirling, Scotland

MURRAY BAY NASTURTIUM CHICKEN

This recipe comes from the collection of the contributor's grandmother, and brings back memories of summertime family reunions on the lower St. Lawrence River. As she recalls, "Lunches and dinners for 20 to 30 people were not unusual. When the chickens were all cooked, cooled and smelling of lemon, laid out on beds of lettuce and garnished with nasturtium flowers, they were indeed a sight to behold."

½ cup butter
2 Tbsp. lemon juice
1 tsp. salt
1 clove garlic, mashed
⅛ tsp. pepper
½ tsp. paprika

Handful mushrooms, sliced
1 Tbsp. nasturtium seeds
2-3 lbs. chicken pieces
Lettuce
Nasturtium flowers

Place butter, lemon juice, salt, garlic, pepper, paprika, mushrooms and nasturtium seeds in skillet and bring to a boil. Add chicken, cover and simmer for 30 minutes, turning chicken several times.

Remove from heat, and as the chicken cools spoon butter mixture over it. When thoroughly cooled, place on bed of lettuce, garnish with flowers and serve.

Serves 3 to 4.

— *Katherine Mackenzie*
Georgeville, Quebec

POULET FRAMBOISE

2 medium onions, thinly sliced
2 Tbsp. water
3 Tbsp. unsalted butter
2-3 lbs. chicken pieces
Salt & pepper

1 large tomato, peeled, seeded & chopped
2 cloves garlic, crushed
2 cups raspberry vinegar
1 cup whipping cream
2 Tbsp. Cognac or Armagnac

Cook onions, water and 1 Tbsp. butter in large frying pan over low heat for 30 minutes. While onions are cooking, season chicken pieces with salt and pepper. Heat remaining 2 Tbsp. butter in another frying pan and cook chicken until golden on both sides. Add tomato and garlic to onions. Place chicken pieces on top of onion mixture and cook, covered, over low heat for 30 minutes, or until chicken is tender.

Remove any excess butter from pan used to brown chicken. Add raspberry vinegar and simmer gently until only ½ cup remains. Place cooked chicken on a warm serving platter. Purée the onion and tomato mixture and add to reduced vinegar in frying pan. Place chicken in the pan and reheat with vinegar mixture for 10 to 15 minutes. Stir in cream and liquor and serve.

Serves 4.

— *Ingrid Birker*
Montreal, Quebec

CHICKEN WITH LEMON-MUSTARD SAUCE

1 chicken, cut up
2 Tbsp. oil
2 Tbsp. flour
½ tsp. salt
⅛ tsp. pepper

1½ cups chicken stock
2 Tbsp. Dijon mustard
1 tsp. tarragon
½ lemon, thinly sliced

Brown chicken in hot oil in large skillet and move to one side. Stir in flour, salt and pepper, then stock, mustard and tarragon until well blended. Cover and simmer for 30 minutes. Add lemon slices; cover and simmer 5 minutes longer or until chicken is tender. Serve over rice or noodles.

Serves 4.

— *Rosy Hale*
Scarborough, Ontario

CHICKEN ADOBE

1 chicken, cut up
2-3 cloves garlic
Soya sauce
15-20 peppercorns

2-3 bay leaves
½ onion, finely chopped
⅓ cup vinegar
Flour

Place chicken in pot and cover with water. Heat water to boiling, add garlic, soya sauce, peppercorns and bay leaves. Cover and simmer for 30 minutes. Add onion and vinegar. Use sufficient flour to thicken the water to a gravy and simmer for another 20 minutes.

Serves 4.

— *Bette Warkentin*
Matsqui, British Columbia

CHICKEN PINWHEELS

THESE PINWHEELS ARE DELICIOUS SERVED HOT OR COLD. FOR A SPECIAL OCCASION, make a cream of mushroom sauce (*Volume 1*, page 92) and pour over the pinwheels. Serve with stir-fried snow peas.

1 cup white flour
½ cup whole wheat flour
3 Tbsp. bran
2 Tbsp. wheat germ
⅓ cup skim milk powder
4 tsp. baking powder
1 tsp. salt
⅓ cup lard or shortening
⅔ cup water

1 Tbsp. butter
2 Tbsp. flour
¼ cup chicken stock
¼ cup milk
2 cups chopped, cooked chicken
¼ cup chopped chives or green onions
Sage
¾ cup grated Cheddar cheese

Mix flours, bran, wheat germ, milk powder, baking powder and ½ tsp. salt. Cut in lard to form a coarse meal. Add water to make a soft dough. Roll on a floured board to a 12-inch by 15-inch rectangle.

Melt butter and stir in flour. Gradually add stock and milk to make a thick cream sauce. Mix with chicken, chives, sage and cheese.

Spread chicken mixture on dough, leaving ½ inch of dough uncovered around the edges. Roll up like a jelly roll and slice every ¾ inch. Place on ungreased cookie sheet.

Bake at 425 degrees F for 12 to 15 minutes or until golden brown.

Makes 12 pinwheels.

— Heather Quiney
Victoria, British Columbia

MEXICAN CHICKEN PIE

QUITE DIFFERENT FROM THE USUAL CRUSTED CHICKEN PIE, THIS IS A FLAVOURFUL AND multi-textured dish.

3 lbs. chicken pieces
12 corn tortillas
3 cups cream of mushroom sauce
  (*Volume I*, page 92)
7-oz. can green chili salsa
1 cup grated Cheddar cheese

Bake chicken pieces, covered, at 400 degrees F for 1 hour in a 9″ x 13″ casserole dish. Remove chicken and debone. Do not wash dish.

Break up 4 tortillas into 2-inch pieces and place in bottom of same casserole dish. Place half the chicken on the tortillas. Combine mushroom sauce with green chili salsa, then pour one-third of this over the chicken. Cut 4 more tortillas into 2-inch pieces and place on top of sauce. Top with remaining chicken and another third of sauce. Cut up remaining tortillas and place on top of sauce. Top with remaining sauce and the cheese. Bake at 375 degrees F for 1 hour.

Serves 6.

— Linda Stanier
Lacombe, Alberta

CHICKEN, LEEK AND SAUSAGE PIE

THIS DELICIOUS MODIFICATION OF AN OLD BASQUE RECIPE MAKES A SUBSTANTIAL dinner. It is easily assembled, especially if one has pastry on hand.

Pastry for double 9-inch pie shell
½ lb. sausage meat
2 Tbsp. oil
2 whole leeks, chopped

2 Tbsp. flour
2 cups chicken stock
2 cups cooked chicken,
  cut into bite-sized pieces

Shape sausage meat into ¾-inch balls and fry in oil until golden. Remove from pan. Pour out all but 2 Tbsp. of oil. In this, sauté leeks for 1 minute. Sprinkle flour on top and stir to blend well. Slowly pour in chicken stock and cook until thickened.

Place cooked sausage balls in bottom of pastry-lined pie plate. Put chicken on top of sausage and pour sauce over top. Cover with pastry and make a slit to allow steam to escape. Bake at 400 degrees F for 35 to 40 minutes, or until golden brown.

Serves 4.

— Terri d'Aoust
Malahat, British Columbia

GOUGERE DE GIBIER

GOUGERE IS A RICH CHOUX-LIKE PASTRY WHICH ORIGINATED IN BURGUNDY, FRANCE. IT can be filled in a variety of ways — this recipe called originally for game (*gibier*) but has been adapted to use chicken.

Filling:
1 small onion, chopped
1 Tbsp. butter
1 Tbsp. flour
⅓ cup chicken stock
¼ cup chopped mushrooms
1 cup diced, cooked chicken
Salt & pepper
½ tsp. thyme
¼ tsp. sage

Paste:
¼ cup butter
½ cup water
½ cup flour
2 eggs
⅛ tsp. prepared mustard
Salt & pepper
⅔ cup grated Cheddar cheese
⅓ cup dry bread crumbs

To make filling, fry onion slowly in butter. Stir in flour, then stock and mushrooms. Boil, stirring frequently, until thick, then add chicken. Season with salt and pepper, thyme and sage. Cool.

For paste, measure butter and water into heavy pot. Bring to a boil until butter melts, then remove from heat. Add flour and beat until smooth. Cool, then beat in eggs. Add mustard, salt and pepper and ⅓ cup cheese.

Spread half of paste in greased pie plate, working it ½ inch up sides. Add filling and spread evenly. Cover with remaining paste, sprinkle with remaining cheese and bread crumbs and bake at 425 degrees F for 25 minutes. Reduce heat to 375 degrees and bake for another 10 minutes.

Serves 4.

— Judy McEwen
Arnprior, Ontario

CHICKEN RICE PIE

2 cups cooked rice
⅓ cup butter, melted
1 tsp. salt
¼ tsp. pepper
2 Tbsp. flour
1 cup milk

2 cups diced, cooked chicken
2 large tomatoes, peeled & chopped
3 stalks celery, chopped
1 small green pepper, chopped
3 Tbsp. dry bread crumbs

Combine rice, 2 Tbsp. butter, half the salt and half the pepper and mix well. Press into deep pie plate to form shell and set aside.

Melt 2 Tbsp. butter, stir in flour and cook until bubbly. Gradually stir in milk until thickened and smooth. Season with remaining salt and pepper. Stir in chicken, tomatoes, celery and green pepper. Pour into rice shell. Mix bread crumbs with remaining melted butter and sprinkle over pie. Bake at 350 degrees F for 25 minutes, or until golden brown.

Serves 6.

— *Inez Atkins*
Agincourt, Ontario

SKILLET CHICKEN

6 chicken legs
2-3 Tbsp. oil
1 cup tomato sauce (*Volume 1*, page 204)
2 Tbsp. finely chopped onion
1 Tbsp. vinegar

2 tsp. Worcestershire sauce
2 tsp. prepared mustard
¼ cup molasses
½ cup water

Split chicken legs in half through joint. Heat oil and brown chicken gently on all sides. Combine tomato sauce, onion, vinegar, Worcestershire sauce, mustard, molasses and water. Drain off excess fat from skillet and add sauce. Cover and simmer gently for 35 minutes, turning occasionally. Remove chicken to warm platter and boil sauce briskly to reduce and thicken it. Pour over chicken and serve.

Serves 4 to 6.

— *Linda Russell*
Exeter, Ontario

HOT CHICKEN LEGS

3 Tbsp. flour
Salt & pepper
2 tsp. turmeric
1 Tbsp. cumin
1 tsp. garlic powder
6 chicken legs

3 hot peppers, sliced, including seeds
3 onions, coarsely chopped
½ cup coarsely chopped Italian parsley
Chunks of Chinese lettuce or celery
2 cups chicken stock

Combine flour with salt and pepper, turmeric, cumin and garlic powder in large plastic bag. Shake chicken pieces in bag to coat them and brown with fat in skillet over high heat. Place in casserole dish and add peppers, onions, parsley and lettuce. Combine stock with 1 heaping Tbsp. coating mixture to thicken and pour over chicken. Cover and bake at 325 degrees F for 1 hour.

Serves 6.

— *Harvey Griggs*
Willowdale, Ontario

CHICKEN WINGS

48 chicken wings
½ cup honey
1 cup soya sauce
6 cloves garlic, minced
⅓ cup cornstarch
½ tsp. pepper
1 cup water

Cut chicken wings in half, discarding tip of wing. Mix honey, soya sauce, garlic, cornstarch and pepper and pour over wings. Marinate for minimum of 1 hour.

Drain wings, keeping marinade to one side. Fry wings in hot, shallow oil until golden brown on both sides. Place wings, marinade and water in baking dish and bake at 350 degrees F for 15 to 20 minutes.

Serves 12.

— *Andrew Camm*
Teeswater, Ontario

HONEY GARLIC CHICKEN

½ cup honey
½ cup soya sauce
2 cloves garlic, crushed
¼ cup butter
1 chicken, cut up

Combine honey, soya sauce, garlic and butter in a saucepan. Bring to a boil, reduce heat and simmer for 5 minutes.

Place chicken in a shallow pan and bake at 375 degrees F for 15 minutes. Cover with sauce and continue baking, turning chicken occasionally, until sauce is absorbed and chicken cooked.

Serves 4.

— *Louise Olson*
Vancouver, British Columbia

CHINESE WALNUT CHICKEN

1 cup coarsely broken walnuts
¼ cup oil
2 chicken breasts, deboned and
  cut into thin strips
½ tsp. salt
1 Tbsp. cornstarch
¼ cup soya sauce
2 Tbsp. sherry
1¼ cups chicken stock
1 cup onion slices
1½ cups celery slices, cut diagonally
1½ cups mushrooms
5-oz. can water chestnuts, drained
  & sliced

In skillet, toast walnuts in hot oil, stirring constantly, then remove and drain on paper towels. Place chicken in skillet and sprinkle with salt. Cook, stirring frequently, for 5 to 10 minutes, or until tender. Remove chicken.

Make sauce by combining cornstarch, soya sauce and sherry in skillet and gradually adding chicken stock. Cook for 2 to 3 minutes until sauce begins to thicken. Add chicken, onion, celery, mushrooms and water chestnuts and cook for 5 minutes, or until vegetables are slightly tender. Stir in toasted walnuts. Serve with hot rice.

Serves 4 to 6.

— *Donna Petryshyn*
Westlock, Alberta

CHICKEN WOKERIES

CHINESE 5-SPICE POWDER, A PUNGENT, SOMEWHAT SWEET MIXTURE OF GROUND SPICES, is readily available in Chinese specialty shops, but it is also very simple to make oneself. Simply grind into a fine powder equal amounts of Chinese star anise, fennel, pepper, cloves and cinnamon. Store in a small jar with a tightly fitting lid.

2 Tbsp. whole wheat flour
2 chicken breasts, deboned & cut
 into pieces
3 Tbsp. soya oil
2 onions, thickly sliced
1 cup mushrooms, halved
1 green pepper, thickly sliced
2 cups peas

1 cup chopped broccoli
1 cup sliced celery
¼ cup sliced water chestnuts
3-4 cloves garlic, sliced
2-3 Tbsp. soya sauce
½ cup chicken stock
¼ tsp. Chinese 5-spice powder
¼ tsp. grated ginger root

Place flour in plastic bag, add chicken pieces and shake bag until chicken is coated. Heat oil in wok, add chicken and cook for 1 or 2 minutes. Set chicken aside. Stir onions, mushrooms, green pepper, peas, broccoli, celery, water chestnuts and garlic into wok, adding more oil if necessary. Cook for 2 minutes, stirring occasionally. Stir in soya sauce, stock, 5-spice powder and ginger root. Add chicken, heat and serve.

Serves 3 to 4.

— Joanne Marcil
Dorval, Quebec

KHAENG KHIEU WAN KAI

A VISIT TO A CHINESE OR INDIAN SPECIALTY STORE MAY BE NECESSARY TO PURCHASE some of the ingredients for this curry, but the resulting flavour is well worth the effort.

Green Curry Paste:
1 large, fresh green chili
1 tsp. peppercorns
1 small onion, chopped
1 Tbsp. chopped garlic
2 Tbsp. chopped fresh coriander
2 tsp. chopped lemon rind
1 tsp. salt
2 tsp. ground coriander
2 tsp. dried shrimp paste
1 tsp. ground turmeric
1 Tbsp. oil

Chicken:
3 cups coconut milk
3 Tbsp. green curry paste
3 lbs. chicken pieces
2 Tbsp. lemon rind
½ tsp. salt
2 Tbsp. oyster sauce
2 Tbsp. finely chopped red chilies
4 Tbsp. finely chopped fresh basil

Prepare paste by chopping green chili, seeds and all, and blending with remaining ingredients to a smooth paste. Add additional oil or water if necessary to make paste smooth.

Prepare chicken by heating the green curry paste and half the coconut milk in saucepan until oil separates — about 10 minutes. Add chicken pieces and cook over medium-low heat for 10 minutes. Blend in remaining coconut milk, lemon rind, salt and oyster sauce. Cook, covered, for 30 minutes. Add red chilies and basil just before serving.

Serves 6.

— Ingrid Birker
Montreal, Quebec

CHICKEN TALUNAN

This Philippine dish originally utilized the tough meat of the losing rooster (called the *talunan*) in a cockfight. The sauce and lengthy stewing time serve to tenderize the meat.

2 cakes tofu
1 cup vinegar
½ cup brown sugar
4 cups water
3½ lbs. chicken pieces
2 lbs. pigs' feet, or other pork bits
1 clove garlic, crushed

1 cucumber, sliced
1 bay leaf
1 Tbsp. oregano
1 whole clove
1 star anise
1 stick cinnamon

Mash tofu and mix with vinegar and sugar. Combine water, chicken, pigs' feet and tofu mixture in large saucepan. Simmer until meat is tender and remove meat.

Add garlic, cucumber, bay leaf, oregano, clove, star anise and cinnamon to stock, cover and simmer until thick. Place meat on serving dish and pour sauce over.

Serves 6.

— *P.S. Reynolds*
Guelph, Ontario

TURMERIC CHICKEN & RICE BAKE

1 cup uncooked rice
2 cups boiling water
2 tsp. salt
1½ tsp. turmeric
¼ tsp. pepper

1 bay leaf
2 Tbsp. chopped onion
1 Tbsp. lemon juice
3 lbs. chicken pieces

Mix all ingredients except chicken in 2-quart casserole dish, stir well, then add chicken pieces. Cover and bake at 325 degrees F for 1½ hours.

Serves 5 to 6.

— *Mary Barrett*
Dollard des Ormeaux, Quebec

CHICKEN TANDOORI

This is an East Indian recipe traditionally served with curried rice, crisp vegetables and yogurt shakes.

2 cups yogurt
2 tsp. chili powder
6 cloves garlic, crushed
¼-½ tsp. red pepper
6 tsp. vinegar
Juice of 1 lime
1 tsp. salt

1 tsp. ginger
1 tsp. coriander
1 tsp. cumin
1 tsp. cardamom
2 tsp. honey
Pepper
4-5 lbs. chicken pieces

Combine all ingredients except chicken and mix well. Marinate chicken in this mixture for about 8 hours, turning frequently. Remove from marinade and bake at 375 degrees F for 60 to 75 minutes, basting with marinade.

Serves 4 to 6.

— *Randi Kennedy*
Amherst Island, Ontario

INDIAN CHICKEN CURRY

1 chicken
Salt & pepper
Cornstarch
Oil
1 Tbsp. soya sauce
4 onions, chopped

6 cloves garlic, minced
1 green pepper, chopped
3 cups mushrooms, sliced
3 tomatoes, peeled & chopped
4 Tbsp. curry

Cut chicken into small pieces, season with salt and pepper and dust with cornstarch. Brown in hot oil and set aside.

In chicken drippings and soya sauce, brown onions and garlic. Add green pepper and mushrooms and cook for 4 minutes. Add tomatoes and cook for 2 more minutes. Return chicken to pot, sprinkle with curry and cook for 10 minutes, turning chicken frequently. Add ½ cup boiling water, cover, reduce heat and simmer for 1 hour.

Serves 4 to 6.

— *Judith Goodwin*
Tamworth, Ontario

CHICKEN APPLE CURRY

½ cup chopped onion
1 clove garlic, minced
3 Tbsp. butter
1 Tbsp. curry
1 cup chopped apple
½ cup chopped celery

¼ cup flour
1 cup chicken stock
¾ cup milk
½-¾ tsp. salt
2 cups cooked, diced chicken

Sauté onion and garlic in butter with curry until onion is tender. Add apple and celery and cook for about 3 minutes longer. Stir in flour, then stock, milk and salt. Stir while heating until mixture boils. Add chicken; heat and serve over rice.

Serves 4.

— *Jane Lott*
Toronto, Ontario

CURRIED FRUIT CHICKEN

4 pieces chicken
½ cup oil
½ cup brown sugar
4 tsp. curry

1 Tbsp. flour
2 peaches, pitted & cubed
2 pears, pitted & cubed
2 plums, pitted & cubed

Brown chicken in ¼ cup of oil. Arrange the chicken, skin side up, in a baking dish. Combine the sugar, curry, flour and remaining oil and stir into the fruit. Let stand for 15 minutes, stirring occasionally. Spread fruit over chicken. Cover and bake at 350 degrees F for 30 minutes. Uncover and bake until the chicken is tender — about 50 minutes.

Serves 4.

— *Maureen Marcotte*
Farrellton, Quebec

CURRIED CHICKEN WITH SHRIMP

3 lbs. chicken pieces
Salt & pepper
2 Tbsp. butter
¾ cup finely chopped onion
½ cup finely chopped celery
1 tsp. finely minced garlic
2 Tbsp. curry

1 bay leaf
1 cup cubed apple
⅓ cup diced banana
2 tsp. tomato paste
1½ cups chicken stock
½ cup whipping cream
12 large shrimp

Sprinkle chicken with salt and pepper and brown in butter. Add onion, celery and garlic and cook briefly. Add curry, bay leaf, apple and banana. Cook for 5 minutes, then stir in tomato paste. Add stock and stir to blend. Cover and cook for 20 minutes longer, or until chicken is tender.

Remove chicken. Strain sauce through fine sieve. Reheat with cream. Return chicken along with shrimp to sauce and simmer until shrimp are pink.

Serves 6.

— *Linda Thompson*
Sudbury, Ontario

CHICKEN SATAY

1 cup finely chopped onion
1 clove garlic, crushed
¼ cup soya sauce
¼ cup oil
¼ cup peanut butter

2 Tbsp. brown sugar
3 Tbsp. lemon juice
¼ tsp. cayenne
1 tsp. coriander
1 chicken, cut up

Blend all ingredients, except chicken, until smooth. Marinate chicken in mixture for at least 2 hours, then bake at 350 degrees F for 30 to 45 minutes.

Serves 4.

— *Cynthia Gilmore*
Toronto, Ontario

CHICKEN WITH RAISINS & ALMONDS

5-lb. chicken
2 onions, chopped
¼ cup honey
1 Tbsp. butter
1 tsp. cinnamon

1 tsp. turmeric
Ginger
½ cup raisins
1 cup almonds, blanched,
  peeled & toasted

Place chicken in pot with water to half cover. Add remaining ingredients except raisins and almonds, bring to a boil and cook until chicken is done — about 1 hour. Add raisins and almonds and boil until liquid is about 1 to 2 inches deep. Place chicken in serving dish and pour sauce over it.

Serves 4.

— *Dale Fawcett*
Wyebridge, Ontario

CHICKEN WITH DATES

2 chickens, deboned & cut up
2 Tbsp. butter
2 Tbsp. oil
Salt & pepper
1 cup orange juice
2 cups chicken stock
3 Tbsp. cornstarch
1 tsp. salt

½ tsp. pepper
1 tsp. curry
1 medium onion, chopped
Juice of 1 lemon
Pitted dates
Green pepper rings
Orange slices

Brown chicken in butter and oil. Place in casserole dish and sprinkle with salt and pepper. Place orange juice, stock, cornstarch, salt, pepper, curry, onion and lemon juice in pot where chicken was browned. Heat to boiling, stirring constantly, until slightly thickened sauce results. Pour over chicken and bake at 350 degrees F for 35 minutes. Arrange dates, pepper rings and orange slices on casserole and bake for 10 more minutes.

Serves 6.

— *Eleanor Wallace Culver*
North Vancouver, British Columbia

BARBECUED CHICKEN BURGERS

3 lbs. chicken, skinned & deboned
1-2 strips bacon
1-2 slices dry whole wheat bread

Salt & pepper
4 slices mozzarella cheese
4 sesame seed buns

Put chicken meat through meat grinder along with bacon. When all meat has been ground, put bread through grinder and add to meat. Season with salt and pepper, mix gently and form into 4 patties. Grill over hot coals, turning when well-browned on one side. Place a slice of cheese on each patty and continue grilling until other side is browned. Serve on toasted buns with your choice of toppings.

Serves 4.

— *Karen Ritchie*
Cranbrook, British Columbia

CHICKEN LOAF

1½ lbs. finely ground, cooked chicken
¼ cup Parmesan cheese
½ cup bread crumbs, softened
  with ½ cup water
1 small onion, minced
½ tsp. basil

½ tsp. garlic powder
Salt & pepper
1 Tbsp. parsley
½ cup milk
3 eggs, lightly beaten
¼ cup melted butter

Mix together chicken, Parmesan cheese, bread crumbs, onion, basil, garlic powder, salt and pepper and parsley. Blend milk, eggs and melted butter together, then add to above mixture. Pat down lightly into greased loaf pan and bake at 350 degrees F for 45 minutes. Invert on a meat platter and slice to serve.

Serves 4 to 6.

— *Judy Black*
St. Andrews, New Brunswick

HOT CHINESE CHICKEN SALAD

8 chicken thighs, skinned, boned
  & cut into 1-inch chunks
¼ cup cornstarch
¼ cup oil
⅛ tsp. garlic powder
1 large, ripe tomato, cut into chunks
4-oz. can water chestnuts, drained
  & sliced (optional)

½ cup sliced mushrooms
1 bunch green onions, coarsely chopped
1 cup celery, sliced diagonally
¼ cup soya sauce
2 cups finely shredded lettuce

Roll chicken in cornstarch. Heat oil over high heat, add chicken and brown quickly. Sprinkle with garlic powder and stir in tomato, water chestnuts, mushrooms, onions, celery and soya sauce. Cover and simmer for 5 minutes, then toss in lettuce. Serve hot with rice.

Serves 6.

— Carol Weepers
Windsor, Ontario

CHICKEN SALAD VERONIQUE

2½ cups diced, cooked chicken
2½ tsp. lemon juice
1¼ cups diced celery
⅔ cup green seedless grapes
3 hard-boiled eggs, cut into quarters

¾ cup slivered, toasted almonds
⅔ cup mayonnaise
Bibb lettuce
Paprika

Combine chicken, lemon juice, celery, grapes, eggs, almonds and mayonnaise and mix well. Heap in bowl lined with lettuce and sprinkle with paprika.

Serves 6.

— Nan & Phil Millette
Corunna, Ontario

HOT CHICKEN SALAD

2 cups cooked chicken pieces
1 cup diced celery
½ cup slivered almonds
1 Tbsp. lemon juice
3 hard-boiled eggs, sliced
1 cup cream of mushroom sauce
  (*Volume I*, page 92)

2 tsp. minced onion
1 tsp. salt
¼ tsp. pepper
½ cup mayonnaise
2 cups cracker crumbs

Combine all ingredients, except cracker crumbs, in greased casserole dish. Top with crumbs and bake at 350 degrees F for 20 minutes.

Serves 4.

— Ingrid Magnuson
Winnipeg, Manitoba

CHICKEN SALAD

EITHER YELLOW SUMMER SQUASH OR ZUCCHINI CAN BE USED SUCCESSFULLY IN THIS recipe. Yellow beets are advised as they do not bleed and therefore result in a more attractive presentation.

2 cups cooked chicken
3-4 radishes
1 cup green or yellow beans
1 cup snow peas
1 small summer squash
6 pickling-sized yellow beets, cooked
  until tender

1 onion
1 head lettuce
½ cup mayonnaise
4 leaves red cabbage

Chop chicken and vegetables, except cabbage, into bite-sized pieces. Toss together. Add mayonnaise and mix well. Place in serving bowl lined with cabbage.

Serves 4 to 6.

— *Cindy Majewski*
Pansy, Manitoba

CHICKEN LIVER & CORN

2 Tbsp. flour
½ tsp. salt
¼ tsp. savory or rosemary
1½ lbs. chicken livers

2-3 Tbsp. butter
1 cup corn
½-1 cup water

Mix together flour, salt and seasoning. Rinse liver in very cold water and drain. Melt butter and add liver so pieces are lying flat. Sprinkle with half the seasoned flour, turn and sprinkle with remainder. Fry until lightly browned, then add corn and water and simmer until just tender, about 10 to 15 minutes. Add more water, if necessary, to make a light gravy.

Serves 4.

— *Rose Hurlbut-Wilson*
Ignace, Ontario

CHICKEN GIBLET CURRY

2 lbs. chicken giblets
2-3 onions, chopped
Butter
1-2 tsp. garlic powder
1 tsp. salt
½ tsp. crushed red pepper
1 tsp. ground coriander
12 cloves
4-5 bay leaves

1 tsp. finely chopped ginger root
2 tsp. cumin
12 peppercorns
3-4 cardamom seeds
1 tsp. turmeric
1 tsp. cinnamon
3-4 tomatoes, peeled & chopped
1 cup water

Cut giblets into small pieces. Brown onions in butter, then add giblets, garlic powder and salt. Cook for 5 minutes, add remaining spices and cook for a few minutes. Add tomatoes and water, lower heat and simmer for 45 minutes.

Serves 4 to 6.

— *Sue Griggs*
Willowdale, Ontario

CHICKEN LIVERS IN BEER SAUCE

2 lbs. chicken livers, rinsed & drained
4 Tbsp. butter
4 Tbsp. flour
1 cup chicken stock
1 medium onion, finely chopped
1 clove garlic, crushed

2 Tbsp. chopped parsley
½ cup sliced mushrooms
Salt & pepper
¼ tsp. thyme
½-¾ cup beer (or red wine)

Sauté livers in butter for 5 minutes on medium-high heat, then set aside. Lower heat, add flour to remaining juices and stir to make a smooth paste. Add chicken stock gradually, stirring over medium heat until a thickened sauce forms. Add onion, garlic, parsley, mushrooms and seasonings, and simmer for 5 minutes, stirring occasionally. Add beer or wine and livers; simmer for a few more minutes until livers are done. Do not overcook.

Serves 6.

— *Janet Drew*
Odessa, Ontario

MOTHER'S GEHACKTE LEBER

THIS IS A BASIC TRADITIONAL RECIPE FOR CHOPPED LIVER.

1 lb. chicken livers
2 onions, coarsely chopped
1 hard-boiled egg
1 slice bread

1 Tbsp. brandy
Dry mustard
Salt & pepper
Mayonnaise

Fry chicken livers and 1 onion until liver is cooked. Put through meat grinder with remaining onion, egg and bread. Mix in brandy, a little mustard and salt and pepper to taste. Add enough mayonnaise to hold mixture together. Chill and serve with crackers.

Makes approximately 2 cups.

— *Jeannie Rosenberg*
Huntingdon, Quebec

CHICKEN PATE WITH SORREL & DILL

1 lb. ground white chicken meat
½ cup diced fresh sorrel
1 tsp. freshly ground pepper
½ tsp. dry mustard

1 tsp. finely chopped fresh dill weed
1 cup dry white wine
1 egg
2 sprigs fresh dill

Mix chicken, sorrel, pepper, mustard and chopped dill and pour white wine over mixture. Cover and refrigerate for at least 4 hours.

Drain wine from mixture. Beat egg and mix into meat. Using a deep, narrow baking pan, place 1 sprig of dill on bottom, fill with chicken mixture and place remaining sprig of dill on top. Cover with aluminum foil and bake in water bath at 325 degrees F for 1 hour.

Remove pan from water bath and uncover. Drain any liquid that has accumulated. Leaving pâté in pan, place weight on top, cover and refrigerate for at least 4 hours.

To serve, remove pâté from pan and discard dill from top and bottom. Remove any gelatin that has formed. Slice very thinly and arrange on a bed of fresh sorrel and garnish with sprigs of fresh dill.

Makes 25 thin slices.

— *Arthur Grant*
Toronto, Ontario

TURKEY ARTICHOKE PIE

1 lb. spinach, steamed & chopped
2 cups cooked rice
4 Tbsp. butter
¼ cup chopped toasted almonds
15-oz. can artichoke hearts, drained
1½ cups chopped, cooked turkey
1 cup grated jack cheese
¼ lb. mushrooms, sliced

2 Tbsp. flour
½ tsp. curry
½ tsp. garlic powder
1 tsp. dry mustard
Salt & pepper
1 cup milk
Paprika

Combine spinach, rice, 2 Tbsp. butter and almonds and press into greased pie plate. Chill for 1 hour. Arrange artichokes, turkey and cheese in shell.

Melt remaining 2 Tbsp. butter and sauté mushrooms. Stir in flour, curry, garlic powder, mustard, salt and pepper and milk and cook until thickened. Pour over pie and top with paprika. Bake at 350 degrees F for 45 minutes.

Serves 6.

— *Gillian Barber-Gifford*
Rossland, British Columbia

TURKEY RING

3 cups diced, cooked turkey
1 cup soft bread crumbs
1 Tbsp. oil
½ tsp. salt
⅛ tsp. pepper

1 cup hot milk
2 eggs, beaten
¼ cup finely chopped celery
2 Tbsp. finely chopped green pepper
2 Tbsp. finely chopped pimento

Combine all ingredients and mix thoroughly. Pour into greased ring mould and bake at 350 degrees F for 35 to 40 minutes. Let stand for 5 minutes; remove from mould.

Serves 6.

— *Christine Curtis*
Bowmanville, Ontario

SWEET & SOUR RABBIT

3 lbs. rabbit pieces
Flour
1 tsp. salt
¼ tsp. pepper
1 cup pineapple juice
¼ cup vinegar
1 cup pineapple chunks

1 green pepper, cut into chunks
½ red pepper, cut into chunks
1 cup bean sprouts
1 cup diced celery
1½ Tbsp. cornstarch
½ cup brown sugar
½ cup water

Roll rabbit pieces in flour and brown. Add salt, pepper, pineapple juice and vinegar and simmer until tender — about 40 minutes. Add pineapple, green and red peppers, bean sprouts and celery. Simmer for 10 minutes. Mix cornstarch and sugar and stir into water. Gradually stir this mixture into liquid containing rabbit. Cook slowly until thickened — about 5 minutes.

Serves 4 to 6.

— *Marian Page*
Chesterville, Ontario

RABBIT PIE

WORK ON THIS DISH MUST BEGIN A DAY AHEAD AS THE COOKED RABBIT AND STOCK NEED to be refrigerated overnight.

Pastry for double 9-inch pie shell
5-6 lb. rabbit
1 Tbsp. salt
½ tsp. pepper
1 cup chopped celery leaves
1 large onion, quartered
½ tsp. crumbled savory or thyme
1 bay leaf
6 cups boiling water

3 cups sliced carrots
2 cups diced celery
12-24 small white onions
¾ cup butter
¾ cup flour
2 cups milk
1 cup whipping cream
1 Tbsp. lemon juice
½ cup minced parsley

Place rabbit in large pot with salt, pepper, celery leaves, onion, savory or thyme, bay leaf and boiling water. Cover and simmer over low heat until rabbit is tender — 1½ to 2 hours. Leave rabbit in stock until cool enough to handle. Pull meat off bones and place in a large bowl. Put bones back in pot and boil stock, uncovered, until reduced to two-thirds its original quantity. Strain stock over rabbit, cover and refrigerate overnight.

The next day, place carrots and celery in bowl and cover with boiling water. Let stand for 1 hour. Peel onions and boil for 15 minutes.

Heat rabbit just until stock can be strained, measure out 3 cups. Melt butter, add flour and stir until blended. Add milk, cream and 3 cups stock and cook until sauce is creamy. Add drained onions, carrots, celery, rabbit, lemon juice and parsley. Place in deep pie plate lined with pastry. Top with pastry, crimp edges, make steam holes and bake at 400 degrees F for 40 to 50 minutes, or until golden brown.

Serves 6 to 8.

— Marian Page
Chesterville, Ontario

SPICY RABBIT

THIS RECIPE RESULTS IN A FLAVOURFUL, AROMATIC DISH THAT NEEDS ONLY A BOWL OF rice and a salad to make a full meal.

2 Tbsp. oil
2 Tbsp. butter
1 large onion, thinly sliced
1 large clove garlic, minced
1 tsp. ginger
1½ tsp. cumin
1 tsp. salt
½ tsp. paprika
½ tsp. pepper

⅛ tsp. saffron
⅛ tsp. cayenne
1 rabbit, cut up
¾ cup pitted prunes
1 Tbsp. honey
1-2 Tbsp. lemon juice
2 Tbsp. toasted sesame seeds
Chopped coriander

Heat oil and butter in heavy pot with tightly fitting lid. Add onion and sauté until translucent, then add garlic. Combine ginger, cumin, salt, paprika, pepper, saffron and cayenne and add. Stir in rabbit pieces. Place lid on pot, reduce heat and simmer for 1 hour, turning meat occasionally and adding water if meat becomes too dry. Add prunes and cook for 15 minutes longer. Gently stir in honey and cook for 5 more minutes. Remove meat and prunes and keep warm. Raise heat to high and reduce liquid to thick sauce. Stir in lemon juice, pour over meat and sprinkle with sesame seeds and coriander leaves.

Serves 4 to 6.

— Ann Jeffries
La Ronge, Saskatchewan

LAPIN AU CITRON

DEVELOPED BY THE CONTRIBUTOR FOR A POTLUCK SUPPER IN HOPES OF INCREASING sales for her rabbit business, this dish, presented to the guests as chicken lest they be squeamish about eating rabbit, was the pièce de résistance of the meal.

4-5 lbs. deboned rabbit pieces
2 Tbsp. butter
1 Tbsp. olive oil
Juice & grated rind of 2 lemons
1 tsp. salt
Pepper
2 Tbsp. chopped parsley
2 Tbsp. chopped chives

1 tsp. marjoram
1 Tbsp. paprika
Butter
1 cup chicken stock
¼ cup dry vermouth
2 Tbsp. cornstarch dissolved
  in 3 Tbsp. cold water

Brown rabbit pieces over medium heat in butter and oil. Transfer rabbit with butter and oil to large, shallow baking dish. Add lemon juice and rind, salt and pepper. Cover and bake at 350 degrees F for 45 minutes. Add herbs, dot with butter and broil for 5 minutes. Pour juices into saucepan, add stock and vermouth and bring to a boil. Add cornstarch-water mixture and simmer until thickened – about 5 minutes. Pour over rabbit.

Serves 6 to 8.

— *J.M. Bowden*
East Selkirk, Manitoba

RABBIT DIABLE

2-3 lbs. rabbit pieces
4 Tbsp. butter
½ cup honey

¼ cup prepared mustard
1 tsp. salt
1 tsp. curry

Wash rabbit pieces and pat dry. Melt butter in shallow baking pan. Stir in remaining ingredients and roll rabbit in mixture to coat all sides. Bake at 375 degrees F for 1 hour.

Serves 4.

— *Barbara Wilkinson*
Winlaw, British Columbia

YOGURT BAKED RABBIT

⅓ cup flour
1 tsp. salt
1 tsp. paprika
½ tsp. thyme
½ tsp. cayenne
½ tsp. pepper
¾ cup chopped celery

½ cup chopped onion
2 cups sliced mushrooms
Butter
1½ cups plain yogurt
Shortening
2½-3 lbs. rabbit pieces

Combine flour, salt, paprika, thyme, cayenne and pepper in plastic bag and set aside. Cook celery, onion and mushrooms in butter until tender. Add yogurt and place in casserole dish.

Heat shortening so there is ¼ inch in skillet. Shake rabbit pieces in flour mixture to coat evenly, then brown in hot shortening. Place in casserole dish with sauce and bake at 375 degrees F for 1 hour.

Serves 6.

— *Diane G. Michaud*
Mallaig, Alberta

BRANDIED ORANGE RABBIT WITH CHANTERELLES

CHANTERELLES, KNOWN IN FRANCE AS *girolles*, ARE EDIBLE MUSHROOMS, IMPOSSIBLE to confuse with any other. They are formed in the shape of a cup with a frilled edge and are the colour of egg yolk. The stalks are so short as to be nonexistent in some cases. Regular mushrooms can be substituted in this recipe.

4 lbs. rabbit pieces
½ cup brandy
½ cup frozen orange juice concentrate
4 Tbsp. butter
2 cups sliced chanterelles
1 Tbsp. cornstarch dissolved
  in ½ cup orange juice

2 cloves garlic, crushed
Curry
Salt & pepper
4 carrots, sliced julienne style

Marinate rabbit in brandy and orange juice concentrate overnight. Melt butter and sauté chanterelles until tender. Thicken juices with cornstarch-orange juice mixture.

Arrange rabbit in baking dish. Add marinade to chanterelle mixture along with garlic, curry and salt and pepper. Bake, uncovered, at 325 degrees F for 1 hour. Add carrots and cook for 1 more hour.

Serves 4 to 6.

— *Dianne Radcliffe*
Denman Island, British Columbia

CORNISH GAME HENS INDIENNE

6 Cornish game hens
1½ tsp. salt
1 tsp. pepper
1 tsp. thyme
½ cup butter, melted
6 strips bacon
3 medium onions, chopped
5 Tbsp. flour
3 Tbsp. sugar
2 Tbsp. curry

2 cups apricot nectar
Juice from 1 lemon
Juice from 1 orange
Stuffing:
½ cup brown & ½ cup wild rice,
  cooked in chicken stock
½ cup chopped mushrooms
2 Tbsp. butter
⅛ cup dry red wine

Wipe hens inside and out. Combine 1 tsp. salt, pepper and thyme and sprinkle ½ tsp. inside each hen. Place hens, breast side up, in pan and brush with ¼ cup melted butter. Roast at 375 degrees F for 50 to 60 minutes, basting with remaining ¼ cup butter and pan drippings.

Meanwhile, sauté bacon until crisp. Drain and crumble. Stir chopped onions into bacon drippings and sauté until soft. Blend in flour, sugar, curry and remaining ½ tsp. salt. Heat, stirring constantly, to boiling point. Stir in apricot nectar, lemon and orange juice, bacon and onions. Bring to a boil and simmer for 5 minutes.

Prepare stuffing by combining cooked rice, mushrooms, butter and wine. Remove hens from pan and discard drippings. Stuff hens, return to pan, pour sauce over top and roast for 10 minutes.

Serves 6.

— *Mary-Lee Chase*
Chipman, New Brunswick

COQ AU CAMBERTIN

THIS RECIPE CALLS FOR A DEMI GLACE. TRADITIONALLY, MAKING THIS IS A FAIRLY complex procedure involving many steps, but for the purposes of this recipe, a somewhat simplified process is provided. The dedicated chef may consult any book of traditional French cooking for more detailed instructions.

Demi glace:
Shoulder of veal
Beef stock
Chicken stock
½ cup butter
½ cup flour
Parsley
Green onions
½ bay leaf
Thyme

2 Cornish game hens
Oil
1 onion, chopped
1 lb. mushrooms, sliced
¼ lb. bacon, chopped
3 cloves garlic, crushed
1 cup dry red wine
2 cups demi glace
Salt & pepper
3 bay leaves
1 tsp. tarragon
½ tsp. thyme

To make demi glace, cover veal with beef stock and cook over high heat until stock is reduced to coating on bottom of pot. Cool. Refill saucepan with chicken stock, heat slowly to boiling point and skim fat. Remove veal and allow stock to cool slightly.

Make a roux by melting butter and stirring in flour. Cook slowly for 2 minutes. Gradually pour stock into roux, stirring constantly. Add parsley, green onions, bay leaf and thyme. Bring to a boil, lower heat and simmer for 1 hour. Skim. Simmer for 30 minutes and skim again. Strain and set aside. This is the demi glace.

Cut hens in half and remove breast and back bones. Braise lightly in a little oil and set aside. In same pan, sauté onion, mushrooms, bacon and garlic. Add wine and demi glace. Add salt and pepper, bay leaves, tarragon and thyme. Place chicken in sauce, cover and cook for 25 minutes.

Serves 4.

— Anne McKenzie
Englehart, Ontario

BRAISED DUCK

WHETHER MADE FROM WILD OR DOMESTIC DUCK, THIS DISH HAS A DELICIOUSLY delicate flavour. Of course, wild duck will result in a stronger, gamier taste.

4½-lb. duck, skinned & quartered
¼ cup soya sauce
¼ cup vinegar
½ cup water
1 small onion, finely chopped
1 tsp. butter

Salt & pepper
2 Tbsp. red currant jelly
2 bay leaves
1 cup chicken stock
1 tsp. ground ginger
½ cup green or red grapes

Marinate duck in soya sauce, vinegar and water for at least 2 hours or overnight. Sauté onion in butter. Add duck and brown. Add marinade plus salt and pepper, jelly, bay leaves, stock and ginger. Cover and simmer until duck is tender – approximately 1 hour.

Remove duck and reduce sauce to ¾ cup over high heat. Strain sauce over duck and add grapes.

Serves 4.

— Dianne Baker
Tatamagouche, Nova Scotia

SHANGHAI DUCK

6 green scallions
2 slices ginger root
4-6 lb. duck
1 Tbsp. sherry

¾ cup soya sauce
½ cup sugar
½ cup water
Anise seeds

Lay scallions and ginger root in bottom of large pan. Place duck on top, breast down. Pour sherry, soya sauce, sugar and water over duck and sprinkle with anise. Bring to a boil, then simmer for 45 minutes, turn duck over and simmer for another 45 minutes. Remove duck, skim fat off gravy and reduce to a thick sauce.

Serves 6.

— Anne Morrell
Margaree Valley, Nova Scotia

PARTRIDGE PIE

Pastry for 9-inch pie shell
3-4 bush partridges, cleaned,
    skinned & cut up
Salt & pepper

Flour
6 hard-boiled eggs, sliced
1 egg yolk, beaten

Cook partridges in salted water until tender. Cool enough to be handled easily and debone. Place in deep pie dish and add salt and pepper. Thicken liquid in pot with flour, then pour over meat. Cover with egg slices and top with pastry. Slash pastry to allow steam to escape and brush with beaten egg yolk. Bake at 375 degrees F for 40 to 50 minutes, or until golden brown.

Serves 4 to 6.

— Janet Bantock
St. Thomas, Ontario

SWEET & SOUR PARTRIDGE

THE CONTRIBUTOR OF THIS RECIPE SPENT THE FALL AND WINTER OF 1981 TRAPPING in northern Ontario. Fresh game was scarce, and, in her words, "It was a special occasion and a real treat, so we turned our plain old partridge into a gourmet meal."

1 partridge
½ cup brown sugar
1 Tbsp. cornstarch
⅓ cup vinegar

⅓ cup pineapple juice
1 Tbsp. soya sauce
¼ tsp. garlic powder
½ cup chopped pineapple

Clean and debone partridge, wrap in foil and refrigerate overnight. Cut into 1-inch cubes, place in pot and cover with water. Cover pan and simmer until tender — 30 minutes.

To make sauce, combine sugar and cornstarch in saucepan. Stir in vinegar, pineapple juice, soya sauce and garlic and cook until thick. Add pineapple and simmer for 2 more minutes. When partridge is cooked, pour off excess liquid and add sauce. Cook for 5 to 10 minutes.

Serves 2.

— Jane Kavelman
Kitchener, Ontario

PHEASANT BREAST AUX VALDEN

ORIGINALLY A NATIVE OF THE CASPIAN REGION OF EASTERN EUROPE, THE PHEASANT IS now found in many parts of the world. It is considered a food for the real gourmet and is described as follows by French gastronome Brillat-Savarin, "Eaten at precisely the right moment, its flesh is tender, sublime and highly flavoured, for it has at once something of the flavour of poultry and of venison. This ideal moment is when the pheasant begins to decompose."

½ lb. lean bacon
2 medium pheasant breasts
½ cup plus 2 Tbsp. flour
2 tsp. garlic powder
2 medium-sized onions
½ tsp. dill weed

1 tsp. ground ginger
¼ tsp. pepper
1 cup water
½ cup red table wine
¾ cup whipping cream
2 Tbsp. brandy

Cut bacon into ½-inch pieces and place in a 4-quart, stoneware or cast-iron oven pan. Fry the bacon on medium heat sufficiently to melt down the fat. Using a slotted spoon, remove the bacon and place on paper towels to drain.

Split pheasant breasts and wash under cold water. Pat dry and place in a paper bag containing ½ cup flour and 1 tsp. garlic powder. Shake to cover. Brown evenly in bacon fat and remove from pan.

Finely chop onions and fry in bacon fat until just turning brown. In small bowl, mix remaining 1 tsp. garlic, dill weed, ginger, pepper, remaining 2 Tbsp. flour and 1 cup water. Add this mixture to onions, stirring constantly as mixture thickens. Add cooked bacon. Place browned pheasant breasts in roasting pan and coat evenly with sauce. Bake at 350 degrees F for 1 hour, turning over after half an hour.

Remove breasts from pan and mix cream and brandy into sauce. Place on serving platter and pour sauce over the breasts.

Serves 4.

— *Valerie Rudyke*
Thunder Bay, Ontario

PHEASANT WITH RICE STUFFING

2 Tbsp. butter
½ cup rice
1 cup chicken stock
¼ tsp. salt
½ cup chopped onion

2 Tbsp. chopped parsley
3 Tbsp. chopped celery
2 pheasants
6 slices bacon

In heavy saucepan, melt 1 Tbsp. butter, add rice and stir constantly for 2 to 3 minutes until most of rice has turned opaque. Pour in chicken stock, add salt and bring to boil. Cover, reduce heat and simmer for 15 minutes, or until rice has absorbed all the liquid.

Sauté onion in remaining 1 Tbsp. butter for 5 to 6 minutes. Add parsley and celery, then combine with cooked rice.

Sprinkle body cavities of pheasants with salt. Stuff and truss. Cover tops with bacon and cook at 350 degrees F for 1 hour, remove bacon and cook until done.

Serves 2.

— *Margaret Fredrickson*
Limerick, Saskatchewan

PHEASANT IN CREAM SAUCE

1½-2 lbs. pheasant pieces
1 medium onion, sliced
2 stalks celery with tops
1 tsp. salt
⅛ tsp. pepper

1 cup whipping cream
1½ Tbsp. flour
2 Tbsp. cold water
2-3 Tbsp. red wine

Combine pheasant, 2 cups boiling water, onion, celery, salt and pepper and simmer, covered, for about 45 minutes, or until pheasant is tender.

Remove pheasant from stock and take meat off bones, leaving it in large pieces. Strain stock and boil down to ½ cup. Add cream to this and heat to boiling. Stir in blended flour and cold water and cook, stirring, until mixture thickens. Add pheasant and heat through. Add red wine and serve immediately.

Serves 3 to 4.

— Tracy Cane
Harwood, Ontario

ORANGE GROUSE

2 grouse, cut up
Flour, seasoned with salt & pepper
2 Tbsp. butter
2 Tbsp. oil
1½ cups white wine

½ cup orange juice
½ tsp. rosemary
½ tsp. dry mustard
Cayenne

Dredge grouse in seasoned flour and brown in butter and oil mixture in heavy skillet. Add wine, orange juice, rosemary, mustard and cayenne. Cover and simmer for 1½ hours, adding a little water if necessary. Thicken with flour and water paste and serve over hot buttered noodles.

Serves 2.

— Judy Cushman
Wells, British Columbia

CORNED BEAR

SERVED EITHER HOT WITH BOILED POTATOES, HOT MUSTARD AND HORSERADISH, or cold on a sandwich, corned bear is a delicious and unusual alternative to other corned meats.

4 quarts hot water
2 cups coarse salt
¼ cup sugar

2 Tbsp. mixed whole spice
5-lb. piece bear meat
3 cloves garlic, peeled

Combine hot water, salt, sugar and whole spice. When cool, pour over bear meat and garlic. Place in enamelled pot, stoneware or glass jar. Weight meat to keep it submerged. Let marinate for 3 weeks in a cool place, turning every few days.

To cook, rinse meat under cold water, cover with boiling water and simmer for 4 hours, or until meat is tender.

— Kass Bennett
Cranbrook, British Columbia

BLACK BEAR STEW

1½ lbs. lean bear meat, cubed
2 quarts water
½ cup vinegar
Salt & pepper
½ small onion, chopped
½ green pepper, chopped

2 medium potatoes, cubed
2 cups diced carrot
3 stalks celery, cut into ½-inch pieces
18-oz. can tomatoes
2 Tbsp. cornstarch

Wash meat in cold water, then soak for 15 minutes in water and vinegar. Dry meat in towel and fry with salt and pepper, onion and green pepper. When well fried, add potatoes, carrot, celery and tomatoes. Simmer for 45 minutes. While simmering, add the cornstarch dissolved in a few tablespoons of water.

Serves 2 to 4.

— Ken Laninga
Grande Prairie, Alberta

MOOSE MEAT PIES

Pastry for 6 double 9-inch pie shells
7 lbs. ground pork
3 lbs. ground moose meat
3 medium cooking onions
4 cups sliced mushrooms
2 tsp. cloves
2 tsp. ground cinnamon

¼ tsp. ground mace
3-4 bay leaves
½ tsp. celery seed
2 Tbsp. sherry
¼ tsp. allspice
Salt & pepper
½ tsp. nutmeg

Combine all ingredients except pastry in large pot. Bring to a boil and simmer until meat turns white. Fill pastry-lined pie plates with meat mixture and cover with top crust. Bake at 425 degrees F for 15 minutes and then at 350 degrees for 30 minutes.

Makes 6 pies.

— Diane Ladoucer
Cochrane, Ontario

ELK MEATBALLS

1 lb. minced elk meat
½ cup cracked wheat
½ tsp. garlic powder
1 onion, minced

2 cups chicken stock
2 cups water
2 Tbsp. tamari sauce
3 Tbsp. cornstarch

Combine meat, wheat, garlic and onion and form into walnut-sized balls. Bring stock, water and tamari sauce to a boil. Simmer meat for 15 minutes. Remove and keep warm. Reduce stock to 2½ to 3 cups. Mix cornstarch and a little cold water and add to stock. Boil for 5 minutes, then pour over meatballs.

Serves 4.

— Linda Townsend
Nanoose Bay, British Columbia

TJALKNOL FRAN MEDELPAD

THIS RECIPE COMES FROM THE PROVINCE OF MEDELPAD IN SWEDEN — *Tjäl-Knöl* MEANS frost-chunk. It can be made from any kind of roast, but is particularly tasty when made with elk.

3-4 lb. frozen elk roast
2½ cups water
5 oz. salt
1 tsp. sugar

Place frozen roast on rack and bake at 150 degrees F for 12 hours. Place meat in plastic bag and add water, salt and sugar. Force out air, tie bag and let roast marinate for 5 hours. Cut thin slices and serve with potato salad.

Serves 8 to 10.

— Maria Ehnes
King City, Ontario

VENISON PATTIES

1 lb. ground venison
½ lb. bacon, chopped
1 small onion, finely chopped
½ tsp. salt
⅛ tsp. pepper

⅛ tsp. thyme
⅛ tsp. marjoram
½ tsp. grated lemon peel
1 egg, beaten
1 cup cracker crumbs

Combine all ingredients and mix well by hand. Form into roll 2 to 3 inches in diameter. Chill or freeze, then cut into slices and fry.

Serves 4.

— Taya Kwantes
Summerland, British Columbia

Meat

Some hae meat and canna eat,
And some wad eat that want it;
But we hae meat, and we can eat,
And sae the Lord be thankit.

– **Robert Burns**
The Selkirk Grace

VEAL ROLLS DIVAN

3 slices bacon
1½ cups dry herbed dressing
¼ cup butter
6 thin veal steaks, pounded
Salt
1 Tbsp. oil

2 heads broccoli, chopped & parboiled
½ cup chicken stock
1 cup cream of mushroom sauce
 (*Volume 1*, page 92)
½ cup cooked shrimp

Cook bacon until crisp and drain. Combine dressing and butter and crumble bacon into mixture.

Sprinkle veal with salt. Place ⅓ cup dressing on each steak, roll and tie securely. Heat oil in skillet and brown veal. Arrange veal and broccoli in greased, shallow baking dish.

Pour chicken stock over casserole, cover and bake at 350 degrees F for 1 hour. Combine mushroom sauce with shrimp in saucepan and heat through. To serve, remove ties from meat and pour sauce over casserole.

Serves 6.

— *Tracy Cane*
Harwood, Ontario

WIENER SCHNITZEL

6 veal scallops
Salt & pepper
2 eggs, slightly beaten
Flour
3 Tbsp. bacon drippings

Juice of 1 lemon
1 Tbsp. flour
1 cup sour cream
Lemon slices

Sprinkle veal with salt and pepper. Dip into beaten eggs then into flour. Brown on both sides in hot bacon drippings, then cover and cook slowly until chops are tender — about 1 hour. Sprinkle with lemon juice and arrange on hot platter.

Blend 1 Tbsp. flour with fat in pan, add sour cream and cook for 3 minutes, stirring constantly. Season with salt and pepper and serve with chops. Garnish with lemon slices.

Serves 6.

— *Lorraine Murphy*
Mississauga, Ontario

VEAL CASSEROLE

2 lbs. boneless veal, cut
 into 1-inch cubes
1 Tbsp. oil
1 Tbsp. butter
½ cup chopped onion
½ cup chopped celery
¼ cup diced green pepper
14-oz. can tomatoes, drained
 with juice reserved

Chicken stock
½ cup white wine
1 Tbsp. parsley
Thyme
Garlic powder
Salt & pepper
½ cup sliced mushrooms

Brown veal in oil and butter in 2-quart casserole dish, removing pieces as they are done. Cook onion and remove from pan. Drain fat from pan and replace meat and onion. Add celery, green pepper and tomatoes.

Add chicken stock to reserved tomato juice to make 1 cup and bring to a boil in a small saucepan. Cool slightly and add wine. Pour over casserole and add seasoning.

Cover and bake at 325 degrees F for 1¾ hours. Add mushrooms and bake for a further 15 minutes.

Serves 4.

— *Florence Hutchison*
Clearbrook, British Columbia

VEAL & HAM PIE

Pastry:
½ tsp. salt
⅓ cup very cold water
2 cups flour
1 egg
⅔ cup butter, softened

Filling:
2 lbs. cooked veal
1 lb. cooked ham
2 eggs, hard-boiled & peeled
1¾ cups veal stock
1 egg yolk, beaten
1 envelope gelatin

To make pastry, dissolve salt in water. Sift flour into a ring on working surface and place egg, butter and salt water in centre. Mix these together, then work in flour to make dough. Wrap in wax paper and refrigerate for 2 hours. Line a greased, 9-inch cake pan with two-thirds of the pastry.

Cut veal and ham into bite-sized pieces and place in pie shell in alternate layers, packing around eggs. Add 3 to 4 Tbsp. stock.

Top with remaining one-third of pastry. Make central hole to allow steam to escape. Brush with egg yolk and bake at 375 degrees F for 1 to 1½ hours. Cool.

Dissolve gelatin in remaining stock. Pour stock carefully into pie through central hole. Refrigerate. When jelly is set, remove pie from dish and serve.

Serves 4.

— *Ruth Leir*
Ottawa, Ontario

KOREAN VEGETABLES & BEEF

3-4 Tbsp. soya sauce
1 Tbsp. oil
1 tsp. honey
1 clove garlic, crushed
½ lb. beef, thinly sliced
Sesame oil

1 onion, chopped
2½ cups chopped assorted vegetables
 (green beans, zucchini, cauliflower, broccoli)
3 Tbsp. crushed sesame seeds

Combine soya sauce, oil, honey and garlic. Marinate beef in this for 15 minutes.

Heat oil in wok. Stir-fry drained beef and onion. Add vegetables and fry until bright in colour. Add sesame seeds and leftover marinade. Heat through and serve with rice.

Serves 3 to 4.

— *Gwen Miller*
Barrhead, Alberta

CARBONNADE OF BEEF

⅓ cup flour
1 tsp. salt
¼ tsp. pepper
3 lbs. round, chuck or blade steak,
 cut into stewing pieces
¼ cup oil
¼ cup butter
6 large onions, thinly sliced

1½ bottles beer
2 cloves garlic, crushed
2-3 bay leaves
¼ tsp. thyme
¼ tsp. basil
¼ tsp. marjoram
Parsley
½ tsp. salt

Combine flour, salt and pepper in plastic bag. Place meat, a few pieces at a time, into bag to coat with flour. Heat oil and butter in heavy casserole dish and add meat, browning on all sides. Add onions and cook until limp. Add any extra flour and the beer. Add spices and mix thoroughly. Bring to a boil, cover and place in oven. Cook at 300 degrees F for 2 hours.

Serves 6.

— *Sheri Lemire*
St. André est., Quebec

BRAISED BEEF WITH TOMATOES & HERBS

3 lbs. lean chuck steak,
  cut into 1½-inch cubes
Salt & pepper
3 Tbsp. olive oil
2 Tbsp. finely chopped garlic
½ lb. onions, chopped
½ lb. whole mushrooms
¼ cup flour

1 cup dry red wine
2 cups canned tomatoes
24 pitted, stuffed green olives
1 bay leaf
½ tsp. thyme
Cayenne
¼ cup finely chopped parsley

Trim fat off meat and sprinkle with salt and pepper. Heat oil in large pan, add beef and cook, stirring often. Add garlic, onions and mushrooms and stir. Sprinkle with flour and stir to coat evenly. Add wine, tomatoes, olives, bay leaf, thyme, cayenne, salt and pepper. Cover and simmer on low heat for 1½ hours. Sprinkle with parsley and serve.

Serves 6.

— *Linda Hodgins*
Calgary, Alberta

GINGERED BEEF WITH RAISIN SAUCE

1½ lbs. round steak
2 Tbsp. flour
1½ tsp. ground ginger
1 tsp. paprika
1 tsp. minced garlic
3 Tbsp. oil

3 Tbsp. catsup
½ cup raisins
2 Tbsp. butter
1 Tbsp. soya sauce
½ cup chicken stock

Cut steak in thin strips. Combine flour, ginger, paprika and garlic, and dredge steak in this mixture.

Heat oil in frying pan and fry steak quickly, stirring constantly, until meat loses pink colour. Remove from pan and keep warm.

Add to pan catsup, raisins, butter, soya sauce and chicken stock, stirring well to combine. Simmer for 10 minutes, return meat to pan and heat through. Serve with rice.

Serves 4 to 6.

— *Irene Louden*
Port Coquitlam, British Columbia

GREEK SLIPPER STEAK

4 ½-lb. steaks
8 Tbsp. chopped, lightly toasted
 almonds
4 Tbsp. chopped stuffed olives
2 tsp. minced hot Greek pickled pepper
1 tsp. minced garlic

½ tsp. cinnamon
Salt & pepper
Butter
Red wine
Onion slices

Slice a pocket in one side of each steak, cutting to within ¼ inch of the edges. Combine remaining ingredients, except butter, wine and onion slices, and stuff steaks. Stitch opening shut.

Sear steaks in butter in frying pan. When cooked, place on warm platter in oven. Deglaze pan with a little red wine. Add onion slices and sauté briefly. Garnish steaks with onion and spoon pan juices over them.

Serves 4.

— *Elizabeth Ballantyne*
Winnipeg, Manitoba

STEAK WITH GREEN PEPPERS

1½ cups raw rice, cooked
1 lb. lean steak
1 Tbsp. paprika
2 Tbsp. butter
2 cloves garlic, crushed
⅛ tsp. cayenne
½ tsp. salt

1½ cups beef stock
1 cup sliced green onions
2 green peppers, cut into strips
2 Tbsp. cornstarch
¼ cup water
¼ cup soya sauce
2 large tomatoes, cut into eighths

While rice is cooking, thinly slice steak across grain. Sprinkle meat with paprika and let sit for a few minutes. Brown in butter in large skillet. Add garlic, cayenne, salt and beef stock. Cover and simmer for 30 minutes. Add green onions and green peppers, cover and cook for 5 more minutes. Blend together cornstarch, water and soya sauce and stir into meat. Cook, stirring, until stock is clear and thickened – about 2 minutes. Add tomatoes and serve over rice.

Serves 3.

— Janice Hyatt
Saskatoon, Saskatchewan

BEEF PARMIGIANA

1½ to 2 lbs. round steak
3 Tbsp. flour
Salt & pepper
½ cup fine dry bread crumbs
¼ cup Parmesan cheese
¼ tsp. basil
1 egg, beaten with 1 Tbsp. water

4 Tbsp. oil
2 cups tomato sauce (*Volume 1*,
 page 204)
1 clove garlic, crushed
½ tsp. oregano
6 slices mozzarella cheese

Cut steak into 4 serving-sized pieces. Combine flour with salt and pepper and dredge meat in it. Pound both sides of meat. Combine bread crumbs with Parmesan cheese and basil. Dip each piece of meat into egg-water mixture and then dredge in crumbs. Brown meat lightly in oil and place in greased 9″ x 13″ baking dish.

Combine tomato sauce, garlic and oregano and pour over meat. Cover with foil and bake for 1 hour or until very tender. Place a slice of cheese on each piece of meat. Bake for a few minutes longer, until cheese is melted.

Serves 4.

— Laurie Gillespie
Finnegan, Alberta

BULKOKI

5 tsp. soya sauce
7 Tbsp. oil
3 Tbsp. sherry
3 cloves garlic, crushed
½ cup chopped onion

1 Tbsp. sugar
2 Tbsp. peppercorns, coarsely ground
¼ cup chopped scallions
2 tsp. dill seed
1-1½ lbs. beef, cut into thin strips

Combine soya sauce, 5 Tbsp. oil, sherry, garlic, onion, sugar, peppercorns, scallions and dill seed and marinate beef in this, covered, for 2 to 3 hours. Sauté in remaining 2 Tbsp. oil over high heat for 3 to 4 minutes.

Serves 4.

— Sheila Livingston
DeBaie's Cove, Nova Scotia

GIRARDI STEAKS

2 lbs. round or sirloin steak
Salt & pepper
Oil
1 medium onion, sliced
½ cup white wine
1 cup beef stock
6 slices bacon

½ lb. mushrooms
1 small onion
1 Tbsp. chopped parsley
1 tsp. capers
1 tsp. lemon rind
1 Tbsp. flour
½ cup sour cream

Season steaks with salt and pepper, sear on both sides in hot oil and set aside.

In remaining oil, add sliced onion, white wine and beef stock. Replace steaks and allow to simmer.

Meanwhile, mince bacon, mushrooms, onion, parsley, capers and lemon rind. Fry all together, sprinkle with flour and stir in cream. Add this to steaks and simmer until tender.

Serves 4.

— *Claudette Spies*
Nakusp, British Columbia

STEAK TERIYAKI

¾ cup oil
¼ cup soya sauce
¼ cup honey
2 Tbsp. cider vinegar

2 Tbsp. finely chopped green onion
1 large clove garlic, chopped
1½ tsp. ground ginger
2 lbs. flank steak

Mix together oil, soya sauce, honey, vinegar, onion, garlic and ginger and pour over meat. Let marinate, turning occasionally, for several hours.

Broil or cook over coals, basting with marinade.

Serves 4.

— *Michèle Raymond*
St. Sulpice, Quebec

ROULADEN

THE IDEAL MEAT FOR ROULADEN, OR BEEF ROLLS, CAN BE BOUGHT IN MOST EUROPEAN butcher shops, but an almost-frozen roast of beef slices easily with excellent results.

⅛-inch-thick slices of beef,
  4-5 inches wide by 8 inches long
Hot mustard
Salt & pepper
Paprika
Thinly sliced onion

Chopped raw bacon
Dill pickle spears
Oil
Bay leaf
Water
Cornstarch

Spread each beef slice thinly with hot mustard and sprinkle with salt and pepper, paprika, onion and bacon. Place dill pickle spear at one end of slice and roll up lengthwise over pickle. Insert toothpicks right through the roll or tie with string to keep from unrolling. In deep, heavy pan containing a little oil, over high heat, darkly brown rolls on all sides almost to the point of burning. Cover with water, add bay leaf and salt and pepper to taste. Bring to a boil, cover and simmer for about 30 minutes. Thicken gravy with cornstarch before serving.

Allow 1 to 2 rolls per person.

— *Mary Dzielak*
Calumet, Quebec

ITALIAN STEAK

3 lbs. steaks
¾ cup bread crumbs
1 Tbsp. oregano
1 egg, beaten
Seasoned flour
Oil
28-oz. can tomatoes

1 green pepper, chopped
1 clove garlic, minced
1 large onion, thinly sliced
1 cup sliced green olives
1 cup sliced black olives
1 lb. mushrooms, sliced
Chopped capers

Cut steak into serving-sized pieces. Combine bread crumbs and oregano. Dip meat in egg, flour, egg again, then bread crumbs. Brown in oil in heavy skillet.

Blend remaining ingredients together. Place meat and sauce in alternating layers in greased casserole dish. Bake at 350 degrees F for 1 hour.

Serves 6.

— Marni Olson
Lumby, British Columbia

BEEF AND PORK CURRY

4 Tbsp. oil
1½ lbs. round steak, cubed
1½ lbs. pork butt or shoulder, cubed
2 onions, peeled & chopped

3 cloves garlic, crushed
2 potatoes, peeled & cubed
4 Tbsp. curry
2 tsp. salt

Sauté beef and pork in oil until browned.

Add onions and garlic and cook until soft. Add curry powder and salt and continue cooking, stirring frequently, for one minute. Add potatoes and cover with water. Let simmer on low heat with lid slightly ajar for 1½ to 2 hours. Serve on bed of rice.

Serves 6.

— Terry Pereira
Sunderland, Ontario

BEEF MACINTOSH

4 cups dry apple cider
1 cup cider vinegar
2 cloves garlic, minced
2 Tbsp. chopped ginger
2 Tbsp. dry mustard

1 apple, diced
6 prunes, diced
5-lb. roast of beef
2 large onions, sliced
Butter

Combine cider, vinegar, garlic, ginger, mustard, apple and prunes. Marinate roast in this, covered, overnight in the refrigerator.

Take out of refrigerator and allow to come to room temperature. Brown onions in butter and transfer to deep saucepan just large enough to hold roast. Take beef out of liquid and pat dry. Brown on all sides in butter and place in saucepan. Add marinade. If beef is not covered by liquid, add cider to cover. Bring to a boil and simmer gently for 3 or 4 hours. Remove from heat and let stand until cool enough to handle. Remove beef, strain out onions and fruit and degrease stock. Pour back into pot with beef and heat through. Serve with broth, onions and fruit.

Serves 8.

— Elizabeth Ballantyne
Winnipeg, Manitoba

ORIENTAL BEEF POT ROAST

4-lb. roast of beef
1 tsp. garlic powder
½ tsp. dry mustard
¼ tsp. pepper
2 Tbsp. oil
¾ cup water
3 Tbsp. honey

2 Tbsp. soya sauce
1 Tbsp. vinegar
1½ tsp. celery seed
½ tsp. ginger
1 Tbsp. cornstarch, dissolved
  in 2 Tbsp. water

Rub roast with mixture of garlic powder, mustard and pepper. Heat a 6-quart roasting pan, add oil and brown roast well on all sides. Combine water, honey, soya sauce, vinegar, celery seed and ginger and pour over meat. Cover and roast at 325 degrees F for 2½ hours. Transfer roast to heated platter and thicken gravy with cornstarch-water mixture.

Serves 8.

— Midge Denault
Lee Valley, Ontario

CRAB APPLE POT ROAST

3 Tbsp. flour
1½ tsp. salt
¼ tsp. pepper
¼ tsp. allspice
4-lb. beef pot roast

2 Tbsp. butter
14-oz. jar spiced crab apples
2 Tbsp. lemon juice
¼ cup raisins

Combine 1 Tbsp. flour, salt, pepper and allspice. Dredge meat in mixture. In heavy saucepan, heat butter and brown meat on all sides.

Drain crab apples, reserving juice. Add enough water to juice to make 1 cup, then add to meat along with lemon juice. Cover and simmer for 3 hours or until tender. About 15 minutes before meat is done, add crab apples and raisins.

To serve, place meat and crab apples on platter. Blend remaining 2 Tbsp. flour with ½ cup cold water and stir into liquid. Let boil for a few minutes to thicken and serve with meat.

Serves 8.

— Mary Hewson
Fort Smith, Northwest Territories

MEAT IN YOGURT SAUCE

This Lebanese variation of Beef Stroganoff is quickly assembled and much lighter.

1 Tbsp. oil
2 lbs. beef or lamb, cubed
1 medium onion, chopped

½ tsp. each salt, pepper & cinnamon
1 Tbsp. cornstarch
1 quart plain yogurt

Brown meat in oil. Add onions and spices and cook until onion is soft. Set aside.

Mix cornstarch with a little water, then mix with yogurt and pour into a 2-quart saucepan. Bring to a boil over medium-high heat, stirring constantly. When the sauce comes to a boil, reduce heat, cover and simmer for 5 minutes.

Add meat and continue to simmer for 10 to 15 minutes. Serve with rice.

Serves 6.

— Moira Abboud
Guelph, Ontario

ROTI

THIS VERSION OF A WEST INDIAN DISH IS ESSENTIALLY BEEF CURRY WRAPPED IN FRIED pastry. The amount of curry powder used can vary according to personal taste — that listed below produces a medium-hot curry.

3-4 Tbsp. oil
1 lb. beef, cubed
2 cloves garlic, crushed
6 curry leaves (optional)
1½ cups chopped onion
½ cup chopped celery
2 heaping Tbsp. curry
Seeds of 2 cardamom pods
1 heaping tsp. cumin seed
1 heaping tsp. ground turmeric
1 heaping tsp. coriander seed

¼ cup vinegar
2 cups peeled, cubed potatoes
3 cups flour
¼ tsp. salt
¼ tsp. baking powder
⅓ cup lard
½ cup milk
½ cup water
Cornmeal
Oil

Heat oil in heavy skillet. Brown meat, garlic and curry leaves. Add onion and celery and sauté until onion is soft.

Crush curry, cardamom, cumin, turmeric and coriander in mortar with pestle or grind in blender. Mix with vinegar and add to meat. Stir and fry for a few minutes. Add water to cover and simmer for 30 minutes. Add potatoes along with more water if necessary.

Bring to a boil, reduce heat and simmer until potatoes are tender. Salt to taste. Cool slightly before putting on wrap.

Meanwhile, make pastry wraps. Combine flour, salt and baking powder in bowl. Cut in lard until mixture resembles coarse crumbs. Mix together milk and water and add to lard mixture. Stir with fork until dough clumps together. Gather dough and knead for 3 minutes until smooth. Let sit, covered, for 30 minutes.

Cut dough into 10 pieces and form each into a ball. Keep balls covered. Roll each ball into 8-inch circle on a lightly floured board sprinkled with cornmeal. Stack wraps with wax paper in between.

To cook, heat a large heavy pan until hot. Cook one wrap at a time in oil until it bubbles and puffs. Brown spots will appear. Flip over and cook for a few minutes on other side. Wraps should be soft and pliable. Stack, covered with a damp cloth.

To serve, spoon ½ cup meat mixture into the centre of each wrap. This can be topped with a dollop of yogurt or sour cream. Fold up wrap and eat like a sandwich.

Serves 4 to 5.

— Anne MacDonald
Cardigan, Prince Edward Island

AFRICAN BEEF

2 lbs. stewing beef
2 large onions, sliced
1½ cups chopped celery
10-oz. can tomato paste
19-oz. can tomatoes
¼ tsp. pepper

⅓ cup brown sugar
1 tsp. ginger
1 tsp. Worcestershire sauce
¼ cup vinegar
Garlic, mushrooms & green peppers
  to taste

Brown meat. Add remaining ingredients. Cover and bake for 3 hours at 325 degrees F. Serve with rice.

Serves 6.

— Valerie Moore
Georgeville, Quebec

GREEN PEPPER STEAK

4 Tbsp. clarified butter
1 lb. lean stewing beef, cut into
  1-inch cubes
1 large onion, chopped
½ lb. mushrooms, thinly sliced
1 large green pepper, diced
1 tsp. garlic powder

1 tsp. salt
1 tsp. pepper
4 cups beef stock
2 Tbsp. cornstarch
¼ cup dry vermouth

Heat butter in heavy pot, add meat and cook until browned on all sides. Add onion, mushrooms, green pepper, garlic, salt and pepper and cook for 3 to 5 minutes, stirring occasionally.

Add stock and bring to a boil, reduce heat and simmer for 10 minutes. Blend cornstarch with vermouth and stir into pot. Cook for 2 more minutes until sauce thickens. Bring to a boil, reduce heat and cook, covered, for 1 hour.

Serves 4.

— Joyce Hall
Beaverton, Ontario

TEXAS CHILI

2 Tbsp. oil
3 lbs. boneless chuck, cut
  into 1-inch cubes
2-3 cloves garlic, chopped
4-6 Tbsp. chili powder
2 tsp. cumin

3 Tbsp. flour
1 Tbsp. oregano
3 cups beef stock
Salt & pepper
Sour cream
Lime wedges

Heat oil in 4-quart pot over medium heat. Add beef and cook, stirring frequently, until meat changes colour but is not browned. Lower heat and stir in garlic. Combine chili powder, cumin and flour and sprinkle over meat, stirring until meat is evenly coated. Crumble oregano over meat. Add 2 cups stock and stir until liquid is well blended. Add salt and pepper and bring to a boil, stirring occasionally.

Reduce heat and simmer, partially covered, for 1½ to 2 hours, stirring from time to time. Add remaining 1 cup stock and cook for 30 minutes longer. Cool thoroughly, cover and refrigerate overnight. Reheat and serve with sour cream and lime wedges.

Serves 8.

— Joan Hampton
Quesnel, British Columbia

OVEN BEEF BURGUNDY

2 Tbsp. soya sauce
2 Tbsp. flour
2 lbs. stewing beef
4 carrots
2 large onions
1 cup sliced celery

1 clove garlic, minced
¼ tsp. marjoram
¼ tsp. thyme
Salt & pepper
1 cup dry red wine
1 cup sliced mushrooms

Blend soya sauce with flour in a casserole dish. Cut meat into 1½-inch cubes and add to soya sauce mixture. Toss to coat well. Cut carrots into chunks and slice onions. Add to meat along with celery, spices and wine. Cover and bake at 325 degrees F for 1 hour. Add mushrooms and stir gently. Cover and cook for another 1½ to 2 hours.

Serves 4.

— Juliana Crawford
Grand River, Nova Scotia

BEEF AND MUSHROOM RAGOUT

THIS FRENCH-STYLE RAGOUT IS AS EASY TO MAKE AS AN EVERYDAY BEEF STEW, BUT IS impressive enough for an elegant dinner. Serve with a tossed salad of mixed greens topped with finely chopped hard-boiled eggs, warm French bread, and complete the meal with a crème caramel.

3 Tbsp. oil
2 lbs. stewing beef
2 large onions, chopped
1 cup sherry or red wine
1 cup water
2 large carrots, finely sliced
1 bay leaf
2 cloves garlic, whole & unpeeled
1 lb. mushrooms, finely sliced
Salt & pepper
4 cups cooked rice

In a large, deep pan, heat oil and cook meat over medium-high heat, removing pieces as they become well-browned. In same pan, brown onion. Return meat to pan, add sherry or red wine and boil gently until alcohol has evaporated. Add water, carrots, bay leaf and garlic.
Cover and simmer for 2 to 3 hours until meat is tender. Add mushrooms and simmer for 15 more minutes. To thicken, uncover and bring to a boil. Remove garlic and bay leaf and adjust seasoning with salt and pepper.

To serve, place cooked rice around the outside of a large platter. Remove the meat and vegetables from the pot with a slotted spoon and place in the centre of the platter. Serve the sauce in a gravy boat.

Serves 4.

— *Sandra James-Mitchell*
Pickering, Ontario

OXTAIL STEW

OXTAIL SOUP IS THE MOST COMMON USE TO WHICH OXTAILS ARE PUT. THIS RECIPE IS another delicious possibility. They can also be stuffed and braised or grilled. Usually sold skinned, it is possible to buy unskinned oxtails, so this should be checked at the time of purchase.

6 lbs. oxtails
Salt & pepper
½ cup oil
1½ cups diced onions
1 cup diced carrots
¼ cup flour
1 tsp. salt
½ tsp. thyme
½ tsp. pepper
5 cups beef stock
2 cups dry red wine
1 lb. carrots
4 small turnips

Trim excess fat from oxtails and sprinkle with salt and pepper. In large, heavy skillet, brown oxtails in oil over high heat and transfer to a large casserole dish. Sauté onions and carrots in remaining oil in skillet, stirring occasionally, until lightly browned. Place in casserole dish and sprinkle with flour, salt, thyme and pepper. Stir gently to coat. Bake at 450 degrees F, stirring once, for 20 minutes. Remove from oven, add stock and wine and bring to a boil over medium-high heat. Return to oven at 325 degrees F and bake for 3 hours.

Meanwhile, quarter carrots lengthwise and cut into 1¼-inch lengths. Peel and quarter turnips. Mix vegetables into stew. Bake for another 30 minutes.

Let stew cool, chill it, then skim off fat. Bring stew to a boil, heat through and serve.

Serves 8 to 10.

— *Mary Lighthall*
Ottawa, Ontario

MURIEL'S SHORT RIBS AND BEANS

2 cups dry pinto or
  kidney beans
2½-3 lbs. meaty beef short ribs
3-4 Tbsp. oil
2 medium onions, thickly sliced

2 cloves garlic, minced
¾ cup tomato paste
Salt & pepper
1 tsp. chili
2 cups stewed tomatoes

Cook beans until barely tender, then drain, reserving liquid. Trim excess fat from short ribs and cut into serving-sized pieces. Brown short ribs in hot oil in large, heavy pot. Remove and set aside. Add onion and garlic and sauté until tender. Return short ribs to pot and add beans. Mix tomato paste with 1 cup of bean liquid and stir in seasonings. Pour over beans and meat. Add tomatoes and mix slightly. Add bean liquid until mixture is barely covered. Bake, covered, at 275 degrees F for 3 to 4 hours, or until short ribs are tender. Stir occasionally and add more liquid if necessary. Uncover during last 15 to 20 minutes.

Serves 4 to 6.

— A. Dianne Wilson-Meyer
Saskatoon, Saskatchewan

SICILIAN MEAT ROLL

2 eggs, beaten
½ cup tomato juice
¾ cup soft bread crumbs
2 Tbsp. chopped parsley
½ tsp. oregano
¼ tsp. salt

¼ tsp. pepper
¼ tsp. garlic powder
2 lbs. ground beef
4-6 oz. thinly sliced ham
6 oz. sliced mozzarella cheese

In a bowl, combine eggs and tomato juice. Stir in bread crumbs, parsley, oregano, salt, pepper and garlic. Add ground beef and mix well. On wax paper, pat meat into an 8″ x 10″ rectangle. Arrange ham slices on top of meat, leaving a small margin around edges.

Reserve 1 slice of cheese. Tear up remaining cheese and sprinkle over ham. Starting from short end, carefully roll up meat, using paper to lift. Seal edges and ends. Place roll, seam side down, in a 9″ x 13″ baking pan.

Bake at 350 degrees F for about 1¼ hours. Centre of roll will be pink due to ham. Cut reserved cheese slice into 4 triangles, overlap atop meat and return to oven until cheese melts.

Serves 8.

— Patricia A. Leahy
Regina, Saskatchewan

BOBOTI

1 medium onion, minced
2 Tbsp. oil
½ tsp. nutmeg
½ tsp. cinnamon
1 tsp. coriander
1 tsp. cumin

1 tsp. garam masala
1 tsp. turmeric
1-1½ lbs. ground beef
¼-½ cup water
¼ cup raisins
Dash nutmeg

Sauté onion in oil. Add spices and stir into onions. Add ground beef and cook until browned, stirring frequently. Stir in water and raisins. Turn into greased casserole dish. Smooth surface and sprinkle with nutmeg.

Bake at 350 degrees F for 15 to 20 minutes.

Serves 6.

— Pamela Morninglight
Queen Charlotte, British Columbia

LIHAPIRUKAS MURETAINAS

THIS ESTONIAN RECIPE PRODUCES MILD-FLAVOURED MEAT TARTS WITH SOUR CREAM crusts. They can be eaten hot or cold and the individual-sized tarts are easily handled.

5 cups flour
2 tsp. salt
1½ cups butter
1 cup sour cream
2 eggs
4 Tbsp. butter
¾ cup finely chopped mushrooms

⅓ cup finely chopped onion
4 cups ground beef
1 cup grated Cheddar cheese
Dill
Salt & pepper
½ cup milk
1 egg

Sift flour with salt. Cut in chilled butter until mixture resembles coarse meal. Add sour cream and eggs and work until dough is pliable. Chill for at least one hour.

Melt butter in saucepan. Add mushrooms and cook until golden brown. Remove from pan, add onions and ground beef and sauté until beef is cooked. Add mushrooms, cheese, dill and salt and pepper. Mix thoroughly over medium heat until cheese is melted.

Roll pastry out thinly and cut into 4-inch circles. Place 2 tsp. of meat on each circle. Combine milk and egg. Fold circles in half and seal with milk-egg mixture.

Place on greased cookie sheet and bake at 350 degrees F for 15 to 20 minutes.

Makes 36 tarts.

— Donna Hert
Grande Prairie, Alberta

SAMOSAS

IT TAKES A BIT OF TIME AND EFFORT TO ROLL THIS DOUGH AS THIN AS IT SHOULD BE, SO some people may wish to substitute commercial won ton or egg roll wrappers. Available now in most grocery store produce sections, they can be frozen successfully. Samosas also make excellent party fare, as they are delicious hot or cold. When they are to be eaten with the fingers, make them bite-sized. Deep-fry and keep warm in the oven — they will stay very crispy.

Dough:
3 cups flour
2 tsp. salt
1 tsp. cumin seeds
Water

Filling:
2 onions, chopped
Oil
2 lbs. ground beef

½ lb. peas
3 potatoes, chopped
Cayenne
2 tsp. curry
2 cloves, crushed
1 cinnamon stick, crushed
½ tsp. crushed cardamom
½ clove garlic, crushed
4 dried hot chilies, crushed

Combine flour, salt, cumin and water to make a stiff, elastic dough. Roll very thinly and cut into 8-inch triangles.

Make filling by frying onions in oil until browned. Add beef, peas, potatoes and spices. Sauté until meat is well cooked.

Place a spoonful of filling in centre of each triangle. Overlap 3 corners to form a smaller triangle. Seal with water. Deep-fry until golden brown.

Serves 6.

— Ingrid Birker
Montreal, Quebec

CANADIAN SKI MARATHON SAUCE

DEVELOPED TO FEED HUNGRY CROSS-COUNTRY SKIERS ON THE LACHUTE-TO-OTTAWA marathon, this spaghetti sauce makes use of sausage meat as well as ground beef. Once cooked, it can be left to simmer for several hours if desired, or it can be frozen for later use.

1 lb. spicy Italian sausage
1 lb. lean ground beef
½ cup finely chopped onion
2 cloves garlic, crushed & minced
1 Tbsp. salt
2 tsp. basil

½ tsp. fennel
¼ tsp. pepper
¼ cup chopped parsley
28-oz. can tomatoes
13-oz. can tomato paste

Remove sausage meat from casings and mix with ground beef and onion. In large heavy pot, over medium-high heat, sauté meat mixture and garlic, stirring frequently, until well browned. Drain fat.

Add salt, basil, fennel, pepper and parsley and mix well. Chop up tomatoes and add with liquid. Stir in tomato paste and ½ cup water. Bring to a boil, reduce heat and simmer, covered, for at least one hour, stirring occasionally. Serve over noodles.

Serves 8.

— *Louise McDonald*
L'Orignal, Ontario

APPLE MEAT LOAF

THIS IS A VERY MOIST MEAT LOAF WITH AN EXCELLENT FLAVOUR — A GOOD STANDBY for a cold winter night's supper.

2 cooking apples
1½ lbs. ground beef
1½ cups soft bread crumbs
1 onion, finely chopped
Salt & pepper

1 tsp. Worcestershire sauce
2 eggs
Topping:
⅓ cup catsup
2 Tbsp. maple syrup

Peel, core and grate apples and combine with ground beef, onion, bread crumbs and seasonings. Beat eggs and add to meat mixture. Press into loaf pan. Combine topping ingredients and spoon over the meat loaf. Bake at 325 degrees F for 1¼ hours.

Serves 4 to 6.

— *Linda Plant*
Powassan, Ontario

BURGER TRITTINI

THIS RECIPE WILL HELP USE UP AN OVERABUNDANCE OF BEET GREENS OR SWISS CHARD.

2 lbs. ground beef
1 onion, sliced
2 cups tomato sauce (*Volume 1,*
  page 204)
13-oz. can tomato paste
1 cup sliced mushrooms
2 tsp. basil

1 tsp. oregano
¼ tsp. pepper
4 cups chopped, cooked beet greens
  or Swiss chard, very well drained
2 cups cottage cheese
1 cup grated mozzarella cheese

Brown beef and onion. Add tomato sauce, tomato paste, mushrooms, basil, oregano and pepper. Mix greens with cottage cheese.

In greased casserole dish, spoon meat mixture evenly over bottom. Cover with half the mozzarella cheese, then the greens-cottage cheese mixture, then the rest of the mozzarella cheese. Bake at 375 degrees F for 25 to 30 minutes.

Serves 6.

— *Paula Compton*
Sointula, British Columbia

EAST INDIAN MEATBALLS

1 large onion, chopped
  (reserve 2 Tbsp. for meat)
2 Tbsp. butter
½ tsp. cinnamon
½ tsp. mace
¾ tsp. curry
1 tsp. whole peppers in
  cheesecloth bag
⅓ cup seedless raisins
¼ cup slivered blanched almonds

1½ cups water
1 tsp. salt
½ cup soft bread crumbs
¼ cup milk
1 lb. ground beef
2 Tbsp. chopped parsley
1 egg
1 tsp. Worcestershire sauce
¼ tsp. pepper

In a large skillet, cook onion in butter until lightly browned. Add cinnamon, mace, curry, peppers, raisins, almonds and water and simmer for 15 minutes. Remove pepper bag.

Mix remaining ingredients and shape into 1-inch balls. Brown on all sides in a skillet, using a small amount of fat. Pour off excess fat and add sauce to meatballs. Cover and simmer for 20 minutes.

Serves 4.

— *Anita Cunningham*
Belwood, Ontario

TOMATOES AND BULGUR

¾ lb. ground beef
1 tsp. salt
½ tsp. pepper
½ tsp. cinnamon
1 medium onion, chopped

¾ lb. tomatoes, peeled & chopped
2 Tbsp. tomato paste
1 cup water
1 cup bulgur

Brown beef with spices. Add chopped onion and cook until soft. Add tomatoes, tomato paste and water and bring to a boil.

Add bulgur, cover and simmer until bulgur is soft, about 20 minutes. Stir occasionally and add water if necessary to prevent sticking.

Serves 4.

— *Moira Abboud*
Guelph, Ontario

HOT TAMALE PIE

Filling:
1 lb. ground beef
1½ cups corn
2 cups tomatoes
Salt & pepper
¾ cup chopped onion
1 Tbsp. chopped chili pepper

Crust:
¼ cup shortening
1 egg
1½ cups flour
2 cups corn meal
2 tsp. baking powder
1 cup milk

Combine filling ingredients in a heavy pot and bring to a boil. Reduce heat and simmer until meat is cooked through — 15 to 20 minutes.

To make crust, cream shortening and beat in egg. Combine flour, corn meal and baking powder and stir into creamed mixture. Add milk to make a soft, smooth dough.

Place ground beef filling in greased casserole dish and top with dough. Bake at 400 degrees F for 35 to 40 minutes.

Serves 4.

— *Anne McKenzie*
Englehart, Ontario

GROUND BEEF & SQUASH

3 acorn squash, cut in half & cleaned
2 lbs. ground beef
2 eggs
2 tsp. lemon juice

Salt & pepper
2 Tbsp. grated onion
1½ cups cooked rice
6 Tbsp. chili sauce

Bake squash at 250 degrees F for 30 minutes. Combine remaining ingredients, spoon into squash and bake for another 40 minutes.

Serves 6.

— Susan Boehm
Aylmer, Ontario

BEEF PATTIES A LA LINDSTROM

INSPIRED BY THE CONTRIBUTOR'S VISIT TO SCANDINAVIA, THIS DISH HAS GONE ON TO become a family favourite.

4 oz. cooked beets
2 Tbsp. vinegar
4 oz. cold, boiled potatoes
1½ lbs. lean ground beef
2 egg yolks

Salt & pepper
2 Tbsp. grated onion
2 Tbsp. chopped capers
3 oz. butter
Parsley

Slice beets and marinate in vinegar for 20 minutes. Drain and chop finely. Dice potatoes.

Place meat in bowl and mix in egg yolks and salt and pepper. Stir in potatoes, beets, onion and capers and form into 12 patties.

Fry the patties in butter then pour browned butter over them. Serve with chopped parsley.

Serves 4 to 6.

— Kay Barclay
Burlington, Ontario

PEPPER STEAK PATTIES

1 lb. lean ground beef
1 Tbsp. cracked peppercorns
½ tsp. salt
1 cup sliced mushrooms
½ cup chopped onion

2 Tbsp. butter
1 tsp. Worcestershire sauce
2 Tbsp. lemon juice
2 Tbsp. Cognac

Shape beef into 4 patties. Spread peppercorns on wax paper, then press patties into pepper until both sides are coated. Sprinkle salt over bottom of heavy skillet. Set over medium-high heat and add mushrooms and onions. Cook patties to suit individual preference.

In a separate pan, heat butter, Worcestershire sauce and lemon juice. Pour off drippings from meat, pour butter mixture over meat and flambe with Cognac. Serve.

Serves 4.

— Nan & Phil Millette
Corunna, Ontario

BAKED STUFFED LIVER

½ cup soft bread crumbs
½ Tbsp. diced onion
¼ tsp. sage
Salt
Milk

½ lb. liver, cut into wide slices
2 Tbsp. flour
Butter
1 cup tomato sauce (*Volume 1*, page 204)

Combine bread crumbs, onion, sage, salt and enough milk to moisten. Place on slices of liver, roll up and secure with toothpicks. Roll liver in flour and brown in butter. Place in greased casserole dish. Pour tomato sauce over top. Cover and bake at 350 degrees F for 1 hour.

Serves 3.

— Pat Leary
Kingston, Ontario

EGG DUMPLINGS

THESE DUMPLINGS CAN BE ADDED IN THE LAST FEW MINUTES OF COOKING IN ALMOST any stew.

1⅔ cups flour
3 tsp. baking powder
½ tsp. salt
1 Tbsp. butter
½ cup milk
1 egg, beaten

Blend dry ingredients. Rub in butter with fingers, then stir in milk and egg and drop by large spoonfuls into stewpot, cover and simmer for 12 to 15 minutes.

Makes 8 dumplings.

— Robert Brandon
Turner Valley, Alberta

PORK TENDERLOIN WITH APRICOT SAUCE

1½ lbs. pork tenderloin
Flour
Salt & pepper
2-3 cups herbed bread dressing
5-6 strips bacon

2 Tbsp. butter
2 Tbsp. cornstarch
2 cups apricot juice
6 apricot halves

Flatten pork between 2 layers of wax paper to ¼-inch thickness. Cut into 2½" x 3" rectangles, dredge with flour and sprinkle with salt and pepper.

Place a small amount of dressing on each rectangle and roll up like a jelly roll. Secure with toothpicks. Halve bacon strips and drape over pork rolls. Place on rack in shallow pan and bake at 350 degrees F for 1½ hours.

Meanwhile, make apricot sauce. Over medium heat, melt butter, whisk in cornstarch and add 1½ cups juice. Cook, stirring, until mixture comes to a boil and thickens. If sauce is too thick, add remaining ½ cup juice.

When meat is cooked, pour sauce over each roll and bake for 10 more minutes. Top each roll with an apricot half and baste with sauce. Bake for another 10 minutes.

Serves 4 to 6.

— Louise Routledge
Port Coquitlam, British Columbia

ROAST PORK STUFFED WITH APPLES & PRUNES

1 onion, chopped
1 apple, chopped
½ cup chopped, pitted prunes
3 Tbsp. apple butter
1 clove garlic, chopped

½ tsp. thyme
½ tsp. rosemary
Pepper
4-lb. pork loin roast, deboned

Mix together onion, apple, prunes, apple butter, garlic and seasonings. Stuff the roast with this mixture, place in roasting pan and bake at 325 degrees F for 2 hours.

Serves 6 to 8.

— Lynn Biscott
Toronto, Ontario

ROAST PORK & RED CABBAGE

¼ lb. bacon, cut into strips
  1½ inches long & ¼ inch across
½ cup thinly sliced carrots
1 cup sliced onion
3 Tbsp. butter
3 cups red cabbage, cut into
  ½-inch slices

2 cups dry red wine or beer
2 cups beef stock
2 apples, diced
2 cloves garlic, crushed
Salt & pepper
3 lbs. deboned & rolled pork loin,
  tenderloin or shoulder end

Place bacon in saucepan and cover with cold water. Bring to a boil, simmer for 10 minutes and drain. Sauté carrots, onion, bacon and butter in covered pot for 10 minutes. Add cabbage, wine or beer, stock, apples, garlic and salt and pepper and blend; cover and bake at 325 degrees F for 3 hours, stirring occasionally.

After 3 hours, brown the pork loin in small amount of fat and place on cabbage. Cover and return to oven for 2 hours. Remove pork and let sit, covered with foil, for 15 to 20 minutes. Place cabbage on a warm platter, slice pork and arrange on cabbage. Serve with cooking juices in a gravy boat.

Serves 6.

— Jeff Greenberg
Ottawa, Ontario

MARINATED PORK ROAST WITH CURRANT SAUCE

½ cup soya sauce
½ cup sherry
2 cloves garlic, minced
1 Tbsp. dry mustard
1 tsp. ginger
1 tsp. thyme

4-5 lbs. pork loin roast,
  deboned, rolled & tied
Currant Sauce:
10 oz. currant jelly
2 Tbsp. sherry
1 Tbsp. soya sauce

Combine soya sauce, sherry, garlic, mustard, ginger and thyme. Place roast in plastic bag in deep bowl. Pour in marinade and close bag. Marinate for 2 to 3 hours at room temperature, pressing bag occasionally. Remove from bag and place in roasting pan with marinade and roast, uncovered, at 350 degrees F for 2½ to 3 hours, basting with marinade during last hour.

Meanwhile, make sauce by melting currant jelly. Add sherry and soya sauce and simmer for 2 minutes. Serve roast with sauce.

Serves 8.

— Susan Bates Eddy
St. Andrews, New Brunswick

APPLE GLAZED ROAST PORK

4-5 lbs. pork roast
1 Tbsp. butter
1 small onion, grated
1 Tbsp. cornstarch

1 Tbsp. brown sugar
1 Tbsp. soya sauce
½ tsp. ginger
1 cup apple juice

Place pork fat side up on rack in shallow roasting pan. Score fat layer in diamonds and roast, uncovered, at 325 degrees F for 1 hour.

While roast is in oven, prepare glaze. Melt butter in saucepan and sauté onion until soft. Thoroughly mix together cornstarch, brown sugar, soya sauce, ginger and juice. Pour into pan with sautéed onions and cook over low heat, stirring constantly, until thick. Brush part of glaze over meat, then continue brushing every 15 minutes for the next hour, or until meat is done.

Serves 8.

— *Donna Sopha*
Belleville, Ontario

SWEET RED CURRY

1 Tbsp. oil
1 lb. cubed pork
1 medium onion, chopped
1 28-oz. can tomatoes, mashed
2 Tbsp. brown sugar
1 tsp. curry

2 Tbsp. water
3 apples, diced
1 cup peas
½ cup shredded coconut
6-8 mushrooms

Heat oil in large skillet and brown meat. Add chopped onion and cook, stirring, for 3 minutes. Add tomatoes. Bring to boil and add brown sugar. Mix curry with water and add. Simmer for 30 minutes.

A few minutes before serving, add diced apples, peas, coconut and mushrooms and heat through. Serve over rice.

Serves 4.

— *Denise Aspinall*
Wolfville, Nova Scotia

PORK AND APPLE PIE

Pastry for double 9-inch pie shell
3 cups diced, cooked pork
5 tart apples, peeled,
  cored & thinly sliced
1-2 medium onions, thinly sliced
3 Tbsp. flour

¼ tsp. salt
2 Tbsp. brown sugar
½ tsp. cinnamon
½ tsp. nutmeg
1 Tbsp. lemon juice
Milk

Line pie plate with one-half of pastry.

Combine pork, apples and onions in a large bowl. Mix flour, sugar, salt, cinnamon and nutmeg. Toss together pork and flour mixtures with lemon juice. Spoon into shell. Cover with second half of pastry, flute edges and cut slits in top for steam. Brush with milk.

Bake at 425 degrees F for 45 to 60 minutes.

Serves 4 to 6.

— *Janie Zwicker*
Bond Head, Ontario

PORK CUBES IN APPLE CIDER

¼ cup flour
½ tsp. salt
¼ tsp. pepper
¼ tsp. paprika
Garlic powder

2 lbs. pork, cubed
¼ cup butter
2 cups chopped onion
2 cups unsweetened apple cider

Mix flour and seasonings in paper bag. Add pork a few cubes at a time and shake to coat. Melt butter in skillet and brown cubes a single layer at a time, placing in an ovenproof casserole dish as they brown. Cook onions until limp but not brown and add to pork cubes. Pour cider over all, cover and bake at 350 degrees F until pork is tender − 1 to 1½ hours.

Serves 4.

— Mary Lennox
Collingwood, Ontario

ADOBONG BABOY

THIS RECIPE FOR PORK ADOBO IS FROM THE PHILIPPINES, WHERE THE CONTRIBUTOR spent some time on a youth exchange.

6 pork chops
8-10 cloves garlic
1 cup vinegar
1 cup water

1½ tsp. salt
2 bay leaves
½ tsp. pepper
Oil

Cut fat from pork and discard. If chops are large, cut into bite-sized pieces. Place pork and all other ingredients except oil into heavy saucepan and marinate for at least 1 hour. Bring to a boil, then reduce heat and simmer for 40 minutes, or until pork is tender. Remove pork from pan, boil liquid over high heat until reduced and thickened, then strain into small bowl. Place oil in the bottom of skillet and fry meat until evenly browned and crisp. Arrange on heated serving platter, pour sauce over the top and serve with rice.

Serves 6.

— Gemma Laska
Whitehorse, Yukon Territory

MEDITERRANEAN PORK CHOPS

6 large pork butt chops
6 Tbsp. flour
½ tsp. salt
¼ tsp. coarsely ground pepper
¼ tsp. oregano

2 oz. tomato paste
12 leaves fresh sage
2 oz. dry white wine
3 cloves garlic, minced

Remove fat from chops and set aside. Mix together flour, salt, pepper and oregano and coat chops with this mixture. Let sit on a rack for 1 hour to help flour adhere.

Place scraps of fat in large shallow pan which can be tightly covered and heat them until bottom of pan is covered with a thin film of liquid fat. Discard scraps.

Put chops in pan and brown lightly on both sides. Spread tomato paste evenly on top of each chop. Add water to cover bottom of pan and simmer meat for 45 minutes with the lid on the pan. Remove lid, place 2 sage leaves on each chop, add wine and place garlic on bottom of pan. Bring to a boil, then cover, decrease heat, and simmer for an additional 5 minutes. Discard sage and garlic and serve immediately.

Serves 6.

— Glenn McMichael
Goderich, Ontario

DEVILLED PORK CHOPS

4 very thin pork chops
3 Tbsp. chili sauce
1½ Tbsp. lemon juice
2 tsp. Worcestershire sauce
¼ tsp. paprika

¼ tsp. dry mustard
⅛ tsp. curry
⅛ tsp. pepper
½ cup water

Trim excess fat from chops. Heat strips of fat in large skillet until they liquify. Brown chops well on both sides and pour off fat.

Combine chili sauce, lemon juice, Worcestershire sauce, paprika, mustard, curry, pepper and water and pour over chops. Bring to a boil, lower heat, cover and simmer until chops are tender — about 20 minutes.

Serves 4.

— Jane Morrissey
Fort McMurray, Alberta

PORK CHOPS WITH WHITE WINE & HERBS

1 Tbsp. chopped oregano
1 Tbsp. chopped marjoram
1 clove garlic, chopped
Salt & pepper
4 large pork loin chops

¼ cup butter
½ cup dry white wine
1 tsp. cornstarch
1 Tbsp. chopped parsley

Mix together oregano, marjoram, garlic and salt and pepper. Coat both sides of chops with herb mixture, pressing it on well.

Melt butter and fry chops for 3 minutes on each side. Pour in half of wine and bring to a boil. Cover and cook for 30 to 40 minutes or until tender. Transfer to warmed serving dish and keep hot.

Dissolve cornstarch in remaining wine, stir in a little of the hot liquid, then add to the pan, stirring constantly. Bring to a boil and simmer for 3 to 5 minutes. Pour over chops and sprinkle with parsley.

Serves 4.

— Elizabeth Clayton Paul
Nepean, Ontario

PORK CHOPS WITH PEACHES

4 pork chops
¼ cup brown sugar
1 tsp. ginger
1 large onion, sliced
1 cup water

2 Tbsp. soya sauce
¼ cup cider vinegar
1 Tbsp. cornstarch, dissolved
  in cold water
2 fresh peaches, peeled & sliced

Brown pork chops in hot pan. Sprinkle sugar and ginger over chops, top with onion slices and cover with water, soya sauce and vinegar. Cover tightly and simmer for 35 minutes, turning chops once. Thicken sauce with cornstarch mixture, add peaches and heat until warm.

Serves 4.

— Judy Wuest
Cross Creek, New Brunswick

STEAMED SPARERIBS WITH BLACK BEAN SAUCE

1½ lbs. spareribs, cut
  into 2"-3" pieces
4-5 Tbsp. cooked black beans
6-10 cloves garlic
1 tsp. salt
3 Tbsp. sherry

3 Tbsp. water
3 Tbsp. vinegar
2 Tbsp. oil
4 Tbsp. sugar
6 spring onions, chopped into
  1-inch pieces

Boil ribs for 5 minutes and drain. Blend remaining ingredients except onions and pour over ribs. Marinate for 4 hours.

Place ribs in steamer, add onions and steam for 45 minutes.

Serves 6 as an appetizer or 3 to 4 as a meal.

— Harvey Griggs
Willowdale, Ontario

SPARERIBS CANTONESE

4 lbs. pork spareribs
1 cup orange marmalade
½ cup soya sauce
½ tsp. garlic powder
½ tsp. ginger
Orange slices

Cut ribs into serving-sized pieces. Arrange in a rectangular casserole dish. Brown at 400 degrees F for 15 minutes. Drain off fat.

In a bowl, combine marmalade, soya sauce, garlic powder, ginger and ¾ cup water. Mix well. Pour over ribs, cover casserole dish and bake at 350 degrees for 1 hour, or until the ribs are done to your liking, basting occasionally.

Place ribs on serving dish and garnish with orange slices.

Serves 4 to 6.

— Irene Louden
Port Coquitlam, British Columbia

HERBED SPARERIBS

3 lbs. spareribs
Salt & pepper
2 Tbsp. oil
1 clove garlic, crushed
½ cup chopped onion
2 Tbsp. brown sugar
1 Tbsp. vinegar
1 Tbsp. lemon juice
1 tsp. dry mustard

½ tsp. salt
⅛ tsp. red pepper
¼ tsp. thyme
¼ tsp. oregano
¼ tsp. basil
½ bay leaf
1 cup tomato sauce (*Volume 1*, page 204)
½ cup water

Cut spareribs into serving-sized pieces and sprinkle with salt and pepper. Heat oil in saucepan and sauté garlic and onion until tender. Add remaining ingredients and simmer for 10 minutes.

Parboil spareribs, then place in shallow pan and cover with sauce. Bake at 375 degrees F until done — about 30 minutes.

Serves 6 to 8.

— Helene Conway-Brown
Elnora, Alberta

FAVOURITE PORK SPARERIBS

THE CONTRIBUTOR OF THIS RECIPE SAYS, "THIS HAS BEEN A FAVOURITE IN OUR FAMILY for 30 years. In fact, each of my married children has sent home for the recipe."

4 lbs. pork spareribs, cut up
1 large onion, minced
1 clove garlic, crushed
3 Tbsp. butter
2 Tbsp. cider vinegar
2 Tbsp. orange juice
6 Tbsp. brown sugar
3 tsp. salt

1 Tbsp. mustard
1 tsp. cinnamon
4 Tbsp. Worcestershire sauce
2 cups catsup
1½ cups diced celery
1 cup water
8-oz. can crushed pineapple

Cover ribs with water, boil for 15 minutes and drain. In another pan, simmer onion and garlic in butter until tender. Add remaining ingredients and cook for 5 to 10 minutes. Add ribs and cook gently until meat is tender — about 1 hour.

Place ribs in broiling pan, cover with sauce and broil until brown.

Serves 4 to 6.

— *Ritta Wright*
Elmsdale, Nova Scotia

DRY GARLIC SPARERIBS

1 lb. pork spareribs, cut
  into 1" x 1½" pieces
Salt & pepper
1 Tbsp. soya sauce

½ tsp. sugar
2 Tbsp. cornstarch
2 tsp. oil
2 Tbsp. crushed garlic

Place ribs in bowl and add salt and pepper, soya sauce and sugar. Stir, then add cornstarch and stir to mix. Marinate for at least 15 minutes.

Heat oil until very hot. Add ribs and brown, stirring occasionally. Lower heat, cover and cook for 5 minutes. Drain off excess liquid. Increase heat to high, add garlic and stir-fry until it is golden — about 2 minutes. Transfer to broiler pan and broil until crisp, turning once — 5 to 10 minutes.

Serves 4 as an appetizer.

— *Judith & Bob Brand*
Pender Island, British Columbia

ZUCCHINI PORK BAKE

1 lb. ground pork
½ tsp. garlic powder
3 Tbsp. Parmesan cheese
½ cup yogurt
4 small zucchini, sliced
½ lb. mozzarella cheese, grated

Fry pork until browned, drain. Add garlic, Parmesan cheese and yogurt.

Place half of zucchini in shallow greased pan, cover with meat and top with remaining zucchini. Cover with grated mozzarella cheese. Bake at 375 degrees F for 20 to 25 minutes.

Serves 4.

— *Linda Townsend*
Nanoose Bay, British Columbia

SAUSAGE & SPINACH PIE

Pastry for 9-inch pie shell
1 lb. sausage meat, cooked
3 large eggs
1 lb. spinach, cooked, drained & chopped
½ lb. mozzarella cheese, grated

⅓ cup cottage cheese
¼ tsp. salt
⅛ tsp. pepper
¼ tsp. garlic powder
½ tsp. oregano

Combine all ingredients and mix well. Pour into unbaked pie shell and bake at 375 degrees F for 1 hour.

Serves 4 to 6.

— J. Kristine MacDonald
Baddeck Bay, Nova Scotia

SAUSAGE ZUCCHINI CASSEROLE

1½ lbs. garlic sausage
1 large onion, diced
2-3 small zucchini, cubed
4 small potatoes, cooked & cubed
1 green pepper, diced

6 small tomatoes, peeled & cubed
Pepper
Garlic powder
1 cup grated old Cheddar cheese

Remove sausage from casing and sauté until no longer pink. Add onion and zucchini and sauté for a few minutes. Layer this mixture with potatoes, green pepper and tomatoes in greased casserole dish. Sprinkle with pepper and a dash of garlic powder. Cover and cook at 350 degrees F for 30 minutes. Remove cover, sprinkle cheese on top and broil until bubbly.

Serves 4 to 6.

— Doris Hill
Ayr, Ontario

LECHO

THIS IS A CZECHOSLOVAKIAN MEAL IN ITSELF AND IS DELICIOUS SERVED WITH A HEARTY rye bread.

2 lbs. onions, finely chopped
Oil
2 lbs. green peppers, finely chopped
2 lbs. tomatoes, chopped

Salt & pepper
1½ lbs. Ukrainian sausage
1 egg, beaten

Place onions in large pot with enough oil to prevent sticking and cook until transparent. Add green peppers and cook until colour changes. Add tomatoes and cook for 1 hour. Season with salt and pepper. Cut sausage into ¼-inch rounds and add. Cook 30 minutes longer. Just before serving time, stir in the beaten egg to thicken.

Serves 6.

— Faye Hugar
Eholt, British Columbia

RUMAKI

½ lb. pork liver
10-oz. can water chestnuts
½ cup soya sauce
¼ cup firmly packed brown sugar

2 cloves garlic, finely chopped
¼ tsp. ginger
1 Tbsp. tarragon
1 lb. bacon

Rinse liver and pat dry. Slice into 36 thin pieces. Cut water chestnuts into 36 pieces.

Combine soya sauce, sugar, garlic, ginger and tarragon in plastic bowl. Stir in liver and chestnuts. Cover, refrigerate and marinate for at least 2 hours. Drain.

Cut bacon slices in half. Lay a slice of liver and a piece of chestnut on each bacon strip. Roll up and secure with toothpicks. Bake at 400 degrees F for 25 to 30 minutes, turning once. Drain well.

Serves 12 as an appetizer.

DANISH LIVER PASTE

1½ lbs. pork liver
2-3 large onions
1 lb. bacon fat
½ cup butter

½ cup flour
Milk
Salt & pepper
2 eggs

Grind liver, then onions, then bacon fat to desired smoothness. Melt butter, add flour and stir until smooth. Add milk to make a thick gravy. Add salt and pepper and eggs. Stir in meat, mix well and bake in a loaf pan at 325 degrees F for 1¼ hours.

Makes 3 to 4 cups.

— Mary Alice Self
Tatlayoko Lake, British Columbia

BACON WRAPPED CHUTNEY BANANAS

2 bananas
1 lb. bacon
Lemon juice
1 cup mango chutney

Slice bananas into halves lengthwise, then into quarters crosswise. Dip bacon in lemon juice, roll around a piece of banana and secure with toothpick. Repeat until all banana pieces are used up.

Place on cookie sheet and bake at 375 degrees F for 20 minutes. Remove from oven, dip into chutney and bake for another 10 to 15 minutes.

Serves 4 as an appetizer.

— Joanne McInveen
Whistler, British Columbia

SOUTHERN ONTARIO PIG TAILS

5 lbs. pig tails
4 Tbsp. sugar
4 Tbsp. vinegar
½ cup chopped onion

2 Tbsp. brown sugar
2 Tbsp. soya sauce
1½ cups tomato juice

Boil pig tails until tender, then cut off most of the fat. Make sauce by combining remaining ingredients and cook until onions are tender.

Place pig tails in a casserole dish, pour sauce over them and bake at 275 degrees F, basting occasionally, for an hour.

Serves 6.

— Linda Halford
Maidstone, Ontario

ORANGE GLAZED HAM

4-5 lbs. ham
1 Tbsp. grated orange rind
1 cup orange juice
¼ cup brown sugar

1½ Tbsp. soya sauce
½ tsp. ginger
1 Tbsp. cornstarch

Bake ham on rack in roasting pan at 325 degrees F for 45 minutes. Remove excess fat and any rind with a sharp knife, leaving ¼ inch fat layer. Score fat in a diamond pattern. Combine orange rind, juice, sugar, soya sauce and ginger in small bowl. Remove and reserve ⅔ cup for orange sauce.

Brush ham with remaining glaze. Continue roasting, brushing with glaze every 15 minutes for an hour longer. Remove roast from oven to a heated platter.

For orange sauce, combine reserved glaze with ⅔ cup water and the cornstarch in a small saucepan. Heat, stirring constantly, until mixture thickens and bubbles. Cook for 1 minute. Slice ham and serve with sauce.

Serves 6 to 8.

— Valerie Gillis
Renfrew, Ontario

LEEKS WITH HAM AND CHEESE

12 small leeks, cleaned
½ lb. cooked ham, chopped
½ cup grated Swiss cheese
¾ cup whipping cream
Salt & pepper

Simmer leeks in water for 15 minutes and drain. Arrange in greased baking dish. Sprinkle with salt and pepper and cover with chopped ham. Sprinkle with cheese and pour cream over all.

Bake at 400 degrees F for 10 to 15 minutes.

Serves 4.

— Denyse Fournier
Ottawa, Ontario

COLD HAM PIE

THIS PIE IS PERFECT TAKE-ALONG FOOD FOR A PICNIC. SERVED WITH A SALAD, IT IS ALSO delicious summer luncheon fare.

Pastry for double 9-inch pie shell,
  with ½ tsp. mustard &
  pinch thyme added
1 egg
1 tsp. dry mustard
1 cup sour cream

2 lbs. ham, cooked & ground
1½ cups sliced mushrooms, cooked
⅔ cup grated Swiss cheese
¼ cup thinly sliced green onion
3 Tbsp. minced parsley
1 egg, beaten with a little milk

Beat together egg, mustard and sour cream. Add ham, mushrooms, cheese, onion and parsley and mix well.

Place in pastry-lined pie dish and top with remaining pastry. Slit top crust to allow steam to escape. Brush top with beaten egg and milk. Bake at 425 degrees F for 30 minutes, reduce heat to 350 degrees and bake for 10 minutes longer. Cool, then chill in refrigerator.

Serves 4 to 6.

— *Trudy Mason*
Meaford, Ontario

MUSTARD MOUSSE

AN ELEGANT ACCOMPANIMENT TO BAKED HAM.

¾ cup sugar
3 tsp. dry mustard
4 eggs
½ cup vinegar

1 envelope gelatin
2 Tbsp. cold water
1 cup whipping cream

Combine sugar and mustard and beat in eggs. Add vinegar. Cook in top of double boiler over boiling water, stirring frequently, until mixture coats spoon.

Meanwhile, soak gelatin in water. Add to thickened mustard mixture, stirring until dissolved. Let cool.

Whip cream until soft peaks form, and fold into cooled mustard mixture. Chill well in mould. Serve with ham.

Makes approximately 2 cups.

— *Heather Bonham*
Kingston, Ontario

ROAST MUSTARD LAMB

4-lb. leg of lamb
12 Tbsp. oil
1 Tbsp. soya sauce

4 Tbsp. mustard
¼ tsp. garlic powder
½ tsp. rosemary

Trim away most of the fat from the leg of lamb and place the lamb in a shallow roasting pan. Mix together remaining ingredients and spread over the surface of the leg. Leave at room temperature for about an hour, then roast at 325 degrees F for 20 to 30 minutes a pound, or until an internal temperature of 175 degrees is reached.

Serves 6.

— *Adele Dueck*
Lucky Lake, Saskatchewan

LEG OF LAMB WITH CORIANDER & GARLIC

6-lb. leg of lamb
6 cloves garlic, peeled
1 Tbsp. crushed coriander seeds

1 tsp. salt
½ tsp. pepper
2 Tbsp. butter

With the tip of a sharp knife, make six incisions in the leg of lamb near the bone. Press the garlic cloves and the coriander into the incisions and rub lamb with salt and pepper. Place meat in medium-sized roasting pan. Cut butter into small pieces and dot it over the meat.

Roast meat at 375 degrees F for 20 minutes per pound, or until juices run out faintly rosy when meat is pierced with the point of a sharp knife.

Serves 8.

— *Dolores de Rosario*
Hamilton, Ontario

HONEY SOYA LEG OF LAMB

6-lb. leg of lamb
Salt & pepper
5-6 Tbsp. liquid honey
4-6 Tbsp. soya sauce

Remove fat and membrane from lamb. Liberally salt and pepper the meat, rubbing in well. Place leg of lamb on a rack in roasting pan and apply honey as a glaze. Add 1 inch of water to pan and roast, uncovered, at 425 degrees F for 30 minutes. Reduce heat to 350 degrees and pour 2 Tbsp. soya sauce over lamb. Repeat every 45 minutes. Total roasting time is 2½ hours. Remove lamb to platter and keep warm.

Remove any fat from sauce in roasting pan and serve sauce with lamb.

Serves 8.

— *Lynne Zahariuk*
Winnipeg, Manitoba

PHIL'S LAMB

6-lb. leg of lamb
6 cloves garlic, peeled & sliced in half
1 lemon
1 orange
1 cup liquid honey

Tarragon
Salt & pepper
1 cup orange juice
1 cup water
1 onion, quartered

Make slits in lamb with sharp knife and place half a clove of garlic in each. Cut lemon and orange in half and rub over meat, squeezing out the juice. Place fruit pieces into roasting pan with lamb. Pour honey over lamb, then sprinkle with a generous amount of tarragon. Add salt and pepper, then orange juice, water and onion. Let marinate, refrigerated, overnight, basting from time to time.

Roast at 325 degrees F for 18 to 20 minutes per pound, basting every 15 minutes.

Serves 8.

— *Philip Wood*
Harrowsmith, Ontario

RIVERSLEA SHOULDER OF LAMB

3-4 lbs. boneless shoulder of lamb
1 cup bread crumbs
2 Tbsp. melted butter
1 onion, finely chopped
1 clove garlic, crushed

1 cup dried apricots, chopped and
  soaked in water to soften
1 Tbsp. parsley
1 egg, beaten
Salt & pepper

Have your butcher debone and roll (but not tie) a shoulder of lamb. Combine all other ingredients, mixing well. Lay the meat out flat and spread the mixture over it. Roll the meat up and tie several times to hold together.

Roast in an open pan at 350 degrees F for about 20 to 30 minutes per pound.

Serves 6.

— Jean Rivers
Russell, Ontario

APRICOT STUFFED LAMB

1 cup dried apricots
2 cups strong, hot tea
2 cups coarse bread crumbs
3 Tbsp. chopped parsley
½ cup coarsely chopped walnuts
1 egg

Grated rind of lime or lemon
1 tsp. salt
½ tsp. pepper
2 Tbsp. gin
6-lb. shoulder of lamb, deboned

Cut apricots into dime-sized pieces and soak in hot tea for 30 minutes. Drain, reserving liquid. Place fruit in a bowl and add remaining ingredients, except lamb. Mix well and moisten with reserved liquid until damp but not soggy. Spread on meat and roll and tie with cotton cord. Secure loose ends with toothpicks, to be removed when roast is firm.

Roast, covered, at 350 degrees F for 30 minutes, then uncovered for a total of 20 minutes per pound. Baste meat with tea if it starts to look dry.

Serves 8.

— Randi Kennedy
Stella, Ontario

TURKISH GLAZED ROAST LAMB

THIS UNUSUAL GLAZE IMPARTS ALMOST NONE OF ITS OWN FLAVOURS TO THE MEAT, BUT heightens the flavour of the meat itself, as well as keeping the meat tender and juicy. It originated among the nomadic shepherds who carried very little food. They took what they needed from the flocks they were tending — fresh milk and meat.

⅔ cup strong coffee
⅔ cup sugar
⅔ cup milk or cream
4-lb. lamb roast

Combine coffee, sugar and milk and brush freely over lamb while cooking at 350 degrees F for 20 minutes a pound.

Serves 6.

— Randi Kennedy
Stella, Ontario

TENDERLOIN WITH OYSTER SAUCE

½ cup beer
½ cup oil
2 cloves garlic, chopped
1 medium onion, chopped
½ tsp. dry mustard
1 large bay leaf
Pepper
2 small lamb tenderloins
Oil for cooking

2 stalks celery, diagonally sliced
½ cup sliced mushrooms
½ cup sliced green pepper
2 scallions, chopped
2 Tbsp. oyster sauce
3 Tbsp. water
1 Tbsp. cornstarch
Pepper

Combine beer, oil, garlic, onion, mustard, bay leaf and pepper. Cut meat in ¼-inch slices and marinate for 1 hour in above mixture, then drain.

Heat oil in skillet and add meat. Fry until browned, then add vegetables and fry until celery is softened. Combine last 4 items and add to meat, bring back to boil and serve over brown rice.

Serves 3 to 4.

— *Charlene Skidmore*
Medicine Hat, Alberta

LAMB STEAK BIGARADE

2 lamb steaks, cut from the leg
1 tsp. salt
2 unpeeled oranges, sliced
2 Tbsp. brown sugar
1 Tbsp. orange rind

½ tsp. ginger
¼ tsp. ground cloves
1 tsp. dried mint
¼ cup melted butter

Place steaks in a 2-inch-deep baking dish, rub with salt and cover with orange slices.

Mix together remaining ingredients and pour over the orange slices. Bake at 325 degrees F for 40 minutes, basting frequently.

Serves 4.

— *Carol Frost*
Chilliwack, British Columbia

PINEAPPLE SOYA LAMB CHOPS

1 small onion, chopped
2 cloves garlic, chopped
⅓ cup oil
½ cup soya sauce

⅓ cup pineapple juice
Pineapple rings
2 Tbsp. brown sugar
6 2-inch lamb chops

Combine onion, garlic, oil, soya sauce, pineapple juice, pineapple and sugar and marinate meat for at least 4 hours, turning once. Broil for 12 minutes on each side. Serve topped with pineapple rings.

Serves 2 to 3.

— *Barbara Littlejohn*
Niagara Falls, Ontario

MUTTON CURRY

THIS DISH IS PARTICULARLY TASTY SERVED OVER RICE, WITH SIDE DISHES OF YOGURT, almonds, coconut and sliced bananas.

3 Tbsp. oil
2 onions, chopped
2 cloves garlic, chopped
1½ lbs. mutton, cut into small pieces
Flour
2 cups boiling water
¼ cup stewed tomatoes

2 tsp. salt
2 tsp. curry
1½ tsp. cumin
1 tsp. ginger
Pepper
1 apple, peeled & diced
½ cup raisins

Heat oil in heavy pot and brown onions and garlic. Dredge meat in flour and brown. Add boiling water, tomato, salt, curry, cumin, ginger, pepper, apple and raisins. Simmer for 2 hours.

Serves 4.

— Jeannie Rosenberg
Huntingdon, Quebec

BAKED LAMB & SUMMER SQUASH CASSEROLE

2-3 small summer squash
1-2 green peppers
1 tomato
1 lb. chopped lamb
1 tsp. salt
¼ tsp. pepper
1 tsp. basil

¼ cup oil
1 clove garlic, crushed
Sauce:
2 cloves garlic, crushed
1 cup yogurt
Cayenne
Crushed mint leaves

Cut up squash, green peppers and tomato. Toss in a greased casserole dish with lamb, seasonings, oil and garlic. Mix well and bake, uncovered, at 425 degrees F for 45 minutes.

Meanwhile, make sauce. Mix garlic, yogurt and dash of cayenne. Stir into casserole when cooked and sprinkle with mint leaves.

Serves 4.

— Rhonda Barnes
Saltspring Island, British Columbia

IRISH STEW

3-4 Tbsp. shortening
1 medium onion, chopped
1 clove garlic, minced
1-1½ lbs. stewing lamb
¼ cup flour

1 tsp. salt
¼ tsp. pepper
8-10 medium potatoes, chopped
3 large carrots, cut in strips
¼ large cabbage, chopped

Melt 1 Tbsp. shortening in large pot. Brown onion and garlic and set aside. Melt another tablespoon of shortening. Coat meat with flour, salt and pepper and brown, adding shortening as needed. Combine meat and onion mixture, add water to cover and simmer, covered, for 2 to 3 hours or until tender. Add potatoes and carrots and cook for 30 minutes. Add cabbage and cook until tender. Thicken with a little flour and water mixture if desired.

Serves 4.

— Lucille Kalyniak
Elmwood, Ontario

APPLE MINT LAMB SHANKS

THESE ARE EASY, DELICIOUS AND ECONOMICAL. THE GLAZE CAN BE USED AS A marinade, a roasting sauce or a barbecuing glaze and can be used on any cut of lamb with good results.

1 cup boiling water
3 Tbsp. dried or 1 cup
  fresh mint leaves

6-oz. can frozen apple juice
  concentrate, thawed
3 Tbsp. honey
4 lbs. lamb shanks

Combine water and mint leaves in a saucepan and let steep for 15 minutes to make a strong tea. Add apple juice and honey and heat gently to blend.

Marinate shanks in this for at least 1 hour and as long as 24 hours. Remove shanks from marinade and roast, uncovered, at 325 degrees F for 1 to 1½ hours, turning and basting frequently.

Serves 4.

— *Randi Kennedy*
Stella, Ontario

MOUSSAKA

OF GREEK ORIGIN, THE DELICATE FLAVOUR OF THE EGGPLANT MINGLING WITH THE succulence of the spring lamb makes this dish well worth the work.

1½ lbs. potatoes
2 medium eggplants
Olive oil
4 large tomatoes, peeled &
  thinly sliced
Basil
1 large white onion, thinly sliced

1 lb. ground spring lamb
Mint
Garlic powder
2 Tbsp. butter
2 Tbsp. flour
1 cup milk, heated
½ cup grated Emmenthal cheese

Peel potatoes, slice ¼-inch thick and parboil for 10 minutes. Drain and place half in bottom of greased casserole dish.

Trim eggplant and slice ½-inch thick. Fry a few at a time in oil until lightly browned on both sides. Place half the eggplant over the potatoes. Place half the sliced tomatoes over top of eggplant and sprinkle lightly with basil.

Sauté onion in same skillet as eggplant in small amount of oil until transparent, and top tomatoes with half the onions.

In same skillet, adding more oil if necessary, brown lamb and season lightly with mint and garlic. If meat seems dry, add a few tablespoons water or stock. Spread meat evenly over onions. Add remaining layers in this order: onions, tomatoes sprinkled with basil, eggplant and potatoes.

Melt butter in small saucepan, add flour and stir roux for a minute or so over medium-low heat. Whisk in heated milk over medium heat until thick, then stir in cheese and cook until melted. Pour over casserole and bake at 375 degrees F for 30 to 35 minutes, or until top is lightly browned. Remove from oven and cool for 10 minutes before serving.

Serves 6.

— *Veronica Green*
Beausejour, Manitoba

LAMB YOGURT TARTS

Crust:
8 oz. cream cheese
8 Tbsp. unsalted butter
2 cups flour
½ tsp. salt

Filling:
2 tsp. butter
1 cup finely chopped onions

1 lb. ground lamb
1 cup pine nuts
¼ tsp. salt
½ tsp. pepper
½ tsp. ground allspice
2 Tbsp. chopped parsley
1½ cups unflavoured yogurt

To make crust, blend together cream cheese and butter and work in flour and salt. Wrap in wax paper and chill for at least 2 hours.

Meanwhile, make filling. Melt butter and cook onions until transparent. Add meat and cook until red is gone, but do not brown. Drain and cool.

While filling is cooling, roll out dough and cut to make 24 tart shells. When meat is cool, add remaining ingredients, reserving ½ cup yogurt. Mix until smooth, fill tart shells and bake at 350 degrees F for 30 minutes. Serve with remaining yogurt.

Serves 24 as a party snack, or 8 as a main dish.

— Randi Kennedy
Stella, Ontario

LAMB LOAF

THIS LOAF SLICES WELL COLD AND IS DELICIOUS ON RYE BREAD WITH ALFALFA SPROUTS and Dijon mustard.

1 lb. ground lamb
⅛ tsp. celery seed
⅛ tsp. cloves
¼ tsp. savory
¼ tsp. cinnamon
⅛ tsp. pepper
¼ tsp. salt

¼ green pepper, diced
1 small onion, diced
1 medium tomato, peeled & diced
2 slices bacon, browned & diced
½ cup oatmeal

Combine all ingredients, mix well and bake at 350 degrees F for 45 minutes to 1 hour.

Serves 6 to 8.

— Kathryn MacDonald
Yarker, Ontario

LAMB & APPLE STEW

4 Tbsp. oil
1 onion, finely chopped
1½ lbs. lean stewing lamb, cubed
1 tsp. salt

White pepper
Cinnamon
1½ cups water
4 small cooking apples

Heat half the oil in a heavy pot and sauté onion until wilted. Add lamb and brown on all sides. Add seasonings and water and bring to boil. Reduce heat, then cover and simmer for 1 hour. Heat remaining oil in a skillet and sauté apples gently for 2 minutes. Add apples to stew and continue to simmer for 15 minutes.

Serves 4.

— Margaret Babcock
Kemble, Ontario

JANET'S LAMB KIDNEYS

6 lamb kidneys
3 Tbsp. butter
¼ lb. mushrooms, sliced

¼ cup sherry
2 thick bread slices

Remove outer skin from kidneys, split them lengthwise and remove the Y-shaped ligaments inside with scissors. Melt butter in large skillet and sauté mushrooms until nearly done. Push them to cooler side of pan and add the kidneys, cooking and turning until the red is gone. Push them to cool side of pan. Toast 2 slices of bread. Place mushrooms and kidneys on toast, heat pan up and deglaze with sherry, then pour over toast.

Serves 2.

— *Randi Kennedy*
Stella, Ontario

CHEVON STEW

2 lbs. goat meat, cubed
6 Tbsp. olive oil
6 Tbsp. flour
2 tsp. salt
¼ tsp. pepper
2 cloves garlic, crushed
1 bay leaf
2 Tbsp. parsley
2 cups beef stock

2 cups water
1 cup dry red wine
1 cup sliced carrots
1 cup diced potatoes
½ cup diced turnip
½ cup diced parsnip
1 cup peas
6 medium onions, chopped

Brown meat in oil in large pot, then remove and set aside. Stir flour and spices into oil in pot. Gradually stir in beef stock, water and wine, stirring until smooth. Return meat to pot, add onions and simmer for 1 hour. Add remaining ingredients and cook over low heat for 3 to 4 hours.

Serves 4.

— *Maria Nisbett*
Peterborough, Ontario

Pasta

Noodles, Alfredo?

— M. Bosworth
The Alsatian Affair

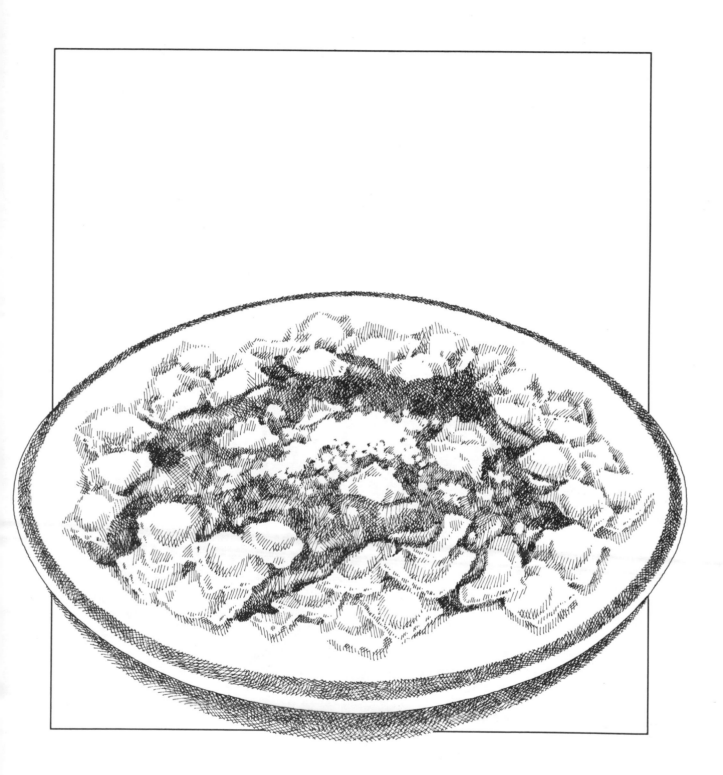

VEGETABLE PASTA

ALMOST ANY COOKED, PUREED VEGETABLES CAN BE ADDED TO BASIC EGG NOODLE dough. For a green pasta, use broccoli, spinach or peas. Tomatoes or carrots result in a red or orange noodle. Even lemon or orange rind and juice can be added for an unusual, light taste. When puréeing vegetables, leave them coarse enough that the pasta will have texture as well as flavour.

It is possible to make many shapes of noodles as well. With an inexpensive hand-crank pasta machine, it takes almost no effort to roll the dough to the desired thinness. From this point, the dough can be cut either by machine or by hand. *Fettuccine* is a flat noodle cut about ½-inch wide. *Spaghetti* is a round noodle, which can be cut only by machine. *Pappardelle* is similar to fettuccine except that it is cut with a fluted ravioli wheel, which provides a fancier noodle. To make *farfalle*, or bow ties, simply roll out dough to desired thinness, cut into 2″ x 1″ rectangles with ravioli wheel and pinch long sides together. Of course, only the cook's imagination is the limit when contemplating flavour and shape possibilities. Here is a basic recipe for vegetable pasta.

3 cups flour
4 eggs
½ cup vegetable purée
1 Tbsp. oil

Place flour in large, flat-bottomed mixing bowl and make a well in the centre. Combine eggs, purée and oil and pour into well. Using a spoon first, then hands, work flour in to form a smooth, not sticky, dough. Additional flour may be necessary. Cover dough and let sit for 30 minutes.

If making pasta by hand, begin rolling, adding flour as needed until dough is thin and translucent. If using a pasta maker, begin with rollers on widest setting and gradually narrow until desired thinness and smoothness are reached. Let dough sit for a few minutes until it is slightly dried out. Cut into desired shape. Place noodles over broom handle until time to cook. Fresh noodles will take only 2 to 3 minutes of cooking in boiling water. If the noodles are to be stored, allow to dry *thoroughly*, then bag and store in refrigerator or freezer.

Makes 3 pounds.

— *Linda Palaisy*
Cantley, Quebec

BASIL BUTTER BALLS

SIMPLE IT IS, BUT SEASONED, BUTTERED PASTA IS ONE OF THE MOST DELICIOUS TREATS possible. These butter balls can be assembled and stored in the freezer, removed at the last minute and served with cooked fresh pasta for a quick and easy supper. All else that is needed is a tossed salad.

½ cup unsalted butter
10 basil leaves
1 clove garlic
¼ tsp. black pepper

In blender or food processor, purée ingredients. Shape into small balls, place on cookie sheet and freeze. When balls are well frozen, remove from cookie sheet and store in covered container in freezer.

— *Louise McDonald*
L'Orignal, Ontario

PESTO

2 cups fresh basil
2 cloves garlic
½ cup parsley

½ tsp. salt
⅓-½ cup olive oil
¼ cup Parmesan cheese

Place basil, garlic, parsley, salt and ⅓ cup oil in blender. Process, adding more oil if necessary to make a smooth paste. Add cheese and blend for a few seconds. Serve over cooked, buttered spaghetti.

Serves 4.

SPINACH SAUCE

¼ cup butter
10 oz. spinach, finely chopped
1 tsp. salt
1 cup cottage cheese

¼ cup Parmesan cheese
¼ cup milk
⅛ tsp. nutmeg

Melt butter, add spinach and salt and cook until spinach is limp – about 5 minutes. Lower heat to simmer, stir in cottage and Parmesan cheeses, milk and nutmeg, and cook, stirring, until mixture is heated through. Serve with cooked spaghetti.

Serves 6.

SPAGHETTI WITH GARLIC & OIL

QUICK AND SIMPLE, THIS DISH ALLOWS THE DINER TO REALLY APPRECIATE THE FLAVOURS of the pasta and the garlic.

4 oz. spaghetti
½ cup olive oil
4 cloves garlic, peeled & crushed
Black pepper

Cook spaghetti in boiling, salted water. When almost cooked, heat oil in heavy pot. Add garlic and cook until browned. Drain and rinse spaghetti. Mix with garlic-oil mixture and serve topped with black pepper.

Serves 2.

ARTICHOKE HEART SAUCE FOR SPAGHETTI

THIS IS A VERY SPICY TOPPING, PARTICULARLY GOOD WITH FRESH FETTUCCINE. Served as an appetizer, it provides a tangy beginning to a meal.

1 large tin artichoke hearts, sliced
½ cup olive oil
1 tsp. crushed, hot red pepper
1 tsp. salt
3 cloves garlic, minced

4 Tbsp. chopped parsley
Juice of 1 lemon
Black pepper
Parmesan cheese

Combine artichoke hearts, oil, red pepper, salt and garlic in heavy pot. Cook, stirring, until hot. Add parsley and lemon juice. Serve over cooked noodles, topped with black pepper and Parmesan cheese.

Serves 4.

FRIED NOODLES WITH BEEF & SNOW PEAS

ALTHOUGH GENERALLY CONSIDERED AN ITALIAN FOOD, PASTA HAS ALSO BEEN A STAPLE of Chinese cuisine for thousands of years. This dish utilizes fried noodles, rather than just boiled, which provides quite a different texture.

16 oz. fine egg noodles
¾ cup oil
2 lbs. round steak, cut into thin strips
1 medium onion, sliced
2 cups beef stock

1 cup chopped mushrooms
2 Tbsp. dry sherry
2 Tbsp. soya sauce
3 Tbsp. cornstarch
8 oz. snow peas

Cook noodles in boiling, salted water until tender. Drain, rinse and drain again. Heat ½ cup oil in heavy skillet. Add noodles and cook, turning occasionally, until browned — about 20 minutes.

Meanwhile, in another skillet, heat remaining ¼ cup oil. When hot, cook steak and onion until meat is browned, stirring constantly. Add stock, mushrooms, sherry and soya sauce. Combine cornstarch with ½ cup cold water and gradually stir into skillet mixture. Cook, stirring, until thickened. Add snow peas and cook until heated through. Serve over noodles.

Serves 6.

NOODLE SALAD

AN EXCELLENT AND EASY WAY TO USE UP LEFTOVER PASTA, THIS DISH CAN EVEN utilize pasta with sauce on it — just rinse thoroughly in cold water before mixing with dressing.

½ cup yogurt
½ cup mayonnaise
1 Tbsp. Dijon mustard
1 Tbsp. dill
3-4 cups cooked pasta

Combine yogurt, mayonnaise, mustard and dill. Mix with rinsed pasta and chill well.

Serves 4.

CHICKEN & VEGETABLE SAUCE FOR MACARONI

1 Tbsp. cornstarch
½ tsp. salt
Pepper
2 Tbsp. soya sauce
½ cup chicken stock
2 Tbsp. vegetable oil
1 clove garlic, peeled
½ lb. raw chicken meat, cut into strips

1 medium onion, sliced
1 cup sliced celery
1 cup sliced mushrooms
2 cups broccoli, cut into florets & steamed
  until tender-crisp
1 tomato, cut into 8 pieces
2 green onions, chopped

Combine cornstarch, salt, pepper, soya sauce and chicken stock and set aside.

Heat oil in wok or heavy skillet. Sauté garlic until golden, then discard. Add chicken and sauté for 3 or 4 minutes, stirring constantly. Remove and set aside. Add onion, celery, mushrooms and broccoli and sauté until celery is tender — 4 minutes. Add chicken, tomato, green onions and cornstarch mixture. Cook until thickened, stirring constantly. Serve over cooked macaroni.

Serves 4.

PORK MEATBALLS AND SPAGHETTI SAUCE

A VARIATION OF THE TRADITIONAL BEEF MEATBALLS, PORK MEATBALLS PROVIDE a flavourful addition to this spaghetti sauce, which is also enhanced by the addition of zucchini.

Meatballs:
1 lb. ground pork
¼ cup Parmesan cheese
¼ cup oatmeal
½ cup chopped onion
3 Tbsp. chopped parsley
1 tsp. oregano
½ tsp. salt
¼ tsp. pepper
2 drops Tabasco sauce
1 Tbsp. oil

Sauce:
28-oz. can tomatoes
6-oz. can tomato paste
¾ cup chopped celery
½ cup chopped green pepper
½ cup chopped green olives
1 tsp. oregano
1 tsp. basil
2 drops Tabasco sauce
¾ cup grated zucchini
1 cup chopped mushrooms

To make meatballs, combine pork, cheese, oatmeal, onion, parsley, oregano, salt, pepper and Tabasco sauce. Mix well and form into small balls. Refrigerate for 1 hour to allow to set. Heat oil in skillet and brown meatballs on all sides. Drain on paper towels.

For sauce, combine tomatoes and tomato paste in large saucepan. Stir in celery, green pepper, olives, oregano, basil and Tabasco sauce. Bring to a boil, then drop in meatballs, zucchini and mushrooms. Simmer for 10 minutes and serve over cooked spaghetti.

Serves 6 to 8.

FETTUCCINE PRIMAVERA

THIS RECIPE MAKES USE OF EARLY SPRING VEGETABLES — THEY *must* BE FRESH — IN A white sauce. Additions or changes may be made according to personal taste. Green beans and cauliflower are good, as is the addition of shrimp. Because so many vegetables appear in the sauce, it is best to use unflavoured fettuccine noodles.

½ large head broccoli, cut
  into florets
1 zucchini, thinly sliced
½ cup sliced mushrooms
10 snow peas
1 medium onion, sliced
1 carrot, sliced
8 oz. fettuccine

¼ cup butter
2 cloves garlic, minced
2 Tbsp. basil
¼ cup cream
¼ cup white wine
2 Tbsp. parsley
½ cup Parmesan cheese

Steam broccoli, zucchini, mushrooms, snow peas, onion and carrot for 10 minutes. Cook fettuccine in boiling, salted water for 10 minutes.

Meanwhile, prepare sauce. Melt butter and brown garlic. Add remaining ingredients, mix thoroughly and heat through. Remove from heat, and toss with vegetables and fettuccine.

Serves 4.

— Janis Scattergood
Arthur, Ontario

CHICKEN & SAUSAGE SPAGHETTI SAUCE

3 Tbsp. olive oil
4 cloves garlic, peeled & crushed
2 medium onions, chopped
1 lb. hot Italian sausage,
  cut into ½-inch slices
3 stalks celery, chopped
1 green pepper, chopped
6 leaves basil

1-2 tsp. oregano
Salt & pepper
Bay leaf
½ lb. mushrooms, sliced
28-oz. can tomatoes
13-oz. can tomato paste
1 chicken, boiled, removed from bones
  & chopped

Heat oil and fry garlic and onions until onions are limp. Add sausage and cook, stirring occasionally, until browned. Stir in celery, green pepper, basil, oregano, salt and pepper and bay leaf. Cook for 5 to 10 minutes. Add mushrooms and cook for 5 more minutes. Add tomatoes, tomato paste and chicken and mix well.

Lower heat to simmer, cover and cook for at least 1 hour, adding water if sauce becomes too thick. Serve over cooked pasta and top with Parmesan cheese.

Serves 8 to 10.

CUCUMBER CLAM SPAGHETTI SAUCE

4 Tbsp. olive oil
1 clove garlic, peeled
10-oz. can clams, with juice reserved
2 seedless cucumbers, sliced

1 tsp. salt
Pepper
1 Tbsp. chopped parsley

Heat oil and sauté garlic until browned, then discard. Drain clam juice into pan, stir in cucumbers, salt and pepper. Cook, uncovered, stirring occasionally, for about 15 minutes. Add clams and cook gently for 5 more minutes. Stir in parsley and cook 1 minute further. Serve over cooked spaghetti.

Serves 4.

— *Judith Goodwin*
Tamworth, Ontario

PASTA E PISELLI

THIS IS A SOUTHERN ITALIAN RECIPE FOR PASTA WITH PEAS, WHICH HAS BEEN IN THE contributor's family for four generations.

2 cloves garlic
⅓ cup olive oil
1 medium onion, sliced
1 lb. tomatoes, coarsely chopped
½ lb. fresh peas
½ tsp. oregano

Salt & pepper
Chili pepper flakes
1 lb. bite-sized pasta
2 eggs
½ cup Parmesan or Romano cheese
2 Tbsp. milk

Peel garlic and brown in oil in large skillet, then remove garlic and discard. Sauté onion in oil until tender. Add tomatoes, peas, oregano, salt and pepper and chili pepper. Cover and simmer slowly as pasta cooks.

Cook pasta in boiling, salted water. While pasta is cooking, beat eggs in bowl and mix in cheese and milk.

Drain cooked pasta and return to pot. Add vegetable mixture, then egg-cheese mixture and heat slowly, stirring constantly, until eggs are cooked.

Serves 6.

— *Anthony Balzano*
Piscataway, New Jersey

SPAGHETTI ALLA CARBONARA

1 lb. ham, cubed
2 Tbsp. butter
8 oz. spaghetti
¼ cup butter
1 Tbsp. flour

1 cup whipping cream
4 eggs, beaten
1 cup Parmesan cheese
Freshly ground pepper

Fry ham in 2 Tbsp. butter until crispy and set aside. Cook spaghetti in boiling, salted water.

While spaghetti is cooking, make sauce. Melt ¼ cup butter and stir in flour. Gradually blend in whipping cream and bring almost to a boil. Add eggs and ham and simmer for 2 minutes, stirring constantly. Add Parmesan cheese and pepper, pour over cooked, drained spaghetti and serve.

Serves 4.

— Fern Acton
Creston, British Columbia

LINGUINI WITH ZUCCHINI AL PESTO

2 small zucchini, cut into strips
2 Tbsp. butter
½ cup fresh basil
½ cup snipped parsley
3 cloves garlic, crushed
4 Tbsp. pine nuts, lightly roasted

Handful Parmesan cheese
1 cup olive oil
6 Tbsp. butter, softened
Salt & pepper
8 oz. linguini

Fry zucchini in oil until limp and golden. Whir in blender basil, parsley, garlic, pine nuts and Parmesan cheese, adding oil and butter a little at a time to keep the sauce thick.

Cook linguini until just tender. Combine linguini, zucchini and sauce. Add salt and pepper to taste.

Serves 4 to 6.

— Cary Elizabeth Marshall
Thunder Bay, Ontario

SPINACH LINGUINI WITH RED CLAM SAUCE

FRESH PASTA, EASILY MADE AT HOME AND INCREASINGLY AVAILABLE IN SPECIALTY stores, offers a flavour and texture that is incomparable to commercial dried noodles. The pasta becomes an integral part of the dish, not just the base for the sauce. Fresh pasta, with a cooking time of less than 5 minutes, is strongly recommended for this recipe.

2 Tbsp. olive oil
2 cloves garlic, minced
1 small onion, chopped
1 tsp. chopped fresh marjoram
1 tsp. chopped fresh basil
3 tomatoes, peeled & chopped

1 Tbsp. tomato paste
4 Tbsp. dry white wine
10-oz. can baby clams
½ lb. spinach linguini
Parmesan cheese

Heat olive oil in heavy pot and sauté garlic and onion for 5 minutes. Add marjoram and basil and sauté for 2 more minutes. Stir in tomatoes, tomato paste, wine and clams; cover and simmer for 20 minutes.

Cook linguini until just tender. Drain, rinse under hot water and serve immediately with clam sauce. Top with Parmesan cheese.

Serves 4.

— Jane Pugh
Toronto, Ontario

ZUCCHINI AND SPAGHETTI CASSEROLE

4 medium zucchini, sliced
1 large onion, chopped
4 tomatoes, peeled & chopped
½ cup butter

½ cup grated Parmesan cheese
Salt & pepper
1 lb. spaghetti, cooked
1 lb. mozzarella cheese, grated

Sauté vegetables in butter until tender. In casserole dish, toss with Parmesan cheese, salt and pepper and spaghetti. Top with mozzarella cheese.

Bake at 350 degrees F for 30 minutes, or until cheese is melted and bubbling.

Serves 6 to 8.

— *Glenda McCawder*
Okanagan Falls, British Columbia

MACARONI WITH SAUSAGE

1 lb. sausage meat
1 onion, finely chopped
1 clove garlic, chopped
¼ cup sliced mushrooms
1 Tbsp. butter
¼ tsp. savory
¼ tsp. celery seed
¼ tsp. oregano

¼ tsp. chili powder
¼ tsp. pepper
¼ tsp. dry mustard
6-oz. can tomato paste
¼ cup water
3 cups cooked macaroni
1 cup cottage cheese

Sauté sausage meat until lightly browned. Drain off fat, separate meat with fork and set aside. Sauté onion, garlic and mushrooms in butter. Add sausage meat, savory, celery seed, oregano, chili powder, pepper and dry mustard. Stir in tomato paste and water and mix well. Add macaroni and stir.

Arrange alternate layers of macaroni-meat mixture and cottage cheese in greased casserole dish, ending with meat on top. Bake at 350 degrees F for 25 to 30 minutes.

Serves 8.

— *Ruth Anne Laverty*
Listowel, Ontario

SAVOURY NOODLE BAKE

2 Tbsp. oil
4 Tbsp. butter
2 onions, finely chopped
1 clove garlic, minced
2 cups canned tomatoes
⅛ tsp. salt

Pepper
¼ tsp. oregano or basil
1 bay leaf
8 oz. egg noodles
3 cups grated Cheddar cheese

Combine oil and 2 Tbsp. butter, place over low heat and, when butter has melted, add onions and garlic. Cook over low heat until soft.

Combine tomatoes, salt and spices. Add to onion mixture; simmer for 15 minutes and discard bay leaf.

Cook noodles until tender; rinse with hot water and drain. Add remaining 2 Tbsp. butter and 2 cups cheese. Add tomato sauce. Turn mixture into greased baking dish and top with remaining 1 cup cheese.

Bake at 350 degrees F for 30 minutes.

— *Georgina Mitchell*
Bainsville, Ontario

KARIN'S RAVIOLI

Pasta:
5 cups flour
1½ tsp. salt
5 eggs
1 Tbsp. oil
1-1½ cups lukewarm water
Filling:
1 lb. ground beef
½ large onion, chopped
2 cloves garlic, chopped
2 pinches oregano
1 pinch basil
½ tsp. coriander
2 Tbsp. flour

Salt & pepper
1 tomato, peeled & chopped
½ cup grated hard cheese
Sauce:
28 oz. stewed tomatoes
1 clove garlic, chopped
½ large onion, chopped
½ green pepper, chopped
2 stalks celery, chopped
Salt & pepper
2 tsp. oregano
1 tsp. basil
1 tomato, peeled & chopped
½ lb. mushrooms, sliced

To make dough, combine flour and salt. Mix together eggs, oil and 1 cup water. Make a well in the middle of the flour mixture and pour in liquid. Stir and then knead by hand to make a firm but pliable dough, adding additional water or flour as necessary. Place in a lightly greased bowl, cover and set aside.

For filling, brown ground beef and drain off fat. Add onion and garlic and continue to cook until onion is limp. Add oregano, basil, coriander, flour, salt and pepper, tomato and cheese. Simmer for 1 to 2 hours, then cool.

Combine sauce ingredients in heavy pot and simmer for 1 to 2 hours.

When filling cools, roll out dough to ⅛-inch thickness and cut into 1½" x 3" rectangles. Place 1 tsp. of filling on each rectangle, fold over and pinch together edges. Cook in boiling, salted water until puffy. Place in simmering sauce and serve with Parmesan cheese.

Serves 6.

— Karin Mayes
Prince George, British Columbia

NEAPOLITAN LASAGNE

1 lb. ground beef
2 hot Italian sausages, out of casings
1 large onion, finely chopped
1 stalk celery, finely chopped
2 cloves garlic, minced
4 cups tomato purée
6-oz. can tomato paste
4 oz. dry red wine
1 tsp. marjoram
1 tsp. basil

Fresh parsley
½ tsp. cinnamon
Salt & pepper
2 eggs
2 cups cottage cheese
½ cup Parmesan cheese
½ lb. mozzarella cheese, thinly sliced
1 lb. spinach, cooked, drained & chopped
1 zucchini, thinly sliced
16 lasagne noodles, cooked

In heavy pot, cook beef, sausage meat, onion, celery and garlic until lightly browned. Stir in tomato purée and paste, then wine, marjoram, basil, parsley, cinnamon, salt and pepper. Simmer for 30 minutes. Meanwhile, combine eggs, cottage and Parmesan cheeses.

Place a little sauce on the bottom of greased 9" x 13" pan. Alternate layers as follows: noodles, cheese mixture, spinach and zucchini slices, mozzarella, meat sauce. Repeat. Bake at 375 degrees F for 30 minutes.

Serves 10 to 12.

— Valerie Marien
Orangeville, Ontario

LASAGNE HAM ROLL-UPS

8 lasagne noodles
8 thin slices ham
2 Tbsp. prepared mustard
1 cup grated Cheddar cheese
Salt & pepper

2 cups tomato or mushroom sauce
 (*Volume 1*, pages 204 & 92)
2 large tomatoes, sliced
Parsley sprigs

Cook noodles until tender. Drain, rinse and lay on sheet of greased foil. Lay slice of ham on each noodle, trimming to fit. Spread with mustard and sprinkle with cheese and seasonings. Roll up each noodle, enclosing the filling. Place in greased shallow baking dish. Pour sauce over top and arrange tomato slices over this. Bake at 375 degrees F for 30 minutes. Garnish with parsley and serve.

Serves 4.

— *Anne Budge*
Belfountain, Ontario

BAKED RIGATONI

16 oz. rigatoni noodles
3 Tbsp. butter
8 oz. mozzarella cheese, diced

4 cups spaghetti sauce
1 cup sliced mushrooms
¾ cup Parmesan cheese

Cook rigatoni in boiling, salted water and place in greased casserole dish. Add 2 Tbsp. butter, cheese, spaghetti sauce and mushrooms and mix well. Sprinkle with Parmesan cheese and dot with remaining butter. Bake at 350 degrees F for 20 to 30 minutes, or until heated through.

Serves 4 to 6.

— *Debbie Anne McCully*
Kingston, Ontario

LOKSHEN KUGEL

KUGEL IS A TRADITIONAL SABBATH DISH. THIS NOODLE PUDDING WAS PREPARED THE day before and slow cooked over a fire until the Sabbath, when fires could not be started. It can also be made as a sweet dish by the addition of raisins and cinnamon.

1 pkg. wide egg noodles
1 sleeve soda crackers
Salt & pepper
3-6 eggs

Cook noodles in boiling, salted water until tender. Drain but do not rinse. Crush crackers and add to noodles. Add salt and pepper to taste. Add eggs one at a time until creamy. Bake in greased, deep baking dish at 400 degrees F for 50 to 60 minutes or until golden brown.

Serves 6.

— *Lisa Mann*
Dundas, Ontario

Desserts

A wilderness of sweets.

– **John Milton**
Paradise Lost

CHOCOLATE AMARETTO CHEESECAKE

ALREADY A RICH DESSERT, THIS CHEESECAKE IS MADE EVEN MORE DELICIOUS BY THE addition of chocolate and amaretto. As cheesecakes are egg-based, it is very important to cook at a low temperature and to store in the refrigerator.

Crust:
1¼ cups chocolate wafer crumbs
  or 1 cup graham wafer crumbs
  & ¼ cup cocoa
2 Tbsp. sugar
¼ cup melted butter

Filling:
16 oz. cream cheese
½ cup sugar
2 large eggs

6 oz. semisweet chocolate,
  melted & cooled
½ tsp. almond extract
1 tsp. vanilla
⅓ cup amaretto
⅔ cup sour cream

Topping:
2 oz. semisweet chocolate
1 tsp. shortening

Combine crumbs, sugar and melted butter and press into bottom and halfway up sides of greased 8-inch springform pan. Chill while making filling.

Beat cream cheese until smooth. Beat in sugar gradually. Beat in eggs one at a time at low speed. Add cooled chocolate, flavourings, amaretto and sour cream. Beat at low speed until thoroughly blended then pour into prepared pan.

Bake at 300 degrees F for 1 hour. Turn off heat and leave cake in oven for 1 hour longer. Cool in pan at room temperature, then chill for at least 24 hours in refrigerator.

For topping, melt chocolate with shortening and spread over top of cake.

Serves 8.

— *Vanessa Lewington*
Timmins, Ontario

FROZEN BLUEBERRY RIPPLE CHEESECAKE

1 cup sugar
⅓ cup water
⅛ tsp. cream of tartar
3 egg whites
16 oz. cream cheese
½ cup sour cream

2 tsp. vanilla
1 Tbsp. grated lemon rind
½-1 cup blueberry preserves
  or blueberry jam
Whipped cream
Blueberries

Combine sugar, water and cream of tartar in a small saucepan and bring to a boil. Boil rapidly until syrup registers 236 degrees F on a candy thermometer — 5 to 9 minutes.

Meanwhile in large bowl of electric mixer, beat egg whites until stiff. Pour hot syrup in a thin stream over egg whites while beating constantly. Continue beating until very stiff peaks form and mixture cools — 10 to 15 minutes.

Beat cream cheese, sour cream, vanilla and rind until light and fluffy. Gently fold meringue into cheese mixture until well blended.

Spoon one-quarter of blended mixture into a decorative serving dish or bowl and drizzle blueberry preserves over this. Continue to layer in this manner, then run knife through completed layering to give a swirl effect. Freeze overnight or until firm. Decorate with whipped cream and berries and serve.

Serves 12.

— *Joann Alho*
Rosseau, Ontario

CHOCOLATE MOUSSE TORTE

THIS DESSERT IS SO RICH THAT IT WILL EASILY SERVE 12 CHOCOLATE-LOVING PEOPLE.

Butter
Fine bread crumbs
6 oz. unsweetened chocolate
2 oz. semisweet chocolate
1 Tbsp. dry instant coffee
¼ cup boiling water

8 eggs, separated
⅔ cup sugar
1 tsp. vanilla
⅛ tsp. salt
1 cup whipping cream, whipped

Butter a 9-inch pie plate and dust with bread crumbs. Place chocolate in top of double boiler over hot water. Dissolve coffee in boiling water and stir into chocolate. Cover and melt over low heat, stirring occasionally. Cool slightly.

Beat egg yolks for 5 minutes or until pale and thickened. Gradually add sugar, beating on high for another 5 minutes. Add vanilla and chocolate mixture. Beat slowly until smooth.

Add salt to egg whites and whip until whites hold shape but are not stiff. Fold half the egg whites into chocolate mixture in three additions, then fold chocolate into remaining whites. Remove 3½ cups of mousse, cover and refrigerate.

Line pie plate with remaining mousse and bake at 350 degrees F for 25 minutes. Turn oven off, but leave torte there for 5 more minutes. Remove and cool completely. Place chilled mousse in baked shell and refrigerate for at least 2 to 3 hours. Top with whipped cream and serve.

Serves 12.

— Brenda Kennedy
Armstrong, British Columbia

DOBOSH TORTE

Cake:
2 cups flour
1 tsp. baking powder
1 tsp. nutmeg
½ tsp. salt
5 eggs
1 cup butter
1 cup sugar
2 tsp. grated lemon rind
1 tsp. vanilla

Icing:
6 oz. chocolate chips
¼ cup hot, strong coffee
¼ cup icing sugar
½ cup soft butter
4 egg yolks
2 Tbsp. rum

Sift together flour, baking powder, nutmeg and salt. Beat eggs until very thick and lemon coloured — 8 to 10 minutes. Cream butter until light, then gradually add sugar. Add eggs, lemon rind and vanilla and mix thoroughly. Add dry ingredients and mix well.

Pour into buttered loaf pan lined with wax paper and bake at 300 degrees F for 1½ hours. Cool thoroughly.

Meanwhile, make icing. Place chocolate in blender at high speed for 6 seconds. Add coffee and blend for another 6 seconds. Add sugar, butter, egg yolks and rum and blend for a final 15 seconds.

Carefully slice cooled cake horizontally into 4 layers. Spread each layer with icing and reassemble. Top with icing.

Serves 10.

— Kitty Pope
Yellowknife, Northwest Territories

ALSATIAN TORTE WITH BERRY FILLING

Base:
1½ cups flour
¼ cup sugar
½ cup butter
1½ tsp. baking powder
1 egg
1 tsp. vanilla

Filling:
3-4 cups blueberries or strawberries
Grated rind of 1 lemon or lime
2 Tbsp. sugar

Custard:
2 cups sour cream
2 egg yolks
¼ cup sugar
2 Tbsp. lemon or lime juice

Combine the ingredients for base in a bowl. Combine well, mixing by hand, and pat evenly in the bottom of a greased, 12-inch springform pan.

Lightly mix berries, rind and sugar and sprinkle evenly over dough. Whisk together custard ingredients and pour evenly over berries.

Bake at 350 degrees F for 1 hour or until firm and golden brown on top. Cool before serving.

Serves 8 to 10.

— Janice Graham
London, Ontario

BAKEWELL TART

Pastry for 9-inch pie shell
2 Tbsp. jam
⅓ cup butter
½ cup sugar
½ cup rice flour

¼ cup ground almonds
1 egg, beaten
Almond extract
Blanched almonds

Line pie plate with pastry and spread with jam. Cream butter and sugar. Add rice flour and ground almonds alternately with beaten egg. Add a few drops of almond extract.

Spread mixture over jam and decorate with a lattice of pastry strips and blanched almonds. Bake at 375 degrees F for 40 to 45 minutes.

— Sue Davies
Golden, British Columbia

RASPBERRY YOGURT CUSTARD TART

Shell:
¾ cup unbleached flour
¾ cup whole wheat flour
¾ cup butter
2 Tbsp. sugar
1 Tbsp. vinegar

Filling:
1 cup sugar
½ cup flour
3 eggs
2 cups yogurt
3½ cups raspberries

Combine shell ingredients until crumbly. Press onto bottom and sides of 10-inch springform pan.

For filling, mix sugar and flour. Stir in eggs and yogurt until well blended. Fold in 3 cups raspberries until blended. Pour into shell and bake at 375 degrees F for 50 minutes. Cool completely and remove from pan. Top with remaining ½ cup raspberries.

— Billie Sheffield
North Gower, Ontario

GRASSHOPPER PIE

Crust:
1¼ cups finely crushed
 chocolate wafers
¼ cup sugar
3 Tbsp. melted butter

Filling:
1½ tsp. gelatin
6 Tbsp. cold water
¼ cup sugar

1 egg yolk, slightly beaten
⅓ cup crème de menthe
¼ cup white crème de cacao
1 cup whipping cream

Topping:
1 cup whipping cream
2 Tbsp. sugar
1 square semisweet chocolate, shaved

Combine crust ingredients and press into bottom and sides of well-buttered 9-inch pie plate. Bake at 450 degrees F for 2 to 3 minutes and cool.

To make filling, sprinkle gelatin over cold water in small saucepan. Place over low heat and stir until dissolved. Combine sugar and egg yolk in a bowl and add gelatin and liqueurs. Chill until the consistency of unbeaten egg whites. Whip cream and fold into gelatin mix. Pour into crust and chill for 3 to 4 hours.

For topping, whip cream and sugar. Spoon onto pie and top with shaved chocolate.

— Kirsten McDougall
Kamloops, British Columbia

RASPBERRY BLUEBERRY PIE

Pastry for double 9-inch pie shell
1½ cups raspberries
2 cups blueberries
⅔ cup sugar

2 Tbsp. instant tapioca
½ tsp. grated lemon rind
2 Tbsp. lemon juice
2 Tbsp. butter

Lightly toss together berries, sugar, tapioca, lemon rind and lemon juice. Place in pastry-lined pie shell and dot with butter. Cover with top crust, flute edges and cut vents. Bake at 425 degrees F for 15 minutes, reduce heat to 350 degrees and bake for 30 more minutes.

— Valerie Gillis
Renfrew, Ontario

CREAMY CHOCOLATE RUM PIE

Pastry for 9-inch pie shell
1 oz. unsweetened chocolate
1 Tbsp. butter
2 eggs
1 cup sugar
½ cup maple syrup
½ tsp. vanilla

½ cup pecan halves
3 egg yolks
½ cup cold water
1 Tbsp. gelatin
⅓ cup dark rum
1½ cups whipping cream
Chocolate curls

Combine chocolate and butter in a small saucepan and set over low heat until melted.

Beat eggs, ⅓ cup sugar, syrup, chocolate mixture and vanilla together until blended. Stir in pecans and pour into pastry-lined pie plate. Bake at 375 degrees F until filling is set and pastry browned — 15 to 20 minutes. Cool.

Beat egg yolks until foamy. Gradually beat in remaining ⅔ cup sugar. Combine cold water and gelatin in a saucepan. Let stand for 5 minutes, then heat, stirring, just to boiling point. Gradually beat into egg yolk mixture and stir in rum. Set bowl aside in ice water to cool, then chill until it begins to hold its shape when dropped from a spoon. Whip cream until stiff and fold into gelatin mixture. Place in ice water and chill until mixture holds peaks. Spoon over cooled chocolate mixture in pie shell. Garnish with chocolate curls and chill until shortly before serving time.

— Marian da Costa
Islington, Ontario

ALMOND LEMON TART

Base:
3 eggs, separated
¾ cup sugar
Grated peel of 1 lemon
1 cup finely ground almonds
1 Tbsp. flour
Salt

Topping:
3 lemons
2 egg whites
¼ cup sugar
¾ cup finely ground almonds

To make base, beat egg yolks until pale yellow. Beat in sugar, then stir in lemon peel, almonds, flour and salt. Beat egg whites until stiff and fold into batter. Butter a 10-inch springform pan, pour in batter and bake at 350 degrees F for 30 minutes, or until light brown and pulling away from sides of pan.

Meanwhile, make topping. Peel lemons and separate them into segments, removing pith. Beat egg whites, adding sugar 1 Tbsp. at a time. Fold in ground almonds.

Cover base of cake with lemon segments and spread almond mixture over top. Return to oven for another 15 minutes to brown.

— Lucetta Grace
Toronto, Ontario

ORANGE CHIFFON PIE

Pastry for 9-inch pie shell
3 Tbsp. flour
⅓ cup sugar
Salt
3 eggs, separated
2 Tbsp. lemon juice
1 cup orange juice
½ tsp. vanilla
1 Tbsp. butter
3 Tbsp. cream
Sesame seeds

Line pie plate with pastry and bake at 325 degrees F for 20 minutes, or until golden. In top of double boiler, combine flour, sugar, salt, egg yolks, lemon juice and orange juice. Cook, stirring, over boiling water until very thick. Remove from heat and stir in vanilla, butter and cream. Cover pan and set in cold water. Beat egg whites until stiff and fold into orange mixture. Pour into pie shell and garnish with sesame seeds. Bake at 400 degrees F for 10 minutes. Cool before serving.

— Lisa Calzonetti
Elora, Ontario

GERRI'S BANANA CREAM PIE

Pastry for 10-inch pie shell
¾ cup sugar
¼ cup cornstarch
½ tsp. salt
1 Tbsp. gelatin
4 egg yolks
3 cups milk
2 Tbsp. butter
1 tsp. vanilla
1 cup whipping cream
4 medium bananas, thinly sliced
Lemon juice

Line pie plate with pastry and bake at 325 degrees F for 20 minutes, or until done. Combine sugar, cornstarch, salt and gelatin. Beat in egg yolks and milk until very smooth. Cook mixture over low heat until thickened — 15 minutes — stirring constantly. Stir in butter and vanilla. Cover and chill.

Whip cream. Reserving some banana for garnish, fold cream and bananas into custard and spoon into pie crust. Chill.

Dip remaining banana slices into lemon juice and garnish top of pie.

— Eila Koivu
Thunder Bay, Ontario

Baked Trout with Almond Cream, 125

Assorted Cookies, pages 273-280

Spinach and Fruit Salad with Piquant Dressing, page 57

Sesame Yogurt Chicken, page 147

Crunchy Broccoli, page 79

From top right, *Nanaimo Bars, page 281, Cape House Inn Iced Buttermilk with Shrimp Soup, page 48, Devilled Eggs, page 24, Almond & Mushroom Pâté, page 76, Artichoke Salad, page 52, Watermelon Boat Salad, page 59*

BLACK BOTTOM EGGNOG PIE

Pastry for 9-inch pie shell
1 Tbsp. gelatin
⅓ cup cold water
4 tsp. cornstarch
1⅓ cups light cream
4 egg yolks, beaten
¼ cup honey
¾ Tbsp. dark rum

¼ cup carob powder
2 Tbsp. oil
1 tsp. vanilla
3 egg whites
Salt
1 Tbsp. liquid honey
1 cup whipping cream, whipped

Line pie plate with pastry and bake at 325 degrees F for 20 minutes or until golden. Cool.

Sprinkle gelatin over cold water to soften. In top of double boiler, dissolve cornstarch in light cream. Add beaten egg yolks and ¼ cup honey. Cook over boiling water, stirring constantly, until custard begins to thicken. Remove from heat, remove 1 cup custard and set aside.

Stir gelatin into remaining hot custard to dissolve completely. Add rum and set aside to cool, then refrigerate until nearly set.

Combine carob and oil and dissolve in reserved 1 cup custard. Add vanilla and pour into pie shell.

Beat egg whites and salt, adding honey gradually to make a stiff meringue. Fold meringue carefully into chilled custard. Pile on top of carob mixture, refrigerate for 1 hour, then top with whipped cream.

— Anne-Marie Dupuis
Harcourt, New Brunswick

MAI TAI PIE

THIS DISH IS SO NAMED BECAUSE IT CONTAINS MANY OF THE SAME INGREDIENTS AS THE Mai Tai drink — pineapple juice, rum and orange liqueur. Curaçao, the generic name for orange liqueurs, has been produced by the Dutch since the 16th century using the dried peel of green oranges from the West Indian island of Curaçao. It is now made in a number of different ways and marketed under several names — Grand Marnier, Triple Sec and Cointreau to name a few.

Crust:
1 cup coconut
6 Tbsp. butter, melted

Filling:
1 envelope gelatin
½ cup sugar

4 eggs, separated
¾ cup pineapple juice
¼ cup lime juice
⅓ cup light rum
2 Tbsp. orange liqueur
½ cup whipped cream

Combine coconut and butter and press into 9-inch pie plate. Bake at 300 degrees F for 25 minutes.

Blend gelatin with ¼ cup sugar, then beat in egg yolks until well blended. Gradually blend in pineapple juice. Cook until slightly thickened, remove from heat and stir in lime juice, rum and liqueur. Chill, stirring often, until thickened.

Beat egg whites, slowly adding remaining ¼ cup sugar. Fold into gelatin mixture along with whipped cream, then spoon into cooled pie shell. Chill for at least 3 hours.

— Anna J. Lee
Sault Ste. Marie, Ontario

MAPLE SYRUP BABA

1 tsp. sugar
½ cup warm water
1 Tbsp. yeast
1½ cups flour
½ cup butter
¼ cup sugar

4 eggs, beaten
½ tsp. salt
1½ cups maple syrup
⅓ cup water
1 Tbsp. rum
Whipped cream

Dissolve sugar in warm water, sprinkle with yeast and let stand for 10 minutes. Stir well. Beat in ½ cup flour. Cover and let rise until double in bulk — about 30 minutes.

Cream butter and sugar. Beat in eggs alternately with remaining flour and salt until batter is smooth. Beat in yeast mixture. Turn into greased 8-inch tube pan. Cover and let rise until doubled in bulk — ½ to 1 hour.

Bake at 350 degrees F until nicely browned. Cool in pan, then turn onto plate. Bring syrup, water and rum just to a boil. Prick baba all over with skewer and pour syrup over. Continue basting until baba is well soaked. Serve with whipped cream.

Serves 10.

— Renée Porter
Brockville, Ontario

DANISH RICE DISH

THIS DISH IS TRADITIONALLY SERVED AS PART OF A DANISH CHRISTMAS DINNER.

¾ cup brown rice
4 cups milk
2 tsp. vanilla
2 tsp. almond extract

1½ Tbsp. sugar
1 cup whipping cream
1 cup ground almonds
2 cups raspberries

Cook rice in milk over low heat until tender — this will take a long time. Cool. Add vanilla, almond extract and sugar. Blend well. Whip cream and fold into mixture along with almonds. Refrigerate.

When ready to serve, warm raspberries and serve on top of pudding.

Serves 8.

— G.L. Jackson
Geraldton, Ontario

ORANGE BLOSSOM PUDDING

2 Tbsp. gelatin
2 cups sugar
¼ tsp. salt
2½ cups orange juice
4 egg yolks, beaten

1 Tbsp. grated orange peel
3 Tbsp. lemon juice
1 cup orange sections
2 cups whipping cream

Combine gelatin, sugar and salt. Stir 1 cup orange juice into egg yolks and then stir into gelatin mixture.

Bring to a boil over medium heat, stirring constantly. Remove from heat and stir in orange peel, remaining orange juice and lemon juice.

Chill, stirring occasionally, until mixture falls from spoon in lumps. Stir in orange sections. Whip cream until stiff and fold in.

Pour into 1-quart mould and chill until set.

Serves 10.

— Beth Killing
Midland, Ontario

BURNT ALMOND SPONGE

THIS IS DEFINITELY A DESSERT FOR A SPECIAL OCCASION. THE WONDERFUL TASTE makes the work worthwhile.

½-¾ cup chopped almonds
1 Tbsp. gelatin
1¼ cups milk
1¼ cups sugar

½ tsp. salt
1 cup whipping cream
1 tsp. vanilla
1 Tbsp. sherry (optional)

Toast almonds and set aside 1 Tbsp. for garnish. Sprinkle gelatin in ¼ cup cold water, then warm to dissolve.

Scald milk. Caramelize sugar in heavy saucepan, being careful not to burn it. Remove pan from heat when all the sugar is liquid.

Add milk to caramelized sugar a little at a time. The mixture will boil up each time. Stir constantly as milk is being added. Add salt and gelatin.

Refrigerate mixture and chill until partially set — the consistency of egg whites. Beat until spongy. Without washing beaters, whip cream until stiff, adding vanilla and sherry. Fold into spongy mixture along with almonds. Spoon into serving bowl and sprinkle with reserved almonds. Chill until set.

Serves 6 to 8.

— *Megan Sproule*
Bath, Ontario

RICH RICOTTA CUSTARD

1 cup ricotta cheese
3 egg yolks
1 cup milk

⅓ cup sugar
1 Tbsp. rum
Grating of orange rind

Beat together cheese, egg yolks, milk and sugar. Add rum and orange rind to flavour.

Bake at 325 degrees F until set — about 45 minutes.

Serves 4 to 6.

— *Elizabeth Templeman*
Heffley Lake, British Columbia

MANDARIN MOUSSE

2 10-oz. cans mandarin orange sections,
  well drained
2 Tbsp. lemon juice
2 Tbsp. orange liqueur
1 tsp. vanilla

¼ cup cold water
1 envelope gelatin
½ cup sugar
2 cups whipping cream

Purée mandarins until smooth. Turn into large bowl and add the lemon juice, liqueur and vanilla. Pour water into measuring cup and add gelatin to soften. Turn into saucepan and heat, stirring constantly, over medium heat until mixture becomes almost clear — approximately 2 minutes. Add sugar and stir until dissolved.

Stir into fruit mixture and cool to room temperature. Whip cream until it will hold soft peaks. Stir in quarter of mixture, then fold in remaining cream. Turn into dessert dishes and chill until set, approximately 2 hours.

Serves 6.

— *Judy Black*
St. Andrews, New Brunswick

DANISH RUM SOUFFLE

3 eggs, separated
1 egg yolk
1 cup sugar
¼ cup rum

1 envelope gelatin
¼ cup cold water
1 cup whipping cream
Unsweetened chocolate

Beat egg yolks and ½ cup sugar until light lemon colour. Add rum. Dissolve gelatin in water and heat over boiling water. Stir into yolk mixture. Beat cream until stiff.

In another bowl, beat egg whites until stiff but still moist. Add remaining ½ cup sugar gradually. Fold cream into yolk mixture then fold in whites. Pour into serving dish and chill for 4 to 6 hours. Serve with curls of unsweetened chocolate sprinkled on top.

Serves 4 to 6.

— *Ruth Burnham*
Stirling, Ontario

LEMON SNOW PUDDING WITH CUSTARD SAUCE

4 Tbsp. cornstarch
1 cup sugar
Salt
½ cup cold water
1¾ cups hot water
4 Tbsp. lemon juice
2 tsp. grated lemon peel
2 egg whites

Custard Sauce:

2 egg yolks
1 tsp. cornstarch
2 Tbsp. sugar
Salt
¾ cup milk

Mix cornstarch, sugar and salt in saucepan. Add cold water, mix until smooth and then add hot water. Stir over medium heat until thickened.

Remove from heat and add lemon juice and peel. Fold into stiffly beaten egg whites and chill.

To make custard sauce, combine all ingredients and heat slowly, until mixture coats spoon. Chill. Serve over pudding.

Serves 6 to 8.

— *Patricia E. Wilson*
Belleville, Ontario

BLINTZ SOUFFLE

Batter:
½ cup butter
1 cup sugar
6 eggs
1½ cups sour cream
½ cup orange juice
1¼ cups flour
2 tsp. baking powder
½ tsp. baking soda

Filling:
8 oz. cream cheese, softened
16 oz. small curd cottage cheese
2 egg yolks
1 Tbsp. sugar
1 tsp. vanilla

Cream butter and sugar together. Add remaining batter ingredients and mix well. Pour half of the batter into a greased 9" x 13" pan.

Combine filling ingredients and mix well. Pour over batter and spread. Pour remaining half of batter on top. Bake at 350 degrees F for 50 to 60 minutes.

Serves 8.

— *Nancy Chesworth Weir*
Kensington, Maryland

GRAND MARNIER MOUSSE

1 cup sugar
1 envelope gelatin
6-oz. can orange juice
  concentrate, thawed

5 egg yolks
3 Tbsp. Grand Marnier
8 egg whites
1 cup whipping cream

Mix ½ cup sugar with gelatin in heavy pot. Add orange juice concentrate and heat over medium-low heat until warm, stirring often.

Beat yolks until blended and stir in about ¼ cup hot orange mixture. Slowly add this mixture to pot, stirring constantly. Continue to cook and stir over medium-low heat until thickened − 5 to 10 minutes. Add Grand Marnier. Remove from heat and cover with wax paper. Let cool at room temperature.

Beat egg whites in large bowl. Gradually add remaining ½ cup sugar and continue beating until it will hold soft peaks. Whip cream until it will hold soft peaks. Fold orange mixture into whipping cream, then into egg whites. Refrigerate until firm or freeze for 2 hours, then store in refrigerator.

Serves 6 to 8.

— Heather Petrie
Pitt Meadows, British Columbia

PINA COLADA CUSTARD

IF AVAILABLE, 2 CUPS FRESH PINEAPPLE COULD BE SUBSTITUTED FOR THE CANNED pineapple indicated in the recipe.

3 eggs
¼ cup honey
Salt
2 cups scalded milk

½ cup grated coconut
1 tsp. vanilla extract or 1 Tbsp. rum
14-oz. can unsweetened pineapple
Toasted pecans

Place eggs in heavy pot and whisk to just blend. Add honey and a pinch of salt and slowly pour in the hot milk, stirring constantly. Add coconut and cook over medium heat until thickened − about 10 minutes. Stir in vanilla or rum.

To serve, place pineapple in bottoms of bowls and ladle on custard. Sprinkle with pecans.

Serves 4.

— Bertha B. Bumchuckles
Thunder Bay, Ontario

PAVLOVA AND YOGURT CHANTILLY

2 egg whites
1 tsp. white wine vinegar
3 Tbsp. hot water
1 cup sugar
1 tsp. cornstarch

1 tsp. vanilla
⅔ cup whipping cream
⅔ cup unflavoured yogurt
2 Tbsp. confectioners' sugar
2 kiwi fruit, peeled and sliced

Combine egg whites, vinegar, water, sugar, cornstarch and ½ tsp. vanilla in large bowl and beat until mixture holds a firm peak. Mark an 8-inch circle on a piece of foil on a cookie sheet. Heap the meringue onto the foil and spread it evenly within the circle. Bake at 250 degrees F for 1½ hours. When cool, transfer to a serving plate.

Whip the cream until stiff. Fold in yogurt, sugar and remaining ½ tsp. vanilla. Chill well. Just before serving, pile the whipped cream mixture onto the meringue and top with sliced fruit.

Serves 6 to 8.

— Sylvia Petz
Willowdale, Ontario

CREAMY AMBROSIA

THIS RECIPE RESULTS IN A RICH, CREAMY ICE CREAM THAT, ONCE TASTED, WILL destroy the appeal of all commercial products. The flavouring can be varied to include other liqueurs and/or fruits. Some particularly tasty combinations are raspberry liqueur and raspberries, Tia Maria and peach, amaretto and slivered almonds — anything that appeals. The ice cream can be removed from the mould and garnished with fruit if desired.

¾ cup sugar
3 eggs
3 egg yolks
2 Tbsp. amaretto liqueur
2 cups whipping cream

Combine sugar, eggs and yolks in top of double boiler. Heat slowly over hot water until just warm, stirring constantly — about 10 minutes.

Place in large bowl and beat on high speed until thickened and somewhat stiff — 15 minutes. Beat in liqueur. (If using fruit, add most at this point, saving a few pieces to stir in by hand at the end.)

Whip cream until soft peaks form. Fold gently but thoroughly into egg mixture. Place in freezer container and freeze for at least 6 hours.

Serves 6.

MARBLE GELATIN

THIS LIGHT, NUTRITIOUS DESSERT MAY ALSO BE SERVED AS A REFRESHING SUMMER SNACK if poured into popsicle moulds and frozen.

3 Tbsp. gelatin
1 cup cold apple juice
2 cups hot puréed zucchini
½ cup maple syrup

Salt
½ cup mashed strawberries
Whipped cream

Soften gelatin in cold fruit juice, then add hot puréed zucchini, maple syrup and salt. Stir until dissolved, then add mashed strawberries in a swirl for desired marble effect. Refrigerate until firm. Dot with whipped cream and serve.

Serves 6 to 8.

— *Anne-Marie Dupuis*
Harcourt, New Brunswick

PRIMAVERA SHERBET

2 bananas
2 eggs, separated
2 cups sugar
¾ cup orange juice

¼ cup lemon juice
1 cup unsweetened pineapple juice
1 cup unsweetened grapefruit juice

Mash bananas, then add egg yolks and sugar and mix thoroughly. Beat egg whites until stiff and mix gently into banana mixture. Add fruit juices and combine. Pour into refrigerator trays and freeze until beginning to set. Put mixture back into bowl and beat again. Return to trays and freeze until set.

Serves 8 to 10.

— *Elma MacLachlan*
Kingston, Ontario

MELISSA'S ORANGE SHERBET

½ envelope gelatin
¼ cup orange juice
⅓ cup honey
1 cup whipping cream
¾ cup & 2 Tbsp. orange juice

Heat gelatin and orange juice over low heat until gelatin dissolves — about 5 minutes — stirring constantly.

Mix remaining ingredients and add to gelatin mixture. Freeze in pie plate until firm. Beat with mixer or in blender until smooth, then refreeze in covered container.

Serves 4.

— Linda Townsend
Nanoose Bay, British Columbia

STRAWBERRY SORBET

½ cup water
½ cup honey
4 cups strawberry purée
1 Tbsp. lemon juice

Heat together water and honey until just mixed. Let cool. Add remaining ingredients and mix well.

Freeze in large pan until edges are solid but middle is still mushy. Cut up and blend until smooth and opaque.

Pour into serving bowl and freeze until firm. Remove from freezer and let sit for 10 minutes before serving.

Serves 4 to 6.

— Linda Townsend
Nanoose Bay, British Columbia

KIWI SHERBET

INVENTED AT CHRISTMASTIME, WHEN KIWI ARE VERY CHEAP, THIS IS A LIGHT, FRUITY dessert, the perfect end to a heavy meal.

1 envelope gelatin
½ cup cold water
½ cup boiling water
Juice of 1 lemon
1 cup milk
1 cup sugar
7 kiwi fruit
¼ cup white rum

Soften gelatin in cold water. After 20 minutes, add boiling water and whisk to dissolve. Add lemon juice, milk and sugar. Mash 3 peeled kiwi and add to mixture. Add about ¼ cup white rum and place sherbet in freezer in a shallow pan or metal bowl.

Rewhisk when it forms crystals — at least twice. Do not let it freeze hard — keep breaking up the crystals. Allow about 4 hours for freezing. Just before serving, slice 1 kiwi into each of 4 individual serving dishes, placing slices in bottom and up sides. Add sherbet and top with a kiwi slice.

Serves 4.

— Randi Kennedy
Stella, Ontario

FROZEN TORTONIES

1 egg white
4 Tbsp. sugar
1 cup whipping cream
2 tsp. vanilla

½ cup semisweet chocolate chips
1 tsp. shortening
¼ cup chopped nuts

Beat egg white until stiff. Gradually add 2 Tbsp. sugar and beat until satiny. Whip cream, add remaining 2 Tbsp. sugar and vanilla. Fold cream mixture into egg white mixture, pour into freezing tray and chill well.

Melt chips and shortening in double boiler over hot water and fold in nuts. Drizzle chocolate mixture over cream mixture. Fold gently and freeze. Allow to soften slightly before serving.

Serves 4.

— André-Gilles Chartrand
Aylmer, Quebec

FROZEN ORANGE SOUFFLE

THIS DESSERT WILL LOOK BEAUTIFUL IF ORANGE SHELLS ARE USED AS THE SERVING dishes. Cut off the top quarter of each orange, remove fruit, dry well and fill.

3 egg yolks
¾ cup icing sugar
2 tsp. grated orange peel

¼ cup fresh orange juice
¾ tsp. orange liqueur
1 cup whipping cream, whipped

Beat egg yolks and sugar until smooth — about 1 minute. Stir in orange peel, juice and liqueur. Fold in whipped cream. Pour about ¾ cup of the soufflé mixture into each serving dish. Freeze until firm — 4 to 6 hours.

Serves 6.

— Pam Collacott
North Gower, Ontario

APFELSTRUDEL

1 Tbsp. oil
1 egg
⅓ cup warm water
¼ tsp. salt
1½ cups flour
⅓ cup melted butter
6 Tbsp. fine dry bread crumbs
8 cups thinly sliced, peeled apples

3 Tbsp. sugar
½ tsp. cinnamon
2 Tbsp. dark rum
½ tsp. nutmeg
½ cup seedless raisins
Icing sugar
Whipped cream

Beat together oil, egg, water and salt. Add flour while beating, until a firm dough is formed which pulls away from the bowl. Knead until smooth and elastic. Cover and allow to rest for 30 minutes, then cut into 2 equal portions. Roll out each piece on a floured surface to 12″ x 18″ rectangle. Brush each with melted butter and sprinkle bread crumbs evenly over the surface. Spread apples down centre of each portion lengthwise. Mix sugar, cinnamon, rum, nutmeg and raisins together, divide in half and sprinkle each portion with the mixture. Fold the dough over the filling, first one side, then the other. Slide rolls onto greased baking sheet and brush each with melted butter. Bake at 400 degrees F for 45 minutes. Slice rolls when warm and serve warm or cold, sprinkled with icing sugar and topped with whipped cream.

Serves 8.

— Margaret & Christopher Babcock
Kemble, Ontario

MONGO'S PUMPKIN ROLL

¾ cup flour
2 tsp. cinnamon
1 tsp. baking powder
1 tsp. ginger
½ tsp. salt
½ tsp. nutmeg

3 eggs
1 cup sugar
⅔ cup cooked, mashed pumpkin
Icing sugar
4 cups vanilla ice cream, softened

Mix together flour, cinnamon, baking powder, ginger, salt and nutmeg and set aside. Beat eggs until thick, about 5 minutes, then gradually beat in sugar. Mix in pumpkin and flour mixture.

Line a 10" x 15" jelly roll pan with greased wax paper. Spread batter in pan and bake at 375 degrees F for 15 minutes, or until top springs back when touched. Turn cake onto towel sprinkled with icing sugar. Remove paper and roll cake end to end. Cool.

Unroll cake, spread with ice cream and reroll. Wrap and freeze. Let stand at room temperature for 10 to 15 minutes before serving.

Serves 8.

— Kathy Major
Cherhill, Alberta

PEACH SOUFFLE

3 eggs, well beaten
½ cup milk
½ cup whole wheat pastry flour
½ tsp. salt
2 Tbsp. butter, melted

1 Tbsp. lemon juice
2 cups peaches, peeled & sliced
3 Tbsp. sugar
Sour cream
Cinnamon

Beat eggs, milk, flour and salt until smooth. Melt butter in 9-inch pie plate and pour in batter. Bake at 450 degrees F on lower shelf of oven for 15 minutes, pricking several times to collapse some of the puffiness. Reduce to 350 degrees and continue baking for another 10 minutes or until golden brown on top.

Remove from pan and drizzle with lemon juice. Spoon sweetened fruit over the top and garnish with sour cream and cinnamon.

Serves 6.

— Lisa Calzonetti
Elora, Ontario

PEACH CREAM KUCHEN

2 cups flour
¾ cup sugar
¼ tsp. baking powder
1 tsp. salt
½ cup butter

6 large peaches, peeled &
 thinly sliced
1 tsp. cinnamon
2 egg yolks, beaten
1 cup sour cream

Sift together flour, ¼ cup sugar, baking powder and salt. Cut in butter until mixture resembles fine crumbs.

Press firmly against bottom and sides of greased, 9-inch springform pan. Arrange peaches evenly over crumbs. Combine remaining sugar and cinnamon and sprinkle over peaches.

Bake at 400 degrees F for 15 minutes. Blend egg yolks and sour cream and spoon over peaches. Bake for another 20 minutes or until golden.

Serves 8.

— Midge Denault
Lee Valley, Ontario

PLUM KUCHEN

5 large or 10 small plums
½ cup sugar
¼ cup butter
2 eggs
1 cup flour
1½ tsp. baking powder

½ tsp. salt
¼ cup milk
3 Tbsp. butter
1 tsp. cinnamon
¼ tsp. nutmeg
Apricot or currant jelly

Cut plums into halves or quarters, depending on size. Place ¼ cup sugar, butter, eggs, flour, baking powder, salt and milk in large bowl. Beat at low speed until mixture leaves sides of bowl, scraping bowl constantly. Spread dough in lightly greased, 9″ x 13″ baking pan. Arrange plums, skin side up and overlapping, on top of crust.

Melt butter, stir in remaining ¼ cup sugar, cinnamon and nutmeg and spoon over plums. Bake at 375 degrees F for 30 to 35 minutes. While still hot, brush with melted jelly.

Serves 8.

— Elsie Marshall
Mississauga, Ontario

ICELANDIC VINARTERTA

THIS IS A TRADITIONAL ICELANDIC RECIPE. THE COOKIELIKE LAYERS OF CAKE ARE stacked with a prune filling spread between them.

Cake:
3½ cups flour
1 tsp. cardamom
2¼ tsp. baking powder
1 cup unsalted butter
1 cup sugar

1 tsp. vanilla
3 eggs
Filling:
2 lbs. extra large prunes
1 tsp. cinnamon
1 tsp. almond extract

Combine and sift flour, cardamom and baking powder. Cream butter and sugar until light. Add vanilla, then eggs one at a time, beating well after each addition. Add dry ingredients, half a cup at a time, to make a medium stiff dough.

Divide dough into 5 equal parts. Form each into a round ball, flatten evenly on a floured board and carefully roll into a circle. Place each in a greased, 9-inch cake pan. Bake two at a time at 375 degrees F on separate racks for 6 minutes. Cool.

For filling, cook prunes until tender. Remove pits and add cinnamon and almond extract. Mix well and chill. Spread between layers of cake, building evenly, and refrigerate overnight.

Serves 6 to 8.

— Mrs. N.E. Udy
Abbotsford, British Columbia

HOT FUDGE CAKE

1 cup flour
2 tsp. baking powder
¼ tsp. salt
¾ cup sugar
5 Tbsp. cocoa

½ cup milk
2 Tbsp. melted butter
1 cup brown sugar
2 cups boiling water

Sift together flour, baking powder, salt, sugar and 1 Tbsp. cocoa. Stir in the milk and melted butter. Place in an ungreased, square cake pan. Combine the brown sugar and 4 Tbsp. cocoa. Spread over the mixture in the pan. Pour the boiling water over the whole mixture just before putting it into the oven. Do not stir.

Bake at 350 degrees F for 45 to 55 minutes.

Serves 4 to 6.

— Catherine Gardner
Montreal West, Quebec

FRESH ORANGE CAKE

4 medium oranges
1½ cups sugar
½ cup shortening
2¼ cups flour
2 tsp. baking powder
¼ tsp. baking soda
1 tsp. salt
2 egg whites

Icing:
½ cup butter, softened
2 egg yolks
⅛ tsp. salt
¼ cup orange-sugar mixture
1 tsp. grated orange rind
¼ tsp. grated lemon rind
3½ cups icing sugar

Grate rind from 2 oranges. Peel and section 3 oranges, then cut into tiny pieces. Squeeze remaining orange and add juice to cut up oranges. To 1¼ cups of this add ½ cup sugar and stir well. Set aside ¼ cup for the icing.

Cream shortening and remaining 1 cup sugar well. Sift dry ingredients, then add to creamed mixture alternately with orange juice mixture. Add 1 Tbsp. grated orange rind.

Beat egg whites until stiff and fold into mixture. Pour into 2 greased and floured 8-inch round cake pans and bake at 350 degrees F for 25 minutes.

For icing, mix together all ingredients and fill and frost cooled cake.

Serves 8 to 10.

— Jane Hess
Kemptville, Ontario

RHUBARB APPLE COMPOTE

THIS RHUBARB-APPLE SAUCE IS DELICIOUS SERVED WITH WARM CUSTARD FOR DESSERT, or served over pancakes for Sunday brunch.

5 rhubarb stalks, chopped
½ cup water
5 apples, diced
½ tsp. cinnamon
⅛ tsp. coriander
¼ cup honey

Cook rhubarb in water for 10 minutes. Add diced apples and spices. Cook for 20 more minutes, then add honey.

Serves 6.

— Louise Carmel
Rapide-Danseur, Quebec

HONEY CAKE

3 eggs
1 cup sugar
¾ cup oil
½ cup honey
¼ cup maple syrup
3 cups flour

2 tsp. baking powder
1 tsp. cinnamon
1 cup warm coffee or tea
1 tsp. baking soda
1 tsp. vanilla

Combine eggs and sugar on high speed of mixmaster. Add oil, honey and maple syrup on low speed. Sift together flour, baking powder and cinnamon. Combine coffee or tea and baking soda and let cool. Add to creamed mixture alternately with dry ingredients. Add vanilla.

Bake in greased tube pan lined with wax paper at 350 degrees F for 1¼ hours. Let cool for at least 1 hour before removing from pan.

Serves 10 to 12.

— Kathryn MacDonald
Yarker, Ontario

APPLE GINGERBREAD COBBLER

4 medium apples, peeled, cored & sliced
½ cup brown sugar
1 cup water
1 Tbsp. lemon juice
¼ tsp. cinnamon
¼ cup sugar
1 egg
½ cup buttermilk
¼ cup molasses

2 Tbsp. oil
1 cup flour
½ tsp. baking soda
½ tsp. baking powder
½ tsp. ginger
¼ tsp. nutmeg
¼ tsp. salt
2 tsp. cornstarch

Combine apples, brown sugar, water, lemon juice and cinnamon. Cover and cook until apples are tender.

Beat together sugar, egg, buttermilk, molasses and oil. Stir together flour, baking soda, baking powder, spices and salt. Add to egg mixture and beat until smooth.

Combine cornstarch and 1 Tbsp. cold water and stir into apple mixture. Pour into 1½-quart casserole dish. Spoon gingerbread mixture on top.

Bake at 350 degrees F for 30 minutes.

— Carole Creswell
St. Chrysostome, Quebec

BLUEBERRY COBBLER

3 cups blueberries, fresh or frozen
½ cup water
½ cup sugar
1 tsp. lemon juice
½ tsp. cinnamon
1½ cups flour

2 Tbsp. butter
2 tsp. baking powder
¼ tsp. salt
2 Tbsp. sugar
⅓-½ cup milk

Wash blueberries and mix with the water, sugar and lemon juice in bottom of 8-inch pan. Sprinkle with cinnamon.

Stir together flour, butter, baking powder, salt and sugar with a fork until mixture is consistency of corn meal. Stir in milk. Roll dough on floured board, cut into serving-sized squares to fit pan and place over berries. Sprinkle with a little sugar and brush with some melted butter.

Bake uncovered at 400 degrees F for 25 minutes.

Serves 6.

— Janet Ueberschlag
Breslau, Ontario

BAKED APRICOTS

6 apricots
1 cup brown sugar
1 cup sour cream

Halve apricots and place in shallow baking dish. Sprinkle with brown sugar and top with sour cream. Cook at 325 degrees F for 15 to 20 minutes or until apricots are soft but not mushy.

Serves 6.

— Dee Clarke
Port Chalmers, New Zealand

BAKED PEARS

4 pears
½ cup sugar
1 cup water
Grated peel of ½ lemon
Ginger

Whipped cream sauce:
½ cup sugar
¼ cup Grand Marnier
½ cup whipping cream
2 egg yolks

Cut pears in half and core. Combine sugar, water, lemon peel and ginger and heat to dissolve sugar. Pour over pears and bake at 350 degrees F for 20 minutes. Drain and cool.

Prepare cream sauce by combining all ingredients and whipping until stiff peaks form. Spoon over pears.

Serves 4.

— *Jill Harvey-Sellwood*
Toronto, Ontario

MAPLE BAKED APPLES

6 apples
⅔ cup chopped walnuts
½ cup maple syrup
¼ cup raisins

3 Tbsp. butter, melted
Nutmeg
½ cup apple cider
Whipping cream

Trim a slice from bottom of each apple so it will stand upright in pan. Core apples to within ½ inch of bottom and make a shallow cut around the middle of each to allow for expansion during cooking. Fill centres with equal amounts of nuts and raisins and set apples in a shallow pan so that they do not touch one another.

Pour some syrup into each apple, then a bit of the melted butter. Sprinkle nutmeg over top and bake at 375 degrees F for 30 to 40 minutes, basting frequently with apple cider while cooking.

Serve hot with cream.

Serves 6.

— *Lynn Tobin*
Thornhill, Ontario

CANTALOUPE ALASKA

3 ripe cantaloupes, chilled
4 egg whites
Salt

½ cup sugar
2 cups firm vanilla ice cream
2 Tbsp. halved, blanched almonds

Cut cantaloupes in half, remove seeds and level base. Beat egg whites and salt until stiff and gradually beat in sugar until meringue is very glossy.

Place melons on cookie sheet, put 1 scoop of ice cream in each half and spread meringue over ice cream and top edge of melon. Sprinkle with almonds. Bake at 500 degrees F for 2 minutes, or until meringue is golden. Serve immediately.

Serves 6.

— *Pam Collacott*
North Gower, Ontario

ELEGANT GRAPES

2 cups seedless grapes
1 cup sour cream
½ cup brown sugar
Grated orange rind
Tia Maria

Combine grapes and sour cream, and sprinkle with brown sugar. Chill for at least 2 hours. Add Tia Maria to taste, sprinkle with orange rind and serve.

Serves 4.

— Elsie Marshall
Mississauga, Ontario

FRUIT FRITTERS

2 eggs, separated
½ cup milk
1 cup flour
½ tsp. salt
2 tsp. sugar
2 Tbsp. melted butter
Oil

2 bananas, sliced
2 apples, peeled, cored & quartered
2 pears, peeled, cored & quartered
2 peaches, peeled, pitted & quartered
Sugar
Custard

Beat egg yolks until light, then add milk. Sift together flour, salt and sugar and add to milk-egg mixture. Add butter. Beat egg whites until stiff and fold into batter.

Heat oil. Dip fruit in batter and fry in hot oil a few at a time. Cook until golden brown. Remove and drain on paper towels. Roll in sugar, then keep warm while making remaining fritters. Serve with custard if desired.

Serves 4.

— Patricia E. Wilson
Belleville, Ontario

CHOCOLATE DIPPED STRAWBERRIES

NUTS AND OTHER FRUITS CAN ALSO BE USED WITH THIS RECIPE. A SIMPLE BUT ELEGANT dessert is to fill a fondue pot with chocolate, melt it at the table and supply guests with bowls of assorted fruit for dipping.

1 quart large, well-shaped & firm strawberries
12 oz. semisweet chocolate chips

Leave stems on berries and make certain that they are completely dry. Melt chocolate in top of double boiler over hot, not boiling, water.

One at a time, dip pointed end of berries halfway into chocolate. Place on cookie sheet lined with wax paper and place in freezer for a few minutes, then refrigerate until set. Serve within a few hours.

— Louise McDonald
L'Orignal, Ontario

Baking

'A loaf of bread,' the Walrus said,
  'Is what we chiefly need. . . .'

– Lewis Carroll
Through the Looking-Glass

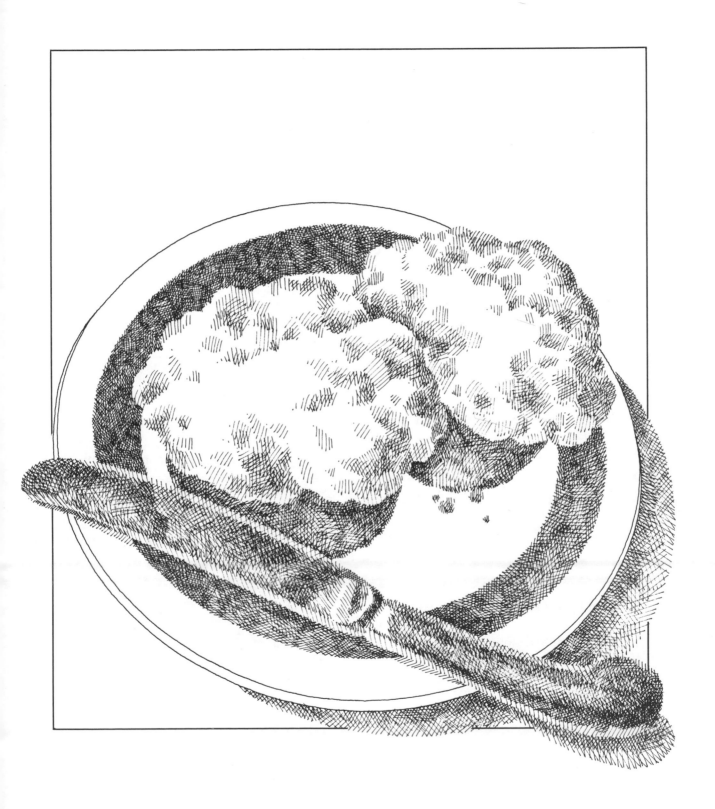

BANANA BRAN MUFFINS

1 cup sour milk
2 Tbsp. molasses
1 egg
2 Tbsp. butter
⅔ cup raisins
½ cup walnuts
1½ cups bran

1 cup whole wheat flour
½ cup brown sugar
½ tsp. salt
½ tsp. baking soda
2 tsp. baking powder
1 cup mashed bananas

Combine milk, molasses, egg, butter, raisins, walnuts and bran in a bowl and stir to blend. Sift together dry ingredients and add to moist mixture. Add bananas and stir only enough to moisten.

Fill greased muffin tins three-quarters full and bake at 375 degrees F for 20 to 25 minutes.

Makes 24 muffins.

— *Kathy Crawley*
Calgary, Alberta

RED BRAN MUFFINS AT UNIWAT

1½ cups whole wheat flour
¼ cup soya flour
1½ cups raw bran
¼ cup wheat germ
1½ tsp. baking powder
1½ tsp. baking soda
1 tsp. salt
¼ cup brown sugar

2 eggs
½ cup oil
¼ cup molasses
1½ cups buttermilk
1 tsp. vanilla
½ cup each raisins & currants
½ cup chopped nuts or sunflower seeds

Combine flours, bran, wheat germ, baking powder, baking soda, salt and brown sugar and blend.

Beat together eggs, oil, molasses, buttermilk and vanilla. Add to dry ingredients and blend. Stir in raisins, currants and nuts or seeds.

Fill well-greased muffin tins three-quarters full. Bake at 400 degrees F for 20 minutes.

Makes 24 large muffins.

— *Jacqueline Dysart*
Espanola, Ontario

BANANA OAT MUFFINS

1 cup unbleached flour
½ cup brown sugar
2½ tsp. baking powder
½ tsp. salt
¼ tsp. baking soda
¾ cup oats

1 egg, beaten
3 Tbsp. oil
½ cup milk
½ cup mashed banana
⅓ cup chopped nuts

Combine flour, sugar, baking powder, salt and baking soda. Stir well to blend. Stir in oats. Add remaining ingredients and stir with a fork until dry ingredients are just moistened.

Fill well-greased muffin tins two-thirds full. Bake at 400 degrees F for 18 to 20 minutes.

Makes 12 muffins.

— *Nan & Phil Millette*
Corunna, Ontario

BLUEBERRY OAT MUFFINS

1 cup rolled oats
1 cup buttermilk
1 cup flour
1 tsp. baking powder
½ tsp baking soda
½ tsp. salt
¼ cup brown sugar
1 egg, beaten
4 Tbsp. melted shortening
1 cup blueberries

Combine oats and buttermilk and let stand for 1 hour. Stir together flour, baking powder, baking soda, salt and sugar.

Add egg and shortening to oat mixture. Stir this into dry ingredients until just mixed. Fold in blueberries. Fill greased muffin tins two-thirds full. Bake at 400 degrees F for 20 minutes.

Makes 12 large muffins.

— Eva Whitmore
St. John's, Newfoundland

CRANBERRY OATMEAL MUFFINS

¾ cup unbleached flour
¾ cup whole wheat flour
1 cup rolled oats
½ cup brown sugar
1 Tbsp. baking powder
1 tsp. salt
1 tsp. cinnamon
1 cup fresh or frozen cranberries
¼ cup butter
1 cup milk
1 egg

Combine dry ingredients. Toss the cranberries with 1 Tbsp. of dry ingredients and set aside. Melt butter and combine with milk and egg. Stir butter mixture into dry ingredients and then add cranberries.

Fill muffin tins two-thirds full and bake at 425 degrees F for 15 to 20 minutes. Let stand 5 minutes before removing from pans.

Makes 12 muffins.

— Kathleen Walker
Vaudreuil, Quebec

CRANBERRY MUFFINS

¾ cup halved, raw cranberries
½ cup icing sugar
1 egg
1 cup milk
¼ cup oil
1 cup whole wheat flour
1 cup unbleached flour
3 tsp. baking powder
½ tsp. salt
¼ cup sugar

Mix cranberries and icing sugar well and set aside.

Beat egg, milk and oil together. Add whole wheat flour, then sift together and add remaining ingredients. Stir just to blend. Fold in cranberries with as few strokes as possible.

Fill greased muffin tins two-thirds full. Bake at 350 degrees F for 20 minutes.

Makes 18 muffins.

— Ann Fraser
Ottawa, Ontario

RASPBERRY OATMEAL MUFFINS

1 cup flour
3 tsp. baking powder
½ tsp. salt
¾ cup rolled oats
¼ cup brown sugar

1 egg
¼ cup melted butter
⅓ cup milk
1 cup mashed, fresh or frozen raspberries

Measure dry ingredients into a large mixing bowl. Stir with a fork until well blended.

Whisk or beat egg, butter and milk. Stir in dry ingredients and mix briefly. Add raspberries and mix until evenly blended. Fill greased muffin tins two-thirds full. Bake at 400 degrees F for 20 minutes, or until done.

Makes 12 large muffins.

— Linda Palaisy
Cantley, Quebec

CURRANT CORN MEAL MUFFINS

⅓ cup shortening
1 cup sugar
2 eggs
1¼ cups corn meal
¾ cup flour

2½ tsp. baking powder
¾ tsp. salt
½ cup currants
1 cup milk

Cream together the shortening, sugar and eggs. Combine corn meal, flour, baking powder and salt, and add to creamed mixture along with currants. Add milk and stir to just mix.

Place in greased muffin tins and bake at 400 degrees F for 25 minutes.

Makes 12 muffins.

— Linda Fickling
Oshawa, Ontario

ORANGE RAISIN MUFFINS

½ cup shortening
1 cup brown sugar
1 egg
¾ tsp. baking soda
Rind of ½ orange, grated
1 cup sour cream

2 cups flour
1 tsp. baking powder
¼ tsp. salt
1 tsp. cinnamon
1 cup chopped raisins
½ cup chopped nuts

Cream shortening and add sugar and egg. Mix baking soda, orange rind and sour cream. Combine dry ingredients and add to creamed mixture alternately with sour cream. Add raisins and nuts, mixing to just combine.

Fill greased muffin tins two-thirds full. Bake at 350 degrees F for 15 to 20 minutes.

Makes 24 muffins.

— Sally Ireland
Owen Sound, Ontario

DATE ORANGE MUFFINS

1 orange
½ cup orange juice
½ cup chopped dates
1 egg
½ cup butter

1½ cups flour
1 tsp. baking soda
1 tsp. baking powder
⅔ cup sugar
½ tsp. salt

Cut orange into quarters and remove seeds. Place in blender and whirl with orange juice until well blended. Drop in dates, egg and butter and blend until combined.

Sift together flour, baking soda, baking powder, sugar and salt. Pour orange mixture into dry ingredients and mix to just moisten.

Fill greased muffin tins two-thirds full and bake at 400 degrees F for 15 to 18 minutes.

Makes 18 muffins.

— Jane Lott
Toronto, Ontario

LEMON MUFFINS

2 cups flour
½ cup & 2 Tbsp. sugar
1 Tbsp. baking powder
1 tsp. salt

½ cup butter
½ cup fresh lemon juice
Rind of 1 or 2 lemons, grated
2 eggs

Combine flour, ½ cup sugar, baking powder and salt. Blend well.

Melt butter, remove from heat and stir in lemon juice, rind and eggs. Stir into dry ingredients until well moistened.

Fill greased muffin tins. Sprinkle tops with sugar. Bake at 400 degrees F for 15 minutes.

Makes 12 large muffins.

— Linda Charron
Cochrane, Ontario

APPLE HONEY DELUXE GRANOLA MUFFINS

½ cup whole wheat flour
½ cup raw bran
⅓ cup wheat germ
½ cup rolled oats
½ cup ground walnuts
¼ cup soy flour
2½ tsp. baking powder

½ tsp. cinnamon
½ cup milk
1 egg, beaten
⅓ cup honey
2 Tbsp. safflower oil
1 cup finely grated cooking apple

Mix together in a large bowl whole wheat flour, bran, wheat germ, oats, walnuts, soy flour, baking powder and cinnamon. Combine milk, egg, honey, oil and apple and stir into dry ingredients to just moisten.

Fill greased muffin tins two-thirds full and bake at 375 degrees F for 20 minutes.

Makes 12 large muffins.

— Carolyn Cronk
Montreal, Quebec

PUMPKIN MUFFINS

1 cup sugar
⅔ cup oil
2 eggs
1½ cups whole wheat flour
1 tsp. baking powder
1 tsp. baking soda
Cloves

1 tsp. cinnamon
¼ tsp. mace
½ tsp. nutmeg
¼ tsp. ginger
½ tsp. salt
1 cup pumpkin
1 cup raisins

Cream together sugar and oil. Add eggs and mix thoroughly. Combine dry ingredients.

Add pumpkin to moist ingredients, followed by dry mixture. Stir in raisins.

Fill greased muffin tins two-thirds full and bake at 350 degrees F for 25 minutes.

Makes 18 muffins.

— Karen Bowcott
Pansy, Manitoba

RHUBARB MUFFINS

1 cup brown sugar
¼ cup salad oil
1 egg
2 tsp. vanilla
1 cup buttermilk
1½ cups finely diced rhubarb

½ cup walnut pieces
2½ cups flour
1 tsp. baking powder
1 tsp. baking soda
½ tsp. salt

Combine brown sugar, oil, egg and vanilla. Beat until well blended. Stir in buttermilk, rhubarb and nuts.

Sift flour with baking powder, baking soda and salt. Add all at once to the rhubarb mixture and stir until just moistened.

Fill greased muffin tins two-thirds full. Bake at 400 degrees F for 15 to 20 minutes.

Makes 24 muffins.

— Ann Fraser
Ottawa, Ontario

SPICY MUFFINS

1 cup flour
3 tsp. baking powder
½ tsp. salt
½ cup oat flakes
½ cup wheat germ
½ cup sunflower seeds
½ cup raisins
1 tsp. cinnamon & ¼ tsp. cloves or
  1 Tbsp. grated orange rind
  & ½ tsp. ground nutmeg

¾ cup milk
¼ cup oil
¼ cup honey
2 Tbsp. molasses
1 egg

In large bowl, stir flour, baking powder, salt, oat flakes, wheat germ, sunflower seeds, raisins and spices. In small bowl, mix together milk, oil, honey, molasses and egg.

Make a well in the centre of the flour mixture and blend the wet ingredients with the flour mixture until just combined.

Place in greased muffin tins and bake at 350 degrees F for 15 minutes — until muffins are light brown.

Makes 12 muffins.

— Leslie Reid
Balfour, British Columbia

CANADIAN AIR FORCE WHEAT GERM MUFFINS

WHEN PRINCESS ELIZABETH VISITED CANADA IN THE EARLY 1950S, SHE WAS FLOWN ON a Canadian Air Force craft. On board, she was served these muffins, baked especially for her by the Air Force chef.

2½ cups whole wheat flour
1¼ cups wheat germ
7 tsp. baking powder
1½ cups raisins
¾ tsp. salt

¾ cup butter
¾ cup sugar
3 eggs
2 cups milk

Combine flour, wheat germ, baking powder, raisins and salt. Cream together the butter and sugar and add eggs and milk. Add the liquid ingredients to the dry, mixing as little as possible.

Bake in greased muffin tins at 375 degrees F for 15 to 20 minutes.

Makes 24 large muffins.

— Sandra James-Mitchell
Pickering, Ontario

SPICY APPLE WHEAT GERM MUFFINS

1½ cups flour
½ cup lightly packed brown sugar
1 Tbsp. baking powder
½ tsp. salt
¾ tsp. cinnamon
¼ tsp. nutmeg

½ cup wheat germ
1 cup peeled, finely chopped apple
½ cup raisins (optional)
2 eggs
½ cup milk
¼ cup melted butter

Mix together flour, sugar, baking powder, salt and spices. Stir well to blend. Stir in wheat germ, apple and raisins.

Beat eggs, milk and melted butter in small bowl until thoroughly combined. Add all at once to dry ingredients. Stir until all ingredients are just moistened.

Fill well-greased muffin tins two-thirds full and bake at 400 degrees F for 20 to 25 minutes.

Makes 12 muffins.

— Sharon McKay
Riverview, New Brunswick

DATE NUT MUFFINS

1 cup pitted, chopped dates
¾ cup boiling water
1 egg
½ cup sugar
¼ cup butter
¾ tsp. salt
1 tsp. vanilla
½ cup chopped walnuts

1¼ cups flour
¼ cup wheat germ
1 tsp. baking powder
1 tsp. cinnamon
¼ tsp. allspice
¼ tsp. nutmeg
1 tsp. baking soda

Soften dates in boiling water and allow to cool. Beat egg and gradually add sugar, butter, salt and vanilla. Add nuts.

Combine dry ingredients, except baking soda. Stir baking soda into dates and add to egg mixture. Stir in dry ingredients, mixing until just blended.

Spoon into lightly greased muffin tins. Bake at 375 degrees F for 15 to 20 minutes.

Makes 12 muffins.

— Maxine Farr-Jones
Calgary, Alberta

BLUEBERRY BANANA BREAD

1 cup blueberries
1¾ cups flour
2 tsp. baking powder
¼ tsp. baking soda
½ tsp. salt

⅓ cup butter
⅔ cup sugar
2 eggs
1 cup mashed bananas

Toss berries with 2 Tbsp. flour. Sift remaining flour, baking powder, baking soda and salt.

Cream butter and beat in sugar until light and fluffy. Beat in eggs one at a time. Add flour mixture and bananas alternately in 3 parts to butter mixture. Stir in berries.

Spoon into greased loaf pan and bake at 350 degrees F for 50 minutes.

— Gillian Richardson
Regina, Saskatchewan

HONEY WALNUT BREAD

1 cup milk
1 cup honey
½ cup sugar
¼ cup oil
2 egg yolks

1½ cups unbleached flour
1 tsp. salt
1 tsp. baking soda
1 cup whole wheat flour
1 cup chopped walnuts

Scald milk and stir in honey and sugar until sugar dissolves. Cool. Beat in oil and egg yolks. Sift together unbleached flour, salt and baking soda. Stir in whole wheat flour. Add nuts, then milk mixture. Stir to just blend. Spoon into 2 greased loaf pans.

Bake at 325 degrees F for 1 hour, or until toothpick inserted in loaf comes out clean. Cool in pans for 15 minutes, then turn out onto rack.

Makes 2 loaves.

— Ingrid Birker
Montreal, Quebec

FRUITY & NUTTY TEA LOAF

⅓ cup butter
⅔ cup sugar
2 eggs
1 cup mashed bananas
1½ cups flour
2¼ tsp. baking powder

½ tsp. salt
½ cup oatmeal
½ cup blueberries
¼ cup raisins
½ cup chopped pecans

Cream butter and sugar and add eggs. Add mashed bananas. Combine flour, baking powder, salt and oatmeal. Add to creamed mixture. Stir in blueberries, raisins and nuts.

Pour into greased loaf pan and bake at 350 degrees F for 1 hour.

— Audrey Moroso
Puslinch, Ontario

NUTS & SEEDS BREAD

2 cups flour
1 tsp. baking powder
1 tsp. baking soda
½ tsp. salt
1 cup brown sugar
½ cup chopped nuts

2 Tbsp. sesame seeds
2 Tbsp. poppy seeds
1 egg, beaten
1 cup milk
¼ cup oil

Mix dry ingredients together. Combine egg, milk and oil, then add to dry mixture.

Pour batter into greased loaf pan and bake at 350 degrees F for 45 minutes.

— Linda Purvis
Toronto, Ontario

COCONUT ORANGE LOAF

2½ cups flour
1 cup sugar
¼ tsp. mace
3½ tsp. baking powder
¾ tsp. salt
3 tsp. grated orange rind

½ cup orange juice
¾ cup milk
2 eggs, beaten
2 Tbsp. oil
½ cup coconut
1 cup raisins

Mix together flour, sugar, mace, baking powder, salt and orange rind. Make a well in the centre.

Combine orange juice, milk, eggs and oil and pour into well. Blend well. Add coconut and raisins.

Pour into greased loaf pan and bake at 350 degrees F for 1 hour.

— Jacqueline Dysart
Espanola, Ontario

LEMON SESAME BREAD

¼ cup oil
½ cup honey
3 eggs
Juice of 1 lemon
Rind of 2 lemons, grated
½ cup sesame seeds
¼ cup soy flour

1 cup whole wheat flour
1½ Tbsp. milk powder
½ tsp. salt
2 tsp. baking powder

Topping

Juice of 1 lemon
3 Tbsp. honey

Beat oil and honey together until blended, then beat in eggs, lemon juice and rind. Stir the dry ingredients together, then stir into the liquid mixture.

Bake in greased loaf pan at 350 degrees F for 45 minutes.

To make topping, combine lemon juice and honey, heating if necessary. Poke holes in the warm loaf with a toothpick and pour topping over it. Cool for 10 minutes before serving.

— Norah Ashmore
Kamloops, British Columbia

PEANUT BUTTER BREAD

THIS RECIPE PRODUCES A VERY DENSE, MOIST LOAF WITH A PLEASANT PEANUT BUTTER taste. It could be eaten plain or could serve as the basis for a sandwich.

¾ cup sugar
½ cup peanut butter
1 tsp. vanilla
1¾ cups milk

2¼ cups flour
4 tsp. baking powder
½ tsp. salt

Cream together sugar, peanut butter and vanilla. Add milk and mix well. Combine flour, baking powder and salt. Add to creamed mixture and beat well.

Place in greased loaf pan and bake at 350 degrees F for 45 to 50 minutes, or until golden brown. Allow to cool for 10 minutes before removing from pan.

CARROT NUT LOAF

1½ cups unbleached flour
1 cup whole wheat flour
2½ tsp. baking powder
1 tsp. baking soda
1 tsp. salt
¾ cup brown sugar

2 eggs
1 cup & 2 Tbsp. water
2 Tbsp. melted shortening
½ cup chopped nuts
½ cup raisins
1¼ cups grated raw carrots

Sift flours, baking powder, baking soda, salt and sugar together. Combine eggs, water and shortening and add to dry ingredients. Fold in nuts, raisins and carrots.

Pour into greased loaf pan and let stand for 5 minutes. Bake at 350 degrees F for 1 hour.

— Ruth Hughes
Creemore, Ontario

SAVOURY CHEDDAR BREAD

2 cups flour
4 tsp. baking powder
1 Tbsp. sugar
½ tsp. garlic powder
½ tsp. oregano

¼ tsp. dry mustard
1¼ cups grated Cheddar cheese
1 egg, beaten
1 cup milk
1 Tbsp. butter, melted

Stir together the flour, baking powder, sugar, garlic powder, oregano, dry mustard and cheese. Combine egg, milk and butter and add all at once to dry ingredients, stirring until just moistened.

Spread batter in a greased loaf pan and bake at 350 degrees F for 45 minutes. Cool 10 minutes on a wire rack before removing from pan.

— Nan & Phil Millette
Corunna, Ontario

CRANBERRY LOAF

1 cup white sugar
2 Tbsp. butter
1 egg, beaten
1 cup raw cranberries
1 cup raisins
2 cups flour

½ tsp. baking soda
1½ tsp. baking powder
½ tsp. salt
Juice of 1 orange
Water
½ cup chopped walnuts

Cream sugar and butter and add egg. Toss cranberries and raisins with ¼ cup flour and set aside. Sift together remaining dry ingredients and add to creamed mixture alternately with orange juice that is combined with enough hot water to make ¾ cup. Fold in fruit and nuts.

Place in greased loaf pan and bake at 325 degrees F for 1 hour. Let sit, well wrapped, for one day before using.

— Mary Lou Garlick
Pine Point, Northwest Territories

CRANBAN RING

1 banana, mashed
1 cup fresh cranberries, halved
¼ cup walnuts
1¾ cups flour
2 tsp. baking powder

1 tsp. salt
½ cup sugar
1 egg, beaten
½ cup milk
¼ cup oil

Mix banana, berries and nuts. Combine flour, baking powder and salt. Add sugar, egg, milk and oil. Stir in fruit until just mixed.

Spoon into greased ring mould and bake at 400 degrees F for 35 minutes.

— Andrea Hamilton
Vancouver, British Columbia

CRESCIA

THIS IS A TRADITIONAL ITALIAN EASTER-BREAD RECIPE FROM THE MARCHE REGION OF Italy. It has a strong peppery flavour, and although the recipe makes a very large, round loaf, it will not last long.

3 tsp. sugar
3 Tbsp. yeast
1½ cups warm water
12 eggs
1 lb. butter, melted

12 oz. Parmesan cheese
1 tsp. salt
2 Tbsp. pepper
6-8 cups flour

Dissolve sugar and yeast in water. Cover and let sit for 10 minutes. Beat eggs well and add melted butter. Add yeast mixture, stirring well. Stir in cheese, salt and pepper. Gradually add flour, blending well, until stiff batter dough results.

Pour into a large oiled casserole dish, cover and let rise for 1½ hours, or until doubled in bulk. Bake at 325 degrees F for 1 to 1½ hours.

Makes 1 large loaf.

— Mikell Billoki
Gore Bay, Ontario

CRANBERRY-FILLED BRAID

Bread:
2 Tbsp. sugar
1 pkg. yeast
⅓ cup warm water
3-3½ cups flour
¼ cup sugar
1 tsp. salt
1 tsp. shredded orange peel
⅓ cup orange juice
⅓ cup milk
¼ cup butter
1 egg

Filling:
⅔ cup cranberries
¼ orange, unpeeled
⅓ apple, unpeeled
⅓ cup sugar
1 Tbsp. cornstarch

Icing:
½ cup icing sugar
2 tsp. orange juice
Toasted, sliced almonds

Combine 2 Tbsp. sugar, yeast and warm water. Let sit for 10 minutes. Combine 1 cup flour, sugar, salt and orange peel. Heat together orange juice, milk and butter until warm and add to flour mixture. Add yeast mixture and stir in egg. Add remaining flour to make a soft dough. Knead for 5 to 10 minutes. Place dough in greased bowl, cover and let rise until doubled in bulk — 1 to 1½ hours.

Meanwhile, prepare the filling. Chop all fruit together until fine. Add sugar and stir until dissolved. Add cornstarch and cook until thick and bubbly. Cool.

Punch down dough and let sit for 10 minutes. On lightly floured surface, roll dough into a 9-by-12-inch rectangle. Cut into three 12-by-3-inch strips. Spread cranberry mixture down centre of each strip, bring long edges together and pinch to seal. Place strips side by side, seam down, on a greased baking sheet. Braid and secure ends. Cover and let rise until doubled. Bake at 350 degrees F for 20 minutes, or until golden.

To make icing, combine icing sugar and orange juice. Drizzle over warm braid and sprinkle with toasted almonds.

Makes 1 braid.

— Karen Quinney
Geraldton, Ontario

BRAIDED WHEAT GERM BREAD

1 tsp. sugar
½ cup warm water
2 Tbsp. yeast
½ cup butter
1 cup cottage cheese
1¼ cups wheat germ

1 cup raisins
⅓ cup honey
3 eggs
1 tsp. grated orange rind
1 tsp. salt
4-4½ cups flour

In large bowl, dissolve sugar in warm water. Add yeast and let stand for 10 minutes. Heat butter and cottage cheese until butter melts. Let cool slightly and add to yeast mixture. Stir in wheat germ, raisins, honey, eggs, orange rind and salt. Add 3 to 4 cups flour to make a soft dough. Turn onto floured board and knead, adding flour if it is too sticky. Place in a greased bowl, turning to grease top. Cover and let rise for 1 to 1½ hours, or until doubled in bulk.

Punch down and divide in half. Divide each half into thirds and roll into 12-inch lengths. Braid together, pinching ends. Place on greased cookie sheet, cover and let rise for 1 hour. Bake at 350 degrees F for 30 to 35 minutes.

Makes 2 braids.

— Carolyn Howatson
Victoria, British Columbia

POTICA

THIS IS A TRADITIONAL RECIPE FOR YUGOSLAVIAN CHRISTMAS BREAD.

3½ cups flour
1 pkg. yeast
1 cup milk
2 Tbsp. sugar
2 Tbsp. butter
1 tsp. salt
1 egg

Filling:
2 cups finely ground walnuts
1 egg, beaten
¼ cup brown sugar
2 Tbsp. honey
2 Tbsp. milk
1 Tbsp. melted butter
1 tsp. cinnamon
½ tsp. vanilla

Stir together 1½ cups flour and the yeast. Heat milk, sugar, butter and salt until just warm. Add to flour-yeast mixture. Add egg and beat with electric mixer at low setting. Scrape bowl. Beat for 3 minutes at high speed. Stir in remaining flour to make a moderately stiff dough. Turn out and knead until smooth and elastic. Place in greased bowl and let rise until doubled – about 1½ hours.

Combine filling ingredients and set aside.

Punch dough down and let sit for 10 minutes. Roll out until very thin and approximately 20 by 30 inches. Spread with nut filling and roll up along longer side. Pinch edge to seal. Place in U-shape on greased baking sheet and let rise until doubled. Bake at 350 degrees F for 30 to 35 minutes.

— Marie Yelich
Sardis, British Columbia

GREEK EASTER BREAD

1 pkg. yeast
½ cup warm water
2 cups warm milk
2 cups & 1 Tbsp. sugar
6-8 cups flour
5 eggs

1 orange peel, grated
1 lemon peel, grated
½ tsp. crushed cardamom seeds
½ lb. butter, melted
1 egg white, beaten

Dissolve yeast in water. Add 1 cup warm milk, 1 Tbsp. sugar and 1½ cups flour to make a pudding-like batter. Cover and let stand in warm place for 1 hour.

Meanwhile, combine 2 cups sugar and eggs. Place 5 cups flour in large pan and add orange and lemon peel, cardamom, remaining 1 cup milk and melted butter. Stir in yeast mixture and then sugar-egg mixture. Add flour as needed to make a kneadable dough. Knead gently.

Place dough in clean, oiled pan, cover and let rise for about 8 hours. Punch down, knead lightly again and divide into 9 balls.

Shape each ball into a long strip – 18 to 24 inches – then braid 3 strips together. Place the 3 loaves on a greased cookie sheet, cover and let rise for 2 hours. Brush the top of the loaves with lightly beaten egg white and bake at 325 degrees F for 30 minutes.

Makes 3 loaves.

— Patrick A. Thrasher
Branchton, Ontario

DARK RYE BREAD

3 Tbsp. yeast
1 tsp. brown sugar
1 cup warm water
½ cup dark molasses
½ cup boiling water
2 Tbsp. butter

2 Tbsp. caraway seeds
2 tsp. salt
½ cup wheat germ
2¾ cups dark rye flour
2½-2¾ cups unbleached flour

Dissolve yeast and brown sugar in warm water. In large bowl, combine molasses, boiling water, butter, caraway seeds and salt, stirring until butter melts. Cool to lukewarm. Stir in yeast mixture and wheat germ. Stir in all of rye flour and as much unbleached flour as you can mix in with a spoon. Turn onto floured board. Knead in enough of remaining flour to make a medium-stiff dough that is smooth and elastic. Place in greased bowl, turning once to grease surface. Cover and let rise until doubled — about 1½ hours.

Punch down dough and divide in half. Cover and let sit for 10 minutes. Shape into 2 loaves and place in pans. Cover and let rise again until doubled — about 1 hour. Brush tops of loaves with water. With sharp knife, gently score tops of loaves diagonally at 2-inch intervals. Bake at 350 degrees F for 45 minutes.

Makes 2 loaves.

— Janet Ueberschlag
Breslau, Ontario

CRACKED RYE BREAD

4 cups hot water
1½ Tbsp. salt
¾ cup brown sugar
⅜ cup shortening
1 Tbsp. yeast

⅜ cup warm water
2 cups rye flour
2 cups cracked rye
8 cups unbleached flour

Mix together hot water, salt, sugar and shortening. Let cool to lukewarm. Combine yeast and warm water and let sit for 10 minutes. Pour into hot-water mixture. Add flours until dough cannot be mixed any longer. Knead, adding flour as required, until dough is smooth and satiny. Cover and let rise for 1½ hours.

Punch down and let sit for 10 minutes. Place in greased loaf pans and let rise for 1¼ hours. Bake at 375 degrees F for 45 minutes.

Makes 3 to 4 loaves.

— Lynne Hawkes
Sackville, New Brunswick

ONION RYE BREAD

2 cups milk, scalded
¼ cup sugar
4 tsp. salt
¼ cup oil
1 pkg. yeast
1 cup warm water

6 cups unbleached flour
2 Tbsp. caraway seeds
1 cup chopped onion
2 cups dark rye flour
Cornmeal
Milk

Combine scalded milk, sugar, salt and oil and let cool to lukewarm. Soften yeast in warm water and add to cooled milk mixture. Stir in unbleached flour, caraway seeds, onion and rye flour. Knead until smooth and elastic, adding more rye flour if needed. Place in greased bowl, cover and let rise until doubled — about 1 hour.

Punch down and let rise again until doubled. Place in greased loaf pans that have been sprinkled with cornmeal. Brush tops with milk and let rise for 1 hour, or until doubled. Bake at 350 degrees F for 1 hour.

Makes 3 loaves.

— Lois Jaman
Caliento, Manitoba

OLD FORT HENRY BROWN BREAD

1 pkg. yeast
3 cups lukewarm water
6 cups whole wheat flour
1 Tbsp. salt

Dissolve yeast in water. Mix in flour and then salt. Knead for 2 minutes. Let stand for 10 minutes, then form into loaves and place in loaf pans. Cover and let rise in a warm place for 45 minutes, or until doubled in bulk.

Place in 500-degree-F oven and reduce heat to 375 degrees. Bake for 50 minutes or until done.

Makes 2 loaves.

— St. Lawrence Parks Commission
Old Fort Henry
Kingston, Ontario

SESAME WHEAT BREAD

THIS RECIPE RESULTS IN A SOMEWHAT HEAVY BREAD, WHICH IS PARTICULARLY delicious toasted and spread with honey for breakfast.

4 cups milk, scalded
½ cup packed brown sugar
½ cup honey
5 tsp. salt
¾ cup butter
4 pkgs. yeast

1¼ cups warm water
1 cup sesame seeds, lightly toasted
¾ cup wheat germ
6 cups whole wheat flour
6 cups unbleached flour

Combine scalded milk, sugar, honey, salt and butter and cool to lukewarm. Dissolve yeast in warm water and add to cooled milk mixture. Stir in sesame seeds, wheat germ and whole wheat flour. Add unbleached flour. Knead until dough is smooth and satiny. Cover and let rise until doubled — about 1 hour.

Punch down and let sit for 15 minutes. Divide into 4 loaves and place in greased loaf pans. Let rise until doubled — about 1 hour. Bake at 425 degrees F for 45 to 55 minutes.

Makes 4 loaves.

— Heidi Magnuson-Ford
Leaf Rapids, Manitoba

SPROUTED WHEAT BREAD

2 Tbsp. yeast
½ cup warm water
2½ cups water
1 tsp. salt

¼ cup honey
¼ cup oil
6 cups whole wheat flour
2 cups wheat sprouts

Dissolve yeast in warm water. Add water, salt, honey, oil and 4 cups flour and beat well. Cover and let stand for 1 hour. Stir in remaining flour and sprouts. Knead for 5 to 10 minutes. Place in oiled bowl, cover and let rise for 1½ hours. Punch down and knead for 1 minute.

Shape into 3 loaves and place in oiled bread pans. Let rise, then bake at 350 degrees F for 50 minutes.

Makes 3 loaves.

ENGLISH MUFFINS

1 cup milk
2 Tbsp. sugar
1 tsp. salt
¼ cup butter

1 pkg. yeast
1 cup warm water
5½ cups flour
Cornmeal

Scald milk and stir in sugar, salt and butter. Cool to lukewarm. Sprinkle yeast in warm water in large bowl and stir until dissolved. Add milk mixture and 3 cups of flour and beat until smooth. Add enough flour to make soft dough. On floured board, knead 10 minutes, adding flour as necessary. Place in greased bowl, turning to grease top. Cover and let rise for 1 hour.

Punch down and divide in half. On board, roll out dough to ½-inch thickness. Cut with 4-inch round cutter. Roll in cornmeal and let stand for 30 minutes. Cook on medium-hot griddle for 15 minutes. Turn and cook for another 15 minutes.

Makes 24 muffins.

— *Reo Belhumeur*
Gatineau, Quebec

HONEY WHOLE WHEAT BUNS

1 tsp. honey
2 pkgs. yeast
½ cup warm water
2 eggs, beaten
½ cup melted shortening
¾ cup honey

¼ cup sugar
1 Tbsp. salt
2 cups milk, scalded & cooled
4 cups unbleached flour
3 cups whole wheat flour

Combine honey, yeast and water and let sit for 10 minutes. Mix together eggs, shortening, honey, sugar, salt, milk, 2 cups unbleached flour and whole wheat flour. Add yeast mixture. Knead dough with remaining 2 cups unbleached flour. Let rise until doubled in size — 1½ hours.

Punch down. Shape into rolls and place on greased cookie sheet. Let rise for another hour. Bake at 400 degrees F for 10 to 15 minutes.

Makes 24 rolls.

— *Laine Roddick*
Brockville, Ontario

BREAD PRETZELS

2 cups warm water
1 Tbsp. dry yeast
½ tsp. sugar

4½ cups whole wheat flour
1 egg yolk, beaten
Coarse salt

Dissolve yeast and sugar in warm water. Stir in the flour and knead for 8 to 10 minutes. Cover and let rise in a warm place until doubled in bulk.

Punch down and form into 12 small balls. Roll each out into a sausage shape, then form into pretzel shape. If desired, brush with beaten egg yolk and sprinkle with coarse salt. Allow to rise until not quite doubled. Bake at 475 degrees F for about 10 minutes.

Makes 12 pretzels.

— *Mary Flegel*
Montreal, Quebec

OATMEAL JUMBLES

1¾ cups flour	1 cup shortening
½ tsp. baking soda	⅔ cup brown sugar
½ tsp. salt	1 egg
½ tsp. ginger	½ cup molasses
½ tsp. nutmeg	2 cups rolled oats
½ tsp. cinnamon	½ cup raisins
½ tsp. cloves	

Sift together flour, baking soda, salt, ginger, nutmeg, cinnamon and cloves. Cream together shortening and sugar, then stir in egg and molasses. Add dry ingredients a third at a time. Stir in oats and raisins and drop by teaspoonful onto greased cookie sheets. Flatten with fork. Bake at 350 degrees F for 15 minutes.

Makes 3 dozen large cookies.

— Judith Goodwin
Tamworth, Ontario

ZUCCHINI OATMEAL COOKIES

½ cup softened butter	¼ tsp. cloves
¾ cup honey	¼ tsp. nutmeg
1 egg	1 cup oats
2 cups whole wheat flour	1 cup raisins
1 tsp. baking soda	1 cup grated zucchini
½ tsp. cinnamon	

Cream butter, honey and egg in a large bowl.

Combine flour and spices in small bowl, and the oats and raisins in another bowl. Add both to moist ingredients a little at a time. Stir in zucchini gradually until well mixed.

Drop by teaspoonful onto greased cookie sheets and flatten with a fork. Bake at 375 degrees F for 10 to 12 minutes.

Makes 5 dozen cookies.

— Sue Summers
Enderby, British Columbia

STEPHEN'S CHOCOLATE OATMEAL COOKIES

½ cup shortening	1 egg
½ cup white sugar	5 Tbsp. cocoa
½ cup brown sugar	2 Tbsp. melted butter
1 cup flour	1 tsp. almond extract
1 tsp. baking powder	1 cup oatmeal
½ tsp. salt	

Cream together shortening and sugars. Sift together flour, baking powder and salt and add to creamed mixture. Beat in egg, cocoa, butter and almond extract. Stir in oatmeal.

Drop by teaspoonful onto greased cookie sheets and flatten with a fork. Bake at 350 degrees F for 8 to 10 minutes.

Makes 4 dozen cookies.

— Valerie Arnason
Cheverie, Nova Scotia

CHOCOLATE GOODIES

1 cup brown sugar
¼ cup butter
2 Tbsp. cocoa
¼ cup milk
½ tsp. vanilla

1 cup rolled oats
¼ cup wheat germ
½ cup coconut
¼ cup sesame seeds
½ cup sunflower seeds

Combine sugar, butter, cocoa and milk in a large saucepan and stir over medium heat until butter melts. Bring to a boil and cook for 2 minutes, stirring occasionally. Remove from heat and stir in remaining ingredients.

Drop by spoonfuls onto wax paper and allow to cool.

Makes 3 dozen cookies.

— S. Pedersen
Thunder Bay, Ontario

ORANGE CHOCOLATE COOKIES

½ cup butter
½ cup sugar
1 egg
2 tsp. grated orange rind
2¼ cups flour

½ tsp. salt
1½ tsp. baking powder
Melted semisweet chocolate
Finely chopped nuts

Cream butter and add sugar, egg and orange rind. Mix flour, salt and baking powder and add to butter mixture.

Roll out on floured surface to about ⅛ inch and cut into desired shapes. Bake at 350 degrees F for 10 minutes. Spread melted chocolate on cooled cookies and top with chopped nuts.

Makes 4 dozen cookies.

— Barbara & Dana Leahey
Toronto, Ontario

DELUXE COOKIES

1 cup white sugar
1 cup brown sugar
2 eggs
1 cup peanut butter
2 tsp. vanilla
1 lb. butter
2½-3 cups flour

2 Tbsp. baking soda
3 cups rolled oats
1½ cups chocolate chips
1½ cups raisins
1½ cups chopped walnuts
1 cup sesame seeds

Cream together sugars, eggs, peanut butter, vanilla and butter until smooth. Add flour and baking soda and mix until dough does not stick to hands. Mix in remaining ingredients.

Roll into balls, place on greased cookie sheets and flatten with a fork. Bake at 350 degrees F for 15 minutes.

Makes 8 to 9 dozen cookies.

— Karen Diemert
Telkwa, British Columbia

PEANUT BUTTER CHOCOLATE CHIP COOKIES

½ cup shortening
½ cup brown sugar
½ cup white sugar
½ cup peanut butter
1 egg, beaten
½ tsp. vanilla

1½ cups flour
½ tsp. salt
½ tsp. baking soda
⅔ cup chocolate chips
¼ cup chopped peanuts

Cream together shortening and sugars. Add peanut butter and blend. Stir in egg and vanilla.

Mix together remaining ingredients in a separate bowl, and then combine with creamed mixture.

Place by teaspoonful on greased cookie sheets and flatten with a fork. Bake at 350 degrees F for 12 to 15 minutes.

Makes 3 to 3½ dozen cookies.

— Jane Lott
Toronto, Ontario

RICE COOKIES

1 cup rice flour
¼ cup salt
1½ tsp. baking powder
4 Tbsp. sesame oil
¼ cup maple syrup

1 tsp. vanilla
¼ cup water
½ cup coconut
½ cup finely ground pecans

Combine flour, salt and baking powder and work oil into this mixture. Mix together maple syrup, vanilla and water. In another bowl, combine coconut and pecans. Add water and nut mixtures alternately to dry ingredients. Shape into roll, wrap well and chill until firm. Slice and place on greased cookie sheets. Bake at 350 degrees F for 10 minutes, or until light gold.

Makes 2 dozen cookies.

— Hazel Baker
Coombs, British Columbia

GERMAN SPRINGERLE COOKIES

6 eggs
3 cups sugar
6 cups flour
¾ cup whole anise seed

Beat eggs and sugar together with electric mixmaster on high until thick and creamy — about 4 minutes. Reduce speed to low and slowly add flour, scraping down and mixing thoroughly. Dough will be stiff.

Liberally flour a pastry board and scoop dough out onto it. Knead dough until it has a smooth surface, incorporating as much flour as necessary to keep it from sticking.

Clean off board and reflour. Using a regular rolling pin, roll dough into ¾-inch-thick rectangle. Flour springerle rolling pin and evenly press down design into dough. Cut cookies apart and place on greased cookie sheet that has been sprinkled with anise seed. Set aside overnight to dry.

Bake at 300 degrees F for 10 minutes, or until bottoms are golden brown.

— Edith Cumming Coe
St. Louis, Missouri

CARDAMOM CINNAMON NUGGETS

1¼ cups butter
½ cup sugar
2 cups unbleached flour
½ cup whole wheat flour

Salt
2 tsp. cinnamon
2 tsp. cardamom
¾ cup walnuts

Cream butter and sugar and gradually add flours, pinch of salt, cinnamon, cardamom and walnuts. Divide dough into quarters. Shape into logs and chill well. Cut into ¼-inch slices, place on greased cookie sheets and bake at 375 degrees F for 10 minutes.

Makes 4 dozen cookies.

— Gwen Miller
Barrhead, Alberta

GRANDMA'S MAN-SIZED COOKIES

2 cups raisins
1 cup water
1 cup shortening
2 cups sugar
3 eggs
4 cups flour

1 Tbsp. baking soda
1 Tbsp. baking powder
1 Tbsp. salt
1½ Tbsp. cinnamon
¼ Tbsp. allspice
½ cup nuts

Boil raisins in water until almost dry, then cool. Cream shortening and sugar and add eggs. Beat well.

Combine dry ingredients and add to creamed mixture. Stir in raisins and nuts and mix well.

Form into balls, place on greased cookie sheets and flatten with a fork. Bake at 350 degrees F for 10 minutes.

Makes 10 dozen cookies.

— Crystal Burgess
Kincardine, Ontario

WHEATY WALNUT TRAILBLAZERS

1 cup rolled oats
2 cups whole wheat flour
1 cup unbleached flour
½ cup skim milk powder
2 tsp. baking soda
1½ tsp. cinnamon
¼ tsp. salt

1 cup butter
1¼ cups brown sugar
2 eggs
1 Tbsp. grated orange rind
1½ cups chopped walnuts
1 cup raisins

Combine rolled oats, flours, milk powder, baking soda, cinnamon and salt. Cream together butter, sugar, eggs and orange rind. Stir dry ingredients into creamed mixture and add walnuts and raisins.

Drop by teaspoonful onto greased cookie sheets and bake at 375 degrees F for 10 to 15 minutes.

Makes 8 to 10 dozen cookies.

— Bertha B. Bumchuckles
Thunder Bay, Ontario

ITALIAN ANISE COOKIES

2½ cups flour
½ cup sugar
3 tsp. baking powder

1 tsp. ground anise
⅓ cup soft butter
3 eggs

Sift together dry ingredients and cut in butter. Beat in eggs with fork until dough is smooth. Mix well with hands.

Wrap in plastic and refrigerate overnight. Roll to ¼-inch thickness and cut into circles.

Bake on greased cookie sheet at 350 degrees F for 8 to 10 minutes, until lightly browned.

Makes 3 to 4 dozen cookies.

— Linda Townsend
Nanoose Bay, British Columbia

ORANGE CURRANT COOKIES

2¼ cups flour
1 tsp. baking soda
½ tsp. salt
½ tsp. ginger
½ tsp. cinnamon
½ cup butter, softened

⅓ cup brown sugar
1 egg
½ cup molasses
¼ cup orange juice
½ cup currants

Combine flour, baking soda, salt, ginger and cinnamon. Cream butter and sugar, then add egg. Beat in molasses and orange juice, then dry ingredients. Stir in currants.

Drop by teaspoonful onto greased cookie sheets and bake at 350 degrees F for 10 minutes.

Makes 3 to 4 dozen cookies.

— Cheryl Lenington Suckling
Athens, Georgia

ITALIAN JAM & NUT COOKIES

4 eggs
1 cup oil
1¼ cups sugar
2 Tbsp. lemon juice
Flour

4 tsp. baking powder
Plum jam
1 cup raisins
1½ cups coarsely chopped walnuts

Beat together eggs, oil, sugar and lemon juice. Add enough flour to form soft dough. Add baking powder. Continue adding flour until a soft, but not sticky, dough is formed. Knead dough a little, then cut into 4 pieces.

Roll each piece of dough out ¼-inch thick. Spread jam on the dough, then sprinkle with raisins and nuts. Roll up like a jelly roll and seal the edges. Bake on a cookie sheet for 20 minutes at 350 degrees F. Remove from oven and cut 1-inch thick at an angle. Turn off oven and return cookies to it until oven has completely cooled.

Makes 4 dozen cookies.

— Mary Andrasi
Acton Vale, Quebec

PERSIMMON COOKIES

PERSIMMON, AN ORIENTAL FRUIT, IS UNFAMILIAR TO MANY NORTH AMERICANS.
As in this recipe, the persimmon can be used to make a very tasty cookie. It is also delicious eaten raw. One serving method is to place the raw, ripe (very soft) fruit in a paper towel and freeze it until it is hard. Cut off the top and eat — it will resemble sherbet.

2 cups whole wheat flour
1 tsp. baking soda
¼ tsp. salt
1 tsp. cinnamon
½ tsp. nutmeg
½ tsp. cloves
½ cup butter

½ cup sugar
1 tsp. grated lemon or orange rind
1 egg, beaten
1 tsp. vanilla
1 cup persimmon pulp
  (approximately 2 persimmons)
½ cup raisins

Sift together flour, baking soda, salt, cinnamon, nutmeg and cloves. Cream butter and sugar, then add rind, egg, vanilla and pulp. Blend well and add dry ingredients. Stir in raisins.

Drop by teaspoonful onto greased cookie sheets and bake at 350 degrees F for 20 minutes.

Makes 3 dozen cookies.

— Lisa Calzonetti
Elora, Ontario

CRANBERRY COOKIES

THIS RECIPE RESULTS IN A FLAVOURFUL AND COLOURFUL CHRISTMAS COOKIE WHICH IS not overly rich or sweet.

½ cup butter
¾ cup white sugar
¾ cup brown sugar
1 egg, beaten
¼ cup milk
3 cups flour

1 tsp. baking powder
¼ tsp. baking soda
½ tsp. salt
1 tsp. lemon juice
3 cups chopped cranberries
1 cup chopped nuts

Cream together butter and sugars. Add egg and milk. Sift together flour, baking powder, baking soda and salt and add to creamed ingredients, mixing well. Add lemon juice, cranberries and nuts.

Drop by teaspoonful onto greased cookie sheets and bake at 375 degrees F for 15 minutes.

Makes 8 dozen cookies.

— Helen Hawkes
Moncton, New Brunswick

BANANA COOKIES

2¼ cups flour
2 tsp. baking powder
½ tsp. salt
¼ tsp. baking soda
⅔ cup butter

1 cup sugar
2 eggs
1 tsp. vanilla
6 oz. chocolate chips
1 cup mashed ripe banana

Sift together flour, baking powder, salt and baking soda. Cream together butter, sugar, eggs and vanilla. Add dry ingredients and blend well. Stir in chocolate chips and banana. Drop by teaspoonful onto greased cookie sheets. Bake at 400 degrees F for 12 to 15 minutes.

Makes 4 dozen cookies.

— Linda Charron
Cochrane, Ontario

DATE PINWHEEL COOKIES

½ cup butter
¼ cup honey
½ cup brown sugar
1 egg
2 cups flour
¼ tsp. baking soda
¼ tsp. salt

Filling:
1½ cups chopped dates
Rind of 1 orange, grated
¼ cup honey
1 cup orange juice
Salt

To make cookie dough, cream together butter, honey and sugar. Beat in egg. Sift together flour, baking soda and salt and add to creamed ingredients. Mix to form a dough.

Meanwhile, combine dates, orange rind, honey, orange juice and salt. Cook over low heat until fairly dry. Cool.

Roll dough into an oblong shape about ¼-inch thick. Spread with date mixture and roll up like a jelly roll. Wrap in wax paper and refrigerate for a few hours, or overnight. Slice and bake at 375 degrees F for 12 minutes.

Makes 2 dozen cookies.

— Christine Griffiths
Whitehorse, Yukon Territory

ALMOND SHORTBREAD

THESE COOKIES ARE COMMON CHRISTMAS FARE IN FINLAND, WHERE MOST SHORTBREADS contain almonds.

¾ lb. butter
2 cups sugar
1 egg

½ tsp. vanilla
¾ cup finely ground almonds
3 cups flour (approximate)

Cream butter and sugar. Beat in egg and vanilla and stir in almonds and flour.

Place dough in cookie press or pastry bag and squeeze into desired shape on cookie sheets. Bake at 350 degrees F for 10 minutes, or until light gold.

Makes 4 dozen cookies.

— Eila Koivu
Thunder Bay, Ontario

KOURABIEDES

THIS IS A TRADITIONAL RECIPE FOR GREEK SHORTBREAD COOKIES.

1 lb. unsalted butter, softened
1 cup icing sugar
1 Tbsp. brandy
Juice of 1 orange

1 tsp. vanilla
1 tsp. almond extract
5-6 cups flour
½ cup ground almonds

Whip butter for 10 minutes, until light and fluffy. Gradually add ½ cup icing sugar. Combine brandy, orange juice, vanilla and almond extract. Add liquid and part of flour alternately to butter-sugar mixture, ½ cup of flour at a time, until all liquid has been added. Add ground almonds. Add remaining flour ¼ cup at a time until dough forms a ball, and sides of bowl come clean. Form into 1-inch balls, flatten on greased cookie sheet and poke with finger to form a dent.

Place in oven preheated to 350 degrees F and immediately reduce temperature to 200 degrees F. Bake for 1½ hours. Sift remaining icing sugar over cooled cookies.

Makes 6 to 8 dozen cookies.

— Patricia Forrest
Rosemont, Ontario

EAT MORES

1 cup peanut butter
1 cup honey
1 cup carob powder
½ cup raisins

½ cup coconut
1 cup sunflower seeds
1 cup sesame seeds

Melt peanut butter and honey in top of double boiler. Add carob powder and mix. Add remaining ingredients.

Press into lightly buttered 9″ x 9″ pan. Cover and refrigerate for 2 to 3 hours, then cut into squares.

— Dorothy McEachern
Halton Hills, Ontario

BANANA BARS

½ cup butter
1 cup sugar
2 eggs
1 tsp. almond extract
2 cups sliced ripe bananas
2 cups flour

1 tsp. baking powder
¼ tsp. salt
¼ tsp. baking soda
½ cup chopped almonds
1 cup chopped dates
Icing sugar

Cream butter and sugar. Beat in eggs one at a time until fluffy. Add almond extract and bananas. Sift together dry ingredients and stir into batter. Add almonds and dates.

Spread in greased 9″ x 13″ baking pan and bake at 350 degrees F for 30 minutes. While still warm, sprinkle lightly with icing sugar.

Makes 4 to 5 dozen bars.

— Ann Budge
Belfountain, Ontario

MOM'S CHOCOLATE SHORTBREAD

¾ cup flour
2 Tbsp. cocoa
½ cup butter
2 Tbsp. white sugar
1½ tsp. salt
2 eggs
1¼ cups brown sugar
1 Tbsp. flour
½ tsp. baking powder

½ cup coconut
¾ cup chopped nuts
1 tsp. vanilla
Icing:
1 cup icing sugar
2 Tbsp. butter
1 heaping Tbsp. cocoa
Boiling water

Combine flour, cocoa, butter, white sugar and 1 tsp. salt. Press into greased 8-inch-square cake pan. Bake at 300 degrees F for 20 minutes.

Cream together eggs, remaining ½ tsp. salt, brown sugar, flour and baking powder. Add coconut, nuts and vanilla and mix well. Pour over shortbread base. Raise oven temperature to 350 degrees F and bake for 20 minutes.

To make icing, combine icing sugar, butter, cocoa and enough boiling water to make a creamy mixture. Pour over baked shortbread. Cut into squares.

Makes 2 to 3 dozen squares.

— Dianne Radcliffe
Denman Island, British Columbia

CHOCOLATE CHIP BARS

½ cup butter
1¼ cups brown sugar
¼ cup white sugar
2 eggs, separated
½ tsp. vanilla

1 cup flour
1 tsp. baking powder
⅛ tsp. salt
Chocolate chips
1 cup coconut

Cream together butter, ¼ cup brown sugar, white sugar and egg yolks. Add vanilla. Sift together flour, baking powder and salt and add to creamed mixture. Spread in greased 9" x 13" pan. Sprinkle with chocolate chips.

Beat egg whites and remaining 1 cup brown sugar until stiff. Fold in coconut. Spread evenly over mixture in pan. Bake at 350 degrees F for 20 to 30 minutes. Cut into bars while still warm, then cool in pan.

Makes 3 dozen bars.

— Pauline Longmore
Chilliwack, British Columbia

NANAIMO BARS

¾ cup & 1 Tbsp. butter
5 Tbsp. sugar
5 Tbsp. cocoa
1 tsp. peppermint extract
1 egg

2 cups finely crushed graham crackers
½ cup vanilla pudding
2 cups icing sugar
2 oz. unsweetened chocolate

Heat ½ cup butter, the sugar, cocoa and peppermint in saucepan. Beat in egg and stir until consistency of custard. Remove from heat and stir in crushed graham crackers. Press mixture into a greased 8-inch square pan.

Cream together ¼ cup of remaining butter, the pudding and icing sugar. Spread over graham cracker layer.

Melt chocolate with remaining 1 Tbsp. butter, then pour over second layer. Let sit for a few minutes, then refrigerate for an hour before cutting.

Makes 3 dozen squares.

— Margie Hancock
Cambridge, Ontario

ORANGE SQUARES

½ cup shortening
1 cup sugar
1 egg
Juice & grated rind of 1 large orange
2 cups flour

1 tsp. baking soda
1 tsp. baking powder
½ tsp. salt
1 cup sour milk
1 cup raisins

Cream together shortening and sugar. Add egg and orange juice and rind. Sift flour, baking soda, baking powder and salt and add to creamed mixture alternately with sour milk. Stir in raisins. Place in greased 9" x 13" baking pan and bake at 350 degrees F for 35 minutes. Let cool before cutting and removing from pan.

Makes 3 to 4 dozen squares.

— Orian Steele
Winchester, Ontario

SCOTTISH CURRANT SLICES

Pastry for 2 double 9-inch pie shells
1½ cups currants
½ tsp. cinnamon
¼ tsp. allspice
1 Tbsp. butter
1 Tbsp. lemon juice

½ cup sugar
2 tsp. cornstarch
½ cup water
3½ cups thinly sliced apples
Milk
Sugar

Combine currants, cinnamon, allspice, butter, lemon juice and sugar in saucepan. Stir together cornstarch and water until smooth. Add to currant mixture and bring to a boil, stirring constantly, then simmer for 5 minutes until very thick. Cool.

Divide pastry in half. Roll out one half and line a jelly roll pan with it, pressing the dough part way up the sides. Spread with cooled currant mixture and top with sliced apples. Roll out remaining pastry and lay on top, sealing edges so that the filling is enclosed.

Brush top with milk and sprinkle with sugar. Bake at 450 degrees F for 10 minutes, reduce heat to 375 degrees and continue baking for 20 minutes. Cut into squares when cool.

Makes 6 dozen squares.

— Elma MacLachlin
Kingston, Ontario

CARROT GRANOLA BARS

⅓ cup butter
¾ cup brown sugar
1 egg
¾ cup flour
¼ cup skim milk powder
1 tsp. baking powder
1 tsp. salt

½ tsp. cinnamon
1 cup grated carrots
1-1½ tsp. maple extract
1 tsp. vanilla extract
1½ cups granola
½ cup raisins

Cream together butter and sugar. Add egg and beat until fluffy. In separate bowl, stir together flour, milk, baking powder, salt and cinnamon. Stir into creamed mixture. Add carrots, maple and vanilla extracts, granola and raisins. Mix thoroughly. Turn batter into greased 9" x 13" pan and bake at 350 degrees F for 30 minutes. Cut into bars while still warm, then allow to cool thoroughly before removing from pan.

Makes 4 dozen bars.

— Sue Summers
Enderby, British Columbia

COCONUT SQUARES

3 eggs
2 cups brown sugar
1 tsp. vanilla
2 cups coconut
½ cup chocolate chips

½ cup currants or raisins
½ cup chopped walnuts
½ cup wheat germ
½ cup flour

Beat eggs until foamy. Add remaining ingredients and mix well. Spread in greased 9" x 13" pan and bake at 350 degrees F for 30 minutes.

Makes 4 dozen squares.

IRENE CABLE'S FIG BARS

2 cups dried figs
1½ cups water
Sugar
2 tsp. vanilla
1 cup shortening
1 cup brown sugar

2 eggs, beaten
3 cups flour
¾ tsp. salt
1 tsp. cream of tartar
½ tsp. baking soda
1 Tbsp. hot water

Soak figs in water overnight. Chop well, cook until thick and add sugar to taste. Cool. Add 1 tsp. vanilla.

Cream shortening and sugar. Add eggs and beat until light and fluffy. Sift together flour, salt and cream of tartar. Add half of this to creamed mixture, then add remaining 1 tsp. vanilla, baking soda and hot water. Stir in remaining flour mixture. Chill dough.

Roll out to ⅛-inch thickness on floured surface and cut into 3-inch strips. Place fig mixture down centre and fold each side over the filling. Cut into 1½-inch pieces, place on floured cookie sheets and bake at 375 degrees F for 12 to 15 minutes.

Makes 4 to 5 dozen bars.

— Karin Mayes
Prince George, British Columbia

CHOCOLATE CHEESE BROWNIES

8 oz. cream cheese
⅓ cup white sugar
3 eggs
½ tsp. vanilla
2 oz. unsweetened chocolate

½ cup butter
1 cup brown sugar
¾ cup flour
¾ tsp. baking powder
¼ cup chopped nuts

Blend cream cheese, white sugar, 1 egg and vanilla until smooth. Melt chocolate and butter and cool. Cream together remaining 2 eggs and brown sugar and beat in chocolate mixture. Sift together flour and baking powder and mix into chocolate.

Pour half the batter into a greased 9-inch cake pan. Spoon cream cheese mixture on top, spread out carefully and pour remaining batter over all. Sprinkle with nuts. Bake at 350 degrees F for 45 to 50 minutes.

Makes 1 to 2 dozen brownies.

— Linda Townsend
Nanoose Bay, British Columbia

BOTERKOEK

THIS IS A WELL-KNOWN AND MUCH LOVED RECIPE TO MANY DUTCH-CANADIANS.

1 cup butter
1 cup sugar
1 egg
1 tsp. almond extract

2 cups flour
Milk
Slivered almonds

Cream together butter and sugar. Add egg, almond extract and then flour, mixing well by hand. Press evenly onto cookie sheet, making a ½-inch-thick layer. Wet the surface lightly with milk and press in almond slivers. Bake at 375 degrees F for 30 minutes. Cut into squares while still warm.

Makes 20 squares.

— Wilma Zomer
Forillon, Quebec

PLUM SQUARES

3 cups flour
3 tsp. baking powder
1 tsp. salt
¼ cup sugar
⅓ cup butter, softened

2 eggs, beaten
6 Tbsp. milk (approximately)
½ cup plum jam
3 cups fresh or frozen plums, pitted &
   sliced in half

In large bowl, mix flour, baking powder, salt and sugar. Add butter and cut in finely. Add eggs and enough milk to make a dough that will cling together, but is not too sticky. Gather into a ball and cut into 2 pieces.

On floured surface, roll out one piece of dough to fit cookie sheet. Spoon jam over dough and then arrange plums with skin side down. Roll out next piece of dough to cookie-sheet size and cut into strips to make a lattice top. Bake at 350 degrees F for about 30 minutes, or until golden.

Makes 4 dozen squares.

— Julie Herr
Acton Vale, Quebec

CRANBERRY COFFEE CAKE

½ cup butter
1 cup sugar
2 eggs, beaten
1 tsp. baking powder
1 tsp. baking soda
2 cups flour
½ tsp. salt
1 cup sour cream

½ Tbsp. almond extract
1 cup cooked cranberries
½ cup chopped nuts
Topping:
¾ cup icing sugar
½ tsp. almond extract
1 Tbsp. warm water

Cream together butter, sugar and eggs. Sift dry ingredients together, then add to creamed mixture. Add sour cream and almond extract.

Place half the batter in greased 9" x 9" cake pan. Spoon cooked cranberries evenly over this, then top with remaining batter. Sprinkle nuts on top. Bake at 350 degrees F for 55 minutes.

To make topping, combine icing sugar, almond extract and warm water to form a thin paste. Drizzle over warm cake.

— Helen Hawkes
Moncton, New Brunswick

SHAKER PLUM COFFEE CAKE

¾ cup sugar
1 egg
¼ cup shortening
½ cup milk
1½ cups flour
2 tsp. baking powder
½ tsp. salt
8-10 plums, pitted & halved

Topping:
½ cup brown sugar
3 Tbsp. flour
1 tsp. cinnamon
3 tsp. melted butter
½ cup chopped nuts

Cream sugar, egg and shortening until fluffy, then stir in milk. Sift dry ingredients together and beat into creamed mixture. Spread dough in greased 9" x 9" cake pan. Top with rows of plums.

To make topping, combine remaining ingredients until crumbly. Sprinkle over plums. Bake at 375 degrees F for 35 minutes.

— Carole Zobac
Eagle Bay, British Columbia

RHUBARB SOUR CREAM COFFEE CAKE

½ cup butter
1½ cups brown sugar
1 egg
1 cup whole wheat flour
1 cup unbleached flour
1 tsp. baking soda
½ tsp. salt
1 cup sour cream

1½ cups rhubarb, cut into ½-inch pieces
½ cup chopped walnuts or pecans

Topping:
½ cup butter
1 cup sugar
½ cup light cream
1 tsp. vanilla

Cream together butter, brown sugar and egg until light and fluffy. Combine flours, baking soda and salt. Add to creamed mixture alternately with sour cream, mixing well after each addition. Stir in rhubarb and nuts.

Spoon into well-greased 9" x 13" cake pan. Bake at 350 degrees F for 35 to 40 minutes.

To make topping, combine butter, sugar, cream and vanilla in small saucepan. Heat until butter melts, then pour over cooled cake.

— Valerie Gillis
Renfrew, Ontario

APPLE GINGERBREAD

4 apples, peeled & sliced
2 cups flour
1½ tsp. baking soda
½ tsp. salt
½ cup sugar
1 tsp. ginger

1 tsp. cinnamon
½ cup butter
¾ cup molasses
1 egg
1 cup boiling water

Place apples in greased 9" x 9" cake pan. Sift together flour, baking soda, salt, sugar, ginger and cinnamon. Add butter, molasses and egg and mix well. Add boiling water and beat well. Pour mixture over apples and bake at 350 degrees F for 30 minutes.

— Judy Wuest
Cross Creek, New Brunswick

APPLE BLACKBERRY CAKE

¾ cup butter
¾ cup sugar
4 eggs
3 cups flour
1½ tsp. baking powder
¾ tsp. salt
1½ tsp. baking soda

1½ cups sour cream
1½ tsp. vanilla
1 tsp. cardamom
2 cups peeled, chopped apples
1 cup blackberries
½ cup firmly packed brown sugar

Cream butter and sugar until fluffy. Add eggs one at a time, beating well after each addition. Sift together flour, baking powder, salt and baking soda. Add to creamed ingredients alternately with sour cream. Stir in vanilla and cardamom, then fold in apples.

Pour half the batter into greased 9" x 13" cake pan. Cover with blackberries and sprinkle with brown sugar. Top with remaining batter. Bake at 325 degrees F for 40 to 50 minutes.

— Grietje Waddell
Havelock, Quebec

VEGETABLE CAKE

3 eggs, separated
1½ cups sugar
1 cup oil
3 Tbsp. hot water
1 cup shredded carrots
1 cup shredded beets

½ tsp. salt
1 tsp. cinnamon
2 cups flour
1 tsp. vanilla
2½ tsp. baking powder

Cream together egg yolks, sugar, oil and hot water. Add carrots, beets, salt, cinnamon, flour and vanilla. Beat egg whites with baking powder until stiff, then fold into batter. Place in greased 9″ x 13″ pan and bake at 350 degrees F for 40 minutes.

— *Joanne Graham*
Camrose, Alberta

ORANGE SPONGE CAKE

3 eggs, separated
¼ tsp. cream of tartar
1 cup sugar
2 tsp. grated orange rind
⅓ cup orange juice
1¼ cups flour

1½ tsp. baking powder
¼ tsp. salt
Glaze:
Juice of 1 orange
¼ cup sugar

Beat egg whites with cream of tartar until stiff. Add yolks one at a time, beating well after each addition. Add sugar gradually, beating well. Add rind and juice.

Sift together flour, baking powder and salt and fold into liquid ingredients. Place batter in greased tube pan and bake at 325 degrees F for 18 to 20 minutes.

Combine orange juice and sugar to make glaze and pour over warm cake.

— *Lee Robinson*
Victoria, British Columbia

HAZELNUT CAKE

THIS CAKE IS LOW IN FLOUR AND SUGAR, BUT HIGH IN PROTEIN. IT IS ESPECIALLY delicious served with whipped cream.

2 Tbsp. flour
2½ tsp. baking powder
4 eggs
½ cup sugar
1 cup hazelnuts

Sift together flour and baking powder. Place eggs and sugar in blender and process until smooth. Add hazelnuts gradually and continue to process until all nuts are finely ground. Add flour mixture and mix well. Pour into two 8-inch layer cake pans with greased wax-paper-lined bottoms. Bake at 350 degrees F for 20 minutes.

— *Kass Bennett*
Cranbrook, British Columbia

ANISE SEED CAKE

1½ cups flour
½ tsp. salt
½ cup butter
1 cup sugar

2 eggs, separated & beaten
½ cup milk
1 tsp. anise seeds
1 tsp. baking powder

Sift together flour and salt. Cream butter and sugar and add egg yolks. Add milk, alternating with flour-salt mixture. Fold in stiffly beaten egg whites and anise seeds. Add baking powder and mix well. Pour into greased loaf pan. Bake at 350 degrees F for 55 minutes.

— Katherine Dunster
Golden, British Columbia

GREAT AUNT BESSIE'S MAPLE CAKE

THIS RECIPE WAS DEVELOPED BY THE CONTRIBUTOR'S GREAT AUNT BESSIE. IT BECAME such a favourite of the young members of the family that she continued to bake it on her birthday each year, when the family gathered for a reunion.

½ cup butter
½ cup sugar
½ cup maple syrup
1 tsp. vanilla
2 eggs, well beaten
1¾ cups flour
½ tsp. salt
2½ tsp. baking powder

¼ cup milk
½ cup chopped walnuts
Frosting:
1 cup maple syrup
2 egg whites
Salt

Cream together butter and sugar. Gradually add maple syrup and vanilla and cream well again. Add eggs and mix well. Sift together dry ingredients and add to creamed mixture alternately with milk. Stir in chopped nuts.

Pour into 2 greased and floured 8-inch cake pans. Bake at 375 degrees F for 25 to 30 minutes.

To make frosting, cook maple syrup to soft ball stage. Beat egg whites with pinch of salt until peaks form. Add cooled syrup in fine stream, beating constantly. Frost cooled cake.

— Joyce Barton
Cawston, British Columbia

SOUR CREAM SPICE CAKE

1 cup shortening
½ cup brown sugar
2 eggs, beaten
1 cup molasses
1 cup sour cream
1 tsp. salt
½ tsp. nutmeg

½ tsp. ginger
1 tsp. cloves
1 tsp. baking soda
1 tsp. cream of tartar
3 cups flour
1 cup raisins
½ cup chopped nuts

Cream together shortening and sugar. Add eggs, then molasses and sour cream. Combine salt, nutmeg, ginger, cloves, baking soda and cream of tartar with flour and add to creamed ingredients. Mix well, then stir in raisins and nuts. Place in greased 9-inch cake pan and bake at 350 degrees F for 1 hour.

— Jan Johnson
Welland, Ontario

SPICED YOGURT POUND CAKE

1 cup butter, softened
2 cups sugar
3 eggs
⅔ cup plain yogurt
1 tsp. vanilla
2¼ cups flour
½ tsp. baking soda

½ tsp. salt
1 tsp. mace
½ tsp. allspice
½ tsp. cinnamon
¼ tsp. cloves
2 oz. unsweetened chocolate, grated

Cream butter until fluffy, then gradually beat in sugar. Add eggs one at a time, beating well after each addition. Stir in yogurt and vanilla.

Sift together flour, baking soda, salt, mace, allspice, cinnamon and cloves and stir into creamed mixture. Beat for 4 minutes, then fold in chocolate.

Place batter in greased and floured bundt pan. Bake at 325 degrees F for 70 minutes. Cool in pan for 10 minutes, then turn onto rack to finish cooling.

— Elizabeth Clayton Paul
Nepean, Ontario

CARROT WALNUT CUPCAKES

1 cup oil
¾ cup brown sugar
2 eggs
1 tsp. vanilla
1½ cups flour
1½ tsp. baking soda

½ tsp. salt
1 tsp. cinnamon
½ tsp. nutmeg
2 cups finely shredded carrots
1 cup finely chopped walnuts

Combine oil, sugar, eggs and vanilla in large bowl. Beat until thick. Sift together flour, baking soda, salt, cinnamon and nutmeg and add to creamed ingredients. Stir in carrots and walnuts. Place in prepared muffin tins and bake at 350 degrees F for 20 minutes.

Makes 18 to 20 cupcakes.

— Anne Sanderson
London, Ontario

BANANA YOGURT CUPCAKES

½ cup butter
1 cup honey
2 eggs
2 ripe bananas, mashed
2 tsp. lemon juice
1 tsp. grated lemon rind

1 cup whole wheat flour
1 cup & 2 Tbsp. unbleached flour
1 tsp. baking soda
½ tsp. salt
½ cup yogurt

Cream butter, then add honey and mix. Add eggs one at a time, beating well after each addition, then bananas. Stir in lemon juice and rind.

Sift together flours, baking soda and salt and add to creamed mixture alternately with yogurt. Spoon into prepared muffin tins and bake at 350 degrees F for 15 to 20 minutes.

Makes 24 cupcakes.

— Linda Ewert
Pouce Coupé, British Columbia

COCONUT POUND CAKE

1 cup butter
2 cups sugar
5 eggs
3 cups flour
¼ tsp. salt

1 cup milk
1½ cups coconut
1 tsp. lemon juice
½ tsp. vanilla

Cream butter and sugar together until fluffy. Add eggs one at a time, beating well after each addition. Sift flour with salt and add alternately with milk to creamed mixture, beating after each addition. Add coconut, lemon juice and vanilla. Turn into greased and floured tube pan. Bake at 325 degrees F for 90 minutes. Cool for 10 minutes, then remove from pan and cool on rack.

— Sheila Couture
Trenton, Ontario

CHESTNUT CAKE

THIS TRADITIONAL FRENCH CAKE TAKES A CONSIDERABLE AMOUNT OF WORK, BUT THE result — an almost fondant-fudge-like cake — is well worth it. When selecting chestnuts, pick fresh, plump, shiny nuts without insect bites. Vanilla sugar is made by placing a vanilla bean in a jar of sugar for a few days.

60 chestnuts (1½ lbs.)
1 cup skim milk
1 lb. fruit sugar
1 tsp. vanilla sugar

½ lb. unsalted butter
6 eggs, separated
Salt

To prepare chestnuts, make 2 incisions crosswise at the top of each nut and place them in a skillet. Cover with water and boil for 8 minutes. Remove from heat, but leave in water. Peel chestnuts, then place in another skillet with 3 cups water and 1 cup skim milk. Simmer for 30 minutes. Drain and force through fine-mesh sieve a few at a time to make a purée the consistency of fine noodle threads.

Blend chestnut purée with fruit sugar and vanilla sugar. Beat in the butter until smooth. Beat in egg yolks one at a time.

Combine salt and egg white and beat until stiff peaks form. Take one-quarter of this and beat it into the chestnut paste. Fold remaining egg whites gently into batter.

Place batter in greased tube pan and bake at 375 degrees F for 30 to 45 minutes.

— J.A. Guy Bacon
Montreal, Quebec

Beverages

Now is the time for drinking,
now the time to beat
the earth with unfettered foot.

– **Horace**
Odes

ELDERFLOWER CRUSH

THIS IS A COOLING SUMMER DRINK WHICH IS ESPECIALLY GOOD DURING HAYING.
The elderflower bushes bloom in June, and the florets should all be open when the head is picked.

4 lbs. sugar
2½ oz. citric acid
20 elderflower heads
2 lemons, sliced
5 cups boiling water

Place sugar in bottom of bucket, with citric acid on top. Add elderflower heads and lemons. Pour boiling water over top, then stir with wooden spoon until sugar is completely dissolved. Cover pail with a cloth and keep in a cool place. Stir once or twice a day for 5 days.

— Meg Weber-Crockford
Cantley, Quebec

TIGER'S MILK

1 large banana
½ cup yogurt
3 Tbsp. honey
1½ cups milk
½ tsp. cinnamon

Blend all ingredients together and serve.

Serves 2.

— Sandra Cameron
Kemptville, Ontario

MINT LEMONADE

4 cups sugar
5 cups water
Juice of 12 lemons

Juice of 4 oranges
Grated rind of 2 oranges
2 cups crushed mint leaves

Simmer sugar and water for 5 minutes, then cool. Add lemon and orange juices. Pour mixture over orange rind and mint leaves. Strain into jar and store in refrigerator. To serve, mix with equal amounts of water and add ice.

Makes 20 to 24 servings.

— Cheryl Lenington Suckling
Athens, Georgia

BANANA COW

1 banana
½ cup milk
1 Tbsp. honey
⅛ tsp. vanilla
1 cup crushed ice

Place all ingredients in blender and blend until smooth.

— S. Pedersen
Thunder Bay, Ontario

PINEAPPLE PUNCH

THE APPEARANCE OF THIS FRUIT PUNCH IS ENHANCED IF AN ICE RING IS PLACED IN THE punch bowl. Into a tube cake pan, pour 1 inch of any fruit juice and freeze. Arrange fruit slices on frozen juice and cover with another inch of juice. Freeze thoroughly. Place in punch bowl at serving time.

8 cups lemon juice
5 cups lime juice
4 cups sugar
24 cups unsweetened pineapple juice
10 cups orange juice

2 cups chopped mint leaves
45 cups ginger ale
16 cups club soda
6 cups quartered strawberries

Heat lemon and lime juices with sugar until sugar is completely dissolved. Combine with pineapple and orange juices. Add mint leaves and chill thoroughly. Add ginger ale, club soda and strawberries just before serving. Place in punch bowls with ice ring.

Makes 28 quarts.

— Donna Petryshyn
Westlock, Alberta

PINK BANANA WHIP

2 cups chilled cranberry-apple juice
2 cups fresh orange juice
1 ripe banana
6 ice cubes, crushed

Buzz all ingredients in blender and serve immediately.

Serves 3.

— Kathleen Walker
Vaudreuil, Quebec

CASTILIAN HOT CHOCOLATE

½ cup unsweetened cocoa
2 Tbsp. & 1 tsp. cornstarch
½ cup water
¾ cup honey, melted
1 quart milk

Combine cocoa, cornstarch and water in blender. Gradually add honey and blend. Whisk this mixture with milk in saucepan, continuing to stir as you bring it to a simmer.

Simmer, stirring often, for about 10 minutes. It will be glossy, smooth and almost as thick as pudding. Serve hot.

Serves 6.

— Lorna Wollner
Moberly Fire Lookout, Alberta

ENERGY DRINK

2 cups fresh-squeezed orange juice
1 banana
1-2 slices fresh pineapple
1 tsp. honey
⅔ cup crushed ice

Mix orange juice, banana, pineapple and honey in blender. Add ice and blend again.

Serves 2.

— Irma Leming
Meaford, Ontario

BLUEBERRY DRINK

THIS HOT FRUIT DRINK IS PARTICULARLY TASTY AFTER A DAY OF OUTDOOR WINTER activity.

2 cups blueberries
3 cups water
1 cup sugar
2 Tbsp. cornstarch

Combine all ingredients and blend well. Heat to boiling and serve.

Makes 6 cups.

— *Devon Anderson*
Maple Creek, Saskatchewan

SIERRA SUNRISE

THIS MAKES A PLEASANT SUNDAY BRUNCH DRINK.

6-oz. can frozen orange juice concentrate
1 cup cream
¾ cup sherry
1 egg
Salt
4 ice cubes, crushed

Place all ingredients in blender and mix at high speed until frothy and well blended.

Serves 2.

— *Louise Oglaend*
Hjelmeland, Norway

TOM'S SPECIAL SUMMER DELIGHT

1 large bag frozen strawberries
40 oz. white rum
Ice cubes
Ginger ale or club soda

Place strawberries in 64-oz. plastic container. Pour rum over top, cover tightly and refrigerate for at least 3 months.

To serve, fill tall glasses one-third full with strawberry-rum mixture, add 2 ice cubes and fill with ginger ale or club soda.

Makes 32 servings.

— *Kirsten McDougall*
Kamloops, British Columbia

CRANBERRY SPRITZERS

2 cups cranberry juice
1 cup white wine, chilled
Ice cubes
Soda water or mineral water, chilled
Mint leaves & lemon slices

Mix juice and wine. Pour into glasses with ice until two-thirds full. Top with chilled soda or mineral water. Garnish with lemon slices and mint leaves.

Serves 6.

— *Louise McDonald*
L'Orignal, Ontario

YOGURT SIP

1 cup frozen peaches, thawed slightly
2 bananas, very ripe
2 cups plain yogurt
¼ cup peach brandy

¼ cup light rum
2 Tbsp. honey
Nutmeg

Blend together fruit and yogurt. When smooth, add remaining ingredients. Blend for a few more seconds and serve cool.

Serves 4.

— Charlene Skidmore
Medicine Hat, Alberta

BANANA PUNCH

48 oz. orange juice
4 eggs
5 bananas
26 oz. club soda
13 oz. vodka
Ice cubes

Mix orange juice, eggs and bananas in blender until smooth. Just before serving, add club soda, vodka and ice cubes.

Makes 36 cups.

— Sonja Machholz
Vancouver, British Columbia

RICH & CREAMY EGGNOG

½ cup sugar
¼ tsp. cinnamon
Nutmeg
3 eggs, separated

2 cups whole milk
1 cup light cream
Rum

Combine sugar, cinnamon and dash of nutmeg. Beat egg whites to soft peak stage, then gradually beat in half the sugar mixture until stiff peaks form.

Beat egg yolks until lemon coloured, then add remaining sugar mixture and beat until thick and smooth. Fold gently but thoroughly into beaten egg whites. Stir in milk and cream and mix well.

To serve, place 1 oz. rum in each glass, and fill with eggnog.

Serves 4.

— Linda Plant
Powassan, Ontario

MULLED ALE

1 orange peel spiral
Whole cloves
6 small, red apples
3 12-oz. bottles ale

3 cups dark rum
⅔ cup sugar
⅛ tsp. ginger

Stud orange spiral with cloves ½-inch apart. Place in shallow pan along with apples and bake, uncovered, for 20 minutes.

In large, heavy saucepan, combine ale, rum, sugar and ginger and bring to a boil, stirring until sugar is dissolved. Place hot orange spiral and roasted apples into ale mixture and keep at low heat. Serve.

Makes six 10-ounce servings.

— Susan Shaw
Annapolis Royal, Nova Scotia

LA PONCE DE GIN DE GRAND-PERE

IN THE 18TH CENTURY, FREDERIC TOLFREY, ORIGINALLY FROM FRANCE, WAS OFFERED this drink in Canada and wrote down the recipe in his diary. Ever since, the recipe has been passed on from generation to generation not only as a tonic against the harshness of Canadian winters, but also as a cold and flu remedy.

¼ cup gin
3 Tbsp. lemon juice
1 tsp. honey
1 whole clove
⅔ cup boiling water

Combine all ingredients and let steep for a few minutes before drinking.

Serves 1.

— Nicole Morin
Aylmer, Quebec

ALMOND LIQUEUR

3 oz. chopped raw almonds
Cinnamon
1½ cups vodka
½ cup sugar syrup

Place almonds, pinch of cinnamon and vodka in sterilized glass jar. Shake well to combine ingredients, then cover and steep for 2 weeks. Strain, then sweeten with sugar syrup. Replace in jar and let sit for a few weeks more.

Makes 16 ounces.

— Rosy Hale
Scarborough, Ontario

MAPLE SYRUP LIQUEUR

4 oz. maple syrup
8 oz. rye whiskey

Combine ingredients in jar with tight-fitting lid. Shake for 2 minutes. For the next 2½ to 3 weeks, shake the container daily for 1 minute.

Serve as a liqueur or an aperitif poured over crushed ice.

Makes 12 ounces.

— Don Smillie
Calgary, Alberta

IRISH CREAM LIQUEUR

3 eggs
1 cup whipping cream
1 cup condensed milk

3 Tbsp. chocolate
¼ tsp. almond extract
12 oz. rye

Place all ingredients in blender and blend. Bottle and store in the refrigerator. This will keep for up to 3 weeks.

Makes 32 ounces.

— Anne Nuttall
Ridgetown, Ontario

GLOGG

1½ cups gin
2 cinnamon sticks
3 Tbsp. cardamom seeds
10 cloves
Almonds
Raisins

Fruit peel
1½ cups port
1 cup sugar
1 cup water
Juice of ½ lemon
15 cups red wine

Combine gin, cinnamon sticks, cardamom seeds and cloves and soak for at least 3 days. Soak almonds, raisins and fruit peel to taste in port for 1 day.

Make syrup by boiling together sugar, water and lemon juice until sugar is dissolved.

Place wine in large, heavy pot, add strained gin (discard spices), port and fruit and heat slowly, adding syrup. Heat until very hot, but do not boil.

Serves 20.

— *Ulrika Schmidt*
Calgary, Alberta

Suggested
MENUS

Summer Solstice

Artichoke Heart Sauce
(Vol. 2, 217)

Buttered Fettuccine

Phil's Lamb
(Vol. 2, 206)

Garden Rice
(Vol. 1, 111)

Dill & Creamed Spinach
(Vol. 2, 93)

Cauliflower Pecan Salad
(Vol. 2, 56)

Raspberry Flan
(Vol. 1, 225)

Strawberry Shortcake
(Vol. 1, 223)

Barbecue for Eight

Shrimp & Artichoke Tarts
(Vol. 2, 133)

Barbecued Arctic Char
(Vol. 2, 125)

Hot German Potato Salad
(Vol. 2, 90)

September Garden Zucchini
(Vol. 1, 70)

Spinach Orange & Mango Salad
(Vol. 2, 57)

Creamy Ambrosia with Fresh Fruit
(Vol. 2, 246)

Picnic to Travel

Devilled Eggs
(Vol. 2, 24)

Cold Ham Pie
(Vol. 2, 205)

Cold Barbecued Chicken
(Vol. 1, 152)

Shrimp Cooked in Beer
(Vol. 2, 130)

Nancy's Dill Dip
(Vol. 2, 75)

Assorted Raw Vegetables

Fresh Fruit

Raspberry Bars
(Vol. 1, 282)

Peanut Butter Chocolate Chip Cookies
(Vol. 2, 275)

Candlelight Dinner for Two

Coquilles St. Jacques
(Vol. 1, 130)

Pheasant with Rice Stuffing
(Vol. 2, 173)

Caesar Salad
(Vol. 1, 86)

California Corn
(Vol. 2, 82)

Burnt Almond Sponge
(Vol. 2, 243)

Harvest Dinner

Dilled Tomato Soup
(Vol. 2, 43)

Cornish Game Hens Indienne
(Vol. 2, 170)

Broccoli with Wild Rice
(Vol. 2, 80)

Tossed Salad
with Chili French Dressing
(Vol. 2, 63)

Baked Corn
(Vol. 2, 82)

Pumpkin Pie
(Vol. 1, 230)

Yogurt Fruit Mould
(Vol. 1, 216)

Party Menu for Twenty

Rumaki
(Vol. 2, 203)

Almond Mushroom Pate
(Vol. 2, 76)

Herbed Cheese Dip
(Vol. 1, 29)

Crudites

Cheese Stuffed Meatballs
(Vol. 1, 184)

Rabbit Pate Camille
(Vol. 1, 159)

Olive Ball Snacks
(Vol. 2, 26)

Angels on Horseback
(Vol. 2, 135)

Herbed Leg of Lamb
(Vol. 1, 196)

Paella
(Vol. 2, 138)

Scalloped Potatoes
(Vol. 1, 66)

Three Bean Salad
(Vol. 1, 85)

Salpicon
(Vol. 2, 53)

Family Christmas Dinner

Rich & Creamy Eggnog
(Vol. 2, 295)

Crab Delight
(Vol. 1, 128)

Raw Vegetables & Crackers

Roast Turkey with Russian Dressing
(Vol. 1, 156)

Cranberry Sauce

Potato Casserole
(Vol. 2, 89)

Crunchy Broccoli
(Vol. 2, 79)

Tossed Salad
with Creamy Garlic Dressing
(Vol. 2, 64)

Pavlova & Yogurt Chantilly
(Vol. 2, 245)

Chocolate Cheesecake
(Vol. 1, 218)

Buffet Brunch

Piraeus Shrimp
(Vol. 2, 129)

French Bread

Tomato Basil Tart
(Vol. 1, 11)

Vegetable Cheese Pie
(Vol. 2, 14)

Terrine of Pork
(Vol. 1, 190)

Artichoke Salad
(Vol. 2, 52)

Turkish Yogurt & Cucumber Salad
(Vol. 2, 55)

Tossed Salad
with Olga's Dressing
(Vol. 1, 93)

Orange Blossom Pudding
(Vol. 2, 242)

Sesame Seed Cookies
(Vol. 1, 277)

New Year's Eve Buffet

Cape House Inn Chilled Buttermilk with Shrimp Soup
(Vol. 2, 48)

Beef Wellington
(Vol. 1, 172)

Stuffed Snapper with Orange & Lime
(Vol. 2, 124)

Potatoes Moussaka
(Vol. 2, 91)

Marinated Mushrooms
(Vol. 1, 90)

Cauliflower Spinach Toss
(Vol. 2, 56)

Lithuanian Napoleon Torte
(Vol. 1, 219)

Post Cross-Country Skiing Dinner

Mulled Ale
(Vol. 2, 295)

Chicken Liver Pate Casanova
(Vol. 1, 158)

Crackers

Canadian Ski Marathon Sauce
(Vol. 2, 192)

Buttered Noodles

Tossed Salad
with Celery Seed Dressing
(Vol. 1, 95)

Assorted Cheeses

After Theatre Supper

Tiopetes
(Vol. 2, 25)

Mulligatawny Soup
(Vol. 2, 32)

Flaky Biscuits
(Vol. 1, 255)

Ruth's Fall Vegetable Vinaigrette
(Vol. 2, 54)

Chocolate Dipped Strawberries
(Vol. 2, 254)

Dinner for Two

Parsley Soup
(Vol. 2, 34)

Scallops in Wine
(Vol. 2, 134)

Donna's Rice Pilaf
(Vol. 1, 113)

Green Bean Timbales
(Vol. 2, 78)

Syllabub
(Vol. 1, 216)

Index